The
Spanish
Anarchists

THE HEROIC YEARS   1868-1936

The Spanish Anarchists

THE HEROIC YEARS 1868-1936

Murray Bookchin

Louis Herber

FREE LIFE
EDITIONS
41 UNION
SQ. WEST
NEW YORK
N.Y. 10003

THE SPANISH ANARCHISTS
The Heroic Years 1868-1936

Copyright © 1977 by Murray Bookchin
All rights reserved, Free Life Editions, Inc.

First Edition

Published 1977 by Free Life Editions, Inc.
41 Union Square West
New York, N.Y., 10003

Library of Congress Number 75-10121
ISBN 0-914156-14-4

Book designed by Raymond Solomon

The publisher wishes to thank
The International Institute of Social History in Amsterdam
and the author
for use of the pictures in this volume.
The map of Spain was taken from
The Revolution and the Civil War in Spain by Pierre Broué and Emile Témime
with the kind permission
of the MIT Press in Cambridge, Ma.

En memoria de Russell Blackwell
—mi amigo y mi compañero

OTHER BOOKS BY MURRAY BOOKCHIN

Lebensgefahrliche, Lebensmittel (1955)
Our Synthetic Environment (1962)
Crisis in Our Cities (1965)
Post-Scarcity Anarchism (1971)
The Limits of the City (1973)
Pour Une Société Écologique (1976)

IN PREPARATION

The Ecology of Freedom
Urbanization Without Cities

Contents

Illustrations

Introduction

It is not widely known to the general reader that the largest movement in pre-Franco Spain was greatly influenced by Anarchist ideas. In 1936, on the eve of the Spanish Civil War, approximately a million people were members of the Anarchosyndicalist CNT (*Confederacion Nacional del Trabajo,* or National Confederation of Labor)—an immense following if one bears in mind that the Spanish population numbered only twenty-four million. Until the victory of Franco, the CNT remained one of the largest labor federations in Spain.

Barcelona, then the largest industrial city in Spain, became an Anarchosyndicalist enclave within the republic. Its working class, overwhelmingly committed to the CNT, established a far-reaching system of syndicalist self-management. Factories, utilities, transport facilities, even retail and wholesale enterprises, were taken over and administered by workers' committees and unions. The city itself was policed by a part-time guard of workingmen and justice was meted out by popular revolutionary tribunals. Nor was Barcelona alone in this radical reconstruction of economic and social life; the movement, in varying degrees, embraced Valencia, Malaga, CNT-controlled factories in the large Basque industrial cities, and smaller communities such as Lerida, Alcoy, Granollers, Gerona, and Rubi.

Many of the land laborers and peasants of Andalusia were also Anarchist in outlook. During the first few weeks of the Civil War, before the south of Spain was overrun by fascist armies, these rural people established communal systems of land tenure, in some cases abolishing the use of money for internal transactions, establishing free, communistic systems of production and distribution, and creating a decision-making procedure based on popular assemblies and direct, face-to-face democracy. Perhaps even more significant were the well-organized Anarchist collectives in Republican-held areas of Aragon, which were grouped into a network under the Council of Aragon, largely under the control of the CNT. Collectives tended to predominate in many areas of Catalonia and the Levant, and were common even in Socialist-controlled Castile.

These experiences alone, so challenging to popular notions of a

libertarian society as an unworkable utopia, would warrant a book on
Spanish Anarchism. But they also have a certain intrinsic interest. To
anyone with a concern for novel social forms, the Anarchist collectives of Spain raise many fascinating questions: how were the collective farms and factories established? How well did they work? Did
they create any administrative difficulties? These collectives,
moreover, were not mere experiments created by idle dreamers; they
emerged from a dramatic social revolution that was to mark the
climax—and tragic end—of the traditional workers' movement. High-
lighting the reconstructive efforts of the Anarchists was the Spanish
Civil War itself, an unforgettable conflict that was to last nearly three
bitter years, claim an estimated million lives, and stir the deepest
passions of people throughout the world.

No less significant was the development of the Spanish Anarchist
movement from the 1870s to the mid-1930s—its forms of organization, its influence on the lives of ordinary workers and peasants, its
internal conflicts, and its varied fortunes. For Spanish Anarchism
remained above all a peoples' movement, reflecting the cherished
ideals, dreams, and values of ordinary individuals, not an esoteric
credo and tightly knit professional party far removed from the everyday experiences of the villager and factory worker. The resiliency and
tenacity that kept Spanish Anarchism alive in urban *barrios* and rural
pueblos for nearly seventy years, despite unrelenting persecution, is
understandable only if we view this movement as an expression of
plebian Spanish society itself rather than as a body of exotic libertarian doctrines.

The present volume (the first of two that will trace the history of
the movement up to the current period) is primarily concerned with
the organizational and social issues that marked the years of Spanish
Anarchism's ascendency and, finally, of its drift toward civil war—a
span of time I have designated as its "heroic period." Despite the
fascination that the collectives of 1936-39 hold for us, I believe it is
immensely rewarding to explore how ordinary workers and peasants
for nearly three generations managed to build the combative organizations that formed the underpinning of these collectives; how they
managed to claim for themselves and incorporate in their everyday
lives revolutionary societies and unions that we normally relegate to
the work place and the political sphere. Quite as significant in my
eyes are the organizational structures, so libertarian in character, that
made it possible for workers and peasants to participate in these
societies and unions, to exercise extraordinary control over their
policies, and to gain for themselves a new sense of personality and
inner individual strength. Whatever our views of Spanish Anarchism, it has far too much to teach us to remain so little known to the

general reader, and it is primarily for this reader that I have written the present volume.

To a certain extent I have been researching the materials for this book since the early 1960s. In 1967 I began systematically to gather data with a view toward writing it during a lengthy trip to Europe, where I interviewed exiled Spanish Anarchists. The present volume was almost entirely completed by 1969. At that time virtually no literature existed in English on Spanish Anarchism except for Gerald Brenan's empathetic but rather incomplete accounts in *The Spanish Labyrinth* and the largely personal narratives of Franz Borkenau and George Orwell. Apart from these works, the scanty references to the Spanish Anarchists in English seemed appallingly insensitive to the ideals of a very sizable section of the Spanish people. Even today, most of the works on Spain by conservative, liberal, and Marxist writers offer no serious appraisal of the libertarian viewpoint and exhibit shocking malice toward its so-called "extreme" wing as represented by the Anarchist action groups. It may well be felt by many students of Spanish Anarchism that I have gone to another extreme. Perhaps—but it seemed especially important to me, whatever my personal reservations, that the voices of these groups be expressed with a greater degree of understanding than they have generally received.

The Spanish Civil War, in fact, was very much part of my own life and affected me more deeply than any other conflict in a lifetime that has seen a terrible international war and the decades of nearly chronic warfare that followed it. My sympathies, indeed my utter devotion, lay with the Spanish left, which I initially identified as a very young man with the Communist Party and, later, as the Civil War came to its terrible close, with the POUM *(Partido Obrero de Unificacion Marxista)*. By the late 1950s, however, I had become more informed about Spanish Anarchism, a movement that had been little known to American radicals of the 1930s, and began to study its origins and trajectory. As one who had lived through the Spanish Civil War period, indeed, who vividly recalled the uprising of the Asturian miners in October 1934, I thought it all the more necessary to correct the false image that, if it existed in my mind, almost certainly existed in the minds of my less politically involved contemporaries. Thus this book is in part a rediscovery of a magnificent historic experience that culminated in a deeply moving tragedy. I have tried to offer at least an understanding voice to those liberty-loving people who marched, fought, and died by the thousands under the black-and-red banners of Spanish Anarchosyndicalism, to pay a fair tribute to their idealism without removing their organizations from the light of well-intentioned criticism.

Another, more contemporary factor motivated me to write this book. The appearance of the black flag of Anarchism in the streets of Paris and many American cities during the 1960s, the strong anarchistic sentiments of radical youth during that fervent decade, and the wide interest in Anarchist theories that exists today, seem to warrant an account and evaluation of the largest organized Anarchist movement to appear in our century. There are many differences, to be sure, between the Anarchist movement of Spain and the anarchistic currents that seemed to flow in the youth revolt of the 1960s. Spanish Anarchism was rooted in an era of material scarcity; its essential thrust was directed against the poverty and exploitation that had reduced millions of Spanish workers and peasants to near-animal squalor. Not surprisingly, the Spanish Anarchists saw the world through puritanical lenses. Living in a society where little was available for all to enjoy, they excoriated the dissoluteness of the ruling classes as grossly immoral. They reacted to the opulence and idleness of the wealthy with a stern ethical credo that emphasized duty, the responsibility of all to work, and a disdain for the pleasures of the flesh.

The anarchistic youth of the 1960s, on the other hand, held diametrically opposite views. Raised in an era of dazzling advances in technology and productivity, they questioned the need for toil and the renunciation of pleasure. Their credos were sensuous and hedonistic. Whether they were conscious of tradition or not, their plea for enlarging experience seemed to echo the writings of Sade, Lautreamont, the Dadaists, and the surrealists rather than those of the "classical" Anarchists of a century ago.

Yet when I started this book, I could not help feeling that an aging Spanish Anarchist easily could have communicated with the revolutionary youth of the 1960s and with the ecologically oriented young people of today. In contrast to Marxian movements, Spanish Anarchism placed a strong emphasis on life-style: on a total remaking of the individual along libertarian lines. It deeply valued spontaneity, passion, and initiative from below. And it thoroughly detested authority and hierarchy in any form. Despite its stern moral outlook, Spanish Anarchism opposed the marriage ceremony as a bourgeois sham, advocating instead a free union of partners, and it regarded sexual practices as a private affair, governable only by a respect for the rights of women. One must know the Spain of the 1930s, with its strong patriarchal traditions, to recognize what a bold departure Anarchist practices represented from the norms of even the poorest, most exploited, and most neglected classes in the country.

Above all, Spanish Anarchism was vitally experimental. The Summerhill-type schools of recent memory were the direct heirs of experiments in libertarian education initiated by Spanish intellectuals who had been nourished by Anarchist ideals. The concept of living close to nature lent Spanish Anarchism some of its most unique features—vegetarian diets, often favoring uncooked foods; ecological horticulture; simplicity of dress; a passion for the countryside; even nudism—but such expressions of "naturalism" also became the subject of much buffoonery in the Spanish press of the time (and of condescending disdain on the part of many present-day academicians). The movement was keenly preoccupied with all the concrete details of a future libertarian society. Spanish Anarchists avidly discussed almost every change a revolution could be expected to make in their daily lives, and many of them immediately translated precept into practice as far as this was humanly possible. Thousands of Spanish Anarchists altered their diets and abandoned such habit-forming "vices" as cigarette-smoking and drinking. Many became proficient in Esperanto in the conviction that, after the revolution, all national barriers would fall away and human beings would speak a common language and share a common cultural tradition.

This high sense of community and solidarity gave rise to the Anarchist "affinity group," an organizational form based not merely on political or ideological ties, but often on close friendship and deep personal involvement. In a movement that called for the use of direct action, Anarchist groups produced individuals of unusual character and striking boldness. To be sure, I would not want these remarks to create the impression that the Spanish Anarchist movement was a revolutionary crusade of uncompromising, morally unblemished "saints." Like all organizations in Spain, the movement had its fair share of self-seeking opportunists who betrayed its libertarian ideals in critical moments of struggle. But what made it unique, even in a land where courage and dignity have always been highly prized, were those remarkable personalities like Fermin Salvochea, Anselmo Lorenzo, and Buenaventura Durruti, who literally personified different aspects of its temperament and libertarian ideals. It has been my good fortune to meet some of the best living representatives of this movement in their places of exile and to gain their assistance in gathering material for this book.

I do not claim to have written an exhaustive account of Spanish Anarchism. For an author to make such a claim would require the backing of several volumes. The scholarly literature consists of sizable works that deal with periods of a decade or less, a literature that is not likely to command the attention of the general reader. Accordingly, I have chosen to dwell upon the turning points of the movement, especially those moments of social creativity which are likely to have importance for our own time. I have also tried to tell the story of the more outstanding Spanish Anarchists: the saint-like ascetics and fiery *pistoleros*, the defiant terrorists and plodding organizers, the scholarly theorists and untutored activists.

The Spanish Civil War came to an end almost forty years ago. The generation that was so deeply involved in its affairs, whether in Spain itself or abroad, is passing away. A real danger exists that the passions aroused by this immense conflict will disappear in the future literature on the subject. And without that passion, it will be difficult to appraise the largest popular movement in the conflict—the Spanish Anarchists—for it was a movement that made spiritual demands of its adherents that are often incomprehensible today. Leaving aside the changes in life-style I've already noted, I should emphasize that to be an Anarchist in Spain, indeed, to be a radical generally in the 1930s, meant that one was uncompromisingly opposed to the established order. Even Socialists retained this high sense of revolutionary principle, in Spain and in many other countries, despite the reformism of the Communist and Social Democratic parties. To participate in bourgeois cabinets, for example, earned one the epithet of "Millerandism," a harshly derogatory term which referred to the unprecedented entry of the French Socialist Millerand into a bourgeois cabinet prior to the First World War.

Today, an ecumenical reformism is taken for granted by virtually the entire left. If the word "Millerandism" has been dropped from the political vocabulary of the left, it is not because revolutionary "purity" has been restored in the major workers' parties but, quite to the contrary, because the practice is too widespread to require an opprobrious designation. The term "libertarian," devised by French Anarchists to deal with the harsh anti-Anarchist legislation at the end of the last century, has lost virtually all its revolutionary meaning. The word "Anarchist" itself becomes meaningless when it is used as a self-description by political dilettantes so light-minded that they move in and out of authoritarian or reformistic organizations as casually as they change a brand of bread or coffee. Contemporary capitalism, with its "revolutionary" motor vehicles and hand lotions, has subverted not only the time-honored ideals of radicalism, but the language and nomenclature for expressing them.

It is emotionally refreshing as well as intellectually rewarding to look back to a time when these words still had meaning, indeed, when content and conviction as such had definition and reality. People today do not hold ideals; they hold "opinions." The Spanish Anarchists, as well as many other radicals of the pre-Civil War era, still had ideals which they did not lightly discard like the brand names of products. The Anarchists imparted a spiritual meaning, intellectual logic, and dignity to the libertarian ideal which precluded flirtations with their opponents—those not only in the bourgeois world but also in the authoritarian left. However unsophisticated they proved to be in many ideological matters, it would have seemed inconceivable to them that an Anarchist could acknowledge the coexistence of a propertied sector of society with a collective one, ignore or slight differences in class interests and politics, or accept a policy of accommodation with a centralized state or authoritarian party, however "libertarian" their opponents might seem in other respects. Basic differences were meant to be respected, not ignored; indeed, they were meant to be deepened by the logic of dispute and examination, not compromised by emphasizing superficial resemblances and a liberal accommodation to ideological divisions. The slaughter and terror that followed in the wake of Franco's march toward Madrid in the late summer of 1936 and the physical hemorrhage that claimed so many lives in the long course of the Civil War produced a spiritual hemorrhage as well, bringing to the surface all the latent weaknesses of the classical workers' movement as such, both Anarchist and Socialist. I have pointed to some of these weaknesses in the closing chapter of this volume. But a high sense of revolutionary commitment remained and continued for decades. That events involving the sheer physical survival of people may induce compromises between ideals and realities is no more surprising in the lifetime of a movement than it is in that of an individual. But that these very ideals should be casually dismissed or forgotten, replaced by a flippant ecumenicalism in which one deals with social goals like fashions, is unforgivable.

My feeling for the Spanish Anarchist sense of commitment to a highly principled libertarian ideal—organizationally as well as ideologically—forms still another part of my motives for writing this book. A decent respect for the memory of the many thousands who perished for their libertarian goals would require that we state these goals clearly and unequivocally, quite aside from whether we agree with them or not. For surely these dead deserve the minimal tribute of identifying Anarchism with social revolution, not with fashionable concepts of decentralization and self-management that comfortably coexist with state power, the profit economy, and multinational corporations. Few people today seem concerned to distinguish the Spanish Anarchists' version of revolutionary decentralization and self-management from the liberal ones that are so much in vogue. Anselmo Lorenzo, Fermin Salvochea, and the young *faistas* of the 1930s would have been appalled at the claim that their ideas had found realization in present-day Chinese "communes" or in the European trade-union leaders who sit as "workers' representatives" on corporate boards of directors. Spanish Anarchist notions of communes, self-management, and technological innovation are totally incompatible with any system of state power or private property and utterly opposed to any compromise with bourgeois society.

Contemporaneity alone does not, in my view, establish the need for a book on Spanish Anarchism. I could easily have adduced Franco's death as justification for offering this book to the public, and certainly it could be cited as a good reason for reading such a work, but my motives for writing it are not to be explained by the current interest in Spain. The basic question raised by Spanish Anarchism was whether it is possible for people to gain full, direct, face-to-face control over their everyday lives, to manage society in their own way—not as "masses" guided by professional leaders, but as thoroughly liberated individuals in a world without leaders or led, without masters or slaves. The great popular uprising of July 1936, especially in the Anarchist centers of Spain, tried to approximate this goal. That the effort failed at a terrible cost in life and morale does not nullify the inherent truth of the goal itself.

Finally, I would like to remind the reader that Spanish life has changed greatly from the conditions described in this volume. Spain is no longer a predominantly agrarian country and the traditional *pueblo* is rapidly giving way to the modern town and city. This should be clearly borne in mind at all times while reading the book. The image of "eternal Spain" has always been a reactionary one. Today, when Spain has become one of the most industrialized countries in the world, it is simply absurd. Yet there is much of a preindustrial and precapitalist nature that lingers on in Spain, and it is devoutly to be hoped that the old Anarchist dream of melding the solidarity of earlier village lifeways with a fairly advanced technological society will have reality for the Spanish present and future.

Before concluding this introduction, I would like to explain certain unorthodoxies in the writing of the book and extend my acknowledgement to individuals who rendered invaluable assistance in its preparation.

Throughout most of their history, the Spanish Anarchists were adherents of a trade-union form of Anarchism which is generally designated as "Anarchosyndicalism."[1] In contrast to many writers on the subject who see Spanish Anarchosyndicalism as a distinctly twentieth-century development, one that had its origins in France, I am now quite convinced that the Spanish section of the First International was Anarchosyndicalist from its very inception in the early 1870s. This tradition persisted, I believe, in virtually all libertarian unions up to and into the formation of the CNT. The tradition, moreover, applied as much to the land laborers' unions of Andalusia as to the textile workers' unions of Barcelona. French Anarchosyndicalism may have been the source for a comprehensive theory of the syndicalist general strike, but the Spanish Anarchists were practicing Anarchosyndicalist tactics decades earlier and, in many cases, were quite conscious of their revolutionary import before the word "Anarchosyndicalist" itself came into vogue.[2]

Accordingly, I have used the terms "Anarchist" and "Anarchosyndicalist" almost intuitively, ordinarily combining libertarians of all persuasions under the "Anarchist" rubric when they seemed to confront the Marxists, the state power, and their class opponents as a fairly unified tendency in Spanish society and singling out "Anarchosyndicalists" when they were functioning largely from a syndicalist point of view. The mingling of these terms was not uncommon in many works on Spain during the 1930s, as witness Gerald Brenan's *The Spanish Labyrinth* and Franz Borkenau's *The Spanish Cockpit*.

I should also note that I have abandoned the use of the usual accent that appears in many Spanish words. I fail to see why *Lerida* and *Leon* (the latter by no means consistently) have accents, while *Andalusia* and *Aragon* do not. For the sake of consistency, I have removed the accents entirely, all the more because this book is written for an English-reading public.

The Spanish Anarchists were given to acronyms like *faista*, *cenetista*, and *ugetista* for members of the FAI, CNT, and the Socialist-controlled UGT. I have retained this vocabulary in the book but have avoided the more familiar diminutives they used for their periodicals, such as "Soli" for *Solidaridad Obrera*.

Whatever originality this book can claim is due primarily to interviews I have had with Spanish Anarchists and with non-Spaniards who were personally involved with their movement. Although I have consulted a large number of books, periodicals, letters, and reports on the Spanish Anarchist movement, my most rewarding experiences have come from the individuals who knew it at first hand. Space limitations make it possible for me to list the names of only a few. I am deeply grateful to a very kindly man, Jose Peirats, the historian of Spanish Anarchism in its later period, for painstakingly explaining the structure of the CNT and FAI, and for many facts about the atmosphere in Barcelona during the years of his youth. Peirats, whom I view as a friend, has done more to convey the mood of the Spanish Anarchist movement in the pre-Civil War period than any text could possibly do. For this sense of personal contact as well as for his invaluable writings on the trajectory of Spanish Anarchism, I owe him an immeasurable debt.

I have also learned a great deal from personal conversations with

Gaston Leval. He has been an indispensable source of information about the Anarchist collectives in Spain during the Civil War (a field in which his command of the facts is unparalleled); he has also given me the benefit of his insights and, for the purposes of this first volume, of his experiences in the CNT during the 1920s. Leval, who is no apologist for the CNT and FAI, contributed considerably to my appraisal of the exaggerated emphasis on Anarchist *pistolerismo* during that critical time and presented me with a more balanced picture of the early 1920s than I have received from the conventional literature on the subject.

To Pablo Ruiz, I owe a truly immense debt for the detailed account he gave me of the founding and activities of the Friends of Durruti, the small but heroic group that did so much to uphold the honor of Spanish Anarchism during the difficult "ministerial" crisis within the movement in 1936-37. The late Cipriano Mera provided me with invaluable details on the structure of the Anarchist militias during the Civil War and on the movement's activities in Madrid during the early 1930s. Although a movement in exile is ordinarily distorted by its isolation and internal conflicts, I gained some sense of the life of Spanish Anarchism by attending meetings of the CNT in Paris, visiting the homes of its members, and hearing deeply moving accounts of the solidarity these individuals retained in the years following the defeat of their movement in 1939.

I owe a great deal to two friends, Sam Dolgoff and the late Russell Blackwell, for their assistance in assembling data for this book and giving freely of their personal recollections. That I dedicated this volume to the memory of Russell Blackwell is more than act of friendship. Blackwell had fought with the Friends of Durruti in Barcelona during the May uprising in 1937. In time he came to symbolize the melding of Spanish and American libertarian ideals in a form that seemed unsurpassed by anyone I had known. I must also express my appreciation to Federico Arcos and Will Watson for making materials available to me that are very difficult to obtain in the United States; to my good friend, Vernon Richards, for his valuable critical insights; to Frank Mintz for sharing many facts drawn from this own researches; to the custodians of the Labadie Collection at the University of Michigan for permission to freely examine documents and unpublished dissertations on various periods of the movement's history; to Susan Harding for sending me additional European material and offering criticisms that have been useful in preparing the text.

In writing a general narrative of this kind, an author must make a decision on where to draw the limits to his research if he is to complete the work in a reasonable period of time. Despite the comparatively improved climate of Franco's Spain a decade ago, my visit to the country in 1967 coincided precisely with the publication of an article in my own name in a leading European Anarchist periodical, and I decided it would be imprudent to continue the research I had planned in that country. In any case, European archives on Spanish Anarchism are so immense that I could foresee many years of research abroad were I to sacrifice my goal of a general narrative for a detailed history based on primary sources. Accordingly, I decided to shift my research back to the United States after visiting various European cities where I was fortunate to gather much of the material I required to write this book.

Since the late 1960s, a truly voluminous literature has been published on different periods of Spanish Anarchism. Wherever possible I have made use of these new studies to check and modify my own largely completed work. Happily, I have found surprisingly little that required alteration and much that supports generalizations that were partly hypothetical when they were first committed to paper. In so far-reaching a project, it is inevitable that factual errors will occur. I can only hope they will prove to be minimal and insignificant. The historical interpretations in this volume are my responsibility alone and should not be imputed to the many individuals who so generously aided me in other respects.

Murray Bookchin
November, 1976

Ramapo College of New Jersey
Mahwah, New Jersey

Goddard College
Plainfield, Vermont

Notes

1. For an explanation of the different forms of Anarchism, see pages 17-31 below.

2. Engels, it is worth noting, clearly showed an understanding of the Anarchosyndicalist nature of the Spanish section in his article "Bakuninists at Work." Surprisingly, this fact has yet to be adequately reflected in many current works on the Spanish Anarchist movement.

Prologue:
Fanelli's Journey

In late October 1868, Giuseppi Fanelli, a tall, heavily bearded Italian of about forty, arrived at Barcelona after a railroad journey from Geneva. It was Fanelli's first visit to Spain. He had reached the city without incident and he would leave it, a few months later, without any interference by the Spanish authorities. There was nothing in his appearance that would have distinguished him from any other visiting Italian, except perhaps for his height and his intense prepossessing stature.

But Giuseppi Fanelli was not an ordinary visitor to Spain. His brief journey was to have a far-reaching influence, providing the catalyst for what was not only the most widespread workers' and peasants' movement in modern Spain, but the largest Anarchist movement in modern Europe. For Fanelli was an experienced Italian revolutionary, a supporter of the Russian Anarchist Mikhail Bakunin, and a highly gifted propagandist. His journey had been organized by Bakunin in order to gain Spanish adherents to the International Workingmen's Association, the famous "First International" established by European workers a few years earlier.

Fanelli's trip should have been a complete fiasco. Financially, it was conducted on a shoestring. Bakunin had raised barely enough money to pay for the fare, with the result that Fanelli, chronically short of funds, was constantly pressed for time. His knowledge of Spain was limited and he could speak scarcely a sentence in Spanish. In Barcelona, he managed after some difficulty to find Elie Reclus, the distinguished French anthropologist and a firm Bakuninist, who was visiting the Catalan port for journalistic reasons. Otherwise, Fanelli knew no one in the city. Apparently, the two men quarreled over Reclus's accommodating attitude toward his Spanish Republican friends, for Fanelli, much to his host's embarrassment, tried to win them over to Anarchism. After borrowing some money from Reclus to continue his journey, the Italian went on to Madrid where he met Jose Guisascola, the owner of the periodical *La Igualdad*. He put

GIUSEPPI FANELLI (1827-1877). An Italian Anarchist and follower of Bakunin, his visit to Barcelona and Madrid established the first Anarchist nucleus in Spain in 1868. He is on the right in the picture; from the left, the portraits are of Fernando Garrido, Elias Reclus, Jose Maria Orense, and Aristides Rey.

Fanelli in touch with a group of workers with "very advanced ideas," and a small, intimate meeting was arranged in the guest room of one Rubau Donadeu. Fanelli could only address them in Italian or French, and the workers, most of whom knew only Spanish, had neglected to bring along an interpreter. But once the tall, lean Italian began to speak, his rapport with the audience was so complete that all barriers of language were quickly swept away. Using a wealth of Latin gestures and tonal expressions, Fanelli managed to convey with electric effect the richness of his libertarian visions and the bitterness of his anger toward human suffering and exploitation. The workers, accustomed to the moderate expressions of Spanish liberals, were stunned. Decades later, Anselmo Lorenzo, who attended the meeting as a young man, describes the talk with a vividness of memory that time seems to have left undimmed. Fanelli's "black expressive eyes," he recalls, "flashed like lightning or took on the appearance of kindly compassion according to the sentiments that dominated him. His voice had a metallic tone and was susceptible to all the inflections appropriate to what he was saying, passing rapidly from accents of anger and menace against tyrants and exploiters to take on those of suffering, regret, and consolation, when he spoke of the pains of the exploited, either as one who without suffering them himself understands them, or as one who through his altruistic feelings delights in presenting an ultra-revolutionary ideal of peace and fraternity. He spoke in French and Italian, but we could understand his expressive mimicry and follow his speech."

Fanelli scored a complete triumph. All those present declared themselves for the International. He extended his stay in Madrid for several weeks, cultivating his newly won adherents; together they had three or four "propaganda sessions," alternating with intimate conversations on walks and in cafes. Lorenzo recalls that he was "especially favored" with Fanelli's confidences. If this is so, Fanelli showed excellent judgment: Anselmo Lorenzo was to live for many years, and he remained a dedicated revolutionary, earning the sobriquet "the grandfather of Spanish Anarchism." His contribution to the spread of Anarchist ideas in Barcelona and Andalusia over the decades ahead was enormous.

On January 24, 1869, Fanelli met with his Madrid converts for the last time. Although the small group, composed mostly of printing workers, house painters, and shoemakers, numbered little more than twenty, it officially declared itself the Madrid section of the International Workingmen's Association. Lorenzo tried to persuade Fanelli to remain longer, but he declined. The Italian explained that he had to leave because it was necessary for individuals and groups to develop "by their own efforts, with their own values," so that the "great common work will not lack the individual and local characteristics which make for a kind of variety that does not endanger unity," but in fact yields a "whole that is the sum of many different elements." In these few remarks, summarized by Lorenzo, Fanelli touches upon the organizational principle and practice so basic to Anarchism, that order reaches its most harmonious form through the spontaneous, unhampered development of individuality and variety. Ultimately, the vitality of the Spanish Anarchist movement was to depend on the extent to which it made this principle a living force in its social and organizational activites.

Before leaving Spain, Fanelli stopped again in Barcelona. This time he had a letter of introduction from Jose Rubau Donadeu, one of his Madrid converts, to the painter Jose Luis Pellicer, a radical demo-crat with strong Federalist convictions. Pellicer arranged a meeting in his studio that attracted some twenty Republicans, most of whom were individuals with established professional backgrounds. This sophisticated, middle-class audience was more skeptical of Fanelli's impassioned oratory than the *Madrilenos*. Probably no more than a handful of young men, mostly students, were inclined to commit themselves to the Italian's Anarchist ideas, but they included Rafael Farga Pellicer, the nephew of Jose Luis, who was to play an important role in establishing the International in Barcelona. By this time, Fanelli was almost out of funds, and after a brief stay in the Catalan seaport, he departed for Marseilles.

Guiseppi Fanelli never returned to Spain. He died only eight years later, a victim of tuberculosis at the age of forty-eight. Like so many young Italians of his day, Fanelli had given up a promising career as an architect and engineer to work for the revolution, at first serving under Garibaldi and later as an emissary of Mazzini. With the victory of the national cause in 1861, he became a deputy in the Italian parliament. His official position earned him the traditional free rail-way pass to travel all over Italy, and the government provided him with a modest pension for the loss of his health as a political prisoner of the Bourbons. He met Bakunin in 1866 at Ischia, only two years before his journey to Spain, and fell completely under the charismatic spell of the Russian revolutionary. For Fanelli, revolution was a way of life, not merely a distant theoretical goal, and his latter years as a deputy were spent on the railways, preaching social revolution dur-ing the day in peasant villages throughout Italy, later returning to sleep in the train at night.

It is doubtful that he fully recognized the scope of his achievement in Spain. Previous attempts to implant Anarchist ideas there go as far back as 1845, when Ramon de la Sagra, a disciple of Proudhon, founded a libertarian journal in Coruna. But the paper, *El Porvenir*,

was soon suppressed by the authorities and Sagra died in exile without exerting any influence in his native country.

Fanelli's achievement was unique and prophetic. Perhaps there is
hyperbole in this story as it has come down to us. But even that is
important because it shows the passionately imaginative elements
that enter into the Spanish yearnings for freedom. And, we shall see,
Spain was uniquely susceptible to Anarchist visions of liberation.

Chapter One:
The "Idea" and Spain

Background

What was the "Idea," as it was destined to be called, that Guiseppi Fanelli brought to Madrid and Barcelona? Why did it sink such deep and lasting roots in Spain?

Few visions of a free society have been more grossly misrepresented than Anarchism. Strictly speaking, anarchy means without authority, rulerless—hence, a stateless society based on self-administration. In the popular mind, the word is invariably equated with chaos, disorder, and terrorist bombings. This could not be more incorrect. Violence and terror are not intrinsic features of Anarchism. There are some Anarchists who have turned to terrorist actions, just as there are others who object to the use of violence as a matter of principle.

Unlike Marxism, with its founders, distinct body of texts,and clearly definable ideology, anarchistic ideals are difficult to fix into a hard and fast credo. Anarchism is a great libidinal movement of humanity to shake off the repressive apparatus created by hierarchical society. It originates in the age-old drive of the oppressed to assert the spirit of freedom, equality, and spontaneity over values and institutions based on authority. This accounts for the enormous antiquity of anarchistic visions, their irrepressibility and continual reemergence in history, particularly in periods of social transition and revolution. The multitude of creeds that surface from this great movement of the social depths are essentially concrete adaptations to a given historical period of more diffuse underlying sentiments, not of eternally fixed doctrines. Just as the values and institutions of hierarchy have changed over the ages, so too have the anarchic creeds that attempted to dislodge them.

In antiquity, these creeds were articulated by a number of highly sophisticated philosophers, but all the theories were pale reflections of mass upheavals that began with the breakup of the village economy and culminated in millenarian Christianity. Indeed, for centuries, the church fathers were to be occupied with mass heresies that emphasized freedom, equality, and at times, a wild hedonism. The slaves and poor who flocked to Christianity saw the second coming of Christ as a time when "a grain of wheat would bear ten thousand ears," when hunger, illness, coercion, and hierarchy would be banished forever from the earth.

These heresies, which had never ceased to percolate through medieval society, boiled up toward its end in great peasant movements and wildly ecstatic visions of freedom and equality. Some of the medival anarchistic sects were astonishingly modern and affirmed a freedom "so reckless and unqualified," writes Norman Cohn, "that it amounted to a total denial of every kind of restraint." (The specific heresy to which Cohn refers here is the Free Spirit, a hedonistic sect which spread throughout southern Germany during the fourteenth century.) "These people," Cohn emphasizes "could be regarded as remote precursors of Bakunin and Nietzsche—or rather of that Bohemian intelligentsia which during the last half-century has been living from ideas once expressed by Bakunin and Nietzsche in their wilder moments."

More typical, however, were the revolutionary peasant movements of the late Middle Ages which demanded village autonomy, the preservation of the communal lands, and in some cases, outright communism. Although these movements reached their apogee in the Reformation, they never disappeared completely; indeed, as late as the twentieth century, Ukranian peasant militias, led by Nestor Makhno, were to fight White Guards and Bolsheviks alike in the Russian Civil War under Anarchist black flags inscribed with the traditional demand of "Liberty and Land."

Anarchistic theories found entirely new forms as revolutionary passions began to surge up in the towns and cities. The word "Anarchist" was first used widely as an epithet against the *Enragés*, the street orators of Paris, during the Great French Revolution. Although the *Enragés* did not make demands that would be regarded today as a basic departure from radical democratism, the use of the epithet was not entirely unjustified. The fiery nature of their oratory, their egalitarianism, their appeals to direct action, and their implacable hatred of the upper classes, menaced the new hierarchy of wealth and privilege reared by the revolution. They were crushed by Robespierre shortly before his downfall, but one of the most able *Enragés*, Jean Varlet, who managed to escape the guillotine, was to draw the ultimate conclusion from his experiences. "For any reasonable be-

PIERRE-JOSEPH PROUDHON (1809-1865). His federalist
views exercised an enormous influence in France, his native
land, and continued on in Spain where they influenced Pi y
Margall's federalist movement and liberals, and helped pave
the way for Socialism in the labor movement.

ing," he wrote years afterward, "Government and Revolution are incompatible. . . ."

The plebian Anarchism of the towns directed its energies against disparities in wealth, but like the peasant Anarchism of the countryside, its social outlook was diffuse and inchoate. With the emergence of the nineteenth century, these diffuse sentiments and ideas of the past were solidified by the new spirit of scientific rationalism that swept Europe. And for the first time, systematic works on Anarchist theory began to appear.

Perhaps the first man to call himself publicly an "Anarchist" and to present his ideas in a methodical manner was Pierre Joseph Proudhon, whose writings were to exercise a great deal of influence in the Latin countries. Proudhon's use of the word "Anarchist" to designate his views must be taken with reservations. Personally, he was an industrious man with fixed habits and a strong taste for the quietude and pleasantries of domestic life. He was raised in a small town and trained as a printer. The views of this paterfamilias were often limited by the social barriers of a craftsman and provincial, despite his long stays in Paris and other large cities.

This is clearly evident in his writings and correspondence. Proudhon envisions a free society as one in which small craftsmen, peasants, and collectively owned industrial enterprises negotiate and contract with each other to satisfy their material needs. Exploitation is brought to an end, and people simply claim the rewards of their labor, freely working and exchanging their produce without any compulsion to compete or seek profit. Although these views involve a break with capitalism, by no means can they be regarded as communist ideas, a body of views emphasizing publicly owned property and a goal in which human needs are satisfied without regard to the contribution of each individual's labor.

Despite the considerable influence Spanish Anarchists have attributed to Proudhon, his mutualist views were the target of many attacks by the early Spanish labor movement. The cooperativist movement, perhaps more authentically Proudhonian than Anarchist, raised many obstacles to the revolutionary trajectory of the Spanish Anarchist movement. As "cooperativists," the mutualists were to seek a peaceful and piecemeal erosion of capitalism. The Anarchists, in turn, were to stress the need for militant struggle, general strike, and insurrection.

Nevertheless, Proudhon, more than any writer in his day, was responsible for the popularity of federalism in the Socialist and Anarchist movements of the last century. In his vision of a federal society, the different municipalities join together into local and regional federations, delegating little if any power to a central government. They deal with common administrative problems and try to adjudicate their differences in an amicable manner. Proudhon, in fact, sees no need for a centralized administration and at times seems to be calling for the total abolition of the state.

Although his style is vigorous and often ringing, Proudhon's temperament, methods, and his emphasis on contractual relations can hardly be called revolutionary, much less anarchistic. Nevertheless, his theories were to have enormous influence in France and on the Iberian Peninsula.

Mutualism and Proudhon's ideas became firmly rooted in Spain through the work of a young Catalan, Francisco Pi y Margall. In 1854 Pi published *Reaccion y Revolucion*, a work that was to exercise a profound influence on radical thought in Spain. Pi had been a bank clerk in Madrid who, in his spare hours, combined occasional ventures into journalism with the authoring of several books on art. Although he was not an Anarchist and was never to become one, his book contains thrusts against centralized authority and power that could have easily come from Bakunin's pen. "Every man who has power over another," writes the young Catalan, "is a tyrant." Further: "I shall divide and subdivide power; I shall make it changeable and go on destroying it." The similarity between these statements and Proudhon's views has led some writers to regard Pi as a disciple of the Frenchman. Actually, it was Hegel who initially exercised the greatest influence on Pi's thought in the early 1850s. The Hegelian notion of lawful social development and "unity in variety" were the guiding concepts in Pi's early federalist ideas. It was not until later that the Catalan turned increasingly to Proudhon and shed many of his Hegelian ideas. Although keenly sympathetic to the wretchedness of Spain's poor, Pi shunned the use of revolutionary violence. Their living conditions, he argued, could best be improved by reformistic and gradualistic measures.

The book caused a great stir among the Spanish radical intelligentsia. To many, Federalism seemed like the ideal solution to Spain's mounting social problems. The men whom Fanelli addressed in Madrid and Barcelona were largely Federalists, as were most of the Republicans in the two cities. Federalist ideas had become so widespread in Spain, in fact, that its supporters were to provide the most important intellectual recruits to the Anarchist movement.

Mutualism became the dominant social philosophy both of the radical Spanish Republicans of the 1860s and of the Parisian Communards of 1871. But it was largely due to the work of a famous revolutionary exile—the "Garibaldi of Socialism," as Gerald Brenan calls him—that the collectivist and Federalist elements in Proudhon's theories were given a revolutionary thrust—and were carried into Spain as a fiery anarchistic ideal.

Mikhail Bakunin

The man who was most successful in providing the vast plebian elements of Spanish Anarchism with a coherent body of ideas was neither a Spaniard nor a plebian, but a Russian aristocrat, Mikhail Bakunin. Although a century has passed since his death, he remains one of the most controversial, little known, and maligned figures in the history of the nineteenth-century revolutionary movements. He enjoys none of the posthumous honors that are heaped on Marx. To this day, nearly all accounts of his life and ideas by non-Anarchist writers are streaked with malice and hostility. His name still conjures up images of violence, rapine, terrorism, and flaming rebellion. In an age that has made the cooptation of dead revolutionaries into a fine art, Bakunin enjoys the unique distinction of being the most denigrated revolutionary of his time.

That the mere appearance of Bakunin would have evoked a sense of menace is attested by every description his contemporaries hand down to us. All portray him in massive strokes: an immensely tall, heavy man (Marx described him as a "bullock"), with a tousled, leonine mane, shaggy eyebrows, a broad forehead, and a heavily bearded face with thick Slavic features. These gargantuan traits were matched by an ebullient personality and an extraordinary amount of energy. The urbane Russian exile, Alexander Herzen, leaves us with a priceless description of the time when Bakunin, already approaching fifty, stayed at his home in London. Bakunin, he tells us,

> argued, preached, gave orders, shouted, decided, arranged, organized, exhorted, the whole day, the whole night, the whole twenty-four hours on end. In the brief moments which remained, he would throw himself down on his desk, sweep a small space clear of tobacco ash, and begin to write five, ten, fifteen letters to Semipalatinsk and Arad, to Belgrade, Moldavia, and White Russia. In the middle of a letter he would throw down his pen in order to refute some reactionary Dalmatian; then, without finishing his speech, he would seize his pen and go on writing. . . . His activity, his appetite, like all his other characteristics—even his gigantic size and continual sweat — were of superhuman proportions. . . .

This was written after the weary, politically disillusioned Herzen had parted company with the exuberant revolutionary. Nevertheless the description gives us an image of the sheer elemental force that emanated from Bakunin, qualities which were to carry him through trials that would have easily crushed ordinary men. Bakunin's forcefulness, overbearing as it was to Herzen, was softened by a natural simplicity and an absence of pretension and malice which verged on

MIKHAIL BAKUNIN (1814-1876). Bakunin's writings and personal influence had an enormous impact on Spanish Anarchism through the work of Fanelli and others. His eminence was shared with Peter Kropotkin, and their ideas shaped the nature of Spanish Anarchism.

PETER KROPOTKIN (1842-1921). The theoretician of
Anarchist Communism, as distinguished from Bakunin's
Anarchist Collectivism. Kropotkin's influence is still felt
today in the writings of Lewis Mumford, Paul Goodman, and
advocates of decentralism.

childlike innocence. Like so many Russian exiles at the time, Bakunin was kindly and generous to a fault. There were some who exploited these traits for dubious ends, but there were others (among them, young Italian, Spanish, and Russian revolutionaries) who, strongly attracted by the warmth of his personality, were to turn to him for moral inspiration throughout his life.

He was born in May 1814, in Premukhina, a moderately large estate 150 miles northwest of Moscow. A nobleman whose mother was connected by lineage to the ruling circles of Russia, Bakunin abandoned a distasteful military career and the prospect of genteel stagnation on his family estate for a life of wandering and revolutionary activity in Europe. The year 1848 found him in Paris, later in Prague, and finally in Dresden, where he literally journeyed from one insurrection to another in his appetite for action. From May 1849 he was bandied about from one prison to another—Saxon, Austrian, and Russian—before escaping from Siberia to arrive in London in 1863.

Up to the 1860s Bakunin had essentially been a revolutionary activist, loosely adhering to the radical democratic and nationalist views of the day. It was in London, and especially during a long stay in Italy, that he began to formulate his Anarchist views. In the thirteen years of life remaining before him, he never ceased to be the barricade fighter of 1848 and was involved repeatedly in revolutionary plots, but it was also in this period that he developed the most mature of his theoretical ideas.

Bakunin's Anarchism converges toward a single point: unrestricted freedom. He brooks no compromise with this goal, and it permeates all of his mature writings. "I have in mind the only liberty worthy of that name," he writes,

> liberty consisting in the full development of all the material, intellectual, and moral powers latent in every man; a liberty which does not recognize any other restrictions but those which are traced by the laws of our nature, which, properly speaking, is tantamount to saying that there are no restrictions at all, since these laws are not imposed upon us by some outside legislator standing above us or alongside us. These laws are immanent, inherent in us; they constitute the very basis of our being, material as well as intellectual and moral; and instead of finding in them a limit to our liberty we should regard them as its effective reason.

The "immanent" and "inherent" laws that form the basis of human nature, however, do not lead to a rabid individualism that sees social life as a restriction; Bakunin emphatically denies that individuals can live as asocial "egos." People want to be free in order to fulfill themselves, he argues, and to fulfill themselves they must live with others in communities. If these communities are not distorted by property, exploitation, and authority, they tend to approach a cooperative and humanistic equilibrium out of sheer common interest.

Bakunin's criticism of capitalism leans heavily on the writings of Marx. He never ceased to praise Marx for his theoretical contributions to revolutionary theory, even during their bitter conflicts within the International. The basic disagreement between Marx and Bakunin centers around the social role of the state and the effects of centralism on society and on revolutionary organizations. Although Marx shared the Anarchist vision of a stateless society—the "ultimate goal" of Marxian communism, in fact, is a form of anarchy—he regards the historical role of the state as "progressive" and sees centralization as an advance over localism and regionalism. Bakunin emphatically disagrees with this viewpoint. The state, he admits, may be "historically necessary" in the sense that its development was unavoidable during humanity's emergence from barbarism, but it is an "historically necessary evil, as necessary in the past as its complete extinction will be necessary sooner or later, just as necessary as primitive bestiality and theological divagations were necessary in the past."

The point is that Bakunin, in contrast to Marx, continually emphasizes the negative aspects of the state:

> Even when it commands the good, it makes this valueless by commanding it; for every command slaps liberty in the face; as soon as this good is commanded, it is transformed into an evil in the eyes of true (that is, human, by no means divine) morality, of the dignity of man, of liberty. . . .

This intensely moral judgment plays an important role in Bakunin's outlook, indeed, in Anarchism generally. Human beings, to Bakunin, are not "instruments" of an abstraction called "history"; they are ends in themselves, for which there are no abstract substitutes. If people begin to conceive themselves as "instruments" of any kind, they may well become a means rather than an end, and modify the course of events in such a way that they never achieve freedom. In erroneously prejudging themselves and their "function," they may ignore opportunities that could lead directly to liberation or that could create favorable social conditions for freedom later.

With this existential emphasis, Bakunin departs radically from Marxism, which continually stresses the economic preconditions for freedom and often smuggles in intensely authoritarian methods and institutions for advancing economic development. Bakunin does not ignore the important role of technology in ripening the conditions for freedom, but he feels that we cannot say in advance when these conditions are ripe or not. Hence we must continually strive for complete freedom lest we miss opportunities to achieve it or, at least, prepare the conditions for its achievement.

These seemingly abstract theoretical differences between Marx and Bakunin lead to opposing conclusions of a very concrete and practical nature. For Marx, whose concept of freedom is vitiated by preconditions and abstractions, the immediate goal of revolution is to seize political power and replace the bourgeois state by a highly centralized "proletarian" dictatorship. The proletariat must thus organize a mass centralized political party and use every means, including parlimentary and electoral methods, to enlarge its control over society. For Bakunin, on the other hand, the immediate goal of revolution is to extend the individual's control over his or her own life; hence revolution must be directed not toward the "seizure of power" but its dissolution. A revolutionary group that turns into a political party, structuring itself along hierarchical lines and participating in elections, Bakunin warns, will eventually abandon its revolutionary goals. It will become denatured by the needs of political life and finally become coopted by the very society it seeks to overthrow.

From the outset, then, the revolution must destroy the state apparatus: the police, the army, the bureaucracy. If violence is necessary, it must be exercised by the armed revolutionary people, organized in popular militias. The revolutionary movement, in turn, must try to reflect the society it is trying to create. If the movement is to avoid turning into an end in itself, into another state, complete conformity must exist between its means and ends, between form and content. Writing on the structure of the International, Bakunin insists that it

> must differ essentially from state organization. Just as much as the state is authoritarian, artificial, and violent, alien, and hostile to the natural development of the people's interests and instincts, so must the organization of the International be free and natural, conforming in every respect to those interests and instincts.

Accordingly, in the last years of the International, Bakunin was to oppose Marx's efforts to centralize the movement and invest virtually commanding powers in its General Council.[1]

Bakunin places strong emphasis on the role of spontaneity in the revolution and in revolutionary activity. If people are to achieve freedom, if they are to be revolutionized by the revolution, they must make the revolution themselves, not under the tutelege of an all-knowing political party. Bakunin also recognizes, however, that a revolutionary movement is needed to catalyze revolutionary possibilities into realities, to foster a revolutionary development by means of propaganda, ideas, and programs. The revolutionary movement, he believes, should be organized in small groups of dedicated "brothers" (the word recurs often in his discussion of organization) who single-mindedly pursue the task of fomenting revolution. His emphasis on smallness is motivated partly by the need for secrecy that existed in the southern European countries of his day, partly also by his desire to foster intimacy within the revolutionary movement.

For Bakunin, a revolutionary organization is a community of personally involved brothers and sisters, not an apparatus based on bureaucracy, hierarchy, and programmatic agreement. More so than any of the great revolutionaries of his day, Bakunin sought a concordance between the life-style and goals of the revolutionary movement. He was unique in his appreciation of revolution as a festival. Recalling his experiences in Paris, shortly after the 1848 revolution, he writes:

> I breathed through all my senses and through all my pores the intoxication of the revolutionary atmosphere. It was a festival without beginning nor end; I saw everyone and I saw no one, for each individual was lost in the same innumerable and wandering crowd; I spoke to everyone without remembering either my own words or those of others, for my attention was absorbed by new events and objects and by unexpected news.

Bakunin's emphasis on conspiracy and secrecy can be understood only against the social background of Italy, Spain, and Russia—the three countries in Europe where conspiracy and secrecy were matters of sheer survival. In contrast to Marx, who greatly admired the well-disciplined, centralized German proletariat, Bakunin placed his greatest hopes for social revolution on the Latin countries. He foresaw the danger of the *embourgeoisement* of the industrial proletariat and warned of its consequences. Following a predisposition to mistrust stable, complacent, institutionalized classes in society, Bakunin turned increasingly to decomposing, precapitalist classes of the kind that prevailed in Russia and southern Europe: landless peasants, workers with no stake in society, artisans faced by ruin, footloose *déclassé* intellectuals and students. Marx regarded the formation of a stable industrial working class as a precondition for social revolution. Bakunin, however, saw in this process the ruin of all hopes for a genuinely revolutionary movement—and in this respect he proved deeply prophetic.

Bakunin was not a communist. He may have recognized that economic development in his day did not admit of the communist precept, "From each according to his ability; to each according to his needs." In any case he accepted Proudhon's notion that the satisfaction of material needs would have to be tied to the labor contributed by each individual. Bakunin also closely followed Proudhon's federalist approach to social organization. But in contrast to the French mutualist, he regarded the collective, and not the independent artisan, as the basic social unit. He was sharply critical of Proudhonian mutualists

> who conceive society as the result of the free contract of individuals absolutely independent of one another and entering into mutual relations only because of the convention drawn up among them. As if these men had dropped from the skies, bringing with them speech, will, original thought, and as if they were alien to anything of the earth, that is, anything having social origins.

In time this view acquired the name "Collectivist Anarchism" to distinguish it both from Proudhonian mutualism and, later, from the "Anarchist Communism" propounded by Peter Kropotkin. (For a discussion of Kropotkin's Communist views, see pp. 115-116 below.) A mere sketch of Bakunin's theories does not capture the flavor of his writings, the animating spirit that catapulted his personality into the foreground of nineteenth-century radical history. Although a deeply humane and kindly man (indeed because of his intrinsic humanity and kindness) Bakunin did not shrink from violence. He faced the problem with disarming candor and refused to dilute the need for violence—and the reality of the violence which the ruling classes practiced daily in their relations with the oppressed—with a hypocritical stance of moral outrage. "The urge to destroy," he wrote as a young man, "is also a creative urge." His writings exude a sense of violent rebellion against authority, of unrestrained anger against injustice, of fiery militancy on behalf of the exploited and oppressed. There can be little question that he lived this spirit with consistency and great personal daring.

Beneath the surface of Bakunin's theories lies the more basic revolt of the community principle against the state principle, of the social principle against the political principle. Bakuninism, in this respect, can be traced back to those subterranean currents in humanity that have tried at all times to restore community as the structural unit of social life. Bakunin deeply admired the traditional collectivistic aspects of the Russian village, not out of any atavistic illusions about the past, but because he wished to see industrial society pervaded by its atmosphere of mutual aid and solidarity. Like virtually all the intellectuals of his day, he acknowledged the importance of science as a means of promoting eventual human betterment; hence the embattled atheism and anticlericalism that pervades all his writings. By the same token, he demanded that the scientific and technological re-

sources of society be mobilized in support of social cooperation, freedom, and community, instead of being abused for profit, competitive
advantage, and war. In this respect, Mikhail Bakunin was not behind
his times, but a century or more ahead of them.

To the young revolutionary Spaniards of the 1860s, to the militant
workers of Barcelona and the restive land laborers of Andalusia, the
ideas propounded by Bakunin seemed to crystallize all their vague
feelings and thoughts into an inspired vision of truth. He provided
them with a coherent body of ideas that answered admirably to their
needs: a vigorous federalism revolutionary in its methods, and a radical collectivism rooted in local initiative and decentralist social forms.
Even his militant atheism seemed to satisfy the strong wave of anticlerical feeling that was surging through Spain. The prospect of participating in the work of the International held the promise of linking
their destinies to a worldwide cause of historic dimensions. Finally,
Spain had been prepared for Bakunin's theories not only socially, but
also intellectually. If Bakuninist Anarchism was new to Fanelli's audience, some of its elements, such as federalism, were familiar topics of
discussion in Madrid and Barcelona.

No less important than Bakunin's federalist ideas were his atheis-
tic views and his attacks on clericalism. We shall see that the Spanish
church had become the strongest single prop of absolutism and reaction in the early nineteenth century, later rallying around the Carlist
line (the reactionary pretenders to the Spanish throne) and the most
conservative trends in political life. The collusion between the
Catholic hierarchy and the Spanish ruling classes had completely
"undermined the prestige of the clergy among the working classes,"
writes Elena de La Souchere, "and brought about a de-
Christianization of the masses which is in fact the essential
phenomenon of the history of Spain in the late nineteenth and early
twentieth centuries. The Spanish bourgeoisie had constructed a perfect city from which the plebians, kept beyond the walls, enveloped
the clergy in the hate they bore the institutions and castes which were
admitted to that closed city."

Accordingly, as early as 1835, anger against Carlist atrocities in the
north had led to church burnings in many large towns of Spain.
The monks were detested as parasites and the higher echelons of the
hierarchy were seen as simply the clerical equivalents of wealthy
secular landowners and bourgeois. They were hated all the more
fervently because of their religious pretensions and their invocations
of humility and the virtues of poverty.

Bakunin's emphasis on collectivism, so much stronger than
Proudhon's, had a particularly wide appeal to the dispossessed rural
classes. It conformed admirably to their sense of the *patria chica*, the

autonomous village world that had been deserted by the ruling classes for a comfortable life in the larger provincial cities.

Similarly, the Robin Hood mentality that permeates so much of
Bakunin's thought and, in its own way, forms a conspicuous trait of
his own life, doubtless had a strong appeal in areas like Andalusia
where the peasantry had come to venerate the social bandit as an
avenger of injustice. In this land of the "permanent guerrilla"—a
figure that reaches as far back as the Moorish invasion—the lonely
band, striking a blow for freedom, had become especially dear to the
rural poor and nourished a multitude of local myths and legends.

Finally, Bakunin's appeal to direct action found a wealth of precedents in village and urban uprisings. Lacking even a modicum of
protection by the law, the Spanish people increasingly relied on their
own action for the redress of grievances. We shall see that the use of
the ballot in Spain was to become meaningless, even after universal
suffrage had been introduced. In many Spanish villages, local political bosses, the *caciques* (generally, landowners, but often lawyers and
priests) held absolute control over political life. Using their economic
power and, where necessary, outright coercion, the *caciques* appointed
all the local officials of their districts and "delivered the vote" to political parties of their choice. This scandalous system of undisguised
political manipulation, combined with the repeated *coups d'etat*—the
notorious *pronunciamientos*—of Spanish military officers, created an
atmosphere of widespread cynicism toward electoral activity. The
Spanish people did not have to be convinced by a Russian aristocrat
that the state was the private domain of the ruling classes; their education came directly from the arrogant land magnates and bourgeoisie
of their own country.

Thus, the fact that Guiseppi Fanelli could have scored an immediate triumph in Madrid may have been unique, but it need hardly
seem too surprising. The views he brought with him did not require
elaborate theoretical explanation. It sufficed for his audience to grasp
mere shreds of Bakunin's ideas to feel a living affinity between their
social problems in Spain and the passionate ideas of the Russian exile
in Geneva.

Note

1. Perhaps the greatest single failing of Bakunin is his inconsistency in
translating his avowed organizational precepts into practice. For a discussion
of this problem, see pp. 46-50 below.

Chapter Two:

The Topography
of Revolution

We must now try to see how remarkably well Bakunin's ideas suited the needs of a revolutionary workers' and peasants' movement in Spain.

To nineteenth-century liberalism, the problems of Spain could be reduced to a classic formula: a backward agrarian country, faced with the tasks of land reform, industrial development, and the creation of a middle-class democratic state. The parallel with France on the eve of the Great Revolution is unmistakable: a liberal bourgeoisie, demanding a governing voice in the state; an absolute monarchy, passing into an advanced state of decomposition; a stagnant nobility, lost in darkening memories of its past grandeur; a reactionary church, steeped in medievalism; and a savagely exploited working class and impoverished, land-hungry peasantry. The consciousness of this parallel, almost bordering on fatalism, was so strong that Spanish political factions often modeled themselves on Jacobins, Girondins, Royalists, and Bonapartists.

But there were many profound differences between Spain in the nineteenth century and France in the eighteenth. Some of them, such as the emergence of a modern industrial proletariat, could be explained by the passage of time. Others, however, were peculiar to Spain, and had few historical precedents. It is these differences that account for the extraordinary popularity of Bakunin's Anarchism below the Pyrenees.

The most striking characteristic of the Iberian Peninsula is its startling variety—its variety of landscapes, land tenure, cultural features, and social forms. It is the sudden changes in topography that catch the attention of a traveler in Spain. Within a few hours, one can pass from green, rolling country, with well-watered soil and abundant crops, to baked, arid plains, more reminiscent of North Africa than of Europe. "The north western provinces," observed an English traveler a century ago, "are more rainy than Devonshire, while the centre plains are more calcined than those of the deserts of Arabia, and the littoral south or eastern coasts altogether Algerian."

For Spain, this has meant not only different forms of land tenure, but different types of agrarian unrest. In the well-watered mountainous north, the agricultural economy had long solidified around small, well-tended farms, based on mixed crops and dairy produce. Here, the democratic traditions of pre-Moslem Spain were firmly rooted, and independent peasants, tenants, and rentiers mixed on an easy, almost egalitarian basis. The long heritage of communal life, almost neolithic in origin, had produced a deeply conservative outlook whose spiritual focus was the church and whose anti-Christ was the emerging industrial world with its unsettling values, its startling products, and its invasive claims on village autonomy. The small, dun-colored villages of this great northern region, each hugging its hilltop or mountain ledge like a fortress, lived out their fixed cycles of daily life by the incantations of dogmatic, often fanatical priests and by codes that often went beyond the memory of the most venerable myths.

By the nineteenth century, these villages had emerged from lethargy and isolation to face a world of social and economic upheaval. In their volatile response, revolt took the anachronistic form of permanent counterrevolution. United by a passionate Catholicism, by an embattled sense of local independence, and by deeply rooted communal and patriarchal traditions, the peasantry of the northern mountains provided the largest single reservoir of political reaction in Spain. In the years to follow, these parochial villages produced wave after wave of peasant militia—fearsome men armed with scythes, cudgels, and antique guns—led by village priests with a sinister reputation for butchery. The first of these waves rolled against Napoleon, who personified not only the traditional French invader but also the detested French Revolution. Later, in two bloody civil wars, the northern peasantry took up arms in support of the Carlist line. We shall see that as the nineteenth century drew to a close, new social forces were to dilute this reservoir of reaction with liberal, even Socialist, ideals; nevertheless, it was from the small landowners of the mountains of Navarre and nearby areas that General Franco was to recruit the most enthusiastic domestic masses for his infantry in 1936.

If the north could be regarded as the reactionary Vendée of the French Revolution, the Meseta could be regarded as its moderate Gironde. On this great, treeless, windswept plateau of central Spain, reaction shaded into a cautious liberalism. From the time of the Reconquest, when the Moors were driven from the Iberian Peninsula, the Castilians of the central Meseta have regarded themselves as the wellsprings of Spanish culture and the indisputable heirs of the Spanish state. All other inhabitants of Spain are viewed as social inferiors. Yet rarely in history has a "master race" been confined to a more inhospitable region of the country under its control. The Meseta has a harsh, erratic climate. Its soil, in the absence of irrigation works, is poor and demanding. During Fanelli's day, a traveler would have found all the conditions for chronic agrarian revolts: large estates, owned by absentee aristocrats and newly rich bourgeois, existing side by side with small, wretched farms. Usury and land speculation burdened the plateau to a point where many of the lesser nobility were reduced to the material status of a peasant. A large population of tenant families, working the land under precarious, short-term leases, eked out a miserable subsistence livelihood and were totally indifferent to the needs of the soil.

But this potential for agrarian revolt rarely exploded into a major uprising. In contrast to the north, where the church had shrewdly deflected peasant dissatisfaction into reactionary channels, on the Meseta, chauvinism served more as a political instrument of the central government in Madrid (and here any comparisons with the French Girondins end) than as the foundations of a coherent reactionary ideology. Nearly all social classes, wealthy and poor, upheld the supremacy of the central government over Carlism and regionalism, but beyond this chauvinistic umbrella, allegiances tended to follow economic lines. The landed aristocracy of the Meseta, like its peers elsewhere in Spain, remained Catholic and conservative; the rural bourgeoisie tended to support the policies of moderate liberalism, when social unrest did not stampede it into reactionary causes. The great mass of peasants and tenants were politically inert throughout most of the nineteenth century, the objects of manipulation by the large landowners; eventually, however, they drifted into orderly, bureaucratic Socialist unions.

All further analogies with the French Revolution come to an end the moment one passes southward through the Sierra Morena, one of the most important mountain barriers in Spain. North of the Morena lies classical Spain: stern, morally rigid, obsessed by an unyielding sense of responsibility and duty. To the south lies Andalusia: easygoing, pleasure-loving, and delightfully impulsive. This large, populous region had been successively colonized by Phoenicians, Greeks, Carthaginians, Romans, German barbarian tribes, and Moors. The Moors held Andalusia for nearly five centuries and left behind a hedonistic tradition that survived the Holy Inquisition, the auto-da-fé, and the rule of sullen Castilian bureaucrats. The Romans, who held the region even longer than the Moors, left behind the latifundium, a plantation economy based on gang labor and bestial conditions of exploitation.

The latifundium could well be described as the agrarian ulcer of the Mediterranean world and in many respects bears comparison with the plantation economy of the antebellum American South. Historically rooted in slavery, the two shared identical traditions of labor management and common forms of land tenure. In the cotton districts around Seville, even the crops were the same. Most of the Andalusian latifundia cultivated olives, grapes, and grain—the typical crop pattern of Mediterranean agriculture. The long rainless summers of the region posed formidable problems of moisture conservation. In the absence of agricultural machinery, specially adapted to dry farming, large tracts of land had to be left fallow and sown for crops every second or third year. The largest estates tended to congregate in the Guadalquiver valley, the huge triangular basin that lies between the Sierra Morena and the mountain chains of the southern coast. It was here, in the best lands of the most fertile districts of Andalusia, that one found the largest holdings, the immense masses of gang labor, and those grotesque economic contrasts that gave the region its reputation for misery and agrarian rebellion.

In Andalusia, as far back as Roman times, two classes stood opposed to each other: the land magnates and a huge population of landless laborers. If the land magnate lived on his estate, his presence was feared by all. If he lived in the cities, as was so often the case, the task of managing his properties was left to stewards who mercilessly extracted every bit of labor from the gang workers beneath them. Between this handful of land magnates and the great mass of landless there existed a chasm that few of the institutions of official Spain could bridge. The church alone had been capable of doing so, but with its declining influence in the latter part of the nineteenth century, the last links were broken. It was here, on these immense estates of the south, that Spanish Anarchism was to find massive popular support.

To the west of the Meseta, in Estremadura, a traveler found a wild arid region stretching from the central plateau to the Portuguese frontier. Most of the land was held by a few absentee owners and cultivated by the *yunteros,* a class of rural proletarians who owned nothing but their mule teams. Work was seasonal, often uncertain, and rewarded by pittances. Further northward in Galicia, Spain's westernmost province, rural life had sunk to an incredibly low material level. If Andalusia was the land of the latifundium, Galicia could be called the land of the minifundium, of plots so small that they could scarcely support a single family. Turning to the east, along the

Mediterranean coastal region, the provinces of Valencia and Murcia
(the Spanish Levant) included irrigated *vegas* (plains) which were
parceled into small prosperous holdings of orange growers and in-
land mountain areas stricken by bitter poverty. Politically, the landlords of the *vegas* vacillated between the Liberal and Conservative
parties. The peasants of the mountain region were destined to provide some of the most militant Anarchists in Spain.

The uniformity of these major agricultural regions, however, is
more apparent than real. Within Andalusia, for example, mountain
districts contained mostly small holdings and communally owned
pasture. In the lowlands there were many small farmsteads, worked
by peasant owners and tenants. In the mountainous north, the high-
lands of Aragon supported the impoverished sheepherders of the
Maestrazzo—people who were to be drawn to Carlism not because
they shared the material prosperity of their northern brethren, but on
the contrary, because they did not. In the steppe country of Aragon,
the chronic material poverty generated by a combination of large
estates, usury, and land hunger provided a hospitable climate for
Anarchism. In the *vegas* of the south, Granada was to form an enclave
of socialism, despite the surrounding Anarchist sentiment of the rural
laborers, while in the reactionary mountainous north, islands of
Anarchists and Anarchosyndicalist unions were to emerge in distant
Galicia, in Asturias, and in the wine-growing districts of the upper
Ebro valley.

Spain, however, is a land of startling contrasts not only in its
geography and land tenure. The contrasts extend also to cultures
which, in the case of the Basques and Catalans, verge on fairly distinct nations. The Basques occupy the Atlantic area of the north forming a corner with France, in which live another sizeable portion of
their people. Basque is an ancient language unrelated to any other in
Europe. A deeply pious, outwardly stern people, whose sense of
self-discipline is relaxed in buoyant songs and satiric pantomines, the
Basques succeeded in holding firmly to their independence and unique ways of life for centuries. Economically oriented toward Atlantic
Europe, they managed to resist Latinization and only nominally fell
under Roman rule. During the Middle Ages, they successfully kept
Visigothic, Frankish, and Moorish invaders from occupying their an-
cestral lands. For two centuries, between the tenth and thirteenth,
nearly all the Basques of Spain were united in the Navarrese
kingdom—the Christian kingdom that played so large a part in the
reconquest of the Iberian Peninsula from the Moors.

The advance of the Castilian state in the Meseta gradually pared
away their liberties, driving them into unsuccessful revolts and finally
into the Carlist camp. In the meantime, their ports began to grow and

their trade with Europe expanded steadily. Bilboa, owing to its proximity to high-grade iron-ore mines and the Asturian coal fields, soon became the most important steel-producing city in Spain. Basque financiers played a leading role in all phases of the Spanish economy and Basque shipping magnates succeeded in gathering the bulk of Spanish merchant tonnage into their hands. This industrial and financial bourgeoisie, one of the most modern and businesslike in Spain, soon began to subsidize a moderate nationalist movement—devoutly Catholic in religion, liberal in economic policy, reformist in social program and politics. The Basque working class, recruited largely from the conservative peasantry of the coastal mountains, was never infused with the kind of revolutionary fervor that emanated from Barcelona. Although some steel workers turned to Anarchosyndicalism, the majority of the Basque workers divided their loyalties between Catholic and Socialist unions.

Traditionally oriented toward the north, beyond the Pyrenees, Catalonia was never an organic part of Spain. Rather, it belonged to the vigorous, progressive *langue d'oc* civilization of southern France and northern Italy. The Catalan language is akin to Provencal, not to Spanish, although both are Latin tongues. The "crusade" against the Albigensian heresy in the thirteenth century shattered this colorful world but left many of its cultural roots intact. Definitively separated from France, their trade ruined by the Turkish conquest of Constantinople, the Catalans were compelled to turn away from the north and look toward the Iberian Peninsula. They never liked what they saw. A sophisticated merchant people, with an urbane cultural lineage of their own, the Catalans never ceased to harbor separatist tendencies. By the early nineteenth century, the centrifugal forces created by culture were reinforced by industrial development. At a point in history when all the institutions of the Castilian state in Madrid were in visible decomposition, a viable industrial bourgeoisie and proletariat had emerged not in the center of Spain, but on its periphery. The Basque country and Catalonia each presented economic, political, and cultural demands that threatened to undermine the entire traditional structure of Spain as it had been known since the Reconquest.

Even more threatening to the centralized state than regional nationalism is the intense localism of Spanish social life: the *patria chica* (literally, "small fatherland"), an almost untranslatable term that denotes the village and its immediate region—in short, the living arena of the rural Spaniard's world.

The Spanish word for village is *pueblo*. *Pueblo* also means "people," and this is by no means accidental. J.A. Pitt-Rivers, who devoted years of study to Spanish village life in Andalusia, notes that

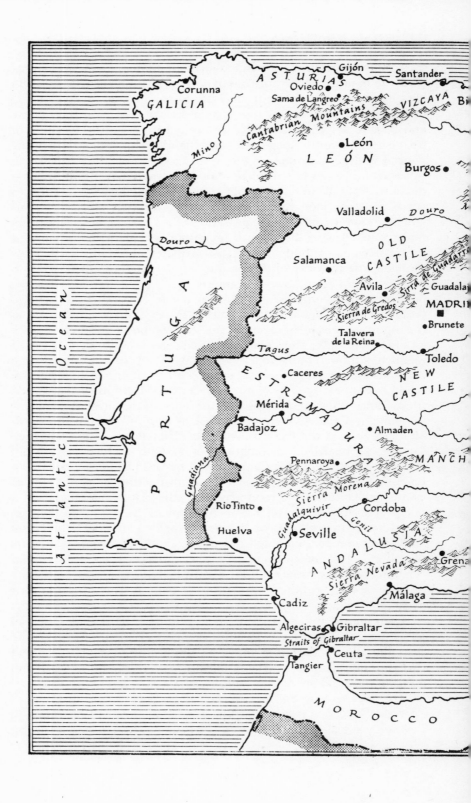

"the Greek word for *polis* far more nearly translates 'pueblo' than any English word, for the community is not merely a geographical or political unit, but the unit of society in every context. The pueblo furnishes a completeness of human relations which make it the prime concept of all social thought."[1]

For the traditional *pueblo*, this completeness involved not only a deep sense of moral unity, common purpose, and mutual aid, but also a body of rights, or *fueros*, which defined the community's autonomy in local affairs and protected it from the encroachment of outside authority. Many *fueros* were born from the needs of the Reconquest, when the kings of Spain granted local privileges for military aid against the Moors. Others were granted by the monarchy in order to gain municipal support against intractable nobles and military orders. But there were *fueros*, such as those of the Basques, which were never "granted" at all, indeed, which go back to a far-distant time when chiefs and later monarchs were democratically elected by popular village assemblies. Elena de La Souchere observes that the Moorish invasion, by shattering the Romano-Germanic state, indirectly fostered the resurrection of these very early social forms. The Iberians of the northern mountains who had successfully resisted Roman, German, and Moorish influence were destined not only to spearhead the Reconquest, "but to perfect and even bring back to other parts of the country their peculiar institutions and customs."

That the *fueros* retained their vitality after the Reconquest was due, ironically, to the nature of the Spanish monarchy and to its impact on economic life. The immense wealth that Spain had acquired from her empire did not go to the Spanish middle classes. It filled the coffers of the absolutist monarchy (perhaps the earliest of its kind in modern times) and was eventually dissipated in imperial adventures to control Europe and the peninsula. This steady drain of potential capital, of resources that might have been invested in industrial development, led to the contraction of domestic trade and the decay of the Spanish bourgeoisie.

Marx, who understood Spain better than many of his Spanish disciples, notes that as commerce and industry declined and as the early bourgeois towns began to stagnate, "internal exchanges became rare, the mingling of different provinces less frequent, and the great roads gradually deserted." This sweeping economic decline in the sixteenth and seventeenth centuries greatly strengthened the local life of the *pueblos* and regions. Spain and the Spanish state began to acquire ineffable qualities. Although the monarchy had all the trappings of absolutism, its control over the country was often nominal or nonexistent. Spain could be defined with geographic exactitude on a map in periods of peace, but an invader soon found, much to his chagrin, that it dissolved into many Spains in times of war. Marx shrewdly observes that Napoleon, who regarded Spain "as an inanimate corpse," was astonished to find "that when the Spanish State was dead, Spanish society was full of life, and every part of it overflowing with powers of resistance."

The *fueros*, which this unique development fostered, helped to provide a sturdiness to the *pueblo* that no amount of bureaucratic structuring could possibly match. They also generated those centrifugal forces that continually threatened the central power, or at least challenged the validity of its functions. What need had Spaniards for a distant, bureaucratic, anonymous state when their *pueblos*, human in scale, intimate in cohesion, with a comforting solidarity and spirit of mutual aid, could meet most of their social and material needs? What need was there for a remote political entity, for vague legal generalities, when the *fueros* provided Spaniards with highly democratic guidelines for social management? Spaniards graded their allegiances from below to above, from *pueblo* to locality, from locality to region, and from region to province, reserving the least loyalty, if any still remained, for the centralized state in Madrid. This intense feeling for community, for the human scale, for self-management, made the Spaniard highly susceptible to libertarian ideas and methods. Transported into an urban environment, this propensity for localism turned the city into a composite of *pueblos*, the trade union into a *patria chica*, the factory into a community.

Note

1. Which is not to say that the *pueblo* did not harbor the petty tyrannies of rigid custom, parochialism, superstition, and the more overt tyrannies of the *caciques*, clergy, and nobility. As we shall see, Spanish Anarchism tried to sift the more positive features of the *pueblo* from its reactionary social characteristics and rear its concept of the future on the mutualism of village life.

Chapter Three:
The Beginning

The International in Spain

As for the nuclei Fanelli left behind in Spain in 1869, little was heard from them for a time.

Before his departure from Madrid, the Italian had given his admiring group of workers a small miscellaneous legacy of written material: the statutes of the International, the program and regulations of the Bakuninist Alliance of Social Democracy, the rules of a Swiss workingmen's society, and several radical periodicals which included articles and speeches by Bakunin. These precious texts were carefully studied, discussed, and passed around (presumably in translation), until the fledgling Madrid Anarchists began to feel assured and confident of their views. They called themselves "Internationalists," and were to do so for years, basking in the mounting prestige of the great workers' International north of the Pyrenees.

They also began to write letters to the International's General Council in London, but rarely received a reply. It may have been that the General Council, dominated by Bakunin's opponent, Karl Marx, was suspicious of the new "official section" in Madrid, or it may have been sheer negligence; in any event, the Madrid Internationalists maintained close ties with Bakunin and his friends in Geneva, and they began to cast around for support in their own city.

But this raised a difficult question: what could a revolutionary group, oriented toward the working class, hope to achieve in the Spanish capital? Madrid, the administrative center of the Spanish crown, had no proletariat in any modern sense of the word. A new city by Iberian standards, Philip II had turned it into a capital in order to provide the country with a sorely needed geographic and political center. It was not until the eighteenth century, under the Bourbon kings, that Madrid reached sizable proportions. At the time of Fanelli's visit, the capital city of Spain had no industry to speak of. Its proletariat consisted of craftsmen, working by traditional standards in small shops, and its market was composed of petty government officials, courtiers, soldiers, an emerging commerical middle class, and a large number of intellectuals attracted by the University of Madrid and by the city's burgeoning cultural life. Anarchism in the Spanish capital was largely to reflect these social traits. The Madrid organization eventually attracted many intellectuals and became one of the major theoretical centers of the Anarchist movement in Spain.

The early Internationalists in the capital, however, began in confusion over their aims and methods. A substantial number of the original group, those who were actually Republicans, Masons, and cooperativists, simply dropped away. The remainder, after sorting out their ideas and the material Fanelli had left behind, began to hold public meetings and attract local attention. The first of these meetings was held in a barn-like warehouse on Valencia Street which the janitor, a newly won supporter by the name of Jalvo, had opened to the Internationalists. Typical of the early enthusiasm and recklessness that marked the movement, Jalvo's gesture could have easily jeopardized his job, possibly exposing him to arrest, for the warehouse was a municipal building used to store materials for public festivals. Fortunately, the authorities did not take the movement too seriously, and Jalvo suffered no reprisals.

The Madrid section of the International expanded rapidly. The early meetings also attracted a number of canny Republican orators who were looking for a base in the labor movement and tried to take over the newly formed section. But Fanelli had done his work well, and they were firmly resisted. Faced with these well-attended meetings, Lorenzo and his comrades now began the difficult task of giving their movement some organizational coherence. They threw their net far, reaching out to the Masons (whom Lorenzo describes sympathetically as "auxiliaries" of the International), cultural groups, mutual-aid societies, and even economic liberals. By early 1870—a year after Fanelli's departure—the Madrid section of the International claimed a membership of two thousand and had started publishing a local periodical, *La Solidaridad*, to propagate its views. This membership figure was probably inflated by the inclusion of many individuals and groups with a very tenuous relationship to the section and with no clear understanding of its revolutionary goals. Yet it is clear that by 1870 the Anarchist movement was firmly rooted in Madrid.

If success is to be gauged by numerical following, the new movement was even more successful in Barcelona. In contrast to Madrid, the great Catalan seaport was a major textile center, the biggest in Spain, with a large industrial working class. Although Barcelona had been renowned for its cloth products for centuries the industrial development of the city in any modern sense of the word did not begin until the late 1840s, when steam-powered cotton factories were widely established. A decade later, engravings show the old port district surrounded by factory chimneys. Most of these concerns were not large; they normally employed between ten and twenty workers and were owned by moderately well-to-do bourgeois families. But there were also spectacular industrial dynasties, such as the Guells, the Muntada brothers, and the Serra brothers, employing thousands of unskilled workers and producing cheap cotton cloth for the villages and towns of Spain.

The average Barcelona factory operative worked long hours and at near-subsistence wages (see pp. 51-52 below), living with his or her family in hovels that often lacked adequate ventilation and sanitary facilities. This degraded way of life, scarred by toil and poverty, was menaced continually by technological unemployment and by lay-offs due to economic slumps. Reduced to an animal level of existence, the Barcelona proletariat seethed with a futile outrage that found partial outlet in "Luddism": the destruction of machinery and factory buildings. In 1836, during an upsurge of working-class unrest, a Barcelona crowd burned down the Bonaplata factory, a new steam-powered enterprise that produced not only fabrics but textile machinery. Factory burnings and the destruction of self-acting spindles also opened the labor struggles of 1854, but this time Barcelona was swept by a general strike in which workers marched under the slogan, "Association or Death." The right to form trade unions, denied by law under nearly all the regimes of that period, had now become a paramount demand of the Catalan working class.

Despite the failure of the strike, the movement toward association was irrepressible. This became evident in the mid-1860s when, under the tolerant administration of a Liberal government, underground workers' organizations suddenly surfaced, established two successful, widely read newspapers, and in 1865 held an impressive congress. The movement was suppressed a year later with the fall of the Liberals, but it thrived below the surface, publicly appearing in such forms as cultural circles and educational societies. Around the time of Fanelli's last visit to Barcelona, the most militant workers' groups were organized around the Federal Center of Workers' Societies (*Centro Federal de las Sociedades Obreras*). Politically, the Federal Center made common cause with the Republicans, supporting their demand for a federal republic. Economically, it favored privately financed cooperatives. A workers' Congress of over sixty societies, held in Barcelona on December 12-13, 1868, declared its support for these moderate forms and circumspectly avoided any demands that might alienate their Republican allies.

It was on this diffuse labor movement, committed to a bourgeois political alliance, that the Barcelona nucleus of the International went to work. The moving spirit of the nucleus was unquestionably Rafael Farga Pellicer, who had been deeply impressed by Fanelli's speech in his uncle's study. The group of Internationalists formed after the Italian's departure was soon reinforced by new, extremely able people: the physican Gaspar Sentinon; Jose Garcia Vinas, a medical student from Malaga; Trinidad Soriano, a technical student; and Antonio Gonzalez Meneses, an engineering student from Cadiz. By May 1869, the nucleus felt strong enough to constitute itself officially as the Barcelona section of the International Workingmen's Association. To the call for a "federal democratic republic," issued by the Workers' Congress, the new group replied with a demand for "Socialism," firmly declaring its dissatisfaction with mere reforms and change in government.

Despite this strong expression of intransigence, the Internationalists proceeded slowly and cautiously. A printer by trade, Farga Pellicer attended the Workers' Congress in December, two months prior to Fanelli's second trip to Barcelona; there, he had openly congratulated the delegates on their support for a federal republic and their plan to establish a newspaper. His relations with the Federal Center were excellent and the pages of its newly established organ, *La Federacion*, were open to the expression of Internationalist opinions. In a letter to Bakunin he describes the basic strategy of the Barcelona nucleus as a threefold approach: to defend Socialism in "a prudent manner" in *La Federacion*, to bring the regulations of the Federal Center into accord with the spirit of the International, and to strengthen the organizational influence of the nucleus on the workers' societies.

Within a few months, this strategy succeeded. Internationalists were elected presidents of several workers' societies and *La Federacion* essentially became an Internationalist organ, the Barcelona counterpart of Madrid's *La Solidaridad*. By 1870, the Federal Center and presumably most of its affiliates declared for the International, bringing thousands of industrial workers into an Anarchist-influenced movement. This influence, it should be stressed, was exercised with care. The great majority of the workers and their leaders were not conscious Anarchists, certainly not in any revolutionary sense of the word. Indeed, as we shall see later, the entry of the Federal Center into the International was an alliance, not an act of organic unity, between a small group of Anarchist militants and a numerically larger trade-union apparatus. But it foreshadowed a time when Anarchist ideas were to saturate the Spanish labor movement and produce a genuinely revolutionary mass organization based on Anarchosyndicalism.

From Madrid and Barcelona, the ideas of the International began to spread into the provinces of Spain. Newspapers and propagandists began to appear in Andalusia, Aragon, the Levant, and in rural areas of Catalonia, the two Castiles, and Galicia. Gradually the movement took hold outside of the two great cities. In February 1870, *La Solidaridad* issued a call for a national congress of all sections of the International in Spain. After consultations with the Catalans over a suitable place, it was decided to convene at Barcelona in late June.

During those few months before the congress the Anarchists did a great deal of careful planning and preparation. After Fanelli's final departure from Barcelona in the winter of 1869, Farga and Sentiñon had carried on a lively correspondence with Bakunin. About a half year later, in September, the two Spaniards attended the worldwide congress of the International in Basel, where Bakunin scored a short-lived triumph over Marx and his supporters. There, Bakunin not only solidified their adherence to Anarchism but initiated them into a secret group, originally named the "International Brotherhood," which the Russian had formed years earlier during his long sojourn in the heady, conspiratorial atmosphere of Italy. (Although the original "International Brotherhood" (*Fraternité Internationale*) was formally dissolved early in 1869, I have retained this name in quotation marks to designate the small group of confidantes who surrounded Bakunin during the later years of his life.)

The key role played the various Bakuninist organizations—the "International Brotherhood" and its successor, the Alliance of Social Democracy—in the development of the International in Spain requires examination here before proceeding with our account of the planned congress in Barcelona.

Bakunin's "International Brotherhood" has been dealt with derisively as a hierarchical, elitist organization which stands in blatant contradiction to his libertarian principles. This contradiction in my view is very real. Bakunin had intended the "International Brotherhood" to be a secret organization of Anarchist militants, led in tightly disciplined fashion by a highly centralized group of initiates—indeed, by what amounted to a revolutionary general staff. The Russian never resolved the need to bring his organizational theories and practices into complete accord with his libertarian social ideals. He seemed quite sincerely to regard both his followers and himself as highly moral and dedicated individuals who could survive the sordid aspects of organizational life without becoming authoritarians, perhaps even shielding weaker individuals and less committed organizations from the temptations of power and authority. Bakunin's followers often rebelled against this obvious contradiction between theory and practice, forcing the Russian to accede to a looser, more libertarian type of organization. The result is that the "Brotherhood" and its

A group portrait of the original Madrid Internationalists who
met and worked with Fanelli during his visit. Fanelli is at the
top. The others include a number of important and lesser
known figures in the history of Spanish Anarchism: Jose
Rubau Donadeu, Angel Cenagorta Mazon, Manuel Cano
Martinez, Francisco Mora Mendez, Marcelino Lopez Fernandez, Antonio Cerrudo Calles, Enrique Borrel Mateo, Anselmo Lorenzo Asperilla, Jose Posyol Urricain, Julio Rubau
Donadeu, Jose Adsuar Fernandez, Miguel Langara Checa,
Quintin Rodriguez Fernandez, Antonio Gimeno Yato, Enrique Simancas Grisnain, Angel Mora Mendez, Tomas Fernandez Pacheco, Benito Rodriguez Fernandez, Nicolas
Rodriguez Fronton, Jose Fernandez Neira.

ANSELMO LORENZO (1842-1914). The "grandfather" of
Spanish Anarchism, and the principal source of information
on its origins and early history. Lorenzo was perhaps the
most dedicated individual in the group that met with
Fanelli in Spain.

RAFAEL FARGA PELLICER, one of Fanelli's ablest Barcelona converts, who was to play a major role in the early
development of Spanish Anarchism.

An etching of the founding congress of the International at the Teatro del Circo in Barcelona, June 1870. Note the elaborate secretariat on the stage, a characteristic feature of Anarchosyndicalist labor meetings up to the present time.

organizational heirs remained nebulous, shadowy, and never developed a hierarchy; indeed, it is doubtful if its numbers ever exceeded a few score individuals.

The "Brotherhood" was expected to play a guiding role in still another organization, the Alliance of Social Democracy which Bakunin's comrades had formed over his objections in 1868, shortly before Fanelli's journey to Spain. Farga Pellicer and Sentiñon, in fact, had helped form the Spanish section of the Alliance months before they knew anything about the "Brotherhood." In contrast to the "Brotherhood," this organization was to be an open, public movement and was clearly Anarchist in program despite the apparent innocence of its name. Declaring itself for the abolition of classes, property, and the right of inheritance, the Alliance recognized "no form of state" and demanded that "all the political and authoritarian states at present should be reduced to mere administrative functions of public services."

To Marx, the presiding spirit of the International's General Council in London, this amounted to a *de facto* rejection of electoral and political activity, a position he strongly opposed. When the Alliance applied for membership in the International late in 1868, its rejection by the General Council was almost preordained. In order to circumvent the Council's decision, the Alliance officially dissolved itself, calling upon its sections to become sections of the International. In reality these sections continued to exist as secret Bakuninist nuclei. In Spain, the Alliance essentially became a small underground organization within the larger, open arena provided by the Spanish sections of the International. By the early summer of 1870, the sections numbered between twenty and thirty thousand members, with scores of groups in different parts of the country.

In the sixty years following Fanelli's visit, the fortunes of Spanish Anarchism were destined to fluctuate sharply and dramatically. During periods of repression, the movement was to contract to a few isolated nuclei of dedicated militants, only to surge forward and embrace ever larger masses of oppressed. Gradually, Anarchist groups were to take root in a multitude of Andalusian villages as well as in major cities and industrial centers. They were to establish tendrils in the mountain communities of Murcia, in the towns of the Ebro valley, in the remote fishing villages of the Galician coast. Long after the Anarchist movement had waned in the rest of Europe, it was to find a rich soil below the Pyrenees, nourished by the devotion of thousands of workers and peasants. Only the scythe of fascism could remove this wild luxuriant growth from the Iberian Peninsula—and with it the revolutionary passion of Spain.

The Congress of 1870

On the morning of Sunday, June 18, 1870, about one hundred delegates representing 150 workers' societies in thirty-six localities of Spain convened in the Teatro del Circo of Barcelona for the first congress of the Spanish section of the International. The congress proposed five months earlier by *La Solidaridad*, the Madrid organ of the International, had now become a reality.

The Teatro was filled to overflowing. The first rows of seats were reserved for delegates, but workers had come in large groups to express their solidarity, occupying every seat, filling the hallways, and spilling out beyond the entrance. A tribune occupied the center of the stage. In the background there was an array of red flags, and overhead, a large red banner proclaiming in gold letters—"No rights without duties, no duties without rights!"[1] Tools were decoratively arranged on both wings to symbolize labor and tables were placed on the extremes of the stage for pro tem secretaries of the congress.

The congress was opened by Rafael Farga Pellicer, who appeared suddenly on the deserted stage, rang a hand bell, and extended the following greetings:

"Comrade delegates: those of you who gather here to affirm the great work of the International Workingmen's Association, which contains within itself the complete emancipation of the proletariat and the absolute extirpation of all injustices which have ruled and still rule over the face of the earth; those of you who come to fraternize with the millions of workers, white slaves and black slaves, under the red banner which covers us; dear bothers, in the name of the workers of Barcelona, peace and greetings!"[2]

The hortatory style with its use of superlatives, its largeness of perspective, its intense internationalism, and its high-minded tone, all sincere and very deeply felt, was to be characteristic of Anarchist speeches in Spain. Farga made no attempt to conceal or subdue his radical views. "The state," he declared, "is the guardian and defender of the privileges that the Church makes divine. . . . We wish to end the rule of the capital, of the state and of the Church by constructing on their ruins Anarchy—the free federation of free associations of workers."

The speaker, we are told, was interrupted continually by "formidable thunderclaps" and the audience was "visibly moved." An atmosphere of "felicity" and enthusiasm pervaded the Teatro, to which greetings from the Swiss and Belgian sections of the International added a sense of historic purpose and worldwide fraternity. In the afternoon, the delegates rose one by one to report on the conditions in their factories. Their accounts leave us a bitter picture of the misery that pervaded the lives of the Spanish workers during the 1870s. The report of Bove, a Barcelona textile worker, is typical. The workers, he tells us, are exploited from five in the morning to late at night. Women work from ten to fifteen hours for less than a dollar, and in some factories, for as much as eighteen hours for little more than a dollar. Other delegates report that eleven, sixteen, and eighteen hours of daily work are typical in the textile enterprises around Barcelona and Tarragona. Farres, a delegate of the steam workers, speaks for "a sad and lamentable group in which the capitalists have declared men useless for work and replaced them with women and children. Take this into consideration, for only the man is useful for this [heavy] work and not the women. The men do not know what to do because they were not born to steal but to work."

These harsh realities contrasted starkly with the glowing hopes that opened and animated the congress. Each session moved along smoothly, often in an atmosphere of spontaneous, even tumuluous enthusiasm, and no restraints were placed on controversy or the free expression of opinion. But as we have seen, the proceedings had been carefully planned and prepared by a conscious, well-organized group of Anarchists, members of Bakunin's Alliance of Social Democracy.

It was these *Aliancistas*—this hidden Anarchist faction in Spain, known perhaps to only a few hundred initiates—that guided the proceedings at the Teatro del Circo. They prepared the agenda of the congress, staffed its key commissions, and provided the most articulate and informed speakers at its sessions. The *Aliancistas* had little need of manipulation for they enjoyed enormous prestige among the delegates to the congress. They were the actual founders of the International in Spain. So closely were the origins of the International linked to the Alliance that Fanelli's disciples had initially adopted the Alliance's program for the Madrid and Barcelona sections. It was not until the spring of 1870, when the Alliance was formally established in Spain as an independent body, that the two organizations became ideologically distinguishable. At the congress of 1870, the *Aliancistas* set about to give the Spanish section of the International a broader program, one that would be more in accord with the needs of a loose federation of workers' and peasants' trade unions.

This new program, however, was not foisted on the congress. It developed out of controversies in the "commissions" on various social issues and in debates on the floor of the Teatro del Circo. In addition to the Anarchists, at least three tendencies surfaced at the congress: an ineffectual miscellany of "associatarians," who were mainly interested in fostering producers' and consumers' cooperative associations within the existing social order; a "political" group which was occupied with mobilizing labor support for the Republican parties; and finally, the most important and enduring tendency of all, the trade unionists "pure-and-simple," a group concerned largely with immediate economic struggles over wages, hours, and working conditions—and a group, as we shall see, that was to function in later periods as a restraining force on the more militant and revolutionary Anarchists. Virtually all of these tendencies employed an expansive revolutionary rhetoric, giving lip-service to a distant egalitarian future, but they divided sharply with the Anarchists on the critical issues of the specifics needed to achieve this new society.

The views of the "associatarians" seem to have evoked very little interest from the congress. A report by a "commission on the theme of cooperation," obviously Anarchist-inspired, dismissed the importance of producers' cooperatives under capitalism: they would represent simply one more institution within the bourgeois framework. But the report did emphasize the practical role consumers' cooperatives could play in promoting "cooperative habits" and a spirit of mutual aid among the workers. In dealing with cooperatives as an educational means, rather than as a social end that could achieve a new society within capitalism, the report scaled down the entire issue, boxing the "associatarians" into a faddist social limbo. On this issue, the congress of 1870 represented a turning point, marking the decline of the Proudhonian tradition which had once been so important in the Spanish labor movement. Henceforth, any discussion of cooperatives was to be tied to problems of social revolution, not piecemeal reform.

Perhaps the sharpest conflict within the congress centered around the attitude of the Spanish section toward politics. The *Aliancistas* advocated political abstention. This position, as Casimiro Marti observes in his study on early Catalan Anarchism, "pointed up in a clear manner the immediate consequences of the new orientation adopted by the workers' movement. It was not now a question of a simple complaint, of a protest, more or less violent, against particular injustices, but of refusing to participate in political activity by virtue of a total and unconditional break with the constituted society." Abstention from politics amounted to unconditional support for "direct action oriented toward the suppression of the State. . . ."

An overstatement, perhaps, but essentially true. Although the non-Anarchist tendencies at the congress were prepared to concede such abstractions as cooperative or communal visions of the future society to their *Aliancista* opponents, they rallied against a strict policy of political abstention and direct action. After much dispute, a compromise was worked out in which the congress, while committing itself organizationally to an antistatist and abstentionist stand, left individual members free to act as they chose in the political arena.

This was a serious setback for the Anarchists. They were not try-ing to make the International's program identical to that of the Al-liance, for that would have confined the International exclusively to revolutionary forms of action. On the contrary, they were eager for the two organizations to be differentiated in many important re-spects, both programmatically and structurally. But they knew that any compromise on the issue of political abstention threatened to open the International to a reformist perspective, involving it largely in the amelioration of existing economic and political abuses. The compromise, in fact, was to have serious implications for the future, for it provided a formula by which the International and its heirs in Spain were to make theoretical acknowledgments to principle but function opportunistically in practice. Although the compromise was carried by the congress, it was scarcely hailed with enthusiasm: nearly 40 percent of the delegates either voted against it or abstained. Most·of these negative votes and abstentions came from delegates of the Barcelona working class.

The most important single achievement of the congress was in the realm of organization. The "commission on the theme of the social organization of the workers" proposed a structure which was to re-main the framework of the Spanish section for several years after-ward and which the *Aliancistas* hoped to advance as a model for the International as a whole at its next conference in London in 1871. This structure is worth examining in some detail. It anticipates in many respects the syndicalist form of organization adopted by the French labor movement in the 1890s, a form that later spread to other Euro-pean countries and surfaced again in Spain.

The commission proposed a dual structure for the Spanish section of the International (or as it was henceforth to be called, the Spanish Regional Federation): organization by trade and organization by local-ity. On the one hand, local trade organizations (*Secciones de oficio*) grouped together all workers from a common enterprise and vocation into a large occupational federation (*Uniones de oficio*) whose primary function was to struggle around economic grievances and working conditions. A local organization of miscellaneous trades (*Secciones de oficio varios*) gathered up all those workers from different vocations whose numbers were too small to constitute effective organizations along vocational lines. On the other hand, in every community and region where the International was represented, the different local *Secciones* were grouped together, irrespective of vocation, into bodies (*Federaciones locales*) whose function was avowedly revolutionary—the administration of social and economic life on a decentralized, libertar-ian basis.

This dual structure forms the bedrock of all syndicalist organization. In Spain, as elsewhere, the structure was knitted together by workers' committees, which originated in individual shops, factories, and agricultural communities. Gathering together in assemblies, the workers elected from their midst the committees that presided over the affairs of the *Secciones de oficio* and the *Federaciones locales;* these were federated into regional, or *comarcal*, committees for nearly every geographic area of Spain. The workers, moreover, elected the delegates to the annual congresses of the Spanish Regional Federation, which in turn elected a Federal Council.

Although all committees were directly accountable to the assemblies that elected them, bureaucratization was a constant possibility and concern. The danger of bureaucracy, manipulation, and centralized control exists in any system of indirect representation. It is not very difficult for an elaborate network of committees, building up to regional and national bodies, to circumvent the wishes of the workers' assemblies at the base of the structure. This actually happened in France, when a corps of opportunistic syndicalists, Socialists, and later, Communists acquired control of the French General Confederation of Labor (CGT).

A bureaucracy never really solidified in the Spanish Regional Federation or its syndicalist heirs, at least not before the Civil War of 1936. Fortunately or not, the periodic waves of government or employer persecution that broke over the Spanish syndicalist unions made a union leader's position an unenviable one. Moreover, the Anarchists functioned as a steady and unsettling counterweight to bureaucratization (despite their own occasional tendencies to manipulate the unions under their control). They kept the labor movement in a state of continual ferment and never ceased to emphasize the need for decentralization, control from below, and direct action. Ultimately, it was their influence on the Spanish labor movement which proved decisive. In the decades to follow, they were to give it a depth of passion and an intensity of revolutionary idealism which has never been equaled by workers' unions elsewhere in the world.

We must look closely at these men and women, these Spanish Anarchists, and try to gain an understanding of their lives, their fervor, and their dedication to the "Idea." Although the founding nuclei of Spanish Anarchism included many intellectuals and students (such figures as Gaspar Sentinon, Trinidad Soriano, Antonio Gonzalez Meneses, and Fermin Salvochea), most of the individuals entering the growing libertarian groups of the cities were ordinary workers. Even the journalists, theoreticians, and historians of this movement were largely self-educated people of proletarian origin who often taught themselves to read and write or attended union and libertarian schools, acquiring their learning by sheer doggedness in the nighttime hours after work. The majority of them had been sent into factory jobs early in life. And later came the responsibilities of family life, of rearing children and maintaining a home. These Anarchists took great pride in their vocational skills and were viewed with immense respect by their fellow workers. Most of them were intensely serious and high-minded individuals. They were also open, candid, and like most Spaniards, passionately devoted to their friends and comrades.

They were individuals with very strong personalities. For example, more dedicated men, once having decided to embrace the "Idea," abjured smoking and drinking, avoided brothels, and purged their talk of "foul" language. They believed these traits to be "vices"—demeaning to free people and fostered deliberately by ruling classes to corrupt and enslave the workers spiritually. It was the duty of every *obrera consciente*, of every conscious worker and especially of an Anarchist, to live by his or her principles, not merely to avow them. By the example of the probity and dignity of their daily lives, such workers would help uplift the rest of their class. Without this moral regeneration of the proletariat, the revolution would eventually be vitiated by all the corruptive realities of bourgeois society.

What these Spanish Anarchists aimed for, in effect, was a "countersociety" to the old one. It is easy to mistake this for an "alternate society," one that would coexist with capitalism as an enclave of purity and freedom, but nothing could be further from the truth. The Spanish Anarchists expressly rejected the concept of an "alternate society," with its hope of peaceful reconstruction and its privileged position in a world of general misery. They regarded the cooperativist movement as a diversion from the main task of overthrowing capitalism and the state. Since social or personal freedom could not be acquired within the established order, they viewed a "countersociety" as a terrain in which to remake themselves into revolutionaries and remove their interests from any stake in bourgeois society. But this terrain was a completely embattled one. Eventually, Anarchist groups formulated their own revolutionary codes, their own concepts of freedom, and created a world of intimate comradeship and solidarity that proved almost impregnable to repression.

The most dedicated Spanish Anarchists not only denied the laws, values, and morality of the existing society, but set out to translate precept into practice. They did not enter into legal marriages. They refused to register the births of their children or to baptize them. The bureaucracy, state, and church were the Anarchists' mortal enemies; any voluntary dealings with these institutions were to be avoided. Children were sent to libertarian or union schools. If these were not available, they went to nonclerical institutions or were taught at home. Parents would often give their children names like "Libertaria" (a favorite for the daughters of Anarchist militants) or "Emancipacion"; they might even exchange their own first names for those of Anarchist heroes or martyrs. They disdained the accumulation of money, and if in later years there was much bank-robbing by Anarchists, the funds went entirely to the movement or to libertarian schools and publishing projects. They did not hesitate to use weapons in defending their own rights or in acts of retribution against official violence.

I shall take up the question of Anarchist violence in its proper context. At this point it might be more appropriate to give attention to the humaneness that permeated the outlook and ideals of Spanish Anarchism. The organized, official violence that the Spanish worker encountered almost daily, even in the form of entertainment, genuinely horrified these earnest libertarians. Shocked by the cruelty and brutalizing effect of the bullfight, for example, the Spanish Anarchists waged a persistent campaign to discourage attendance at the *corrida* and to arouse in the workers and peasants an interest in books, culture, and the serious discussion of ideas. Accordingly, wherever the Spanish Regional Federation had a substantial following it established *centros obreros*, which functioned not merely as union headquarters but as cultural centers. Depending upon its resources, the *centro obrero* might provide literature, books, classes, and meeting halls for discussions on a wide variety of subjects. This institution exercised a profound influence on the personal life of the worker who belonged to Anarchist-influenced unions. Ricardo Mella, one of the most able Anarchist theorists and essayists of that period, recalls that in Seville "with its enormous *centro obrero*, capable of holding thousands of people, morality in the customs [of workers] took hold to such a degree that drunkenness was banished. No worker would have dared or have been permitted to appear drunk at the door of the great popular building."

Anarchist-influenced unions gave higher priority to leisure and free time for self-development than to high wages and economic gains. The expansive humanism of these Anarchists is probably best indicated by the actions they undertook to protest the persecution of revolutionaries abroad, whenever or wherever they might be. Great public rallies and bitter strikes were conducted not only on behalf of their own foreign comrades, such as the Chicago Anarchists of the 1880s and Sacco and Vanzetti decades later, but in support of men who would have strongly opposed their movement and ideas, such as Ernst Thalmann, the German Communist leader imprisoned by the Nazis.

Their generosity of sentiment reached into the most intimate details of personal and family life. A male Spanish Anarchist, for example, rarely wavered in his loyalty to his *companera*. He genuinely respected her dignity, an attitude he extended to his dealings with his children and comrades. The "Idea" was his passion. If he was a committeeman or occupied a union post, he regularly attended meetings and occupied himself with all the details of the movement, for the movement gave meaning and purpose to his life, removing it from the mediocre world of humdrum routine, vulgar self-interest, and banality.

This devotion, however, did not reduce him to an organizational robot. He controlled the movement like everyone else in it and, despite the complexity of its structure at times, it was usually scaled to human dimensions. If this structure threatened to become too complex, he as an Anarchist threw the full weight of his prestige against the development and together with his comrades would rescale it to meaningful, comprehensible dimensions.

Anarchism, moreover, gave his mind a profoundly experimental turn. Spanish Anarchism is rooted in the belief in a "natural man," corrupted by propertied society and the state, who will be regenerated by a libertarian revolution. To many individual Anarchists, this corruption was ubiquitous; it debased not only people's instincts and moral integrity, but also their diet, tastes, and behavior. Hence Anarchists experimented with a wide variety of ideas. They improvised new diets (many turning to vegetarianism), flirted with naturopathy, studied Esperanto, and in some cases practiced nudism. Extolling spontaneity in behavior, they had a fascination for libertarian forms of education and for techniques of child-rearing that promoted the natural proclivities of the young. Their emphasis on freedom became the most serious challenge to the rigid mores and medieval fanaticism of the time.

Many liberal and Marxian writers have described Spanish Anarchism as an atavistic attempt to turn back the historical clock. But in fact, the Anarchists placed a high premium on scientific knowledge and technological advance; they devoured the available scientific literature of their day and expounded continually on such themes as evolution, rationalist cosmologies, and the value of technology in liberating humanity. A very compelling case, in fact, can be made for the argument that Spanish Anarchism refracted the spirit of Enlightenment Europe through an Iberian prism, breaking up its components and then reorganizing them to suit Spain's distinctive needs.

The Spanish Anarchists certainly were eager to preserve the rich, preindustrial tapestry of their country's communal traditions—the emphasis on individuality and dignity, the high spirit of mutual aid, localism, the *patria chica*, and the *pueblo*. But they also realized that Spain needed the technological resources of the advanced capitalist world to create the material bases for a classless society and genuine freedom.

The problem that confronted the Spanish Anarchists was crucial: how to industrialize Spain without destroying her communal heritage, debasing her working class, and rearing the soul-destroying monstrosity that the Industrial Revolution had inflicted on England. The attempt to deal with this problem accounts in part for their puritanical morality.[3] The Spanish Anarchists could not help but absorb the traditional puritanical atmosphere of Catholic, agrarian Spain; but simply to regard their movement as religious, to view it in Brenan's terms as a nineteenth-century Reformation, is a crude oversimplification. In the latter half of the nineteenth century Spain began to undergo an industrial revolution of her own, with many of the demoralizing effects of the Industrial Revolution in England. Technological change and the erosion of traditional social relations began to undermine the family structure and the old system of morality. The demoralization of newly urbanized rural folk who were flocking in great numbers into the cities looking for work and relief from chronic hunger was a visible feature of social life. Drunkenness, prostitution, broken families, and beggary had reached appalling proportions. Not only traditional society but the proletariat itself was in a state of decay.

The Spanish Anarchists were determined to eliminate these demoralizing features from working-class life. They were intent on restoring the moral fiber of the proletariat, on giving it inner solidity and firmness. In a society of scarce resources, where a life of idleness and dissipation was a function of exploitation and privilege, it was inconceivable that a revolution could occur without emphasizing the duty to work. The struggle of the Spanish Anarchists against alcoholism, dissoluteness, and irresponsibility became a struggle for the integrity of the working class, a validation of its moral capacity to reorganize society and manage it on a libertarian basis in an era of material scarcity.

It was individuals of this moral caliber and social outlook who competed with cooperativists, trade unionists, political opportunists, and Socialists for influence in the congress of 1870. And they won this competition, at least until the next congress a year later. By the time Francisco Tomas declared the proceedings closed with "feeling and enthusiastic phrases," the congress had elected a Federal Council of five members: Tomas Gonzalez Morago, Enrique Borrel, Francisco Mora, Anselmo Lorenzo, and Angel Mora. All of these men were Madrid Anarchists who had met Fanelli early in 1869 and were now members of Bakunin's Alliance of Social Democracy. *Aliancistas* also occupied key positions in all leading sections of the Federation and played a decisive role in the forming of their policies. The Spanish labor movement had been founded on essentially libertarian lines and was soon to be plunged into a series of stormy upheavals.

The Liberal Failure

A large gathering of a revolutionary labor organization could not have occurred at a more favorable time than the summer of 1870. The founding congress of the Spanish Federation was held toward the end of an interregnum, when the entire country was in a state of confusion over its political future and its ruling classes were uncertain and faltering. For nearly two years the Spanish throne had been vacant while Madrid afforded the spectacle of politicians quarreling among themselves over the choice of a monarch. This humiliating interregnum revealed with startling clarity the extent to which a permanent crisis had settled into Spanish society. The hurried flight of Isabella II from Spain in September 1868 marks the climax of a historic conflict between an absolutist monarchy and the liberal middle classes, to be succeeded by a duel between the church and the army—the latter being guardian, for a time, of all elements that feared a theocratic government. Each of these conflicts rolled one upon the other like waves, loosening the traditional structure of the Spanish state. The monarchy had failed completely to restore the "old Spain" of the *ancien regime;* the church, to straitjacket the country in a theocracy; the bourgeoisie, to follow in the steps of its predecessors north of the Pyrenees and create the institutional, economic, and cultural bases of a constitutional, democratic state. And now the plebians were beginning to enter the arena in force: the radical middle class, the peasants, and the growing working-class movement.

The details of this succession of failures are too complex to explore in the space of a few pages, but the very fact of their complexity is evidence of the nervous twitching, followed by periodic collapse, that marked Spanish political life from the opening decades of the nineteenth century to Isabella's removal from the throne.

The occupation of Madrid by Napoleon's armies in 1808 completely exploded the last remaining myths of the "Golden Age" when Spain aspired to hegemony in Europe and her empire encompassed vast territories in the New World. For the first time since the Reconquest, her people acquired a vibrant sense of national identity. Every part of the country took up arms against the French invader, each region and locality acting independently under its own juntas and commanders. As noted by Charles Oman, the English chronicler of the peninsular war, "The movement was spontaneous, unselfish, and reckless; in its wounded pride, the nation challenged Napoleon to combat, without any thought of the consequences, without counting up its own resources or those of the enemy." Despite the divisions that pitted juntas, regions, and classes against each other, the long conflict with Napoleon could have created the point of departure for a national renaissance and the reentry of Spain into European society.

It was not to be so. These hopes vanished with the return of Ferdinand VII from captivity in France. Supine before Napoleon, Ferdinand proved to be unrelenting in his efforts to crush the Liberals of Spain. The Constitution of 1812, which the Extraordinary Cortes had promulgated from Cadiz in the midst of the national war, was repudiated. Its provisions for a constitutional monarchy, universal suffrage, a single legislative chamber, and civil liberties were replaced by a harsh absolutism. For nearly six years, Ferdinand's rule lay upon Spain like a shroud. Although the country began to regain its momentum with the successful *pronunciamiento* of Riego and Quiroga in January 1820, the ghost of absolutism was not consigned to its historic mausoleum until Ferdinand's death in 1833. With the demise of absolutist rule, however, Spain now came face to face with the menace of a theocracy. The outbreak of the first Carlist War in October 1833 marked the first blow in the church's attempt to gain mastery over Spanish political life. When violence failed to bring Ferdinand's reactionary brother Don Carlos to the throne, the church turned to systematic penetration of the state. By the late 1860s, the court *camarilla* was riddled with priests and clerical craftiness seemed on the point of achieving what had remained beyond the reach of insurgent peasant militias in years of bloody fighting.

However, neither the church, the army which contested its ambitions, nor the bourgeoisie were to gain lasting control of the Spanish state. The thirty years that followed Ferdinand's death read like the temperature chart of a man in deathly fever. Ministries changed with bewildering frequency, carried away by political maneuvers, civil wars, and above all, by military *pronunciamientos*. The army, initially the defender of Liberalism against absolutism and clerical reaction, began to act alternately as a political master in its own right. Even the word "Liberalism" began to lose its meaning. The bloc that lay claim to this name divided into the Moderates, a reactionary grouping based on the landed bourgeoisie, and the Progressives, a prudent cabal of anticlerical "Europeanizers," who leaned for support on the well-to-do urban middle classes. Welling up from the depths of the disillusioned petty bourgeoisie came the Republicans—a conglomerate of radicals and Federalists, the latter adhering to Pi y Margall's doctrine of a Swiss-like, cantonal state.

There was one thing that united this flotsam of Monarchists, clerics, "liberals," landed oligarchs, and army officers as they scrambled for control of the state. It was fear: a fear of the masses. Franz Borkenau notes that "in Britain, in America, and in Germany, every popular movement originated in the upper stratum of society and then permeated the masses." In Spain, on the other hand,

> no movement in the higher classes ever penetrated deeply the masses. Spain is the country where the spontaneity of the "people" as against the aristocracy, the bourgeoisie, the intelligentsia, and, in the last decades, the clergy, is most conspicuous. Such a deep severance of the people from the ruling groups, such a passing of the initiative to the lowest stratum of society, is always a symptom of deep decay and disintegration of the old civilization.

Sensing their own weakness and decadence, the ruling classes responded to the people with a combination of Olympian contempt and sheer panic. It is reported that after a terrifying experience with a riot, Charles III never overcame his fear of the Madrid "mob"; even street noises frightened him. Although national tradition credits "the people" with driving Napoleon's armies from Spain, a contemporary of the period recalls the panic that seized the middle classes when the ragged militia of the "Valencian Army" entered Madrid.

The job of dealing with the masses, of cultivating a watchful eye and a restraining hand, was left to the Spanish church. The historic isolation of the church from the people in the nineteenth century, a product partly of the Liberals' agrarian policy, completed the isolation of the Spanish ruling classes from Spain.

There had been a time, though, when the popular prestige of the church was enormous. The church bells of Spain had been the tocsins of the Reconquest, rallying the villages to war against the Moorish invaders. Clerics not only blessed the Christian armies but often led them into battle. During the "Golden Age," the clergy provided Spain with its only social conscience, raising its voice on behalf of the exploited peasantry at home and the decimated Indians in the colonies abroad. Inveighing against the ravages of usury, privilege, and greed, it stood foremost among the ruling classes in defense of the communal institutions of Spain and the tribal institutions of the New World.

Despite its imposing hierarchy, the Spanish church probably remained the most democratic institution in a society anchored in political absolutism. To a French nobleman visiting Spain in the early nineteenth century, the structure of the Spanish clergy was virtually republican ("tout a fait republicaine"). Raymond Carr, in a perceptive account of modern Spanish history, reminds us that "one eighteenth-century primate was the son of a charcoal burner, a situation inconceivable in France," and most of the bishops were recruited from "the obscurity of the minor provincial nobility." Nor was there a visible display of clerical luxury and opulence. A bishop, Carr adds,

> was expected to give all his surplus income to charity once his simple houshold needs were satisfied. The average parish priest was poor and remained so throughout the nineteenth and twentieth centuries; he earned less than a well-paid laborer and was often dependent, in rural parishes, on the sale of eggs and on other minor agricultural pursuits.

Lest this trait be overdrawn, however, the fact remains that with the passage of time, the church began to age and fatten, much like the courtiers whose lean, warrior ancestors had helped expel the Moors. By the close of the eighteenth century, the church had become the largest landowner and wealthiest institution in Spain, indissolubly linked with the monarchy and nobility. The gap between what bishops were "expected" to do and what they in fact did widened considerably, but the church's prestige among the masses had not diminished. To the immense number of beggars—*los miserables*—who formed the recruits for "mob" riots and near-insurrections in the streets of Spanish cities, the church provided not only religious circuses but material sustenance. In Madrid, for example, the convents alone provided *los miserables* with 30,000 bowls of soup daily. In Valladolid, according to Carr's estimate, a twentieth of the population depended on the church, "while soup and bread doles from episcopal palaces and monasteries were an important element in the budget of the urban poor."

But ties of this kind could exist only if the church retained the agrarian roots of a feudal estate, roots which nourished the medieval spectacle of public humility and charity toward the poor. When the Liberal premier Mendizabal initiated the confiscation of church lands on a major scale, these traditional roots were pulled up. Ostensibly, the confiscation was undertaken for two purposes: to finance the war against the Carlists and to create an agrarian middle-class base for the Liberals. Actually, the sale of the church lands did not achieve anything near the result intended. The confiscated estates became the object of crass bourgeois speculation, nourishing a new class of lay land magnates. The land hunger of the peasantry, satisfied in France by the Great Revolution and by Napoleon, was to remain an endemic feature of Spanish society.

Having lost its lands and its agrarian roots, the church shifted all its resources to speculation and business. The higher clergy began to neglect its pastoral duties for the more lucrative realms of industry, commerce, urban real estate, and according to the gossip of the day, brothels. The new investments transformed the Catholic Church from the largest landowner in Spain into the largest capitalist; its ideology, the most medieval and atavistic in Western Europe, transformed it from the social conscience of the ruling class into the most reactionary force in social life.

The decline of the church's popular prestige left only one effective institution that could function politically without a popular base—the army. Initially, the army had been a bulwark of Liberalism and its early *pronunciamientos* enforced middle-class interests in Spanish politics. But a half century of meddling and manipulation had made it increasingly suspect as a corps of Praetorians, even to the Moderates. Having exhausted its alliance with the Liberals, embroiled in imperialist adventures in Morocco, the Spanish officer caste began its slow, fatal drift to the right. If the Liberals, who still had illusions of acquiring popular support, regarded the army as an embarrassing and dangerous liability, the reactionaries in later years were only too glad to use it as a lever for social power. The history of the army after 1870 is a numbing account of its growing sense of isolation, its preoccupation with pay, promotion, and graft, and its arrogance toward the *canaille*.

The *canaille*, of course, were the masses of Spain—peasants, farm laborers, craftsmen, industrial workers, *los miserables*—the majority of whom lived in desperate poverty. Thousands of beggars filled the city slums or wandered the country roads. To the ruling classes, the Spanish people were a faceless, anonymous lot, volatile but inchoate, threatening but politically inert; and all the quarreling factions on the summits of society were united in the need to exclude their participation in the processes of institutional change.

But if the word "mass" is meant to convey anything more than sheer numbers, it becomes meaningless in Spain. From the Spanish *pueblo*, with its remarkable sense of community, had emerged a people in which self-assurance, dignity, and a striking individuality seemed like inborn traits. *Dignidad* has a fierceness of meaning in Spanish that has no parallel in any other European language, indeed, a fierceness that the Anarchists were to cultivate in every nuance of behavior and action. They were not unique in this respect. Brenan reminds us that, north of the Sierra Morena at least, the preoccupation with dignity is deeply rooted in Spanish history—the peasant ploughing with a sword dangling from his waist, the cobbler and mason treating the grandee as their equal, the beggars expecting to be addressed as "Your Worship" are images that will be found centuries ago.

It was this people whom the ruling classes finally divested of any meaningful relations with the institutions and values of official Spain. By the late 1860s, a cultural, religious, political, and economic vacuum had been created for the Spanish masses. The church had betrayed its responsibilities and the politicians their promises. There was no way even to faintly reconcile the interests of rural laborers, land-hungry peasants, and bitterly exploited workers with those of the propertied classes. *Caciques* ran the villages with a firm hand. The Civil Guard patrolled the roads, railway stations, and streets. The workers, denied all recognition of their rights to organize, faced an almost solid phalanx of rapacious manufacturers. The guardians of the state, occupied with their narrow political interests, cast a blank stare on the frustrated masses below. For the great bulk of the Spanish people, civil life was as empty as the vacated throne in Madrid. Henceforth, after 1870, all that could fill this vacuum were the Republican politics of the petty bourgeoisie, the Socialist doctrines of the radical intelligentsia, and Anarchist ideals of a proletarian or peasant variety.

Notes

1. In later years, the Anarchists were to adopt the black flag as a symbol of the workers' misery and as an expression of their anger and bitterness. The presence of black flags together with red ones became a feature of Anarchist demonstrations throughout Europe and the Americas. With the establishment of the CNT, a single flag on which black and red were separated diagonally, was adopted and used mainly in Spain.

2. The first and last of the words in this passage—*companeros* and *salud*—have been translated here as "comrades" and "greetings." They became the typical forms of address between Spanish Anarchists in personal encounters and at public meetings. *Companero* has a more endearing and familiar meaning than the formal word *camarada*, which was to be used by the Spanish Socialists and Communists. *Companero* connotes a "mate," a "companion"—one who shares not only common ideas but also a personal relationship. *Salud* could be translated as "your health," "your welfare." It was adopted to replace the usual farewell address, *adios* (literally: "to god"), a reference to the deity that the Anarchists regarded as an invasion by superstition of ordinary discourse. In later years, a gathering of the Spanish Anarch-

ists was to be called *una asemblea de las tribus*—"a gathering of the tribes"—a phrase that anticipates the sense of community sought by the youth culture in our own time. The Spanish Anarchists tended to use more personal, sentimental, and cognatic expressions than those employed by their stolid Marxian opponents.

3. This point should be emphasized. Nearly everyone who comments on the moral emphasis of the Spanish Anarchists treats it as a form of quasi-religious asceticism. Perhaps this was the case among the rural Anarchists, particularly those who lived in *pueblos*, but my own feeling (after discussing the issue with exiled Spanish Anarchists from the industrial cities) is that in the north at least, this moral emphasis was similar to the efforts of black radicals in the United States to elevate their people from the influence of a degrading and enslaving culture.

Chapter Four:
The Early Years

Proletarian Anarchism

The founding of the Spanish Regional Federation opened an entirely new period in the modern history of Spain. Since the respectable Liberal parties had shut themselves off from the masses of Spain the lower classes would try to form organizations of their own. The political polarization of rulers and ruled merely paralleled one that had long since developed on an economic and cultural level, but it was to lead to increasingly bitter confrontations in the years to come.

The earliest of these were mild. The founding congress had evoked press attacks throughout Spain, particularly in Madrid where the Liberals and Republicans viewed the antipolitical stance of the new Federation as a threat to their waning influence on the working class. Fortunately, the most immediate practical result of the Barcelona congress was to furnish the Federation with the nucleus of its own national press; in addition to *La Federacion* in Barcelona and *La Solidaridad* in Madrid, the Internationalists acquired *El Obrera* and *Revolucion* in Palma and *La Voz del Trabajador* in the key industrial city of Bilboa. The propaganda of the Spanish Federation probably represents the most important achievement of its first six months of existence. Its literature reached thousands, evoking an additional press response that gave it wide and continual publicity. The Federation began to acquire larger dimensions in the public mind than it actually possessed in fact, an image which the Federal Council in Madrid and the sections shrewdly reinforced with numerous leaflets, statements, and public meetings.

But other areas of the Federation's activities were less satisfactory. The enormous enthusiasm generated by the founding congress soon gave way to lassitude. The Federal Council's attempt to achieve a working unity between the various sections throughout the country met with a disillusioning lack of response. Letters sent into the hinterlands of Spain went unanswered, responses were often delayed, and a chronic shortage of funds created difficulties for the Madrid organization and severe hardships for members of the Council, most of whom gave generously of their time and resources. This in turn exacerbated relations between some of the *Aliancistas* who constituted the Federation's center and were to lead to serious personal and political frictions.

Even more serious were the problems that faced the Barcelona movement. Although Catalonia provided the largest single bloc of working-class recruits to the Spanish Federation, the Internationalists constituted a very small proportion of the Barcelona proletariat. Perhaps 9 percent of the working class in the city adhered to the new movement. Small as this figure is, it declined drastically when a yellow fever epidemic swept through the Catalan seaport, claiming many lives and stampeding thousands into the countryside. Of the 10,000 members who belonged to the Barcelona movement in July 1870, only 1,800 remained in January 1871, and scarcely more than 2,500 in August, a full year after the founding congress. The commonly repeated notion that the International in Spain enjoyed a spectacular growth during the first year of its existence is a myth, certainly as far as Barcelona—its center of proletarian support—is concerned.

Nominally, the Barcelona organization was controlled by Anarchists. Actually, the number of Anarchists in the sections was very small. In fact many outstanding figures in the Barcelona labor movement were pragmatic trade unionists whose social idealism was shallow at best. The International in the Catalan seaport was based on an alliance between a handful of Anarchists and a larger group of opportunistic unionists who had been driven into an antipolitical, direct-actionist position by the intransigence of the Barcelona textile manufacturers. Between these two tendencies of the Catalan trade-union movement existed an uneasy, even distrustful relationship which was to snap, reknit, and snap again in later years. The nature of this alliance and the maneuvering it entailed disturbed the gallant, honest Anselmo Lorenzo. Lorenzo had never forgotten Fanelli's words on libertarian organization. "How much more beneficial it would have been," he opined, years later, "if instead of finding agreements and solutions by surprise, the Alliance [of Social Democracy] had engaged in a work of education and instruction to show the way of obtaining agreements and solutions as a conscious sum of wills." Instead, the tensions in the fusion of trade-unionist demands with social revolutionary ideals was to have serious consequences throughout the history of the Spanish workers' movement.

Had the Catalan Anarchists rested their hopes solely on an alliance with an opportunistic union leadership, they surely would have lost the Barcelona labor movement to syndicalism of a reformist, French variety. Even the most dense, unreconstructed class of employers could not have deflected this development. What eventually gave Catalan Anarchism a mass following were the hordes of rural folk, the landless peasants and laborers, who streamed into Barcelona looking for work. Each year they came by the thousands, the great majority from the Catalan countryside itself, the next largest group from the Levant (Murcia, Valencia, Alicante, Castellon), followed by Aragonese from Saragossa, Huesca, and Teruel. Contrary to popular myth, only a small fraction of this inflowing labor force came from Andalusia. To the urbane Barcelonese, these destitute emigrants from the hungry Levant, with their country ways and course manners, were indiscriminately lumped together under the name *Murcianos*, in Barcelona a word equivalent to "nigger."

Pariahs in a strange, hostile urban world, the *Murcianos* encamped by the tens of thousands in squalid, miserable shacks. Their hovels ringed the great seaport and penetrated its suburbs, providing a huge reservoir of unskilled, menial labor exploited by the Catalan bourgeoisie. Disdained by nearly all the factions of the Liberals, later manipulated by such Radical demagogues as Lerroux, the *Murcianos* also provided a reservoir for the most volatile recruits to the libertarian movement in Catalonia. Without this transitional proletariat Anarchism would have lost its mass base in a broadly syndicalist labor organization, and it would have been impossible to reorient the reformist tendencies of the skilled and established Barcelona factory workers towards Anarchosyndicalism.

The role of the *Murcianos* in rooting proletarian Anarchism in Spain's largest industrial city, and the near-insurrectionary atmosphere they created, raises many fascinating problems. To Marx, the more the proletariat advanced from a craft to an industrial estate, and the more this class was "disciplined, united and organized by the process of capitalist production itself"—by the factory—the more of a revolutionary force it became. Marx's theory viewed the craft worker as a backward and undeveloped proletarian, a member of a transitional class like the peasantry. It is certain he would have regarded the rural *Murcianos*, not to speak of *los miserables* of the Spanish cities generally, with disdain—as a *déclassé* flotsam, a lumpen proletariat.

This contemptuous attitude toward decaying classes at the base of society is evinced most clearly in his remarks on the Franco-Prussian

War. "The French need a thrashing," he wrote to Engels a day after the outbreak of hostilities.

> If the Prussians win, then centralization of the *state power* is useful to the centralization of the German working class. Furthermore, German predominance in Europe would transfer the center of gravity of the West European labor movement from France to Germany, and one need only compare the movement from 1866 to the present in the two lands to see that the German working class is superior to the French in theory and organization. Its predominance over the French on the world stage would at the same time be the predominance of our theory over that of Proudhon. . . .

As it turned out, Marx was wrong—not only in prospect but also in retrospect. The classes that gave the cutting edge to the revolutions of 1848 were not primarily factory workers, but craftsmen and workers in small shops, precisely those decomposing, preindustrial strata whom Marx viewed with such contempt. The factory workers of Berlin, centered largely in the newly emerging locomotive industry, played a reactionary role in the insurrectionary movement of the period, even by comparison with petty-bourgeois democrats. Later, a year after Marx's letter to Engels, the *déclassés* of Montmartre and the craftsmen and workers in small industry (the "luxury goods workers," as Marx disdainfully called them) raised red flags and died by the thousands on the barricades in defense of the Paris Commune of 1871. And some sixty years afterward, it was not the sophisticated, highly centralized, and well-disciplined labor movement of Germany that was to take up arms against fascism, but the working class and peasants of Spain—both of which were unique in having retained the most preindustrial outlook in Western Europe.

Ironically, the "process of capitalist production itself," which Marx commended in *Capital*, served not only to unite, discipline, and centralize the proletariat, but to vitiate its revolutionary attitudes. The more workers were conditioned to accept the factory routine, to bend their heads before the demands of its overseers, the more they tended to accept hierarchy, authority, and obedience as an unchallengable destiny. And the more the working class acquired a hereditary status in society, knowing no other way of life but the industrial routine, the less revolutionary were its descendants. It was precisely the continual flow of *Murcianos* into Catalan industry, the continual leavening action of decomposing classes from the preindustrial *pueblos*, that renewed the revolutionary fervor of the Barcelona proletariat. These rural folk, uprooted from a precapitalist culture and life-style, imbued with values, codes, and tastes completely antithetical to the enervating culture of the cities, prevented the more stable and coopted sectors of the Catalan working class from hardening into settled social forms. The *Murcianos* were an immense social stratum that had absolutely nothing to lose. Accustomed to illegality, ebullient and riotous almost by nature, they added an electricity to the atmosphere of Barcelona that was to make it the most exciting, unruly, and revolutionary city in Europe.

In the early 1870s, however, these large masses of semiproletarians had yet to be won to Anarchism. The most dedicated early supporters of the Spanish Federation were craftsmen, not *déclassés* or unskilled factory workers. As late as 1872, more than half of the delegates to the Cordoba congress of the Federation were printers, typographers, master masons, shoemakers, and bakers—in short, skilled or fairly skilled craftsmen who worked in small shops. Only one out of five delegates was a factory hand, and an even smaller proportion were peasants. The unruly *miserables* of Madrid, for instance, were by no means uniformly friendly to the Federation. On May 2, 1871, a day which Spain celebrates in honor of the first popular uprising against Napoleon's armies, the Internationalists held a public meeting to counter the chauvinistic, anti-French spirit engendered by the holiday. It was mobbed and broken up by the local poor. A howling crowd laid siege to the Internationalists in a cafe well into the night.

Time was on the side of the Federation, however, and it soon began to make headway among the workers and urban poor. A few successful strikes in Barcelona, coupled with the growing notoriety of the International at home and abroad, brought new, dedicated adherents into the movement. The prospects of rapid growth seemed highly promising. In Barcelona, membership figures began to rise sharply from the low of January 1871; new periodicals were started or planned; and agitation began to spread in earnest beyond the cities into distant reaches of the countryside.

But time was precisely what the Spanish Federation was to lack. When in March 1871, the Parisian workers rose and established the commune, tremors of fear shook all the palaces and chancellories of Europe. In Madrid these fears were compounded by the increasing instability of the government. In December 1870, Amadeo of Savoy had arrived from Italy to occupy the vacant Spanish throne, but instead of bringing peace to the warring political factions, his presence reopened all the infighting and intrigues that had led to the isolation and flight of Isabella. The new regime, high-strung and unsure of itself, became increasingly sensitive to the agitation initiated by the Internationalists. Soon press attacks began to give way to police repression. Internationalists were harrassed and jailed in growing numbers, and the Federal Council, alarmed by the turn in events, decided to emigrate to the less troubled atmosphere of Portugal. In June 1871, on Corpus Christi Day, Lorenzo, Morago, and Francisco Mora departed for Lisbon with the records of the Spanish Federation, leaving Borrel and Angel Mora behind to keep an eye on events.

This flight was probably premature. The government was still too weak and divided to crush the labor organization, and the pressure began to lift. After three months, the Internationalists returned to Madrid. During this brief exile, they went through another bitter round of material hardships and internal friction, but their stay in Lisbon had not been a complete loss. There they met two young intellectuals, Jose Fontana and Antero do Quantal, who helped them establish the first stable nucleus of the International (and Bakuninist Alliance) in Portugal. A year later, the new Portuguese Federation claimed a membership of 10,000 in Lisbon and thousands more elsewhere in the country.

The Spanish Federation, on the other hand, was badly in need of repair. The Federal Council had suffered the loss of two memebers: Borrel, who had dropped out of activity, and Francisco Mora, who remained behind in Lisbon, nursing personal and political grievances that were later to bring him into the Marxian-inspired Spanish Socialist Party. Most of the work in the Council fell on the shoulders of Angel Mora and the indefatigable Anselmo Lorenzo. Although the membership had held its own and *La Solidaridad* in Madrid had been augmented by a new periodical, *La Emancipacion*, the ties between the Federal Council and the various sections in Spain were looser than ever. The very life of the Federation as a national movement seemed in the balance.

To meet this crisis, fifty-four delegates of the Spanish Federation convened in Valencia on September 10, 1871 for a week of intensive organizational work. The conference met in secret owing to the atmosphere of repression that still lingered on from the spring. To firm up the organization, the conference divided the International in Spain into five large regional federations or *comarca* (north, south, east, west, and center). The trade sections or *Secciones de oficio*, which existed in a very decentralized form, were federated on an occupational basis and still further centralized into craft unions. Finally, the powers of the higher committees which knitted the craft unions together were greatly amplified, giving them considerable authority over the local sections.

In time, the new structure was to become so elaborate as to be virtually inoperable. By the end of 1872, the Spanish Regional Federation had turned into a bulky, complex organization composed of five hundred *Secciones de oficio* and *oficio varios*, 236 *Federaciones locales*, and ten *Uniones de oficio*. Each of these bodies had a committee, sub-divided into commissions for administration, correspondence, organization, and propaganda. Anselmo Lorenzo estimates that it would have required nearly 7,500 people to staff all of the committees and local councils—a grave potential for bureaucracy, especially if one bears in mind that many Spanish workers were illiterate. Indeed, many committees could not find a single worker to keep the minutes of the meetings and often had to call upon friendly students and intellectuals for aid.

Had the members of the sections taken the structure and its requirements seriously (which they probably did not do), it would have been virutally impossible to have any concerted action and solidarity on any level beyond the locality. If a group of strikers wished to get support from sections outside their community or tried to draw on the strike funds of the organization, they were required to follow an elaborate procedure of "petitioning" the trade federation to which they belonged. It might easily have taken two months or more before the trade federation responded with some kind of decisive action. If the strike were strictly economic, it probably would have been defeated; if it were the opening act in a revolution, it almost certainly would have been crushed.

Following the return of the Federal Council from Lisbon then, heroic measures were certainly necessary to prevent the Federation from dissolving as a national movement. But the structure adopted at Valencia went far beyond what was needed to preserve the unity of the labor organization. Whence, then, came the impulse for the centralization of the Spanish Regional Federation? Frankly, the Federal Council was not composed entirely of Anarchists. In fact, it included the very men who in later years were to found the Spanish Socialist Party: Francisco Mora, Jose Mesa, and Pablo Iglesias. Within a few months of the Valencia conference, these men—the *Autoritarios* (Autoritarians), as they were called by the Anarchists—were locked in a furious conflict with the so-called *Anti-Autoritarios*. Neither side emerged very creditably.

Although the conflict had obviously been simmering for some time, it was sparked into an open war by events and interference from abroad. In the same month that the Valencia conference was held, Anselmo Lorenzo had gone to London to attend a world conference of the International. There he not only saw Marx, but observed at first hand the bitter infighting that was to culminate in the expulsion of Bakunin at the Hague congress a year later. From the stormy discussions in London it was clear that a split was unavoidable. Two months later, in December 1871, Marx's son-in-law Paul Lafargue appeared in Madrid, a refugee from the repression of the Paris Commune. Lafargue had been raised in Cuba and could speak Spanish fluently. Through Mesa and Iglesias he acquired control over *La Emancipacion* and began to press his attack against the Bakuninists in Madrid.

The conflict, dragging well into the summer of 1872, ended shabbily. The London conference had prohibited the existence of secret organizations within the International. Accordingly, the main thrust of Lafargue's attack was to demonstrate that the Alliance of Social Democracy had never been dissolved and still played a hidden role in guiding the affairs of the Spanish Federation. Lafargue, of course, was correct. The *Aliancistas*, embarrassed by the attacks, dissolved their organization, at least formally. The dispute, however, did not center merely on organizational issues. Lafargue had come to Madrid not only to recover the Spanish Regional Federation for Marx but also to reorient it toward political action. He favored an alliance with the Republicans and the formation of a workers' party. In Madrid, the dispute over these issues assumed a particularly bitter form when, in March 1872, the Marxian editors of *La Emancipacion*, representing virtually no one but themselves, proceeded to use the periodical in the name of the Federal Council to make a rapprochement with the Republicans. The editors were expelled, and the Madrid Federation was faced with the prospect of an open split.

One month later at Saragossa, the Spanish Regional Federation held its second national congress, where an attempt was made to heal the differences between the two factions. The editors of *La Emancipacion* were taken back into the organization. The congress prudently elected a Bakuninist Federal Council, with Lorenzo as secretary general, and transferred its headquarters from Madrid to Valencia. Despite the compromise, within weeks the battle was resumed in full fury—and this time it was waged on both sides without scruple. By publicly casting doubts on the sources of Bakunin's income, for example, the editors of *La Emancipacion* tried to revive the rumor that Bakunin was a police spy. The character assault occurred in September, well after they were expelled from the Madrid Federation, but it affords a glimpse of the murky depths to which the "discussion" had descended. The Anarchists on the Federal Council, on the other hand, were not immune to dishonorable tactics of their own. Suspicious of Lorenzo's personal friendship with Lafargue, they surreptitiously opened his mail from Madrid and surrounded him in an atmosphere of intrigue. Such tactics by his own comrades so infuriated Lorenzo that he resigned from the Federal Council and left

Valencia. But he never gave up his Anarchist principles and soon returned to the Federation.

The serious political differences between the two groups were increasingly obscured by gossip, slander, organizational maneuvering, and bitter invective. The climax of the sordid conflict was reached on June 3, 1872, when the *Autoritarios* were expelled from the Madrid Federation. A month later, they established a "New Madrid Federation" of their own and in reprisal for their expulsion they maliciously published the names of the *Aliancistas* in *La Emancipacion* (July 27), exposing their former comrades to police reprisals. In the end, the conflict achieved virtually nothing for Lafargue, Mesa, Francisco Mora, and Iglesias. The overwhelming majority of the Madrid Federation, indeed of the entire Spanish Regional Federation, supported the *Aliancistas*.

But the skirmishes in Madrid presaged a more historic conflict internationally, one which was to have a profound effect on the revolutionary movement for decades to come. On September 2, 1872, in a memorable congress at The Hague, Mikhail Bakunin and his young Swiss associate, James Guillaume, were expelled from the International for creating a secret organization. The evidence for the charge came from Paul Lafargue. To be certain of his victory over Bakunin, Marx had packed the congress with his supporters, dispatched delegates with highly questionable credentials, made unprincipled deals with men who were soon to become his bitter opponents, and personally participated in the proceedings. He had even charged Bakunin with "swindling" for failing to return a modest publisher's advance for an unfinished Russian translation of *Capital*. "This attempt to rob a famous rebel of his good name, an act of character assassination now condemned, apologetically, by most Marxist historians," observes Max Nettlau, "was to poison well-nigh forever the anarchists' personal feeling toward Marx." Thereafter, Marx had the General Council transferred from London to New York, a move that virtually assured the death of the International.

Two weeks later, the Anarchist delegates to the Hague congress, representing primarily Switzerland, Italy, and Spain, met at St. Imier in the Swiss Jura and formed an International of their own. The delegates from Spain included Farga Pellicer and Gonzalez Morago. After conferring with Bakunin, they hurried home and made plans to affiliate the Spanish Federation with the new International. With all restraints removed by the isolation of the Madrid *Autoritarios* and the split in the International, the *Aliancistas* decided to act boldly. They convened a new congress, four months earlier than the date stipulated by the Saragossa conference of April 1872. On December 25,

Número 264

Año VI

La Revista Social

Año IV.

BARCELONA — 17 DE MARZO DE 1872.

Núm. 136

LA FEDERACION

RECIPROCIDAD
DEBERES
DERECHOS
PROGRESO
INTERNACIONALIDAD
PERSEVERANCIA
MORAL VERDAD
JUSTICIA
HISTORIA
CIENCIAS ARTES
RACIONALISMO
TRABAJO
SOLIDARIDAD
COOPERACION
LIBERTAD

Organo de la Federacion Barcelonesa de la Asociacion Internacional de los Trabajadores.

SE PUBLICA LOS DOMINGOS

The mastheads of *La Federacion* and *La Revista Social*, two of the most important Anarchist periodicals during the 1870s and 1880s.

1872, fifty-four delegates representing 20,000 workers in 236 local federations and 516 trade sections convened in the Teatro Moratin at Cordoba for the third congress of the Spanish Federation. This was to be the last public national gathering of the original International in Spain for the next nine years. In many respects, it was also the most important one.

The Cordoba congress created what is generally regarded as the "typical" form of Anarchist organization in Spain. Although it is hard to speak of "typicality" with respect to the Spanish Anarchist movement, the congress basically abandoned the unwieldly structure created by the Valencia conference of the previous year. The Federal Council was shorn of its authority over local organizations and reduced to a mere "Federal Commission for Correspondence and Statistics." The trade sections and local federations were elevated to "sovereignly independent" bodies, free at any time to renounce their affiliation to the national organization. All restraints were removed from acts of solidarity for local strikes and uprisings. By the same token, no trade section and/or local federation could be coerced into initiating or supporting any actions. Henceforth, the Spanish Federation was to be a formally decentralized organization and its success as a movement was to depend largely upon initiatives from below.

Nevertheless, some kind of cohesion was necessary. The responsibility for knitting the organization together was undertaken by the Anarchists, who, despite the formal dissolution of the Alliance, continued to retain close personal and organizational ties with each other. The Alliance, in effect, continued to exist, which now meant that the Spanish Federation had a *de facto* leadership, albeit a libertarian one. With his typical honesty, Anselmo Lorenzo, refused to sugar-coat this fact. In the late years of his life, he wrote: "When a bourgeois expresses admiration for the working class organizations for not having a president who assumes the responsibility of leadership, the Internationals [Anarchists] smile with superior pride, as though they possess a secret that can not be penetrated by the short reach of the bourgeois interlocutor." This pretension irritated the old Anarchist and he added: "There was no such secret nor was it true that we had a total lack of authority. What we did have was a convention that deceived the very workers who employed it."

Yet in a sense, both Lorenzo and the complacent Anarchists he takes to task miss an essential point. The great bulk of Internationalists worked their jobs for long hours and low wages. They were burdened by the need to make ends meet for themselves and their hungry families. Ordinarily, these workers had little time or energy to give to their organization. Only the most high-minded workingmen could play a routinely active role in the movement, which they did at enormous personal sacrifice. In these circumstances some kind of guidance was both unavoidable and necessary; to deny this fact would have been self-deception or hypocrisy.

Certainly the Spanish Anarchists deceived themselves often enough, and it would have been miraculous if they were free of hypocrites. What deserves emphasis is that they tried to create an organization in which guidance could be exercised without coercion and a leadership, such as it was, removed easily when it was necessary or harmful. They also tried to encourage initiative from below and foster revolutionary elan in the sections, federations, indeed, in the factories and villages themselves. On this score, they were eminently successful, for until the outbreak of the Civil War, the Spanish libertarian movement never developed a bureaucracy. It had its share of those bureaucratic types and authoritarian personalities who are prone to flock into any effective mass movement. These people posed continuous problems for the original International and for its heirs. But their effect was neutralized by a structural flexibility, organizational looseness, and an atmosphere of freedom that has rarely been equaled by a mass labor movement in the history of our time. They had read their Bakunin well.

Brenan gives us a superb account of how well their movement suited Spanish conditions. "The first need," he writes,

> was to get hold of the half-starving, uneducated field laborers and factory workmen and fill them with a consciousness of their own grievances and their own power. These men could not, as a rule, afford to pay a regular subscription and they were suspicious of any influence from outside which might embroil them with their employers. Any regular trade-union organization with a paid secretariat, acting on orders from Barcelona or Madrid and leading its adherents like a bourgeois Republican party to the polling booths, would have been doomed to failure. But the Anarchist leaders were never paid—in 1936, when their trade union, the C.N.T., contained over a million members, it had only one paid secretary. Travelling about from place to place, on foot or mule back or on the hard seats of third-class railway carriages, or even like tramps or ambulant bullfighters under the tarpaulins of goods wagons, whilst they organized new groups or carried on propagandist campaigns, these "apostles of the idea," as they were called, lived like mendicant friars on the hospitality of the more prosperous workmen.
>
> Their first object was simply to enroll groups of poor workers, whatever their political or religious opinions might be, for mutual protection against employers: now and then there would be a small strike, which, if it was successful, would at once double the membership of the section and lead to other small strikes in neighbouring districts. Then gradually the leaders would unfold their anarchist creed with its hatred of the

church, its wild idealism, its generous and humane outlook, and the imagination of the hearers would be kindled. Thus it happened that, at moments of enthusiasm, the number of the workers controlled by the Anarchists would double and treble themselves and, when the inevitable reaction came, would shrink back to a small kernel of convinced militants. This plasticity of the Anarchist movement enabled it to survive persecutions and, soon as they were over, to reappear stronger than ever.

The organizational plasticity created by the Cordoba congress was soon to receive a critical test. The political instability that had led to Isabella's exile and the enthronement of Amadeo was now reaching serious proportions. In this mounting crisis, the agitation and strikes conducted by Spanish Federation did not pass unnoticed. Throughout the closing months of 1871, the Federation, its activities, and the fact of its affiliation to the "sinister" International beyond the Pyrenees had become the subject of increasing discussion within the Cortes. In January 1872, the Federation was officially ordered to dissolve by reason of its ties to a "foreign organization." But the government was too weak to enforce its order and the Federation continued to function as publicly as ever, even calling large rallies to protest the ban. But its days as an open movement were numbered, for if Spain was in upheaval and faced with revolution, she was also faced with a reactionary military *pronunciamiento* that would decide her future for decades to come.

Rebellion and Repression

On February 11, 1873, Amadeo of Savoy abdicated the Spanish throne and returned to Italy. After a reign of little more than two years, the "gentleman king," as the Spaniards called him, had run through six ministerial changes and three general elections without bringing political stability to the country. From the start, Amadeo had never gained the popularity of his subjects. The aristocracy treated him with disdain, Madrid theater audiences openly insulted him, and in the last months of his reign he was virtually isolated in the Cortes. Faced with the choices of completely antagonizing the officer corps, provoking a Republican rebellion, or ruling by decree, this civilized monarch abandoned the throne, opening the way to a bloodless Republican victory.

The declaration of a republic found its adherents as divided as the constitutional monarchists. The Unitarians, a cautious wing led by Garcia Ruiz, favored a centralized republic modeled essentially on French lines. This group found its greatest support in the center of

Spain, especially among the radical middle classes of Madrid. Opposing the centralist Republicans were the Federalists, inspired by Pi y Margall's theories of a decentralized, Swiss-like republic based on the autonomy of the provinces. Not surprisingly, the Federalists acquired the bulk of their adherents from the petty-bourgeois radicals in the provincial cities and towns.

But the Federalists were far from united. The immediate supporters of Pi were prudent men who, echoing his maxim that "force is legitimate only when right fails," believed in achieving a republic by legal means. Together with the Unitarians, they had developed their forces around parliamentary and electoral contests, throwing their support to the more liberal constitutional monarchists in common battles against "reactionaries" in the Cortes. This parliamentary "benevolence" toward supporters of a liberal monarchy earned them the contemptuous sobriquet of *benevelos*. By the end of Amadeo's reign, their tactics had thoroughly infuriated the more militant elements in the Federalist camp—the so-called Intransigents—who now veered toward an antiparlimentary policy of revolutionary action from below.

The Federalists did not have a majority of the country behind them, yet everything favored their success. The anti-Federalist forces had exhausted all the alternatives in their political armory and, after an aborted attempt at a coup in Madrid, sank into complete demoralization. The workers and the great mass of land laborers were highly combustible. A meaningful Federalist program, responsive to their needs, might have easily kindled their support. Reassured by the anticonscription policy of the Federalists, rank-and-file soldiers deserted their regiments in droves, leaving the officer corps with inadequate forces to back up a *pronunciamiento*. The radical petty bourgeoisie of the provincial cities and towns were collecting into paramilitary groups. Only the Carlists were sufficiently armed and cohesive to uphold the interests of reaction, but except for the threat they posed in Catalonia, they were boxed into the northern mountains.

It seemed for a time that the Federalists would succeed. A Constituent Cortes elected a few weeks after Amadeo's abdication provided them with a working majority and the legality necessary to establish a decentralized, cantonal republic. E. Figueras, a cautious Federalist *benevelo* who had functioned as caretaker president since February, was succeeded by Pi y Margall, the father of the Federalist doctrine in Spain. On April 24, 1873, Pi took over the presidency of the new republic. The government and the fate of the Federalist movement he had helped to create lay in his hands. Looking back years later, he recalled that "after April 23 I wielded immense power. . . ." This "immense power" was to melt from his hands like ice under a blazing sun.

In 1873, Francisco Pi y Margall had reached the age of forty-nine. The young, earnest Catalan who had threatened to "divide and sub-divide power" until it was destroyed now found himself ensnared by the very system of power he was pledged to destroy. Nearly twenty years had passed since the publication of *La Reaccion y La Revolucion*. The Federalist cause had grown from a heretical sect into a large movement embracing thousands of enraptured petty bourgeois. The severe repression initiated by Ramon Narvaez after 1856 had convulsed the lower middle classes, alienating them from the Liberal parties. From that point on, the Federalist movement began to grow and in 1869 Pi was elected to the Cortes, where he began to learn the techniques of parlimentary maneuvering.

Having acquired the presidency, Pi began to maneuver with the factions of his own movement. The Intransigents embarrassed him by their "puerile impatience" and were treated cavalierly. This devotee of legality of whom Friedrich Engels offered the curious description, "the only socialist in the Republican camp," could offer the lower classes little more than social abstractions. Although Pi probably had the broadest vision of all the politicians in the Federalist movement, his "socialism," as Raymond Carr has observed, "did not get beyond wage arbitration, a minimum of state action to improve working conditions, agricultural credit, and a 'generalization of property' which would extend the liberal land revolution beyond the 'new feudalism' to the agrarian poor." Thus, if the legal etiquette involved in establishing a federal republic goaded the Intransigents into action, the anemic Federalist program for social reform reduced the working class and peasantry to passivity.

In no sense could Pi be regarded as a revolutionary. His "socialism," consisted of a hash of undeveloped notions, more akin to cooperativism than Anarchism or Marxian Socialism. Although the pressure exercised by the Intransigents was largely responsible for bringing him to power (a fact he well understood and used to advantage), Pi tended to rely on right-wing and centrist Federalists. He was quite prepared to use troops against Intransigent insurrectionaries and abhorred labor strikes. His "conciliatory" policies consisted largely of trying to cajole the Intransigents into making concessions to the moderate wings of the Cortes.[1]

The denouement came on July 12, when armed Cantonalists (as the Intransigents and their allies were known) took over the municipal government of Cartegena and declared themselves autonomous. The Cartegena revolt doomed Pi's legalist "conciliatory" policy. The "father of Spanish Federalism" was now mistrusted by every faction in the movement. The right regarded him as too "socialistic" and "conciliatory"; the Intransigents, as treacherous and lacking in revolutionary zeal, although their deputies in the Cortes were prepared to support him against other tendencies. The Federalist center on which he relied for parlimentary support had divided between the right and the Intransigents, leaving him isolated. On July 18, not three months after taking the presidency, Pi resigned his office and was replaced by Salmeron, who lacked Pi's scruples and was prepared to jettison the federal republic for a more centralized state.[1]

With Pi's resignation, the Cantonalist revolt that had started in Cartagena now spread throughout the south. In a matter of days, July 19 to 22, armed Cantonalists took over the municipal governments of Seville, Cadiz, Valencia, Almansa, Terrevieja, Castellon, Granada, Malaga, Salamanca, Bailen, Andujar, Tarifa, Algeciras, and other smaller communities. The greatest support for the uprising came from Andalusia and the Levant. Madrid and Barcelona remained in the government's hands. The Cantonalist revolt in the south was abetted by the outbreaks of a Carlist revolt in the Pyrenean passes and by disturbances in Madrid, which compelled the government to dispatch its best remaining troops to the north, leaving the key cities in Andalusia virtually unguarded.

What role did the Spanish Federation play in these events? In reality, only a minor one. The Federation had anticipated that the political crisis in Spain would approach an acute stage and took steps to prepare for any contingency. In the spring of 1872, the Federal Council in Madrid sent Francisco Mora and Anselmo Lorenzo on tours of the sections—Mora to the eastern region, Lorenzo to Andalusia—with the aim of establishing an underground organization. The two men asked trusted militants in each section to form a special clandestine group called "Defenders of the International" whose function was to spearhead an insurrection or, in the event of repression, to engage in underground activity. These "Defenders" were the precursors of many other defense organizations that the Spanish Anarchists were to establish in the future.

In the event of a successful insurrection, the "Defenders" were also expected to establish local revolutionary juntas that excluded bourgeois elements "if possible" (to use Lorenzo's words). "Bourgeois elements," of course, included Federalists as well as Liberals. But Lorenzo's qualifying phrase is significant; it reveals the ambiguity that had begun to permeate the Federation's attitude toward the Federalist movement. Clearly, the Federation was nursing hopes for a Federalist victory in Spain, which it believed would provide the labor movement with a politically hospitable atmosphere. But since Anarchist principles required a resolutely antipolitical, class-oriented position, this dilemma was solved by a calculated form of "irresolution." On the eve of the elections to the Constituent Cortes, the Federation affirmed its antipolitical line by refusing to stand candidates. But it allowed the sections and individual Internationalists, if they so wished, to vote for the Federalists and cooperate with them.

In practice, of course the Federation was too weak to follow an independent policy of its own except for Internationalist uprisings in Alcoy, San Lucar, and a few scattered communities in Andalusia. In Barcelona, the proletariat responded to the Federation's plea for a general strike but refused to follow it along the path of social revolution. Intransigents and Internationalists worked together in establishing a Committee of Public Safety in Barcelona's municipal government. The Seville revolutionary junta was headed by the Internationalist, Mignorance. The Cartegena section may have played a role in winning the sailors over to the Cantonalist uprising, and Internationalists cooperated with Intransigents in Granada and Valencia. For the most part, however, the Cantonalist uprisings were followed by sharp recriminations between Anarchists and Federalists of all factions.

The Cantonalists, although capable of mobilizing a much larger following than the Internationalists, were not strong enough to withstand a serious military assault by Madrid. With some three thousand troops, General Pavia captured Seville after two days of heavy fighting and quickly reduced the rebellion in most Andalusian cities. Valencia held out for nearly two weeks against General Campos's forces, and Cartegena, its landside protected by powerful ramparts and the naval base in Cantonalist hands, was enveloped by a long siege. But the city's cause was doomed after the rest of the country had been subdued. After four months it was taken owing to treachery by the officers of a key fortress.

Generally, the Cantonalists dominated the struggle. But in Alcoy a community of thirty thousand people to the south of Valencia, the Spanish Federation managed to etch its own mark on the events of 1873. This old industrial town, a center of paper-making for centuries, and been penetrated and strongly influenced by Internationalists, and by early 1873 already enjoyed the distinction of furnishing outstanding Anarchist militants to the Spanish Federation. The Cordoba congress had decided to locate the Federal Commission at Alcoy because five of the Commission's members came from the town. As a result, the relatively small industrial community became the center of the Spanish Federation on the eve of this nationwide rebellion.

The street fighting in Alcoy preceded by several days the Cantonalist uprising at Cartegena and almost stands out as a precursor of the insurrections that were to follow. Yet Alcoy exploded into insurrection not because of political or regional antagonisms, but as the result of an economic dispute between the paper workers and their employers.

For some time there had been a vigorous agitation for an eight-hour day in the factories of Alcoy. The agitation, conducted by the local Internationalists, reached its climax on July 7, when an assembly of workers decided on a general strike to enforce its demands. On the following day, a delegation of factory employees appeared before the mayor at the City Hall, demanding that he summon the employers and present them with the workers' demands. The mayor, a stolid Federalist by the name of Augustin Albors, decided to play for time. Assuring the workers of his neutrality in the strike, Albors treacherously urged the employers to stand firm and barricade themselves in their homes until military aid could be summoned. After dispatching a request for troops, he reversed his neutral stand and publicly denounced the strikers.

It is doutbful if the Internationalists were really eager to foment an insurrection in Alcoy. They must have realized the vulnerability of an uprising in an isolated and patently indefensible town. Accordingly, they tried to negotiate with the municipal government. The next day a second delegation appeared at the City Hall with the warning that the mayor and his council must either maintain their neutrality or resign if they wished to avoid a conflict. As the delegation was leaving, the police opened fire on an unarmed crowd in the square. It was this stupid provocation rather than any "sinister" Internationalist design that triggered the Alcoy uprising. The senseless shootings infuriated the workers, who quickly gathered arms and besieged the City Hall. The police (numbering little more than thirty) finally surrendered after enduring a siege of twenty hours. They had simply run out of ammunition. Albors, adamant and stupid to the last, was shot and killed after firing his pistol point-blank at the workers who were arresting him.

The Alcoy uprising occurred on July 9, and its chances of enduring were far smaller than those of the later Cantonalist insurrections in the cities. The Internationalists established a Welfare Committee to manage the town, but its most pressing task was to negotiate favorable surrender terms from General Velarde, who was approaching from Alicante. Fortunately the committee received a promise of complete amnesty through the good offices of a Federalist deputy, Cervera, and on July 12, Velarde entered Alcoy without meeting armed opposition.

Many writers have dealt with the Alcoy uprising as a trivial episode that was submerged by the Cantonalist insurrections. In terms of its scope, they are correct. The entire event lasted little more than five days. By comparison with an historic event like the Paris Commune, Alcoy seems like a skirmish. That it occurred at all was due more to the dilatoriness of the military in Alicante than to the revolutionary fervor of the workers in Alcoy. Yet this brief episode created a sensation in Spain. Almost all shades of opinion, including Federalist, joined in condemning it. Doubtless, the well-to-do classes of Spain were haunted by images of the Paris Commune and the possibility of its recurrence in Spain. But there were also internal reasons for the fears Alcoy had aroused. For the first time in Spanish history, an armed uprising had occurred that was orchestrated not by predictable elements such as the military, the church, or the Liberals, but by an avowedly revolutionary working-class organization. For the first time, the industrial proletariat in Spain had acted as an independent insurrectionary force.

The uprising, coupled with the fall of Pi, guaranteed that the Spanish Federation would be physically suppressed. The organization, however, continued to maintain a public, if harrassed, existence for another half year while the bourgeois politicians in Madrid consummated the burial rites of the First Republic. Salmeron, who had taken over the presidency from Pi in July 1873, was replaced in less than two months by Castelar, a Federalist whom the conservative classes and generals regarded as more pliable than his predecessors. Having strengthened the army's position in Spanish politics, neither Salmeron nor Castelar could put it to rest. When it seemed that Castelar would not be able to stem a parlimentary drift back to the Federalists, the generals decided to act openly. In January 1874, General Pavia, the "savior of Spain" from a Cantonalist republic, pronounced against Castelar and installed General Serrano, a conservative military politician. Within a year it was clear that Serrano's government could be little more than a transition to a restoration of the Bourbon monarchy. When a bloodless *pronunciamiento* by Martinez Campos brought Alfonso XII, Isabella's son, to the throne a year later, it surprised no one in Spain or abroad. Even a substantial number of Carlists defected to the new monarch.

The Federalist movement, split irreparably by the Cantonalist uprisings, was to disappear under the Bourbon Restoration. Yet its importance for Spanish Anarchism can hardly be overestimated. Despite the sharp differences that were to emerge between the two movements during the revolt, they overlapped in many key areas. Both sought to weaken the central government (the Anarchists, of course, to abolish it) and to foster a vital regional and community life. The Intransigents, like the Anarchists, were prepared to use the most

Seals from worker and peasant associations of the International from different regions of Spain. Two of the seals repeat the Spanish Region's famous slogan: "No rights without duties; no duties without rights."

desperate insurrectionary methods to achieve their decentralized goals. Anarchists and Cantonalists fought together behind the same barricades in July 1873, and sat on the same revolutionary juntas in the provincial cities and towns. Later, many Federalists were to turn to Anarchism as the logical development of their decentralist aims. The Anarchists, in turn, were to elevate Pi y Margall to the status of a precursor of the libertarian movement in Spain.[2]

No sooner had Serrano become president of the faltering republic in the early months of 1874, when he ruthlessly undertook the suppression not only of the more extreme Federalist groups, but also of the International. The meeting halls and workers' centers of the Spanish Federation were closed down, its militants jailed by the hundreds, and its newspapers outlawed. At its high point in September 1873, the Federation probably numbered no more than 60,000 members, an insignificant fraction of the popular following the Federalists could muster. Even more telling than the arrests of Internationalists were the blows Serrano and the Restoration politicians struck at the movement's base, the working class. Strikes were crushed at gunpoint and the right of workers to form labor unions was prohibited by law. In effect the workers' movement was thrown back nearly twenty years, when the cry "Association or Death" had rung in the streets of Barcelona. Nor did the persecution relent with the passing years. At La Carraca, as late as March 1877, the police placed sixty-six Internationalists in weighted sacks and threw them into the sea. A cloud, thick with fear and repression, had descended on Spain. It would last for nearly eight years.

Somehow the Federation survived these persecutions. National congresses were abandoned for secret regional, or *comarcal*, conferences. Local underground presses replaced the editorial offices of widely distributed public newspapers. Economic strikes were abandoned for revolutionary strikes—which essentially meant no strikes at all. Having drunk heavily from the fount of revolution, the Spanish Federation reorganized itself once again, this time into a small insurrectionary organization.

A new structure geared almost entirely to armed revolt replaced the loose, informal public structure established by the Cordoba congress. In the cities, where it could once count on thousands of adherents and numerous sections, the International was reduced to a few dedicated Anarchists. The "Defenders of the International" were renamed the "Avenging Executive Nucleus," a more aggressive title that accorded with the embattled and violent mood of Anarchism at the time.

The fact is, of course, that the Internationalists in the cities were living on a myth. No revolution was in the offing; indeed, the first signs of mass urban revolutionary unrest were not to reappear in Spain until the turn of the century. Lacking the power to conduct strikes for higher wages and better working conditions, the International had been deserted by the Spanish proletariat; hence it could feed only on ideology, hope, and conspiracy. Many native Catalan workers had never accepted the violent Anarchist theories of the Federation with enthusiasm. They might have entered typical reformistic labor unions in droves were it not for the continual influx of *Murcianos* and the intransigence of the Catalan factory owners. In any case, with the increasing repression, the balance within the International began to shift from the north to the south. By February 1873, when the Spanish Federation's membership had reached a peak of 60,000,two thirds were in Andalusia. It was in the agrarian south, in the mountain *pueblos*, the sun-drenched towns and cities, and on the ancient latifundia of Andalusia and the Levant, that Spanish Anarchism was to survive and grow during the early years of the Bourbon Restoration.

Notes

1. Only after Pi was removed from power did he try to establish a working relationship with the Intransigents, but by this time it was too late. With the collapse of the federal republic and the restoration of the Bourbons, Pi was largely ignored by his erstwhile followers and essentially became a theorist and a Proudhonian ideologue.

2. It was Pi who ordered Velarde to march on Alcoy after the Internationalist uprising. On the other hand, the repression would have been very severe had he not been the president of the republic. In later years, when Anarchist terrorists were to turn public opinion against the libertarian movement, he courageously spoke up on its behalf. As Hennessy points out, Pi was admired by the Anarchists not only because of his moral probity. Pi died in 1901. Generalizing from his life, an obituary in the Anarchist journal *La Revista Blanca* emphasized that "integrity in a corrupting society has a value which only those can appreciate who have wanted and succeeded in maintaining their public and private life untarnished."—a characteristic conclusion for a movement that insisted on a complete unity between the two.

Chapter Five:
The Disinherited

Peasant Anarchism

To claim as some writers have done that Anarchism was imported into Andalusia and the Levant would not be entirely true. Perhaps it would be more appropriate to say that Anarchism was latent there, and the Internationalists evoked it. If the Anarchists of the cities had to build their own countersociety to an inhospitable and corrosive commercial world, the Anarchists of the countryside found one in their very midst. They had only to reshape some of its elements in order to create a living social milieu for libertarian ideas and ways of life.[1]

The International had no difficulty in winning over the *braceros*, the great mass of exploited gang workers who cultivated the latifundia of the Guadalquivir basin. But the real strength lay in the mountain *pueblos*, of Andalusia and the Levant—the "people of the sierra," as J. A. Pitt-Rivers calls them. Here, where a few hundred families lived in compact towns surrounded by bare, jagged peaks, Anarchism struck its deepest and most lasting roots. Tenacity and continuity are among the most striking features of these communities and reveal themselves in many ways. The squat buildings of white-washed granite boulders and uncut stone, so common in the mountains, are made to last, and village traditions often reach back for centuries of embattled Spanish history. The beginnings of some of these *pueblos* can be traced back to the Moorish invasions.

In contrast to the rich Guadalquivir basin, the soil of the sierras is poor and marginal. Fighting an intractable land, the mountain peasants must coax out a mixed crop of vegetables and maize—this by hand labor, for machinery is not only costly but almost useless on the sloping, rocky soil. Olives, fruit, and stock-raising play a key role in the agricultural economy. Most of the mountain peasants own their own land, generally in plots of less than five acres. To compensate for the small size of these holdings, grazing is done on common land. A large *pueblo* of three thousand inhabitants or more, for instance, may own thousands of acres of forest and pasture. A substantial minority of peasants have larger holdings (in excess of five acres). Still another minority are essentially landless laborers who must contract for work in the *pueblo* or on large estates in the valley. The *pueblo's* money is acquired mainly by selling fattened pigs for slaughter, but eggs, poultry, and a large part of the crop also find their way to the market.

Taken as a whole, the mountain *pueblo* is remarkably self-sufficient economically and almost wondrously self-contained culturally. The essential means of life—food, shelter, fuel, and in times past, clothing—come from within the *pueblo* itself; with the result that the mountain peasants are less vulnerable to economic vicissitudes than the *braceros* and industrial workers. The biggest problem they face is drought. In the arid lands of the south, rainfall and access to water are as close as one can come to an agricultural "mystique." In other respects, mountain peasants have no love of nature, no mystical attitude toward the soil, no feeling for agriculture.

Their deepest passion is social life: the joys of talk, argument, and companionship. Hence, houses cluster together, even if this means that peasants may have to walk long distances to their holdings. The virtues that are prized most highly are mutual aid, hospitality, loyalty, and honesty in dealings. So strong is this social cohesiveness that the *pueblo* answers for each of its members as a single community, and each in turn tends to value the good name of the *pueblo* over his or her own petty interests and concerns. Lope de Vega's play *Fuenteovejuna* is based on the real story of a *pueblo* of the fifteenth century that rose against a tyrannical knight and killed him. When the royal judges arrived and tried to determine who was responsible for his death, the only answer they could get was "Fuenteovejuna." It was inconceivable that responsibility for an act by one of its members, which had the approval of the *pueblo*, should be regarded as anything but an act by the *pueblo* as a whole.

This solidarity, reinforced by a harsh environment of sparse means and a common destiny of hard work, produces a fierce egalitarianism. The preferred form of transaction between peasants and laborers is *aperceria*, or partnership, rather than wages. Although they own the land and work as hard as the laborers, the peasants may give as much as half the crop to their temporary "partners." This type of relationship is preferred not only because it is wiser to share what one has in hand rather than to speculate on monetary returns, but also owing to a rich sense of fraternity and a disdain for possessive values. In the life of the *pueblo*, poverty confers absolutely no inferiority; wealth, unless it is spent in behalf of the community, confers absolutely no prestige. The rich who own property in or near the *pueblo* are generally regarded as a wicked breed whose power and ambitions corrupt society. Not only is the *pueblo* immune to their influence, but in reaction, tends to organize its values around the dignity of work and the importance of moral and spiritual goals.

Before the 1870s the more energetic of these peasants might have turned to brigandage in their youth. The mountains were infested with bandits whose exploits as champions of the poor acquired, in some cases, larger-than-life proportions. But after the 1870s, the more capable of the mountain villagers became *"los que tenian ideas"* ("those who had ideas"). They embraced Anarchism with a devotion that was to survive every persecution but the meticulous execution squads of the fascist Falange.

To be an Anarchist in the mountain *pueblos* involved adopting all the personal standards of the Anarchists in the cities. A man did not smoke, drink, or go to prostitutes, but lived a sober, exemplary life in a stable free union with a *companera*. The church and state were anathema, to be shunned completely. Children were to be raised and educated by libertarian standards and dealt with respectfully as sovereign human beings.

But there were also marked differences between the Anarchism of the industrial cities and the Anarchism of the countryside. As proletarian Anarchism drifted increasingly toward syndicalism, it gave a strong emphasis to organizational expediency. Peasant Anarchism retained its intensely moral elements, often conflicting with the values and demands of the cities. As Pitt-Rivers observes, "the telegrams to the congress of 1882 which came from Catalonia and the north ring with phrases like 'anarco-sindicalistas.' Those from the sierra talk only of justice and the cause of the people." Such differences were to reemerge in every major dispute that divided the Spanish Anarchists. City and country were to conflict on the merits of national over local organization, on the value of libertarian communism as against Bakunin's collectivism, on agrarian communes versus the division of the land into individual holdings (the *reparto*). But these disputes belong to later years, when peasant Anarchism began to give way to Anarchosyndicalism.

Living in a world that demanded fewer of the compromises facing their urban comrades, the Anarchists of the sierra walked like unblemished prophets among their people. Their ascendancy was based on no authority or social position. As targets of the clergy, Civil Guard, and large landowners, the Anarchists of the sierra could command no resources other than a respect earned by the exemplary nature of their behavior and the relevancy of their ideas. Lacking any formal influence, they were utterly vulnerable. The Civil Guard often made its own law in the rural hinterland of Spain. That the village

Anarchists could survive the mobilized institutions of the state and
church is compelling evidence of the popular support they acquired.

True, they were semi-educated men, and their ideas often seem
crude to the more literate and sophisticated mind. But it is easy to
forget that during the late nineteenth century in Spain, the village
Anarchists were virtually the sole voices of science and modernism in
the sierra. Only from the Anarchists could the peasants hope to learn
of such men as Darwin, Helmholtz, Laplace—or, for that matter,
Galileo and Copernicus. Always ready to expound upon their views,
they formed the center of all discussions on religion, politics, science,
morality, and education. Many children in the *pueblos* acquired the
rudiments of reading and writing from these conscientious "apostles
of the Idea." And they were the only voices of protest against injustices by the local notables, bringing the complaints of the villagers to
the outside world in the form of letters and articles to the Anarchist
press. The people of the sierra, in turn, consulted them endlessly on
all the petty details of village life. They were the arbiters of personal
disputes and of malfeasances perpetrated by one villager on another—
the source of advice on endless practical questions.

The majority of villagers, to be sure, were never actively occupied
with the Anarchist movement. Although aroused to action in periods
of distress or hope, in ordinary times they went about their daily
business with very little interest in anarchistic tenets. On the other
hand, the convinced Anarchist militants formed a tight nucleus
within the larger arena of the *pueblo*. They became, in effect, a clan,
even "intermarrying" and establishing blood ties. E.J. Hobsbawm,
who made a close study of the Casas Viejas uprising , found that
Maria ("La Liberteria"), the daughter of Curro Cruz, the old Anarchist militant who sparked the uprising, was "engaged" to Jose
Cabanas Silva, the most outstanding of the younger militants.
Another member of the Silva family was the secretary of the Laborers's union. The Cruz and Silva families were united not only by the
relationship of Maria and Jose, but by the tragedy of the uprising
itself.

In the valleys, and at lower elevations in the basin of the Guadalquivir, the smaller farms of the mountain peasants give way to large
estates and finally to the latifundia, the great plantations that characterize the Andalusian countryside. It is here that one encounters the
most glaring extremes of rural wealth and poverty, of extravagant
opulence and chronic hunger. And it is here too, among the landless,
rural proletarians—the *braceros*—that Anarchism found another kind
of mass support, as shifting and changeable as the volatile moods of
the Andalusian poor.

If the tenacity of the Anarchist movement in the sierra can be

explained by the solidity of the *pueblo*, the instability of this movement on the latifundia can be explained by the poverty of social forms
among the *braceros*. Brought together and then scattered by the seasonal demands of plantation agriculture, these great masses of rural
laborers lacked any definable social outlines or institutions. They did
not live on the landlord's estate like serfs, or in villages like peasants,
or even in large cities as did the industrial workers, but rather in the
slums of dismal Andalusian towns of 15,000 inhabitants or more.
These towns were too large and formless to provide the solidarity of a
sierra *pueblo* and too small to afford the stimulation of a Barcelona.

Drab and purposeless, the lives of the *braceros* were completely
unstable. Hired by the season, the week, or the day (they were, in
fact, commonly called *jornaleros*, or day laborers), they worked, with
occasional smoking breaks, for twelve or more hours daily at considerable distances from home. During the plowing and harvesting sea-
sons, when several months of continuous work could be guaranteed,
the *bracero* would be expected to leave his family and live in the
landlord's *ganania*, a shabby, barn-like barracks, where his bed was
some straw on the floor and his companions were lonely, miserable
wretches like himself, torn from their home and families by the need
to work.

Their misery beggars description. The landlord fed them *gazpacho*,
a soup of water, oil, vinegar, bread, and some beans or chick peas.
Bread, eaten as a substitute for virtually all the alimentary staples,
formed the basic diet of the Andalusian poor. A landlord who added
other ingredients to this impoverishing and stunting diet could be
expected to deduct his additional costs from the *bracero's* wages. The
inhuman neglect these people suffered as late as the 1930s is conveyed in an account by E.H.G. Dobby, an English geographer who
spent two years engaged in fieldwork in Spain:

> I recall an incident during a visit to an experimental pig farm in an
> out-of-the-way part of Andalusia. From the darkness at one end of the
> building came a red glow. I went along and found a laborer's family
> crouched on the floor around a twig fire with smoke so thick that breath-
> ing was difficult. The malodorous squalor contrasted with the carefully
> washed sties that I had been seeing. To my query an old woman mum-
> bled: "Yes, we live here. Worse than the pigs." At which the owner
> beside me exclaimed indignantly: "You have a roof over your head.
> What more do you want?"

The response of the owner sums up, with priceless clarity, the
attitude of the Andalusian landed classes toward the *braceros*: they
were regarded as less than animals. And to form a complete picture of
life in the *gananias* during sowing or harvesting time, one must add to

this description twenty or more people of all ages. If a family was present, every member worked, including the children, often to the point of sheer exhaustion.

Economically, the impoverished *braceros* were at the mercy of the landlord, who could lower their wages and break their strikes by hiring scab labor from the mountain villages or by simply cultivating the best land and letting the rest lie fallow. Indeed, large tracts of land were not placed under cultivation: some were returned to game for hunting, others to pasture for breeding fighting bulls. Owing to their extreme poverty, the *braceros* could rarely conduct long attritive strikes; hence the violent, near-insurrectionary dimensions of labor conflicts in Andalusia. Indeed, the strikes had virtually no staying power without support from peasants who owned or leased land in the latifundia regions. If the landowners were not panicked into concessions by the fear of a widespread *jacquerie* or peasant war, the strikers usually lost out. Occasionally, public opinion shifted to their side and the less inhumane landowners made concessions on their own.

To starving, landless proletarians who worked a half year or less for a pittance, the sight of large areas of untilled land could generate only one kind of feeling: a searing hatred for the landlord and the stewards who executed his orders. Their antagonism might have been contained in 1835, when Mendizabal and his Liberal ministry initiated the confiscation of the church lands. In the following years, immense tracts of ecclesiastical and common land were put up for sale in Andalusia. As noted earlier, this enormous legacy was snatched up by the bourgeoisie and turned, for the most part, into latifundia. The *braceros* acquired nothing. Agrarian unrest was answered not by land reform but by the use of the Civil Guard—the detested *Guardia*—against the peasantry and landless laborers.

Historically, the role of this special police force in promoting revolutionary unrest in the countryside has been so important that it must be discussed as a distinct factor in the development of peasant Anarchism. An elite constabulary, carefully selected and well-disciplined, the Civil Guard was established in 1844 to deal with the growing banditry in the south. By this time, the great bulk of Andalusian bandits no longer even remotely approximated the heroic image they had acquired in popular legend. They had become the tools of the *caciques*. They were used to defend property against the upsurge of peasant unrest and intimidate the opponents of their corrupt political bosses in local elections. The alliance between the *caciques* and bandits served not to abate brigandage, but to expand it. Shielded from imprisonment by the patronage of their new employers, the bandits began to raid with impunity. A point was finally reached where travel between Andalusian towns was virtually impossible without an armed escort.

To restore the security of the roads by using the local militia and police would have been useless. Like the bandits, they too had been largely taken over by the *caciques*. Thus, when the Civil Guard was formed, strict measures had to be taken to insulate the new force from local influence. Its men were never recruited from the districts in which they served, and they were expressly forbidden to intermarry or establish familiar relations with the local population. Civil Guards occupied special fortified barrracks within the village. They invariably walked in pairs, fully armed, and exuded a mistrust toward the community that soon enveloped them in hostility. A force apart, increasingly detested, the *Guardia* became easily unnerved and trigger-happy, escalating minor protests into riots and riots into insurrections. Whatever support the revolutionary groups could not mobilize with their literature and oratory, the *Guardia* eventually gained for them with its carbines. Narvaez, who organized this force and sent it on its way into the countryside, deserves to be enshrined as one of the ablest propagandists of the Anarchist and Socialist movements in Spain.

Frustrated by the disposition of the church lands, prodded by the carbines of the *Guardia*, and threatened by the values of a crassly egoistic business civilization, the peasantry and *braceros* of the south were to create their own unique form of social revolt. By the late 1860s, a new kind of restlessness began to stir the *pueblos*, *gananias*, and drab towns of the south: a sense of mounting exaltation that was to surge up at various points, suddenly enveloping the rural masses in hope and sweeping them into local insurrections. Often they occurred not merely for narrow economic gains, but to achieve *comunismo libertario:* the libertarian communism described in Anarchist pamphlets. Writers on the Andalusian uprisings—including the Anarchists themselves—tend to emphasize the millenarian quality of these outbursts; and it is true that in the naive and simple directness of their visions, the insurgent peasants and *braceros* of Andalusia seemed to parallel the rural folk of the late middle ages with their enraptured dreams of a "second coming." Evil and wickedness would be banished from the earth. Rich and poor, enlightened by the bright reality of a new world, would embrace in a spirit of reconciliation and mutual aid. It would be an ascetic world—"a just sharing of austerity rather than a dream of riches," as Hobsbawm notes—but peace, freedom, and equality would reign. Not only would money, wealth, and differences in social rank disappear, but to the more austere adherents, people would cease to partake of tobacco, alcohol, coffee, and other "vice-promoting" luxuries.

This vision would percolate in the *gananias* of the latifundia and the mountain *pueblos*, gradually building up until it seemed that nothing was worth discussing but its merits and possibilities. Then it would boil up, precipitated by a strike or a stupid act by the authorities. There would be a brief period of fighting, followed by a period of repression in which the dream would seem to evaporate. Elation and hope would be succeeded by sullen despair and fatalism. Ricardo Mella, the sensitive Anarchist essayist who lived in Andalusia for many years, recalls the volatile temperament of the people, so quick to rise in boundless enthusiasm and then sink into dejection, lacking doggedness and staying power. Later, however, passions would begin to surge up again, and the dream would reappear. The cycle would be repeated with the same fervor, as though a regeneration had occurred without a background of past defeats.

But granting the cycles of periodic uprising and decline, the agrarian movement in the south had a solid economic core that accounts for its continual revival in the face of unfavorable odds. For many peasants and *braceros*, *comunismo libertario* was equated with the *reparto*—the redivision of the land. In Andalusia, where a vast acreage was needlessly left uncultivated or used with gross inefficiency, a rational redivision of the land would have raised the standard of living enormously and provided a powerful spur to Spain's economic development. In the 1870s and early 1880s, the *reparto* meant the division of the land into individual holdings, not collective farms. Even the peasant Anarchists adhered to this view. Later, with the growth of Anarchosyndicalist unions, the *braceros* and, to a lesser degree, the peasants were won over to a communal system of land tenure.

What doomed the agrarian movement of the period was not the impracticability of its visions but its isolation. The upsurges were usually limited to a few localities, each following the other like firecrackers on a string. Rarely was there an explosion throughout the entire region. The *pueblos* had yet to be linked with the *gananias*. Periodicals were needed to bring tidings of the social movement in one district to the attention of others. Organization was necessary to coordinate the insurrections into a common movement. Finally, and most importantly of all, the barriers separating the industrial cities from the countryside had to be demolished and the workers' movement joined with that of the peasants.

Agrarian Unions and Uprisings

Andalusians such as Trinidad Soriano, Jose Garcia Vinas, and Antonio Gonzalez Meneses were active in establishing the Barcelona nucleus of the International and participated in the founding congress of the Spanish Federation in June 1870. They were students of technology, medicine, and engineering, residents of the Catalan seaport who had gathered around Farga Pellicer in the early days of Internationalist activity and were later to return to their homes in the south where most of them functioned as Anarchist propagandists. In addition, *La Federacion* had begun to reach a number of Andalusian cities, where it had a limited circulation among extreme left-wing Federalists, the more "socialistic" followers of Proudhon and Pi y Margall. Throughout 1870, however, the real strength of the Spanish Federation lay in the north, particularly in Barcelona and nearby textile towns. All seductive preconceptions aside, the fact is that Spanish Anarchism first developed among urban industrial workers and craftsmen, not millenarian peasants. Dreaming millenarians and saintly apostles can, of course, be found but Spanish Anarchism's earliest intellectual adherents contained a fair proportion of technicians and scientists.

In 1871, the Spanish Federation began to make serious headway in the cities of the south, and thereafter it grew rapidly. A year later, Anselmo Lorenzo, touring Andalusia, could report with great satisfaction that viable groups existed in Seville, Carmona, Jerez, Malaga, and Cadiz. The Federation could also claim small groups in Cordoba, Aguilar de la Frontera, and other communities. In the years to come, these towns were to play a key role in the spread of Anarchist ideas among the *braceros* and peasants of the south. By the end of 1872, the Federation could claim close to 28,000 members in Andalusia, more than half its national following.

Andalusia would have provided a fertile ground for the growth of Anarchist ideas even in the absence of any Socialist or Federalist precursors. By the 1860s, the south of Spain was slipping into a condition of chronic social upheaval. The sale of the church properties and particularly of the entailed lands (the latter, mostly held communally by the villages and municipalities) had upset the traditional equilibrium between the ruling classes and the oppressed of the region. For generations the walled, white-washed *cortijo* of the landlord and his overseers had dominated the latifundium like a self-contained fortress of privilege and exploitation. In the first half of the nineteenth century, a relationship still obtained in which the arrogance of the wealthy was pitted against the fatalism of the hungry and impoverished.

It would have been bad enough if the expropriations of the church properties, after opening the prospect of a *reparto*, had cheated the peasants and *braceros* of their last hope to acquire land by legal means. The sale of the confiscated lands, however, not only severed the last

ties between the landless and the state; it strengthened the power of a
grasping bourgeoisie which lacked even the tempering aristocratic
pretensions and paternalism of the traditional nobility. In the large
cities, wealthy middle-class families became absentee landlords,
owners of immense latifundia. In the rural communities, many local
bourgeois (a class of usurers, produce dealers, bailiffs, and lawyers)
acquired smaller but substantial properties of their own. From this
latter stratum came the *caciques* of Andalusia—the men who made a
mockery of every election in the countryside. In their abrasive exploitation and relentless pursuit of profit, this rural bourgeoisie helped
stoke a rebellion that could find relief only in the uprooting of the
entire structure of Andalusian society.

The decay of traditional relations in Andalusia affected not only
the peasantry and *braceros*, but also the lower petty bourgeoisie of the
provincial towns and cities. This large class of school teachers, civil
servants, journalists, professionals, and shopkeepers lived in a genteel poverty that mingled insecurity with humiliation. By the mid-
nineteenth century, the advance of capitalism into the south had
stripped their vocations of all social prestige. They too, reduced increasingly to a reservoir of exploitable labor, began to suffer from the
general exploitation of the area. The superficial unity that Liberalism
had created among all the middle classes during the early part of the
century began to give way to a polarization of prosperous and impoverished classes, driving the petty bourgeoisie—particularly its intellectual stratum—into extreme Federalist and even vaguely Socialist
groupings.

Andalusia, it should be noted, is not lacking in a Socialist tradition
of its own. Even before Fernando Garrido in Madrid had founded *La
Atraccion* (generally described as the first Spanish Socialist—actually
Fourierist—periodical), Juan Abreu had been propagating similar
ideas in Cadiz. Later, he established a Fourierist colony near Jerez de
la Frontera, but it was suppressed by the authorities. The expansion
of a militant Federalist movement into the south had created a great
interest in Socialist ideas, which was fed by pamphlets on
Proudhon's mutualist notions and by translations of his writings. A
strong tradition of *exaltado* Republicanism from the 1820s provided a
certain muscularity to these ideas by emphasizing the bitter antagonism between the rich and poor, the owners of property and the
dispossessed.

This muscularity represents one of the most striking features of
the radical movement in the south. It would be no exaggeration to say
that, during the 1850s and 1860s, the radical petty bourgeoisie of
Andalusia had developed into one of the most insurrectionary strata
in Europe. Only the Parisians could have matched the reckless pro-

pensity of the Andalusians to take up arms, build barricades, and do battle, often against hopeless odds. Major uprisings broke out in southern cities in 1857, in 1861, and again in 1873. The first of these, led by the veterinarian Perez del Alamo in Loja, has earned a place in the annals of Spanish revolutionary history as an *insurreccion socialista*. By the early 1870s the social terrain of the entire region had been thoroughly prepared to receive the most advanced ideas emanating from Madrid and Barcelona. It could be said, in fact, that Anarchism represented not the seed of a new social theory, which found a congenial soil in Andalusia, but the fruition of a great revolutionary development in ideas and social conditons that had been initiated decades earlier.

In some respects, this cumulative development accounts for the slow growth of the Spanish Federation in the southern cities during 1870 and 1871. The Federalist movement almost completely occupied the energies of the Andalusian revolutionaries, leaving little room as yet for the expansion of the International. Inquiries about the International had been received from Montilla, for example, as early as April 1871, but as Diaz del Moral tells us, municipal political conflicts so engrossed the radical movement of the Andalusian city that a viable section could not be formed until nearly two years later. Owing to the work of Diaz del Moral, however, we can form a fairly clear picture of how the earliest Andalusian sections were established and the kind of people they attracted.

One of the most complete accounts of these beginnings can be given for the city of Cordoba. The earliest evidence of Internationalist activity appeared in the summer of 1871, when Rafael Suarez and the newspaperman Jose Navarro Prieto began to correspond with the Federal Council in Madrid. Later, they were joined by three others: the craftsman Francisco Barrado Garcia; a professor of canonical law, Augustin Cervantes, and a municipal employee, Eugenio Gonzalez. This curious assortment of vocations was not unusual in radical groups in the south. All five men were initiated into the Bakuninist Alliance and, by 1872, had established a "section of various trades" and later a local federation in Cordoba. Diaz del Moral leaves us a colorful description of the two intellectuals in the group, Navarro and Cervantes. Their contrasting personalities provide a fascinating picture of the varied human types who were drawn to Anarchism at that period.

Jose Navarro Prieto had barely reached nineteen years of age when he began his correspondence with the Federal Council. As was the case with so many young Andalusian radicals of the day, in his background we see an overlapping of the worlds of craftsman and middle-class intellectual. There was the father, a shoemaker who demanded a higher station in life for his only son; the university education, acquired at great parental sacrifice; the prospect of stagnating as a schoolteacher or a lawyer. Navarro, however, was much too restless and hedonistic to sacrifice his youth to an academic routine. The prospect of a niggardly professional life must have appalled him. He turned to journalism and began to develop a local reputation as a biting satirist. His wit and mental agility soon made him into one of the most outstanding Internationalists in the south, and by 1872 he enjoyed the confidence of the *Aliancistas* in Madrid and Barcelona.

But apparently he also enjoyed a reputation for cowardice in the face of physical danger. The defeat of the Federalist movement in 1873 and the prospect of repression under Serrano began to raise political doubts in his mind which carried him steadily toward the parties of "order." Navarro soon became a complete conservative. In later years, he more than fulfilled his father's aspirations by becoming a leading newspaper publisher and editor. After his death, he was remembered fondly by his conservative friends as an ingenious prankster, a jovial and agreeable character who, in Diaz del Moral's words was "more dedicated to Dionysus than to Apollo."

Navarro's amiable, fun-loving personality was very common in the south, contradicting the stereotype of the mystical Andalusian Anarchist, and many men with his youthful zest and tastes entered the International. Andalusia also had its share of sober figures like Augustin Cervantes, made of more spiritual stuff than Navarro and able to withstand persecution with greater fortitude. The son of a Murcian lawyer, Don Augustin Cervantes del Castillo Valero attended the University of Madrid and finally acquired a doctorate, with degrees in law, philosophy, and letters. He was a serious student, a taciturn young man who presented a reserved and withdrawn mien. This imposing demeanor, coupled with great learning and a varied cultural background, carried Cervantes into the upper strata of the academic world. By the age of thirty he was already a professor in the University of Cordoba. His marriage two years later to Dona Julia Valdivia y Ruiz de Valenzuela brought him into the highest society of the city.

Yet there was a passionate feeling for humanity in Don Augustin that manifested itself in visits to the poorer quarters of the city, where he gave money to the needy. The Cordobese notables knew nothing about these visits. A few months after his marriage, Cervantes openly espoused the cause of the International, and his peers were stunned. He published a propagandistic work, *Three Socialist Discourses on Property and Inheritance*, and participated in the Cordoba congress of the International as a delegate of the local federation of Solana. A social vacuum began to envelop Cervantes. His bourgeois friends—

including Republicans—began to withdraw from him, and he soon found himself almost entirely in the company of the Internationalists. Finally, when he criticized Catholicism from his academic chair, he was savagely attacked by official society. Finding it intolerable to stay at the university, Cervantes left Cordoba to take up an exchange professorship in Badajoz, where he died shortly afterward.

Although their destinies were to differ, Navarro and Cervantes were men of ability; more significantly, they were surrounded by a complement of highly dedicated working-class elements. The Cordoba nucleus began to prosper. After June 1872, it increased to fifty-four members and established itself among the shoe and hat workers of the city. At the Cordoba congress in December, the section played host to leading Internationalists from all over Spain and its members began to acquire a degree of national prominence. The declaration of a republic two months later gave tremendous impetus to the group. It led a successful strike of weavers, established a progressive school, and by June, managed to publish a newspaper of its own, *El Orden*. Riding on the Federalist groundswell of the late spring, the Cordobese Internationalists elected their own candidate, the *Aliancista* Barrado, to the municipal council without any demonstrable qualms over an Anarchist occupying a seat in a bourgeois legislative body.

The agitation during these months was spectacular. Internationalist and Federalist propaganda rolled from the presses. The upheaval spread from the city to the countryside, breaking out in incendiarism. There were rumors of an impending Federalist and Internationalist revolt. Paramilitary groups were formed by Federalists and Monarchists, each threatening to take over the city, which was a strategic southern railroad hub. Anticipating a rising, the military governor, General Ripoll, arrested suspects from both groups. Later General Pavia and his troops took over Cordoba. The Republican militia was disarmed, with the result that the city never rose in the Cantonalist insurrections of July 1873. Their enthusiasm waning, the Federalists suspended the publication of their newspapers and began to make themselves scarce. It was around this time that Navarro began to defect from the workers' movement and drift toward the governmental party. Even the worthy Don Augustin prudently withdrew from Internationalist activity. Led by the craftsman Barrado, the Cordobese section now consisted exclusively of workers. Yet, despite the mounting repression and the desertion of the intellectuals, it continued to grow; *El Orden*, for instance, reached its maximum circulation during the late summer of 1873.

With the accession of Castelar to the presidency, however, a crackdown began in earnest. Constitutional guarantees were suspended, strikers were threatened with gunfire if they refused to return to work, the *centros obreros* were closed down, and the most militant Internationalists found themselves in jail. On October 1, 1873, Barrado was arrested and later deported to Alicante. The Cordoba section now began to decline rapidly. Under Serrano's harsh dictatorship, which replaced the Castelar regime in January 1874, the entire Spanish Federation was forced underground. By April, after weeks of harsh persecution, the Cordobese section disappeared completely as an organized group. The hopes it had engendered throughout the spring and summer of 1873 were to be nursed for years by a handful of isolated, scattered individuals. Not until 1881, when a resurgence of radical activity swept Spain, was the movement to revive in an organized form.

The Cordobese section gives us a fairly typical picture of the development followed by the early Anarchist movement in the Andalusian cities. Intellectuals play the initiating role in establishing a nucleus, but they are soon surrounded by workers, usually craftsmen, who form the lasting bedrock of the local organization. The movement in the cities is not millenarian or wildly apocalyptic. On the contrary, it takes root in a suprisingly stolid manner and grows rapidly only under the impetus of events. When the situation becomes too risky, the majority of intellectuals drop away or undergo a "modification" of their faith that leaves the group in the hands of its working-class adherents. From that point on, the Anarchist movement becomes a predominantly proletarian (or peasant) organization. Its outstanding militants are recruited from the shops and factories.

It is interesting to note how closely the development of the Cordobese section was paralleled by the International in Seville, another major center of Andalusian Anarchism. Here too, a leading role in establishing an organizing nucleus was played by two intellectuals. Trinidad Soriano had by this time returned to his home in Seville and was playing a key role in establishing a movement in the city. Then there was Nicolas Alonso Marselau, a left-wing Republican who had come to Anarchism at the end of the 1860s. He established *La Razon*, the first Internationalist newspaper in the city and one of the earliest in Andalusia. Marselau had been a theology student, and his background was very similar to that of Cervantes. His participation in any major decision of the local group was considered so important that, when Lorenzo visited the city to establish the "Defenders of the International," the *Aliancistas* trooped to the Seville jail where Marselau was confined and conferred with him there. But the onset of blindness and the upheavals of the 1870s shattered all his left-wing convictions. He renounced Anarchism to become a Trappist monk. The movement he helped to create was destroyed by Pavia and Serrano. When it revived, its nucleus and supporters were mainly proletarian. There was, for instance, the cobbler Sanchez Rosa, who had only two years of formal education. After an embattled youth, in which he participated in the famous Jerez uprising and suffered imprisonment, Rosa became an outstanding Anarchist propagandist and educator. He founded progressive and libertarian schools and acquired a certain renown for his simple moral dialogues on the virtues of anarchy and the evils of capitalism.

In the end, Serrano and his successor Canovas were not to prevail in their attempts to repress the Anarchist movement. The crushing of the Cantonalist insurrections were to turn many Federalists into active libertarians. The prestige that the International acquired among the ordinary workers was enormous. Later, with the revival of radical activity, they were to enter its successor organizations in greater numbers than before. No less important is the effect the Federalist movement and insurrections had in disseminating radical ideas among the peasants and *braceros*. The shock waves of Federalist activity and the Cantonalist barricades radiated outward from the cities of Andalusia into the countryside. The rural poor, emulating the revolutionaries in the cities, set fire to the landlord's crops and haylofts, killed his watch dogs, injured his cattle, and tried to destroy some of the *cortijos*. Wandering Anarchist propagandists, many of them refugees or deportees from urban repression, appeared in the *pueblos* and *gananias*, and their role in spreading Anarchist ideas can hardly by overestimated. Years after Serrano suppressed the International in the cities, Anarchist ideas were to percolate deeply into the Andalusian countryside.

The Spanish Federation, however, was now in hopeless decline. Its history between 1874 and 1880 is a humiliating one. The Federal Commission, continually in flight from the police, clawed itself to shreds with internal bickering. A quarrelsome, unstable body with a waning following and obscure leaders, it had finally lost the respect of its small rank and file. Elections to the Commission were treated as a joke, an occasion for a good deal of malicious humor. The once-feared Spanish Federation simply faded away. When the revival of the 1880s came, the Federation was no longer to be seen in the major cities of Spain.

The Federation's sister organizations north of the Pyrenees also declined. The Bakuninist International, founded at St. Imier, held its last congress in 1877 in the Belgian industrial town of Verviers. This libertarian organization had lasted only five years. Its decline is usually atributed to the destruction of the craft industry in the Jura, the famous Swiss watchmakers among whom the Bakuninists had acquired so much support in the previous decade, but this explanation is only partly true. Perhaps a more important reason for the decline of the libertarian International and the Anarchist movement generally in Europe was the economic stabilization that began in the mid-1870s, an upswing that fostered conservative attitudes in the working class. The Marxists, with their policy of electoral activity, parlimentarianism, and reformist unions, were to reap the rewards of the period and win the bulk of the workers outside of Spain and France.

It was not merely police repression that destroyed the International in Spain, but also tactics nurtured by its isolation. In the autumn of 1878 Juan Olivia Moncasi, a young Internationalist from Tarragona, tried to assassinate Alfonso XII by firing two shots at the king in the Calle Mayor in Madrid. The attempt failed, but the government used the occasion to heighten its repressive measures against the labor movement as a whole. Many union militants as well as Anarchists were arrested. The Catalan workers responded with retaliatory strikes and the peasants in Andalusia with a wave of incendiarism. The Spanish Federation's commitment to terrorism and the reprisals provoked by the assassination attempt exacerbated the poor relationship between the Federal Commission and the working class. The greatest strain existed in Catalonia, where the International had its largest proletarian following. When the moderately Liberal government of Sagasta replaced the Canovas ministry in February 1881, the sentiment of the Catalan workers veered sharply away from the violent policies of the Federal Commission.

An attempt was now made to establish a more conventional type of labor federation, avowedly Anarchist in theory but essentially opportunistic in practice. The founding congress of the Workers' Federation of the Spanish Region, as the new organization was called, convened in the memorable Teatro del Circo of Barcelona on September 24, 1881. One hundred and forty delegates representing 162 federations through Spain answered the call—a remarkably large response if one considers that the labor movement had just emerged from years of severe repression. Although more than a decade of rich experiences separated the two founding congresses at the Teatro, the proceedings seem almost like a replay of the disputes that had occurred in 1870. Republicans tried to gain a commitment to political action. Predictably, some of the more forthright trade unionists sought a conventional labor organization, explicitly aimed at reforms and economic gains. The congress rejected both of these positions by large votes, declaring Anarchism to be the social goal of the Spanish working class. It emphatically rejected political tactics as means for achieving its aims. Organizationally, the Workers' Federation modeled itself on the decentralized structure of the old Spanish Federation, but there were modifications in the local unions (*uniones de oficios similes*) which closely resembled the forms that were to be adopted later by the CNT.

The vote accepting Anarchism as an ideal was overwhelming—110 to 8—but the rhetoric could barely conceal a basic shift toward conventional, indeed moderate, unionism. Over strong opposition by the more militant Anarchists, the new Workers' Federation decided as a matter of policy to accumulate a strike fund. It also decided to limit rigorously the use of the strike as a weapon. A strike, when unavoidable, was to be orderly and well-disciplined. It was to rely on attrition rather than compulsion to gain its ends. Essentially, this meant an end to labor violence and sabotage—in short, to militant, quasi-insurrectionary strikes.

This approach marked a decisive defeat for the serious Anarchists in the union. That the more conventional Catalan union leaders could prevail was due in part to the disunity and ideological confusion among the delegates who called themselves Anarchists. The old Bakuninist Alliance of Social Democracy , which played so decisive a role in orienting the Spanish Federation, had gone down together with the International. By the 1880s there was no national Anarchist movement in Spain. Instead there was a quarreling multitude of Anarchist groups whose ideas ranged so far afield that at one extreme they were little more than Republicans and at the other, embattled, individualistic terrorists. There were also many outright reformists who called themselves "Anarchists" because of the prestige and romantic aura that had begun to surround the word among the workers.

Another factor that accounts for the shift toward a policy of conventional unionism was the reprisals that had followed the militant policies of the International. Although already touched upon, this factor needs further explanation. The Catalan unionists viewed the Sagasta regime with extreme suspicion. The new prime minister, a notorious foe of the labor movement, had patched together an uneasy coalition of moderate Liberal groups in order to come to power. The unionists had every reason to fear that he had restored the legality of the trade unions as a kind of democratic window-dressing for the new ministry. However, the Catalan labor leaders were clearly intent on preserving this facade by avoiding any sharp confrontation with the new regime. Despite their revolutionary rhetoric, they dealt prudently with the Sagasta ministry. One of their manifestoes reads more like an appeal for restraint than a call to action; indeed, virtually any advocate of militant tactics is described as a *provocateur*.

As it turned out, the mere growth of the union was enough to doom it. By the time of its second congress, held in Seville in late

September 1882, the Workers' Federation claimed a following of
nearly 58,000 members organized into 218 local federations and 663
sections. The great bulk of the union's membership—more than
38,000—was located in Andalusia, while only 13,000 came from industrial Catalonia. To many delegates from the south, the opportunistic policies of the Catalan labor leaders were nothing less than
treachery. During the three-day congress a furious battle exploded
between the two great regions of Spanish Anarchism. It was here, in
the Seville congress, that the Workers' Federation essentially defined
Anarchism as its long-range goal and the struggle for economic improvement as its day-to-day task—the same dichotomy that had
faced the congress of 1870. Although this explicit formula was presented as a compromise, the Catalan viewpoint essentially prevailed.[2]

But there was deep dissatisfaction among the Andalusians, particularly among the delegates from the southernmost *comarcal* of the
peninsula. One group, calling itself the *Desheredados* (Disinherited),
denounced the Federation's policies and broke away, forming an organization of its own to engage in direct action. The *Desheredados*
were probably one of many secret societies that were proliferating
among the land laborers of the south. The late 1870s and early 1880s
can be described as a period of economic expansion for the industrial
north, but in Andalusia these decades were marked by severe
drought and near-famine conditions. In Jerez, where the workers and
land laborers had clung to Anarchism in the bleakest years of persecution, discontent ran especially high. Here, where the *Desheredados*
had their strongest support, the vineyard workers received extremely
low wages based on piecework and lived in desperate poverty.

Although there may have been more talk than actual violence
among the *Desheredados*, the Jerez district had already experienced
many acts of incendiarism and a number of assassinations. The victims of the assassinations were mostly informers for the police and
occasionally landlords. It is quite possible that the *Desheredados*, together with other secret societies in the area, were involved in some
of the murders. The twilight zone in which these groups operated
makes it impossible to distinguish fact from myth.

A celebrated case of the 1880s points up both the myth-making
that surrounded such incidents and the very real repression that
came in their wake. In the midst of a promising strike by the vineyard
laborers against piecework, a tavern keeper suspected of having been
a police informer was killed. While the strike was still going on, the
Civil Guard suddenly announced that its investigation of the murder
had revealed the existence of an immense secret society, the *Mano
Negra* or Black Hand, which was planning to slaughter all landlords in
Andalusia. Despite recent arguments to the contrary, the sensational

Accused members of the "Mano Negra" in the courtyard of a Cadiz prison. This small group formed one of many hundreds who were arrested throughout Andalusia during 1882-1883 in a sweeping police persecution that finally led to the disappearance of the Workers' Federation of the Spanish Region.

stories that the *Guardia* fed the public are, in my opinion, fictitious. The distinguished Spanish sociologist Bernaldo de Quiros, who investigated the case for the government, doubted that the *Mano Negra* ever existed in Andalusia. But the case was used by the police to round up Anarchists and labor militants throughout the south. Hundreds were tortured to extract confessions, although the majority were finally released for want of evidence. The aftermath of the investigation in 1883 ended in the trial of a hundred alleged conspirators and in the garroting of seven out of the fourteen who had been condemned to death. But the legend of the *Mano Negra* lingered on for years, and Anarchists were arrested and accused of belonging to this spurious organization well into the 1890s.

The *Mano Negra* persecutions destroyed the Workers' Federation in Andalusia and almost certainly contributed to its decline in Catalonia. An atmosphere of fear, nourished by memories of the repression in the 1870s settled over Spain and workers began to desert the movement by the thousands. The third congress of the Federation, held in Valencia in 1883, sharply denounced the violent tactics attributed to the *Mano Negra* but this did not end the continuous decline. Only 3,000 members remained in the now-underground Andalusian sections. *La Revista Social*, an outstanding Anarchist theoretical magazine which had reached a circulation of 20,000, simply faded out of existence for want of subscribers. By 1887, when the Federation held its fourth congress in Madrid, only sixteen delegates showed up. Two years later, the Workers' Federation of the Spanish Region, which had begun with such hope and promise eight years earlier, was officially dissolved.

For the peasant Anarchists of Spain the medieval village had many limitations. As a community, however, it had many vital features. The Andalusian Anarchists valued the *pueblo* because its spirit of mutual aid, solidarity, egalitarianism, and sociability accorded perfectly with the goal of Anarchism, indeed, of any humane society. But they saw the village as a point of departure for a still better way of life, not as an end in itself. For them it was a springboard for a society in which material needs would be satisfied by modern technology and science; the human mind would be liberated by reason and knowledge; the human spirit nourished by cooperation and freedom.

Accordingly, the Anarchists carried on an unrelenting war against the negative features of the *pueblo*—its parochialism, superstition, ignorance, and systems of authority. They encouraged a respect for culture and the boldest ideas in nearly every sphere of life. To the peasants and *braceros* they imparted a sense of dignity and self-worth, of generosity toward the oppressed of their own class, indeed, a view of humanity that was keenly internationalist in spirit and outlook.

They brought to the *pueblos* a knowledge of sciences that had been forbidden by the clergy, a claim to a liberty that had been abrogated by the state, and a demand for material well-being that had been usurped by the ruling classes.

It would be interesting in this respect to compare Andalusian Anarchism with another peasant movement, the Carlism of the northern mountains. Carlism, of course, was primarily an attempt to preserve the *pueblo* and its clerical-patriarchal morality from modernism. Led by the church, this movement was atavistic: it could offer no program other than a return to the past. In sharp contrast to peasant Anarchism, Carlism fostered a mindless obedience to the hierarchy of the church and the authority of the crown—at least the one it hoped to place on the head of the pretender. Provincial and dogmatic, it preached a gospel of hatred and ignorance toward scientific knowledge, experimentation, and intellectual independence. In three civil wars, the Carlist armies marched toward the Liberal cities of the north, burning railroad stations and destroying other "demoniacal" innovations. Fanatical priests, goading their flocks to savage brutalities, terrified the entire peninsula with an example of clerical reaction gone mad. Accordingly, the Carlist Wars served up some of the most frightful butcheries to be seen in the nineteenth century. From this quarter came the demand for censorship of periodicals and books, for clerical control over educational institutions, and for a restoration of the Inquisition.

Both Carlism and rural Anarchism, then, take their point of departure from the *pueblo*. But it would be difficult to conceive of more divergent world outlooks than those of the two peasant movements. One turned toward the past, the other toward the future. Both explored entirely antithetical potentialities in the Spanish *pueblo's* dissatisfaction with bourgeois society. Their common basis in village society is entirely secondary to the fact that they fostered contradictory possibilities and moved in opposing directions.

Notes

1. These libertarian ideas and ways of life, as we shall see, stood in flat opposition to the capitalist relationships that were penetrating the countryside, especially after the communal lands were seized and put up for sale. The challenge of capitalism to the values of the *pueblo* constitutes perhaps the most important single source of agrarian unrest in Spain after the 1850s.

2. The Seville congress was also the scene of an open dispute between the

Bakuninist "Anarchist Collectivists" and the followers of Kropotkin's "Anarchist Communism." The Anarchist Communist position was defended by Miguel Rubio of Seville, the collectivist by Jose Llunas of Barcelona.

Chapter Six:
Terrorists and "Saints"

The 1880s in Spain were a period of rapid industrial growth and overall agricultural prosperity. British and French capital flowed into the mining industry and turned the country into one of Europe's leading producers of iron and copper. The development of Cuba as a market for cheap textiles served to buoy up the Catalan cotton industry, and when the French vineyards were nearly destroyed by the phylloxera virus, Spanish wines enjoyed a brief period of supremacy on the world market. With the coming of the 1890s, however, economic growth became spotty, broken by ominous years of stagnation and decline. If the earlier upswing had brought some limited benefits to the urban and rural working classes, the decline was agonizing for them. What tormented the country were the contrasts between rich and poor. At the one extreme, Spain seemed to have plunged into a world of feverish business in which the wealthy classes were occupied with amassing immense fortunes, while those below lived in chronic destitution, misery, and hopelessness.

This contrast grated against the senses in all the cities of Spain and much of the countryside. In Barcelona, while the textile manufacturers began to raise sumptuous neo-Baroque dwellings on the Tibidabo, the slums of the workers spread outward, joining the hovels of the newly arrived *Murcianos* on the outskirts of the city. Machinery cancerously invaded the traditional universe of the small workshop and threw thousands of craftsmen onto the labor market, skilled workers whose occupations that had been rendered useless by mass manufacture. Even more offensive were the startling economic disparities that prevailed in the south. In many provinces of Andalusia, half the land was held in estates of 5,000 acres or more, while 80 percent of the population was made up of rural landless proletarians. Deficiency diseases from poor nutrition were endemic. The death rate soared. The ruling classes made no effort to provide the people with an education: more than half the men and nearly all the women were totally illiterate.

In addition, the greatest pains were taken to exclude the urban and rural masses from any role in governing the country. Between the 1830s and 1860s, Spanish political life had swung like a pendulum between fairly authentic Conservative and Liberal regimes, presided over by generals, civilians, and, in the late years of Isabella's reign, by a court *camarilla* of priests. But with each oscillation the Conservatives became more liberal and the Liberals more conservative. The two factions were drawn together by a common fear of clerical, military, and radical uprisings. With the premature death of Alfonso XII in March 1885, the Conservative and Liberal parties of the Restoration period came to an agreement to share the state between themselves. A political system of *Turnismo*, or "rotation" was established in which the Liberal Party, under the ebullient Praxedes Sagasta, was given the reins of power whenever democratic window-dressing was needed to absorb social unrest or justify the passage of repressive legislation. The Conservative Party, led by Antonio Canovas del Castillo, occupied the ministry under conditions of relative stability. Except for an anticlerical tradition and an interest in secular education, the Liberals were indistinguishable from their Conservative counterparts. What really distinguished the two parties were the agrarian strata whose interests they reflected: the Conservatives spoke for the Andalusian landowners and the Liberals for the Castilian wheat growers.

The chief architect of *Turnismo* was Canovas, a thorough cynic who combined political astuteness with a broad cultural background almost unmatched by any leading politician of his day. Before entering politics, he had already achieved a reputation of high standing as a historian. Canovas's policy was directed toward the single goal of public order at any cost. This policy of deliberate political stagnation rested in turn on a massive system of corruption in almost every sphere of life. In theory, the Spanish government was a constitutional monarchy based on a limited (later,universal) suffrage with the usual rural *caciques* and urban *jefes* who tailored the vote according to the needs of Madrid. The nominally free press was bought off (almost any prominent journalist had no difficulty obtaining a seat in the Cortes),while the generals were mollified by adventures in Morocco.

The problem of dealing with the bourgeoisie was more complex. Spanish industry had developed not in Castile or Andalusia but on the periphery of the country, in Catalonia and the Basque provinces, the two regions which had been traditional opponents of a centralized state. Somehow, *Turnismo* had to reflect the interests of the strategic industrial bourgeoisie without giving it too much authority in the management of the state. The problem was solved by subterfuge. A political underground of intrigue and pressure groups developed in which the economic demands of the manufacturers were granted after exasperating negotiations and maneuvers. Power, however, continued to rotate between the two large agrarian groups.

By the 1890s, the absurdity of this political structure was evident to almost everyone. In a period of unprecedented industrial growth, the state apparatus was owned and occupied by archaic agrarian interests, thus compelling the "progressive" manufacturing classes to enter it through the back door like beggars. The largely republican petty bourgeoisie was asked to be content with a monarch as the chief tenant and accept a rigged system of elections that effectively denied its entry. The working class and rural poor were simply ignored. Virtually excluded from active political life, they were given the nominal right to bed themselves in "legal" unions which were consistantly harassed by the police and destroyed outright when they became too large.

The unions tried earnestly to accommodate themselves to this arrangement. The Workers' Federation, as we have seen, foundered in its effort to promote legal unionism. It was doomed by the mere fact that it attracted large masses of Andalusian laborers. A more cautious strategy was tried in 1881, the same year that the Workers' Federation was founded, when the *Autoritarios* of the Old International established the Spanish Socialist Party.[1] Although Marxian in rhetoric and organizational structure, it was basically reformist in politics and goals. What probably rescued the party from the fate of the Anarchists were the modest demands of its program, the prudent nature of its tactics, the respectable form of its propaganda. The party soon found itself traveling in a vicious circle. On the one hand, its program and tactics evoked little response from the restive *Murcianos* and *braceros*, who flooded into the Anarchist unions. On the other hand, the skilled workers to whom it appealed, being bourgeois in outlook and political sentiment, placed their confidence in the Republican parties.

Hence it was not until 1888, seven years after the founding of the party, that the Spanish Socialists succeeded in establishing their own labor union, the General Union of Workers or *Union General de Trabajadores* (UGT). Guided by Pablo Iglesias, this cautious, stolidly bureaucratic labor organization made headway among the industrial workers of the Basque cities, the craftsmen of Madrid, and the peasants of Castile. It later developed a large following in Granada, the Andalusian province which Brenan regards as more "Castilian" than any other in the south. The influence of the Socialists on the rebellious miners of Asturias and the Rio Tinto (Anarchist competition was strong in both areas) is more difficult to explain, although it was probably due to conjunctural factors rather than reformist inclinations among the miners themselves. In any event, growth was slow and the UGT numbered less than twenty-five thousand members at the turn of the century, more than a decade after its founding. The union did encounter local hostility in its organizing drives. But it inspired very little fear in the government and escaped the repression that finally shattered the Workers' Federation.

To the European Anarchists of the late nineteeenth century, the ruling classes seemed more firmly in the saddle than ever. An oppressive atmosphere of bourgeois egotism had settled over life. Everything seemed to acquire a dull, gray, tasteless appearance. And Europeans of sensibility were repelled by the smugness and banality of the age. The spirit of revolt, blocked by the massive stability of *fin de siecle* capitalism, began to burrow into the underground of this society. Arthur Rimbaud's poetic credo of sensory derangement, Toulouse-Lautrec's provocatively "lumpen" art, and the flouting of middle-class conventions by Oscar Wilde and Paul Gauguin reflected the compulsion of writers and artists to provoke the bourgeois, to cry out against the deadening complacency of the period. A literary and artistic Anarchism emerged which included men like Barres, Mallarme, Valery, and Steinlen, in whom generous ideals for the liberation of humanity were marbled with a furious anger toward bourgeois mediocrity. The effect of these cultural rebels on the social life of the time was virtually nil. At best, the bourgeois greeted them with scandalized outrage; more commonly they were met with uncomprehending indifference.

There were also some individuals whose desire to provoke led them to terrorist actions. These men were not ignored. They often came from the lowest strata of the working class and petty bourgeoisie—true *Desheredados*, their lives crippled by poverty and abuse. A few—Auguste Vaillant, for example, who exploded a bomb in the French Chamber of Deputies—were members of Anarchist groups. The majority, like the Frenchman Ravachol, were soloists. They called themselves "Anarchists," but belonged to no group, for the word had by this time become a synonym for "terrorist." The identification of Anarchism with terrorism was the result not merely of earlier bombings but of a new emphasis in libertarian circles on "propaganda by the deed."

The disappearance of the Bakuninist International after the Verviers congress of 1877 left behind small, isolated Anarchist groups all over Europe. Many of them lacked any strategy for revolutionary change; their members could oppose the entrenched power of the state with nothing but their writings and speeches. The growing Socialist movements of the day were utterly repellent. Authoritarian in structure and reformist in goals, they seemed to embody the pedestrian bourgeois spirit of the era.

It was in this atmosphere, at a time of defeat and growing hopelessness, that a bold act in Russia illumined the way. On March 1, 1881, on the banks of the Catherine Canal in St. Petersburg, a small terrorist organization, the "People's Will," succeeded in assassinating Czar Alexander II. A politically hybrid group with strong Anarchist leanings, the band of young revolutionaries had publicly sentenced the Czar to death in 1879 and tracked him for two years until they were successful. The duel between a handful of terrorists and the massive Russian state had fascinated the world—and had brought the Czar to the point of nervous collapse.

The assassination electrified Europe. Shortly afterward, when an international congress of Anarchists and left-wing Socialists convened in London, one of the main topics to be discussed was "propaganda by the deed." The delegates concluded that "a deed performed against the existing institutions appeals to the masses much more than thousands of leaflets and torrents of words. . . ." Much discussion centered on "chemistry." It was resolved that "the technical and chemical sciences have rendered services to the revolutionary cause and are bound to render still greater services." Hence affiliated groups and individual supporters were asked to "devote themselves to the study of these sciences."

Among the supporters of the new tactic was a young Russian prince, Peter Kropotkin, who had broken with his class and entered the Anarchist movement. Although temperamentally the very opposite of Bakunin, Kropotkin shared the deep humanity of his predecessor. Despite his aristocratic lineage—or perhaps because of it—he spent two years imprisoned in the dreaded Peter and Paul Fortress for his ideals. His dramatic escape and his distinction as a geographer gave him an international reputation. By the time of the London congress, Kropotkin had become the outstanding spokesman for "Anarchist Communism," a theory he advanced with great ability against the prevalent "collectivism" of the traditional Bakuninists.

Bakunin, it will be remembered, believed that the means of life individuals receive under Anarchism must be tied to the amount of labor they contribute. Although they are to receive the full reward of their labor, the quantity of what they receive is determined by the work they perform and not by their needs. Kropotkin did not differ with Bakunin's overall vision of a libertarian society. He too believed that it would mean a stateless society of free; decentralized communes joined together by pacts and contracts. What distinguished him from Bakunin was his insistence that directly after the revolution each commune would be capable of distributing its produce according to need. "Need will be put above service," he wrote; "it will be recognized that everyone who cooperates in production to a certain extent has in the first place that right to live comfortably." Underpinning this view was the conviction that technology had advanced to a point where everyone's needs could be satisfied. The famous communist maxim, "From each according to his ability; to each according to his needs," would be the rule for guiding distribution immediately after the revolution.

Kropotkin, it has been claimed, favored a purist Anarchist elite and rejected the Bakuninist demand for a close linkage between Anarchist groups and large mass organizations. This is not quite true. In a dispute with a number of Italian Anarchists who advocated a strictly conspiratorial type of organization, Kropotkin insisted that the "small revolutionary group" has to "submerge" itself in the "organization of the people," a view that closely parallels Bakunin's organizational ideas.

The difference between Bakunin's and Kropotkin's organizational views turned primarily around the issue of "propaganda by the deed." As Max Nomad observes:

> That tactic had not been in the armory of the Bakuninists; they believed that the masses were essentially revolutionary, and hence needed no terrorist fireworks to stimulate their spirit of revolt. All that was necessary, according to Bakunin, was an organization of conspirators, who at the proper moment would capitalize on the revolutionary potential of the masses. That view was no longer shared by Kropotkin and his friends. It was replaced by a sort of revolutionary "education" of the masses through acts of revolt, or "propaganda by the deed." Originally that sort of "propaganda," as first discussed at the Berne Congress of the "Anti-Authoritarian" International (1876), referred to small attempts at local insurrection. Somewhat later—after such actions had proven to be quite ineffectual—the term was applied to individual acts of protest.

None of these ideas had any significant effect on Spanish Anarchism until well into the 1880s, when translations of Kropotkin's works were made available. At this time, Italian Anarchist Communist emigres in Barcelona began to promote the purist approach to organization and emphasize the importance of terrorist actions. The bitter controversies among Spanish Anarchists over the new ideas and tactics partly accelerated the breakup of the Workers' Federation.

When the once-promising Workers' Federation dissolved in 1888, its place was taken by a strictly Anarchist organization and by ideologically looser libertarian trade unions. The former, the Anarchist Organization of the Spanish Region, was founded at Valencia in September 1888 and consisted of several libertarian tendencies, mainly Anarchist Communist in outlook. The base of this movement was organized around the *tertulia*: the small, traditionally Hispanic group of male intimates who gather daily at a favorite cafe to socialize and discuss ideas. Anarchist groups were usually larger and assuredly more volatile. They gave themselves colorful names expressive of their high-minded ideals (*Ni rey, ni patria, Via Libre*), of their revolutionary fervor (*Los Rebeldes*), or of their sense of fraternity (*Los Afines*). Like the *tertulianos*, they met in cafes to discuss ideas and plan actions. Such groups had already formed spontaneously in the days of the International, but the new Anarchist Organization consciously made them its basic form of organization. Decades later, they were to reappear in the FAI as *grupos de afinidad* (affinity groups) with a more formal structure. The great majority of these groups were not engaged in terrorist actions; their activities were limited mainly to general propaganda and to the painstaking but indispensable job of winning over individual converts.

The union movement, on the other hand, focused its energies on economic struggles, generally taking its lead from libertarian union officials. A number of these officials, anticipating the death of the Workers' Federation, had decided to retain a loose relationship with each other which they formalized in 1888 as a Pact of Union and Solidarity of the Spanish Region. With the revival of the labor movement in 1891, the Pact of Union and Solidarity convened its first congress in March, attracting Socialists as well as Anarchists. Although the congress was held in Madrid, the new organization was primarily a Catalan movement, influenced by Anarchist collectivists and by militant syndicalists.

The Pact of Union and Solidarity was ill-fated almost from the start, for it emerged at a time when terrorist activity in Spain began to get underway in earnest. Although there had been no lack of bombings and assassination attempts in the 1880s, they had been isolated episodes, occurring as the background of a larger class struggle between unions and employers. The bombings that opened the 1890s were quite different. They exploded across the foreground of the struggle and were destined to become chronic in Barcelona. The first of these bombings occurred in the midst of a general strike for the eight-hour day which the Pact of Union and Solidarity had decided to call on May 1, 1891.

The strike began peacefully enough with a large rally at the Tivoli Theater in Barcelona, followed by a street demonstration down the famous Ramblas to the civil governor's palace. On the following day, however, it began to take on serious dimensions. Many factories closed down and violent clashes occurred between workers and police. Characteristiclly the government responded to the situation with a declaration of martial law. (In Spanish, literally, a "state of war."). The next day a bomb went off before the building that housed the *Fomento del Trabajo Nacional* (the "Encouragement of National

Labor", a euphemism for the powerful, notoriously reactionary association of Barcelona manufacturers).

The strike was broken by violence and treachery, but from that point onward, bombings became a commonplace feature of labor unrest in Barcelona. They were invariably followed by arrests and by beatings of imprisoned militants, yet the explosions themselves did very little damage. Generally, their timing and location were planned to pose the least possible threat to human life. The intention of the "terrorists" was apparently to frighten rather than to kill; indeed, it is not certain how many of these bombings were caused by Anarchists who were protesting against the real injuries inflicted by the authorities on imprisoned labor militants, or by *agents provocateurs* of the *Fomento* and the police.

The increasing drift of Spanish Anarchism toward terrorism was to be reinforced by an episode of agrarian unrest that became memorable in the history of the Andalusian movement. Its locale was Jerez, the center of the *Desheredados* and the alleged *Mano Negra*.

Anarchist ideas had taken root in this famous wine district early in the 1870s and, as we have already seen, held out tenaciously against the long years of repression initiated by Serrano. Pamphlets and periodicals sent by Anarchist emigres in the Americas kept alive the visions of the glorious spring of 1873 long after the movement elsewhere had dwindled to small groups and isolated individuals. The persecutions following the *Mano Negra* investigation did not extirpate the Anarchist groups in the district. On the contrary, the barbarities of the *Guardia* created pent-up feelings of anger and frustration that were certain to find release with the first revival of radical activity.

The revival began in 1890. On May 1 of that year, great demonstrations celebrating the labor holiday swept through Andalusia, bringing thousands of defiant workers and peasants into the streets. The astonished authorities took reprisals: bombs were conveniently "discovered" in the offices of *El Socialismo*, the Anarchist paper of Cadiz, and a new wave of arrests swept through the region. The persecutions continued into the next year when the authorities, invoking the discredited legend of 1883, imprisoned 157 Anarchists and labor militants on charges of being members of the *Mano Negra*. The outraged laborers waited nearly six months before responding to this and other provocations; then they exploded.

Toward midnight on January 8, 1892, a band of about five hundred vineyard workers, laborers, and a sprinkling of craftsmen marched into Jerez crying: "Long live anarchy!" "Death to the bourgeoisie!" "Long live the social revolution!" They were armed with pruning hooks, scythes, and whatever firearms they could gather. Outside, on the plains of Gallina and loitering on the road into the city were some thousands of men, ostensibly a reserve force, but actually stragglers who were too fainthearted to participate in the assault.[2] Precisely what the marchers hoped to achieve in the city is not very clear. There had been a great deal of revolutionary agitation in the area. Several suspicious outsiders, including a young man "from Madrid" (*"El Madrileno"*), had surfaced among the vineyard workers, calling upon them to prepare for a "social revolution."[3] The vineyard owners were patently looking for a confrontation in order to suppress the unrest.

Once inside the town, the marchers broke up into small bands. Disoriented and confused, they were hardly a serious threat to anyone but the few stray passersby who fell into their hands. One group made off for the Jerez jail to free the militants who had been imprisoned as members of the *Mano Negra*. A single shot, presumably fired by the warden's daughter, dispersed them. Others wandered through the city streets looking for "the bourgeoisie." A few well-dressed people were stopped, insulted, and their hands examined for callouses. In the course of this enterprise, two clerks, mistaken for the class enemy, were killed.

During all of this, Civil Guards and cavalry had been carefully posted throughout the city waiting for orders to intervene. The authorities apparently knew all about the thousands on the plains of Gallina, the march into Jerez, and the bands wandering through the nearly empty streets. They did nothing to stop them. With enough "incidents" to justify severe repression, the *Guardia* and cavalry were turned loose on the marchers who quickly dispersed into the countryside after some skirmishes. Despite the triviality of the whole incident, the police dealt with it as a major insurrection. Hundreds were rounded up and many savagely beaten. Sixteen men were tried and condemned to sentences ranging from ten years to life imprisonment. With incredible arrogance, the authorities placed Fermin Salvochea, the revered Anarchist "saint," on trial before a military tribunal and charged him with inciting the Jerez uprising—this despite the fact that he had been locked up in the Cadiz prison throughout the entire incident. The officers unabashedly sentenced him to twelve years of hard labor. A few weeks later on February 16, the Anarchists Lamela, Busique, Lebrijano, and Zarsuela were taken out to the main square of Jerez and garroted before a large, silent crowd. They died defiantly, shouting "Viva la anarquia!" Before he was strangled Zarsuela delivered a prophetic injunction. "People of Jerez!" he cried from the scaffold, "Let no one say we die as cowards. It is your task to avenge us against this new Inquisition!"

With the repression of the Jerez uprising, terrorists activity reached a turning point: the garroting of the four Anarchists incensed revolutionaries throughout Spain and Zarzuela's cry for vengeance did not go unheeded. Seven months later in Barcelona, a young Anarchist tried to assassinate General Martinez Campos as revenge for the Jerez executions. Two bombs were thrown at Martinez Campos, the officer whose *pronunciamiento* had paved the way for Alfonso XII and who now occupied the post of captain general of Catalonia. Martinez miraculously escaped serious injury, but the explosion killed a soldier and five civilian bystanders. The police quickly apprehended the assassin, Paulino Pallas, a young Andalusian Anarchist who had prospected in Patagonia with the famous Italian Anarchist Errico Malatesta. The Andalusian was tried by a court martial and sentenced to execution by a firing squad. From the opening of his trial to the moment of his death, Pallas's behavior was defiant. Before the bullets claimed his life, he repeated the ominous cry of the south: "Vengeance will be terrible!"

The warning became a reality before the year was out. On November 7, during the opening night of Barcelona's opera season, two bombs were thrown from the balcony of the Teatro Liceo into a gilded audience of the city's most notable families. One of the bombs exploded, killing twenty-two and wounding fifty. Panic gripped the bourgeoisie. Unleashed to do their worst, the police closed all the workers' centers and raided the homes of every known radical. Hundreds were arrested and thrown into the dungeons of Montjuich Fortress, the military prison overlooking Barcelona's port area and working-class districts. Five Anarchists, innocent of the bombing, were sentenced to death and later executed.

The real assassin, Santiago Salvador, was not discovered until two months later. Salvador had been a friend of Pallas and was determined to answer his cry for vengeance. After failing at a suicide attempt on his arrest, Salvador succeeded in escaping the tortures that the police ordinarily inflicted on political prisoners by pretending to repent his act and feigning conversion to the church. For nearly a year his execution was stayed while Jesuits and aristocratic ladies petitioned the government for a commutation of sentence. When the young Anarchist finally stood on the scaffold, he abandoned his deception and died with the cry: "Viva la anarquia!"

Salvador's death was followed by another round of bombings, arrests, and executions. To quell the Anarchists with a more effective counterterror, the government established a new unit, the *Brigada Social*, composed of specially assigned police ruffians. This new body of police was openly waiting for an opportunity to throw itself on the Anarchist movement—indeed, on all oppositional groups in Bar-

celona. There are, in fact, strong reasons for suspecting that it manufactured a provocation of its own three years after the Liceo bombing.

On June 7, 1896, while Barcelona's Corpus Christi Day procession
was wending through the Calle de Cambios Nuevos into the church,
a bomb was thrown to the street from a top story window. The
procession was led by the most important notables of the city, such
men as the governor of Catalonia, the Bishop of Barcelona, and the
new captain general, Valeriano Weyler y Nicolau, whose cruelties in
Cuba two years later were to earn him worldwide opprobrium. Yet
with this alluring bait at the head, the bomb was aimed at the tail of
the procession, whose ranks consisted of ordinary people. The explosion killed eleven and wounded forty. The assassin was never found.
The bombing, however, provided Weyler with the excuse for rounding up not only Anarchists and labor militants, but Republicans and
ordinary anticlericals as well. Over four hundred people were thrown
into the Montjuich dungeons and left to the mercy of the *Brigada
Social*.

When revealed in the press, the tortures to which these prisoners
were subjected produced a sensation throughout the world. One of
the victims, Tarrida del Marmol, an Anarchist of a distinguised Catalan family and director of Barcelona's Polytechnic Academy, reported
his eye-witness experiences in a book, *Les Inquisiteurs de l'Espagne*,
that caused a shudder of horror north of the Pyrenees. The tortures
were so severe that several prisoners died before they could be
brought to trial. Men were forced to walk for days at a time without
rest; others were hung from cell doors for hours while their genitals
were twisted with ropes and burned. Fingernails and toe nails were
pulled off and savage beatings inflicted mercilessly all over the body.
After spending the greater part of a year in the prison fortress, ninety
were brought to trial in the spring of 1897. Of twenty-six convictions,
eight received death sentences and the remaining eighteen were
given long prison terms. While the convicted men were obviously
innocent, five were actually executed. Nevertheless, the vindictive
Canovas regime had the acquitted prisoners rearrested and transported to the African penal colony of Rio d'Oro, the Spanish equivalent of France's Devil's Island.

Weyler's attempt to crush oppositional sentiment in Barcelona
backfired completely. Not only did he fail to extirpate the Anarchists,
but a massive protest rolled in from Europe and South America. Mass
meetings against the Montjuich atrocities were held in London, Paris,
and other cities. Leading figures all over the continent expressed their
outrage against the barbarities of *Espagne inquisitorial*. Despite its

shortcomings, the closing years of the nineteenth century were a period when people could be genuinely angered by visible evidence of injustice.

Finally, on August 8, 1897, only a few months after the Montjuich trials, the terror reached the premier personally. Canovas was cornered on the terrace of a mountain resort in the Basque country by Michel Angiollilo, an Italian Anarchist, and shot to death. Although Angiollilo was garroted for the assassination, an unsuccessful attempt by the Anarchist Sempau, to kill Lt. Narciso Portas (one of the Civil Guard officers who had presided over the Montjuich atrocities), ended in quite a different way. Despite the fact that his assassination attempt occurred only a month after the death of Canovas, the Montjuich atrocities had produced such a profound reaction of shock that no judge would convict Portas's would-be assassin and he was released.

The men who performed these Anarchist *atentados* (as the terrorist acts were called) were not cruel or unfeeling like Weyler or Portas, who apparently relished their brutalities. The original bombings of 1891 and 1892 had been relatively harmless acts. They were obviously not meant to claim lives but to shatter bourgeois complacency and provoke a spirit of revolt among the workers. The lethal bombings that followed were reactions to the barbarities of the police and the state. The *atentados* had developed from *opera bouffe* into desperate acts of vengeance. Despite the terrible price they took in life and suffering, these terrorist acts served to damage the "Liberal" facade of *Turnismo* and reveal the cold despotism that lay behind Canovas's mockery of parliamentary government.

The Anarchists had been goaded from a generous humanism into a vengeful terrorism. The trend began early, as we noted, when the Internationalists, almost mortally wounded by the Serrano repression, established an "Avenging Executive Nucleus." When the Cordobese section began complaining frantically to the Federal Commission about police repression, the answer it received is significant: "Take note of the names of your persecutors for the day of revenge and justice." Actually, the "Avenging Executive Nucleus" and the Cordobese section did very little to even the score; the government and police invariably came out ahead. But a time would come when the names collected by the police would be matched by the lists prepared by their opponents; then, the firing squads of the Falange would be echoed by those of the FAI.

Yet one is compelled to ask if this bloody imagery, so common in most accounts of the Spanish Civil War, gives an accurate picture of the Spanish Anarchists. In a period when even the Spanish Socialists began to succumb to the bourgeois spirit of the 1890s, the Anarchist

movement was still developing individuals whose humanity and un-
affected sympathy for the suffering of their fellow human beings has
been aptly described as "saintly." It is fair to say that the deep humanity that turned Pallas into a terrorist served to make a great Andalusian Anarchist Fermin Salvochea into a "saint." The two men
were counterparts, not opposites. Salvochea's "saintliness,"
moreover, had very earthly dimensions.

Fermin Salvochea was a man of broad culture, a rationalist and
humanist whose parents had trained him for a business career, not a
place in the church or the university. He was born on March 1, 1842,
in Cadiz, one of Spain's most important and thriving Atlantic ports,
where his father had made a considerable fortune in commerce. At
fifteen he was sent off to London to learn English and prepare for the
business world. The five years he spent in London and Liverpool
brought him into contact with radical literature. Thomas Paine's
critique of religion and Robert Owen's communist theories influenced
him profoundly. Before he left England in 1864, the young Salvochea
had become a convinced atheist and communist. Once back in Cadiz,
he became active in the Federalist movement, living frugally and
devoting the greater part of his fortune to the revolutionary cause.

Soon he was participating in a host of remarkably audacious conspiracies. In 1866, for example, he plotted to free imprisoned ar-
tillerymen who had participated in a rebellion and were now awaiting
deportation to Manila. Later, he tried to promote a military uprising
in Cantabria. During the period of unrest that opened with Isabella's
flight from the country, Salvochea was elected to the revolutionary
commune of Cadiz and became a commanding officer in the most
radical detachment of the Republican militia. When Republican Cadiz
was attacked by government forces, he characteristically held out to
the last with a poorly armed band against the invading troops.

The courage of the man was extraordinary. When it finally seemed
that resistance was utterly futile, he dispersed the militia and remained behind to assume personal responsibility for the uprising.
His behavior gained the respect even of his enemies. Instead of
executing Salvochea, the general sent him to the Fortress of San
Sebastian as a prisoner of war. By this time, he was already idolized
by thousands of poor in Cadiz. A few months later, while he was still
in prison, they elected him to the Spanish Cortes. The Madrid government refused to recognize the election and Salvochea, denied his
parliamentary seat, remained in jail. He was freed by the amnesty of
February 1869. Eight months later, when Amadeo was offered the
Spanish crown, Salvochea took to the field again, leading six
hundred armed Republicans to a rendezvous with other forces from
Jerez and Ubrique. They clashed with pursuing government forces

An etching of FERMIN SALVOCHEA (1842-1907), perhaps the most be-loved figure in the Spanish Anarchist movement of the last century. He is shown here standing beside a cannon during the uprising of December 1868 in Cadiz.

near Alcala de los Gazules and were defeated after three days of fighting.

The rebels dispersed. Salvochea escaped to Gibraltar and finally made his way to Paris where he entered the radical milieu of the periodicals *La Revue* and *La Repell*. After a brief stay in London, the exile returned to Cadiz following the amnesty of 1871, there to be elected the city's mayor. The Cantonalist revolts of July 1873 found Salvochea involved in an unsuccessful effort to bring Cadiz into the insurrectionary movement.[4] After suffering defeat, he again faced a court martial in Seville for rebellion. Condemned to life imprisonment in the African penal colony of Gomera, he now began to perform those self-denying services that make up the legend of the Anarchist "Christ." He bore the sentence with calm and fortitude, sharing everything he received from his family with his fellow prisoners. When the governor of the penal colony read a pardon that his influential mother, aided by the Cadiz municipality, had finally obtained for him, Salvochea tore up the document and declared that there were only two ways he would leave prison: by an amnesty for all or by a revolt. Nine months later, he escaped and settled in Tangiers.

Until his imprisonment in Gomera, Salvochea was not an Anarchist, although he had a strong affinity for the libertarian movement. He belonged to the International almost from its earliest days in Spain, but it was only in the seclusion of the prison colony that he began to examine Bakunin's theories with care. Having once adopted them, Salvochea became one of the most fervent Anarchist propagandists in Spain. He remained in the libertarian movement until the end of his life.

When Salvochea finally returned to Spain in 1885 after the death of Alfonso XII, it was during a time of intense Anarchist agitation in Andalusia. The libertarian press could now emerge legally and Salvochea established *El Socialismo* in Cadiz, spearheading the movement among the vineyard workers and *braceros* of southwestern Spain. He was arrested repeatedly, but his energetic defense in court proved more damaging to the government than any judicial impediments it could hope to place in his way. His practical abilities in the service of the movement were outstanding; it was Salvochea, apparently, who organized the great May 1 demonstrations that swept through Andalusia in 1890 and 1891. The *Mano Negra* case, followed by the "discovery" of two bombs in the offices of *El Socialismo*, led to widespread arrests throughout the region, and by 1892 Salvochea found himself in prison again. Despite the fact that he was in the Cadiz jail during the Jerez uprising, a court martial sentenced him to twelve years for his alleged role in the event. The civil courts had refused to try him, and Salvochea in turn refused to participate in the proceedings conducted by his military judges. Imprisoned in Valladolid, he was exposed to worse hardships than any he had suffered in the African penal colony. He was placed in solitary confinement and denied the right to write letters. The breaking point came when Salvochea refused the warden's order that he attend mass. He was thrown into a damp, subterranean dungeon for months. Finally growing weak and despairing of release, he tried to commit suicide. This act was intensely human and understandable under the circumstances. It also disquieted the religious and most Christian warden. From that point on Salvochea's prison life began to improve. After a while he was transferred to the jail in Burgos where he turned to intellectual activity, translating a work on astronomy and doing writing of his own.

In 1899 Salvochea was freed in the general amnesty that followed the protest over the Montjuich atrocities. He returned to Cadiz where he was welcomed with enthusiasm and resumed his activities in the Anarchist movement. Now nearly sixty, his health broken by years of imprisonment, he devoted most of his energy to literary activities. His last work was a translation of Kropotkin's *Fields, Factories, and Workshops,* one of the most perceptive studies on the liberatory role of modern technology to emerge from the Anarchist movement.

On September 8, 1907, Fermin Salvochea died in Cadiz, the gleaming white city he loved so dearly. Fifty thousand people, including hundreds from all over Spain, followed in the cortege to the cemetary. The greater part of this immense demonstration was composed of ordinary workmen of the Cadiz and Jerez area who had come to love this man for himself and as the embodiment of their hopes for a better world. As the coffin was slowly lowered into the grave, the great assembly of people, many in tears, suddenly raised their voices in a single, spontaneous cry: *"Viva la anarquia!"* This was a life that spanned the Anarchist movement in Spain from its beginnings to the point where it entered an entirely new phase—the period of Anarchosyndicalism.

Salvochea was a man of rare generosity and sympathy. Anarchists such as Manuel Buenacasa, a historian of the movement, speak of him as *"nuestro santo mayor"*—"our greatest saint"—and recall how he would often be found by his friends without a cap or a topcoat because he had given his own to the needy. He never married and he lived frugally. Yet Salvochea did not seek the ascetic's mortification of the flesh, nor did he find exaltation in hardship. A serene man, he was rarely austere or somber. His demeanor toward his friends was affectionate, and toward his enemies he displayed an equanimity that verged on irony.

Terrorists such as Paulino Pallas and "saints" such as Salvochea were to persist into the 1930s as examples of the dual personality of Spanish Anarchism. As a curious mixture of *pistolerismo* and humanism they were to express the underlying tension that alternately divided the Anarchists and, in moments of crisis, united them in a zealous devotion to freedom and a deep respect for individuality. Perhaps no movement combined such conflicting tendencies in a fashion that served to fuel the enthusiasm and attract the devotion of the most dispossessed elements of Spanish society. Only the most deep-seated changes in the latter-day history of Spain were to erase the memory of the saints and terrorists from the popular legends of the peninsula. For better or worse, the tradition deeply affected the outstanding personalities of the movement itself and profoundly shaped its trajectory for nearly two generations.

Notes

1. The party was actually founded secretly in May 1879 under the name of *Partido Democratico Socialista Obrero*; in 1881 it was refounded, with nine hundred members, under the name of *Partido Socialista Obrero* the "Socialist Workers Party," a name it has retained to the present day. I have followed the rather common custom of designating it simply as the "Socialist Party." The supporters of the party early in the 1880s were almost entirely limited to the printers and typographers of Madrid. Pablo Iglesias was elected its secretary, a position he was to hold for decades. It grew very slowly, acquiring its first weekly, *El Socialista*, five years later.

2. The usual figure given is four thousand (a figure that is often confused with the number who entered the city), but it is doubtful if anything near that number were around. Having decided not to participate in the march, many of them probably went back to their homes.

3. *"El Madrileno"* disappeared completely after the workers marched into Jerez and was not to be found again. Pedro Vallina, an outstanding Spanish Anarchist who was on good terms with some of the participants in the Jerez uprising, regarded the young man as a *provocateur*. He also adds the name of Fernando Poulet, a Frenchman who appeared in Paris among the exiled Anarchists. Poulet, in Vallina's opinion, was a spy in the pay of the Spanish embassy.

4. As mayor, Salvochea had abolished the *consumos* (the onerous excise taxes levied on foodstuffs) and, to recoup the lost revenues, placed the tax burden on the shopkeepers. This act thoroughly alienated the lower middle classes, with the result that he was defeated in his second bid for mayoralty and the attempt to bring Cadiz into the Cantonalist insurrectionary movement failed even before Pavia's troops arrived at the city.

Chapter Seven:
Anarchosyndicalism

The New Ferment

By the closing years of the nineteenth century, an organized libertarian movement in Spain had virtually ceased to exist. Police reprisals against the terrorists, coupled with repressive legislation, led to the dissolution in 1896 of the Pact of Union and Solidarity. The Anarchist Organization of the Spanish Region was in shambles. Workers began to leave libertarian organizations as rapidly as they had entered them several years earlier. In Cordoba, for example, after the promising revival of the 1880s, only a few acolytes could be persuaded to attend the May 1 celebration of 1893. In the following years, the rallies were given up altogether. In vain did leading Anarchists reverse their views and speak out against terrorism. As early as 1891, Kropotkin warned that while "the development of the revolutionary spirit gains enormously from heroic individual acts . . . it is not by these heroic acts that revolutions are made." By 1900, all but a handful of the outstanding Anarchists who had supported "propaganda by the deed" had abandoned terrorist methods as a strategic form of direct action.

Yet the "Idea" was far from dead in Spain, and Anarchist terrorism was never to disappear totally. Libertarian ideas now began to take root among the intellectuals. It was at this time that leading Spanish writers and painters such as the novelist Pio Baroja and a young artist, Pablo Picasso, began to flirt with the "Idea." Others, notably the astronomer Tarrida del Marmol and the engineer Ricardo Mella, were actively involved in the movement itself. *La Revista Social*, an outstanding Anarchist theoretical journal founded in 1896, became a forum for a wide range of professional people from the universities, arts, and sciences. Disillusioned by the failure of terrorist tactics, many Anarchists began to place their strongest emphasis on the importance of education in achieving their social goals. This period was the heyday of libertarian schools and pedagogical projects in all areas of the country where Anarchists exercised some degree of influence. Perhaps the best-known effort in this field was Francisco Ferrer's Modern School *(Escuela Moderna)*, a project which exercised a considerable influence on Catalan education and on experimental techniques of teaching generally. The persecution to which Ferrer was subjected in later years brings into sharp focus the enormous problems and obstacles that faced almost every effort to reform Spanish society. To promote the concepts of the Modern School, Ferrer was obliged to be more than an educator and his personal fate, in turn, became a political event of great importance in the early years of the twentieth century.

There seems to be nothing in Francisco Ferrer y Guardia's background that should have made him an educator or even an iconoclast. He was born on January 10, 1859, in Alella, twelve miles from Barcelona. His parents were devout Catholics who raised their son in the traditional manner of moderately well-to-do peasants (his father owned a small vineyard), and there is no evidence of any rebellion in the boy until he was sent off to work in a Barcelona firm at the age of fifteen. The owner, a militant anticleric, apparently exercised a great influence on his young employee. In any case, by the time Ferrer had reached twenty he had declared himself a Republican, an anticleric, and joined the Freemasons, the traditional haven for liberal thought and political conspiracy in Spain.

The young Catalan caught the attention of Manuel Ruiz Zorrilla, the radical Republican who had been a former premier under Amadeo and who in 1885, was enjoying a lively conspiratorial exile in Paris. Working as a railway employee, Ferrer rode the trains between the French frontier and Barcelona, engaged in the precarious job of smuggling political refugees to France. He also functioned as a courier in Zorrilla's efforts to win over army officers to a Republican coup. When General Villacampa pronounced for a republic in September 1886, Ferrer participated in an aborted Catalan uprising. This was the last insurrectionary attempt to turn Spain into a republic for the next half century. Its failure found Ferrer in Paris, occupying the post of secretary to Ruiz Zorrilla.

It was in the French capital that Ferrer began to abandon the party politics of the Republicans for education. This was a major shift that marked his development toward Anarchism, although he was careful never to describe himself as more than a "philosophical Anarchist," an *acrata*. He was greatly influenced in that direction by Anselmo Lorenzo, whom he met in Paris. In any case, his new interests could not have been better placed. Almost any effort to bring more schools to Spain would have fallen like rain on a parched land. At the turn of the century, nearly 70 percent of the Spanish population was illiterate. Teachers were grossly underpaid, and rural schools (where there were any) were often little more than shacks in which barefooted, ill-nourished children were given only the most rudimentary instruction.

The project that Ferrer was to establish as the Modern School has many elements that would almost seem conventional today, but it was also distinguished by features that even now have scarcely advanced beyond the experimental stage. To understand the remarkable advance scored by the Modern School, one must see it against the background of the Spanish educational system as a whole.

Although Spain had a universal education law, the majority of schools were run by clerics who used brutal teaching methods and emphasized rote instruction in Catholic dogma. These clerics openly inveighed against any political group, scientific theory, or cultural tendency which displeased the church. Coeducation, tolerated in the countryside only for want of school space, was rigorously prohibited in the cities.

To this bleak establishment Ferrer opposed a program and method of instruction that the clerics could regard only as "diabolical." He planned to establish a curriculum based on the natural sciences and moral rationalism, freed of all religious dogma and political bias. Although students were to receive systematic instruction, there were to be no prizes for scholarship, no marks or examinations, indeed no atmosphere of competition, coercion, or humiliation. The classes, in Ferrer's words, were to be guided by the "principle of solidarity and equality." During a period when "wayward" students in clerical schools were required to drop to their knees in a penitent fashion and then be beaten, the teachers in the *Escuela Moderna* were forewarned that they must "refrain from any moral or material punishment under penalty of being disqualified permanently." Instruction was to rely exclusively on the spontaneous desire of students to acquire knowledge and permit them to learn at their own pace. The purpose of the school was to promote in the students "a stern hostility to prejudice," to create "solid minds, capable of forming their own rational convictions on every subject."

To Ferrer, however, "the education of a man does not consist merely in the training of his intelligence, without having regard to the heart and will. Man is a complete and unified whole, despite the variety of his functions. He presents various facets, but is at the bottom a single energy, which sees, loves, and applies a will to the prosecution of what he has conceived." One of the most important tasks of the *Escuela Moderna*, Ferrer insisted, was to maintain this unity of the individual, to see to it that there was no "duality of character in any individual—one which sees and appreciates truth and goodness, and one which follows evil.'' The school itself must be a microcosm of the real world, embodying many different sides and human personalities. Hence, Ferrer insisted not only on coeducation of the sexes but on a representative variety of pupils from all social classes. Every effort must be made to bring the children of workers together with those of middle-class parents in order to create a milieu for the young that is fully liberatory, a "school of emancipation that will be concerned with banning from the mind whatever divides men, the false concepts of property, country, and family. . . .'' Much of this is pure Anarchism and reveals the influence of Lorenzo and Kropotkin on Ferrer's mind.

It was not until September 1901, that Ferrer established the *Escuela Moderna* in Barcelona. He had been a teacher during his long stay in Paris. There he had befriended an elderly student in one of his Spanish classes, Mlle. Ernestine Meunier, who left him a substantial legacy after her death. With these resources, the first Modern School was started with an original class of twelve girls and eighteen boys. Within ten months, the number of students had more that doubled, and in the next few years fifty schools based on the principles of the Modern School were established in Spain, mainly in Catalonia. Ferrer, who had invested Mlle. Meunier's money in well-paying securities, built up sufficient funds to establish a publishing house that turned out small, inexpensive, easily understood books on a variety of scientific and cultural subjects. These were distributed widely throughout Spain to peasants, *braceros*, and workers, often by wandering Anarchist propagandists. It was from these booklets that the poorer classes of Spain acquired their first glimpse into the strange, almost totally unknown world of science and culture that lay beyond the Pyrenees. Although more guardedly than in Paris, Ferrer maintained his association with Anarchists, taking a number of them on his staff and giving employment to his friend, the aged Anselmo Lorenzo, as a translator.

The growth of the *Escuela Moderna* and the wide distribution of its booklets infuriated the clergy. But for years there was little they could do beyond denouncing the school and pouring vituperation on Ferrer's personal life.[1] The opportunity to restrict Ferrer's work finally came in 1906 when Mateo Morral, a member of Ferrer's staff, threw a bomb at the royal couple of Spain. The assassination attempt miscarried, and Morral committed suicide. Ferrer and the Modern School were held responsible, although the young assassin had explicitly denounced the Catalan educator and Anselmo Lorenzo for their opposition to *atentados*. Such was the state of Spanish justice at the time that Ferrer was held in jail for an entire year while police professed to be accumulating evidence of his complicity in the Morral attempt. A review of the case by the civil courts established his innocence, and he was released, but he never reopened the original Modern School in Barcelona.

This strong emphasis on education did not mean that Spanish Anarchism was not still occupied primarily with the tasks of the class struggle and the building of a revolutionary movement. Syndicalism was gaining in popularity. The idea, ostensibly French in origin, that an economic organization of workers—a revolutionary union as distinguished from a political party—can take over society by means of a general strike can be traced back to the days of the Industrial Revolution. In the 1830s, the Chartist movement in England had advanced the proposal of a "Grand National Holiday" (a euphemism for a general strike) to fulfill the demands of the workers. This alluring concept of social change soon faded away once the British labor movement became reformist, only to reappear in 1869 at the famous Basel congress of the International Workingmen's Association. Here, in a debate initiated by the Belgian section with the support of delegates from Spain, the Swiss Jura, and France, the proposal was advanced that the unions should provide the nuclear structure of a future Socialist society. Eugene Hins, the Belgian delegate, outlined the actual form of organization these unions should take. He called for a "dual form of organization": a federation of industry-wide "workers' associations" on the one hand and a federation of local, regional, national, and international "labor councils" on the other. This structure forms the model of the syndicalist type of labor organization. As we have seen, the old Spanish International adopted it from the very outset. The "workers' associations" were the *Secciones de oficio*, or trade sections, and the "labor councils" were the *Federaciones locales*, or local federations.

To understand clearly syndicalist organization, it should be examined in two periods: before a revolutionary change, and afterward, when the "syndicates" are expected to take over the management of the economy. Under capitalism, the federation of "workers' associations," organized by trades, is engaged in conducting the day-to-day class struggle and dealing with the immediate grievances of the workers. In this period, the "labor councils," organized geographically, have the tasks of education, propaganda, and the promotion of local solidarity between the "workers' associations." After the social revolution, the "workers' associations" assume the responsibility for the overall administration and technical coordination of the economy. They see to it that the productive units throughout the country are supplied with raw materials, means of transportation, machinery, etc. The "labor councils," in turn, which contain representatives from each trade and enterprise in the locality, administer the economic operations of the community or region, determine its needs, and arrange for the distribution of goods. In this dual system of organization, the local "workers' associations" and the "labor councils" are federated into parallel municipal, regional, and national bodies until, at the summit of society two councils emerge—one composed of representatives of the trades and the other of the regions—which coordinate the total production and distribution of goods. Inasmuch as representatives of the trades also constitute the "labor councils," the two parallel organizations tend to intersect at every geographic level, but each obviously has separate functions in economic life.

This model, of course, is abstract and overly schematic. Its purpose is to explain the essential structure of a syndicalist organization in the simplest possible terms. In practice, syndicalist federations have been far more flexible than any model could possibly indicate and they incorporated long-established unions that retained distinctly nonsyndicalist features. Moreover, there is no model that, in itself, provides a guarantee that a labor federation is syndicalist in a revolutionary sense. The avowedly reformist American labor movement is also organized on a dual basis. "International" unions in the United States—such as the automobile and steel workers' federations, for example—might be said to correspond in a very rough way to the "workers' associations" and the various city, county, and state labor councils to the "labor councils" described by Hins at the Basel congress. In all other respects, however, the differences between revolutionary syndicalist and reformist unions are more decisive than the similarities.

For one thing, the goal of syndicalism is the elimination of capitalism, not merely the amelioration of the workers' immediate economic problems and labor conditions. Its aim is admittedly revolutionary. Not less important is the syndicalist goal of vesting all economic and social decisions in the hands of the direct producers— the workers in each specific enterprise. The guiding and most important principle of syndicalism is that the management of production occurs at the base of society, not at its summit, and decisions flow from below to above. Hence, syndicalism is anti-authoritarian. The democratic, federalist, and decentralized economic organs of the proletariat replace the political agencies of the state. Authority that is currently vested in political organs is turned over to the economic units of society and the actual producers who operate them.

Accordingly, each enterprise is administered by its own workers through an elected committee whose members are presumably (although not necessarily) removable. The various committees are linked together by delegates on local "labor councils" and on an

FRANCISCO FERRER (1859-1909), the libertarian educator and founder of the "Modern School," whose trial and execution after the "Tragic Week" produced reverberations of shock throughout Europe and America.

industry-wide basis through the "workers' associations," or trade unions. Obviously, the pivotal bodies in this structure are the workers' committees which administer the individual factories, systems of transportation, etc., as well as the "labor councils" which deal with the affairs and needs of the localities. The vocationally structured trade unions (as distinguished from the geographically organized unions), although useful in organizing industry-wide strikes under capitalism, have no real function after the revolution. The task of coordinating production, which the syndicalists vest in the unions, can be handled just as easily by the local, regional, and national "labor councils." Indeed, it was to be symptomatic of the decay of syndicalist ideals in France that increasing authority was vested in the trade unions while the "labor councils" were permitted to atrophy.

In its emphasis on economic control at the base of society, syndicalism is consciously antiparliamentary and antipolitical. It focuses not only on the realities of power but also on the key problem of achieving its disintegration. Real power in syndicalist doctrine is economic power. The way to dissolve economic power is to make every worker powerful, thereby eliminating power as a social privilege. Syndicalism thus ruptures all the ties between the workers and the state. It opposes political action, political parties, and any participation in political elections. Indeed, it refuses to operate within the framework of the established order and the state. What, then, will be the substitute for these traditional methods? Here, syndicalism turns to direct action—strikes, sabotage, obstruction, and above all, the revolutionary general strike. Direct action not only perpetuates the militancy of the workers and keeps alive the spirit of revolt, but awakens in them a greater sense of individual initiative. By continual pressure, direct action tests the strength of the capitalist system at all times and presumably in its most important arena—the factory, where ruled and ruler seem to confront each other most directly.

At the same time that syndicalism exerts this unrelenting pressure on capitalism, it tries to build the new social order within the old. The unions and the "labor councils" are not merely means of struggle and instruments of social revolution; they are also the very structure around which to build a free society. The workers are to be educated in the job of destroying the old propertied order and in the task of reconstructing a stateless, libertarian society. The two go together. When all the conditions have ripened to a point where social revolution is possible, the workers go on a general strike with the avowed aim of toppling capitalist society. All means of production and transportation cease to operate. The capitalist economy is brought to a standstill.

In the 1870s, almost two decades before syndicalism was to become popular in France, Friedrich Engels attributed the concept of the revolutionary general strike to the Bakuninists. His criticism is worth examining. "One fine morning," he writes, "all the workers of all trades in some country, or even all over the world, down tools and thus, in at most four weeks, force the possessing classes either to eat humble pie or let loose their violence against the workers, so that the latter then have the right to defend themselves, and while doing so bring down the whole of the old society." After examining the pedigree of this notion, Engels adds: "On the other hand, the governments, especially if encouraged by political abstention, will never let the organizations or the treasury of the workers get that far; and on the other hand, political events and the excesses of the ruling classes will effect the liberation of the workers long before the proletariat gets to acquiring these ideal organizations and this immense reserve fund. Moreover, if it had them it would not need the circuitous path of the general strike to achieve its aims."

This description, with its crass political perspective and book-keeping, is demagoguery, yet it is interesting that Marx's closest collaborator was compelled to use such an approach. In admitting that the Bakuninists were prepared to "defend themselves" (that is, to rise in insurrection), Engels plainly indicates that the Anarchists were not prepared to stop with a peaceful strike—indeed, that they were only too mindful that a strictly economic test of strength in "at most four weeks" was four weeks too long for the workers to endure. To the Anarchists, the general strike was the steppingstone to an insurrectionary confrontation between the two classes, a confrontation in which the proletariat also exercised its economic power to paralyze the functions of the state and block the movement of troops.

Even more interesting is Engel's remark that the state, "encouraged by political abstention, will never let the organizations or the treasury of the workers get that far." Ironically this statement could apply more readily to a political party than to a syndicalist union. Sixty years later German fascism was to annihilate two huge Marxian political parties with scarcely a flicker of resistance by their leaders and following. The German proletariat, in fact, was to become so completely divested of revolutionary initiative by its well-disciplined Social Democratic and Communist parties that Hitler marveled at the ease with which it was shackled to the totalitarian state.[2]

Syndicalism, to be sure, has many shortcomings, but its Marxian critics were in no position to point them out because they were shared by Socialist parties as well. In modeling themselves structurally on the bourgeois economy, the syndicalist unions tended to become the organizational counterparts of the very centralized apparatus they professed to oppose. By pleading the need to deal effectively with the tightly knit bourgeoisie and state machinery, reformist leaders in syndicalist unions often had little difficulty in shifting organizational control from the bottom to the top. Many older Anarchists were mindful of these dangers and felt uncomfortable with syndicalist doctrines. Errico Malatesta, fearing the emergence of a bureaucracy in the new union movement, warned that "the official is to the working class a danger only comparable to that provided by the parliamentarian; both lead to corruption and from corruption to death is but a short step."[3] These Anarchists saw in syndicalism a shift in focus from the commune to the trade union, from all of the oppressed to the industrial proletariat alone, from the streets to the factories, and, in emphasis at least, from insurrection to the general strike.

In France, where syndicalism initiated a worldwide radicalization of the unions in the 1890s, all the latent dangers in the movement's structure were cultivated to produce a reformist organization. Under Leon Jouhaux, the syndicalist *Confederation Generale du Travail* (CGT) became bureaucratized and, apart from its revolutionary rhetoric, a fairly conventional trade union. Almost exclusively proletarian in composition, it exercised very little influence in rural areas. The word *syndicalisme* acquired a neutral meaning—"unionism"—and revolutionary adherents of the original doctrine by contrast were to be called "Anarchosyndicalists." A few intellectuals were attracted to the promise of the old syndicalist goals and especially to its militancy. Georges Sorel, who sought in proletarian aggressiveness a regenerative force to overcome bourgeois decadence, attempted to give syndicalism a heroic philosophy of its own. But his works exercised very little influence among the French workers and none whatever on the Spanish labor movement. Like the majority of intellectuals who were captivated by syndicalism, Sorel soon became disillusioned with the movement's pragmatic and opportunistic goals.

In contrast to France, syndicalism in Spain developed a fiery elan as far back as the days of the International, and reached out to embrace the countryside. It would be more precise to say that Spanish syndicalism was compelled to evolve in a revolutionary, Anarchosyndicalist direction because of the social and political conditions that prevailed below the Pyrenees. Yet in the opening years of the twentieth century, this overall development was not easily discernable. The Madrid government seemed to be more stable than ever, and economic life had begun a surprising recovery from the low produced by the losses of Cuba and the Philippines in the Spanish-American War. In restive Catalonia, local political life was parceled out between the Lliga Regionalista (Regionalist League), a bloc of right-wing autonomist groups favored by the manufacturers, and the Radical Republican Party, a political machine led by an unscrupulous demagogue, Alejandro Lerroux y Garcia. The Lliga had mustered the support of those well-to-do Catalans who were not committed to the Madrid parties. The Radicals, buoyed up by the inflammatory rhetoric of Lerroux, enjoyed the support of the great majority of workers and middle-class democrats in Barcelona. Apart from its incidental nuisance value, the Anarchist movement, after a brief resurgence in the strikes of 1901-03, had been virtually extirpated by the repression of the Barcelona labor organizations. Indeed for a time, it appeared that the industrial workers of Catalonia would drift toward the Socialist rather than the Anarchist fold.

Yet the very opposite was to occur. The assassination of Canovas in August 1897 produced no change in *Turnismo*, the politically deadening system in which Conservative and Liberal ministries alternated with each other. This blocked any serious parlimentary expression of ferment in the country. In the period between 1899 and 1909, the ministry was occupied by three Conservative premiers, Silvela, Villaverde, and Maura, followed by the Liberals Montero Rios and Moret, and finally, for nearly three years, by Maura again. This final Maura ministry was to undermine *Turnismo* almost completely, opening the way to one of the most stormy periods in modern Spanish history.

For a point was now being reached where Canovas's old strategy of calculated political stagnation could no longer contain the new demands that were emerging in Spanish society. The 1880s and 1890s as we have noted, were decades of major industrialization, indeed, of overexpansion. The Catalan manufacturers, burdened by large surpluses of textiles and by the high price of raw cotton, began to press for tax relief and higher tariffs. When their demands were ignored, they were forced into a fatally discordant strategy: independent political action on the one hand, and wage-cutting on the other.

Although by 1907 the government yielded to the manufacturers' demands, virtually closing the internal Spanish market to foreign competition, irreparable damage had already been done to the political stability of Catalonia. A system of "degenerative feedback" had been initiated which was not to be arrested for the next three decades. Despite its Catalanist pretensions, the right-wing Lliga was opportunistic to the core. The manufacturers who subsidized it could not divest themselves of old habits and continued to make concessions to Madrid in exchange for economic privileges. This vacillating policy promoted the expansion of Lerroux's Radical Party, which now gathered behind it many Republicans who were disillusioned with the Lliga's opportunism. The Lliga had raised the specter of Catalan nationalism to frighten Madrid; Lerroux was eager to rally the great mass of *Murcianos* who were indifferent or even hostile to Catalanism, so he unleashed a violent antinationalist campaign in Barcelona. This campaign was spiced with a bitter anticlericalism, giving the Radical Party an aura of militancy without endangering the position of the bourgeoisie. The Madrid government in turn decided to play the Lliga and Radicals against each other on the principle that the greater the instability in Barcelona, the less likely the Catalans were to unite against the central power.

Mysterious funds began to flow into Lerroux's coffers. At the same time, bombs began to explode on the premises of Catalan textile manufacturers who were known to belong to the Lliga. "Anarchist" terrorism seemed to revive with every upsurge of Catalan nationalist activity. Having raised violence in Barcelona to extravagant proportions, the Madrid government created an ongoing crisis in the city—a crisis it would henceforth be unable to control short of dictatorship or civil war. Lerroux, in turn, was to saddle himself with an irresolvable contradiction between word and deed that eventually undermined the last ties of the Barcelona working class to political parties.

But these factors, undeniably important in themselves, merely exacerbated a mounting class war between the Barcelona working class and the textile manufacturers. Although the cotton industry had expanded greatly over the 1880s and 1890s, it did not expand sufficiently to absorb the enormous inflow of *Murcianos* and rural Catalans into industrial areas. The urban population in Barcelona had increased by 10 percent between 1900 and 1910—an accretion composed overwhelmingly of people from the countryside. For many of the new rural immigrants there was no steady work and no adequate shelter. Demoralized and semistarved, this desperate mass formed an excitable reservoir of discontent that Lerroux stirred with appeals to violent action against the clergy.

No less disaffected were the industrial workers in Barcelona and outlying factory towns. Rising prices had made it impossible for a working-class family to live on the father's wages. Although it required about 112 pesetas for a family of four to satisfy its minimal needs, a day laborer ordinarily received 60 pesetas, a plasterer 96, and a metallurgical worker 108. Three quarters of a worker's wages went to food. To surive, a working-class family had no alternative but to send the wife or children to work. It would have been difficult enough for a worker to accept this bleak situation as a fixed way of life. To also be confronted with a wage-cut hanging over one's head, however, was intolerable. Faced with such grim prospects, the Catalan proletariat was seething with discontent.

The confluence of growing economic problems with syndicalist ideas from France soon led to the formation of a new Anarchist labor organization. On October 13, 1900, a conference of unions, organized on the initiative of a Madrid bricklayers' union, was held in Madrid. Delegates claiming to represent some 50,000 workers were sent from Catalonia, Andalusia, Valencia, Asturias, the Basque country, Coruna, Valladolid, and other areas. Many represented local affiliates of the old Workers' Federation and Pact of Union and Solidarity that had survived the repression of the 1890s. With syndicalism in the air and new union organizations forming throughout the country, the prospects seemed particularly bright for a new labor federation based on Anarchosyndicalist principles.

The organization called itself the Federation of Workers' Societies of the Spanish Region, adopting the structure of its predecessors of 1873 and 1881. It was scarcely in existence for more than a year when it found itself riding a wave of general strikes in Valencia, Seville, Saragossa, and other Anarchist strongholds. In Andalusia, town after town went on strike, in some cases posing only one demand— *comunismo libertario*. There were even minor insurrections reminiscent of the Jerez uprising. The movement in the countryside continued for several years and did not come to an end until 1905, when famine in the south literally starved it into quiescence.

The Federation of Workers' Societies was suppressed, but not before it had initiated one of the most portentous general strikes in the early history of the Catalan labor movement. The strike was to reveal the extraordinary sense of solidarity that by this time had developed among the workers of Barcelona and the intractability of the manufacturers in dealing with labor grievances. It was a portent of the years to come and of the new relationship of forces that was emerging in the great Catalan seaport.

The first skirmishes occurred in the spring of 1901, when the yarn manufacturers of the Ter valley attempted to fix a lower wage scale by replacing men with women on newly installed automatic spinning machines. A strike followed in which the workers fought bitterly with strikebreakers and police. The Ter valley strike was answered with a lockout: the manufacturers closed down the plants in order to starve the workers into obedience. It seemed probable that an employer victory in the Ter valley would lead to lower wage scales not only for textile operatives but for workers in other branches of industry. As the summer of 1901 came to an end, the key unions in Barcelona began to gird themselves for a confrontation with the manufacturing class as a whole.

The obstacles the unions faced were enormous. Less than a third—indeed closer to a quarter—of the city's labor force belonged to labor organizations. In the large textile industry, the overwhelming majority of operatives were women and children—the groups most intractable to union influence. In formulating strategic decisions, the union leadership was sharply divided between syndicalists, Anarchists, and Socialists, not to speak of ordinary unionists whose outlook was shallow and whose capacity for class solidarity was limited. An immense reservoir of unskilled and illiterate rural unemployed was available to the employers as scab labor. The textile workers were scattered over nearly 750 factories, many of them widely dispersed and difficult to coordinate for common actions. Finally the employers were united in a tightly knit organization of their own, the powerful *Fomento del Trabajo Nacional*, and could count on the full cooperation of the police and military. It was with these elements that the Federation of Workers' Societies, a decentralized, libertarian organization, would have had to piece together an effective general strike. Yet the strange dialectic of the strike is that it occurred precisely because the Barcelona proletariat, schooled in direct action and Anarchist tactics, had developed a remarkably high degree of initiative. Without that initiative, the strike would have been virtually impossible.

The strike was touched off by a limited, almost peripheral conflict. On December 6, 1901, the metallurgical workers of Barcelona walked out. Despite the absence of strike funds, they remained out for the next three months pressing their main demand for an eight-hour day. The employers were uncompromising, flatly refusing all offers of mediation and turning a deaf ear to public criticism. The Republican newspaper *El Diluvio* warned that if the workers were defeated, they would interpret this as an indication of the uselessness of peaceful strikes. The observation proved to be acutely perceptive, as the employers were to learn several years later. As the weeks passed and it became clear that the strike was turning into a confrontation between the Barcelona proletariat and the manufacturers, a show of working-class solidarity became absolutely necessary. The municipal organization of the Federation of Workers' Societies thereupon decided to intervene and on Monday morning, February 17, 1902, declared a general strike throughout the entire city.

The strike lasted a full working week. Its scope was enlarged by employers who closed down, fearing damage to their businesses. Some street fighting developed between the strikers and the army, but for the most part the strike was peaceful. On the following Monday, February 24, most of the workers returned to their jobs, and the general strike was over. The strikers had raised no demands and, despite the participation of the Federation of Workers' Societies, had conducted the action without any visible leadership. The general strike, in short, was not only an act of solidarity with the metal workers but a superb demonstration of working-class initiative and capacity for self-organization.

These lessons were not lost on the employers and government, who combined their forces to smash the Barcelona labor movement. More strikes followed in 1903 as the proletariat tried desperately to resist the offensive of the state and manufacturers. Carlos Gonzalez Rothwos, the new governor appointed by the Liberals, arrested more than 350 militants that year and closed down a large number of workers' centers. By 1904, the strike movement had begun to subside. Most of the strikes had been lost, leaving two thousand unemployed. Between 1902 and 1909, Barcelona's union membership had been reduced from 45,000 to 7,000, and the employers could congratulate themselves that the labor movement had been all but obliterated in that city.

The Spanish Socialist Party, which had played no role in the strike, drew its own conclusions. The general strike, it warned, was a threat to public order, inviting grave reprisals that would diminish all possibilities of collective bargaining. This reaction is significant as an indication of the party's policy at the time. Politically and organizationally, the Spanish Socialist Party had become another branch in the tree of European Social Democracy: opportunistic in method and reformist in policy. In Barcelona, where employer and police violence tended to turn every major strike into a near-insurrection, the party was simply irrelevant and its isolation from the workers complete. That the Socialist Party and the UGT did not succeed in remaining consistantly reformist is due more to the mounting crisis in Spanish society than to any latent militancy in the Socialist leadership. Brenan observes that where Anarchist unions were strong, the Socialists were usually reformist; where they were weak, the Socialists behaved as radicals. Perhaps it would be more pointed to say that where the Anarchist unions were strong, they became the brunt of employer offensives while the UGT, shielded by its libertarian rivals, tried to make deals with the employers at the expense of the Anarchists. Where the UGT was the larger organization, it was goaded into militancy by the intransigence of the employers and by the demands of its rank and file.

These traits were not lost on the workers in Barcelona. The UGT tried energetically to bring the Catalan proletariat into the Socialist fold. Indeed, the first national office of the UGT had been established in Barcelona, where the union made some inroads among skilled workers. Caught between Anarchist militancy and employer intransigence, it could make very little headway. In 1898 its headquarters were finally transferred to the more congenial environment of Madrid. Yet here too it encountered Anarchist competition, never gaining complete control over the key construction workers, who eventually drifted into Anarchosyndicalist unions.

In Madrid a vigorous effort was made to get UGT backing for the general strike, and Pedro Vallina leaves us a priceless account of what happened. After a meeting at the Casino Federal del Horno in the capital, where the Anarchists unanimously pledged their support to the Barcelona workers, a committee was appointed to visit the UGT headquarters. "One of the UGT leaders, Largo Caballero, received us in his office," writes Vallina, "and without consulting anyone rejected our demand. In a joking, derogatory manner, he asked if we believed in the possibility of a successful strike. I answered we did, even if the Socialists did not help us, because we had confidence in the good will of the workers of Madrid. The attitude of Largo Caballero was so disagreeable that one of our delegates, becoming indignant, threatened to punch him. In fact, the Socialists declined all participation in the conflict. They were at that time a model of commonsense."

The juxtaposition of the cynical Socialist union boss with the idealistic, volatile Anarchists forms a perfect study in contrasting human types. As it turned out, both the Catalan employers and Madrid Socialist leaders were to be proven wrong in their assessments. The Barcelona union movement would recover and call a second general strike. This would develop into a week of full-scale insurrection. It too would be defeated, becoming known as the "Tragic Week." But instead of falling apart, the Barcelona labor movement would emerge in a more vigorous—and more revolutionary—form than at any time in the past.

"The Tragic Week '

The collapse of the Catalan unions after the general strike of 1902 shifted the center of conflict from the economic to the political arena. In the next few years, the workers of Barcelona were to shift their allegiances from the unions to Lerroux's Radical Party.

The Radical Party was not merely a political organization; it was also a man, Alejandro Lerroux y Garcia, and an institutionalized circus for plebians. On the surface, Lerroux was a Radical Republican in the tradition of Ruiz Zorrilla: bitterly anticlerical and an opponent of Catalan autonomy. Lerroux's tactics, like Ruiz's, centered around weaning the army and the disinherited from the monarchy to the vision of a Spanish republic.

In his younger days, Lerroux may have sincerely adhered to this program. The son of an army veterinary surgeon, he became a deft journalist who could mesmerize any plebian audience or readership. After moving from Madrid to Barcelona in 1901, Lerroux openly wooed the army officers while at the same time, in the *exaltado* tradition of the old Republican insurrectionaries, shopped around Europe looking for arms. Had he found them, however, he probably would never have used them. His main goal was not insurrection but the revival of the dying Republican movement with transfusions of working-class support. This he achieved with dramatic public rallies, violently demagogic oratory, and a network of more than fifty public centers in Barcelona alone. It was Lerroux who introduced into Spain the *Casa del Pueblo* (People's House), an institution of the Belgian Socialists that combined meeting halls, classrooms, a library, and a tavern in a single building. Later the Spanish Socialists were to establish People's Houses of their own as means of expanding their movement. In addition to the People's Houses, Lerroux and the Radicals provided the Barcelona poor with food cooperatives, mutual benefits, day and evening classes, and inexpensive theatrical productions. Part of the money for initiating this costly establishment came from secret government funds that the Liberal premier, Moret, fed to the Radicals in hopes of counteracting the Catalan autonomists.

The masses flocked to the Radicals in droves. More than two-thirds of the party were made up of workers, including tough working-class women who formed their own Radical organizations—the *Damas Radicales* and *Damas Rojas*. The more volatile youth of Barcelona were incorporated into the *Juventud Republicana Radical*—the *Jovenes Barbaros* (Young Barbarians), as they were called—whose task it was to protect Radical rallies and break up those of opponent organizations. This apparatus spread through Barcelona into the workers' suburbs, collecting thousands into a far-reaching political network.

There was nothing to equal this network among Catalan autonomists or the unions. By March 1907, the autonomists had been compelled to join forces against the Law of Jurisdictions which gave the military authorities the power to try by courts martial all civilian acts inimical to the army. The new electoral bloc, named *Solidaridad Catalana*, included moderate Republicans, the business-oriented Lliga, and Carlists. Despite its popularity at the polls, *Solidaridad Catalana* held no attraction for the workers and *Murcianos*, who no longer took elections very seriously in any case.

The unions were still in debris. Many *sindicatos* (as they were now called) had simply disbanded or were shadow organizations, although their leaders retained contact with each other in the years following the general strike. It was not until 1907 that the Barcelona labor movement recovered sufficiently to hold a local congress. In June a commission composed of metallurgical workers, typesetters, bakers, painters, and store clerks gathered in the store clerks' union headquarters to lay plans for a municipal federation. The federation, called Solidaridad Obrera (Worker Solidarity), was founded on August 3 and two months later began publishing a newspaper of the same name. Although the new organization grew slowly, it managed to take hold among workers outside the city. A year later, in September 1908, it was expanded into a regional federation embracing 112 labor syndicates throughout Catalonia with a membership of twenty five thousand workers. The Radical leaders were disconcerted by the emergence of this new rival for working-class support. After an exchange of suspicious cordialities, they began to move against it with the intention of either dominating or destroying it.

Initially, the Radicals had very little to fear. Solidaridad Obrera was a "pure syndicalist" union, organized entirely around immediate demands and collective bargaining. The union declared that it was not under the "tutelage of any political party or . . . either of the two branches of socialism" (Marxism or Anarchism). It enjoyed the favor of the governor, Angel Ossorio y Gallardo, who liked its Socialist members and lamented the weakness of their party in Catalonia. Inevitably, however, the labor federation became a battleground between the Socialists and Anarchists. The Socialists, led by union officials like Antonio Badia Matemola, Arturo Gas, and the Catalan intellectual Antonio Fabra Rivas, were intent on bringing Solidaridad Obrera into the UGT. They strongly approved of the union's opportunism; indeed, as Arturo Gas was to emphasize, "Workers conscious of their position emerge from strong syndicates, and from such workers emerge good Socialists." Like the Radicals, the Socialists regarded *Solidaridad Obrera* as a rival to their own organization and were intent on absorbing it or crushing it. That they were in the new union at all was due to the Catalan Socialist Federation's lack of influence in Barcelona.

The Anarchists in Solidaridad Obrera were Anarchosyndicalists who believed in operating within large labor movements—workers like Jose Rodriguez Romero, Tomas Herreros, and the publicist Leopolda Bonofulla. Encouraged by Ferrer, they opened a concerted attack on the Socialists and tried to guide the labor federation toward revolutionary goals. Their efforts, fostered by the drift of the early French CGT toward revolutionary syndicalism, were to be marked by increasing success. The periodical *Solidaridad Obrera* soon fell under Anarchosyndicalist control and on June 13, 1909, a congress of the labor federation voted overwhelmingly to accept the general strike tactic "depending upon circumstances."

The Anarchosyndicalists were viewed with disdain by the Barcelona Anarchist Communists associated with the periodical *Tierra y Libertad* and the terrorist-oriented *Grupo 4 de Mayo* (May 4th Group). This handful of purists was all that remained of the much larger

Anarchist Communist movement formed in the 1890s. Their ranks had been terribly depleted by arrests and persecutions. Owing to a lack of funds, they were compelled to give up their headquarters and meet in the offices of the newspaper. The editors, Juan Baron and Francisco Cardenal, regarded the Anarchosyndicalists as deserters to reformism and held faithfully to the doctrines that had formed the basis of the old Anarchist Organization of the Spanish Region.

Although there were no visibly organized libertarian federations at this time, Anarchists were numerically significant in the Catalan labor movement. A large number of Anarchosyndicalists were united informally by their common objectives in Solidaridad Obrera. Lerroux's own party contained many ex-Anarchists whose commitment to Republican politics was superficial. These "anarchistic" types (if such they can be called) were to contribute materially to the destruction of the Radical Party merely by doing what it had preached. Yet in the end it was not numerical strength that was to establish Anarchist influence in the Barcelona labor movement, but the sharpening struggle that developed between the Catalan proletariat and the employers.

By the spring of 1909, the class conflict between the Barcelona workers and the textile manufacturers began to look like an uncanny replay of the events that had led to the general strike of 1902. On May 15, the Rusinol factory in the Ter valley was closed down, and 800 workers were discharged. The lockout was the opening blow in another campaign to lower wages throughout the textile industry. At a two-day assembly of Solidaridad Obrera in July, speakers exhorted the delegates to throw the full weight of the labor federation behind the textile workers and to plan for a general strike. There seemed to be broad agreement among the delegates on this proposal. Although most of the workers outside the textile industry were apathetic, the idea of a general strike had been accepted by the union not merely in the abstract but concretely—as a strategy that would be translated into action if there were sufficient provocation from the manufacturers or the government.

It was against this background of mounting crisis in Barcelona that the Maura ministry, on July 11, announced a call-up of military reserves for active duty in Morocco. The call-up was not entirely surprising. Skirmishes and sporadic encounters between Riff tribesmen and Spanish troops had been going on for weeks. The odor of an impending war was already in the air. It was no secret that the Riff forays were menacing the supply routes to valuable iron mines owned by major Spanish capitalists. To the Spanish workers, the prospect of shedding their blood to protect the colonial holdings of a few wealthy magnates was not particularly alluring. Maura's call-up

Coup de grace delivered to executed Anarchists in Barcelona following the "Tragic Week" of 1909.

had produced heartrending scenes in Barcelona, the main port of embarkation for Morocco. Many reservists were desperately poor Catalan workers whose families were in no position to lose their breadwinners even for a few days, much less allow their lives to be endangered in imperialist adventures. Antiwar feeling ran high throughout the country. On July 18, Pablo Iglesias, a man who for decades had made prudence the keystone of Socialist policy, warned an antiwar rally in Madrid that "if it is necessary, workers will go out on a general strike with all the consequences."

But when would it be necessary? On the very day of Iglesias's speech, the Riffs attacked the Spanish supply lines for the first time, turning what had been sporadic engagements into a full-scale war. Demonstrations at the Catalan port spread to train stations in other cities where reservists were being called up. This crisis was raised to acute dimensions in Barcelona when on July 21 *El Poble Catala* published a petition by the Catalan Socialists to their Madrid headquarters, calling for a general strike throughout Spain. Nearly a week had passed since Iglesias's warning without any follow-up action being taken by the UGT. In the meantime, the turmoil in Spain continued to mount. As *El Poble Catala* editorialized: "The valves have been closed and the steam is accumulating. Who knows if it will explode?"

The stalemate was suddenly broken on the night of July 24, when two Barcelona Anarchists, Jose Rodriguez Romero and Miguel Villalobos Morena, decided to constitute themselves as the nucleus of a Central Committee for a strike. Rodriguez Romero was an Anarchosyndicalist official in Solidaridad Obrera, and Villalobos Morena had been a schoolteacher in a mining village who was forced to leave his post for publicizing Anarchist ideas. During the events discussed above, Villalobos was on the staff of Ferrer's Modern School and later represented the "syndicalists" on the Central Committee for a Strike. Both men, of course, were Anarchists in their dedication to a libertarian society and libertarian methods of struggle.[4]

Collecting whatever support they could find among the militant officials of Solidaridad Obrera, they fanned out through the city to gain commitments from other leaders. Faced with a *fait accompli*, the Catalan Socialists, who had been waiting for word from Madrid, now had no choice but to join the Committee. To have remained outside would have cost them the opportunity of playing a leading role in the strike action.

Among the Radicals there was to be a division in attitude between the top leaders and rank-and-file militants. Lerroux had gone abroad in February 1909 to escape trial on an old charge of writing a seditious article. He prudently remained away until October 1909, long after the upheaval had subsided. The leadership of the party fell to

Emiliano Iglesias Ambrosio, a shrewd lawyer and politician whose sole policy was to prevent a revolution without damaging the Radicals' reputation for militancy. In trying to curry favor with both the army officers and workers—two essentially antagonistic camps—the Radical politicians succeeded in satisfying neither group. Although a year later the Radicals were to score a large electoral victory, the Catalan workers were to abandon the party and turn away from politics. The army, for its part, was to develop its own organizations, the *Juntas de Defensa* (Committees of Defense), after which it drifted almost completely toward reaction.

The Central Committee for a Strike had been formed on a Saturday night. By Monday the strike was underway. In the morning hours, strike delegations appeared at the factory gates to call out the workers. To protect their property, the employers closed down the factories, once again swelling the ranks of the strikers as they had in 1902. From the outset the Anarchists associated with *Tierra y Libertad* tried to turn the strike into an insurrection, but their most able activists were quickly arrested by the authorities for inciting crowds to attack the police stations. They were removed from the scene almost as soon as the strike began. The Socialists on the other hand, fearful of "Anarchist turmoil," tried to confine the strike to an antiwar protest and regarded any attempt at a revolt as adventuristic.

The events were to astonish everyone. During the week of July 26 to August 1, Barcelona would present the spectacle of a full-scale insurrection, a largely spontaneous uprising that received little guidance from the union or Radical leaders. As Anselmo Lorenzo wrote to Tarrida del Marmol in London: "What is happening here is amazing. A social revolution has broken out in Barcelona and it has been started by the people. No one instigated it. No one has led it. Neither the Liberals nor Catalan Nationalists, nor Republicans, nor Socialists, nor Anarchists."

Had he known all the details, Lorenzo might have added that the civil government in the city had collapsed. On the first day of the strike, the governor of Catalonia, Don Angel Ossorio y Gallardo, became locked in a feud with his superior, the minister of interior Don Juan de La Cierva and his military counterpart, Santiago, the captain general of Catalonia. He resigned in a huff from his post and withdrew to sulk in his summer mansion on the Tibidabo. Santiago, mistrustful of the local garrison, confined most of his troops to their barracks, abandoning the streets to the revolutionaries.

Whatever leadership emerged came from the militants in the Radical Party and Solidaridad Obrera. "By default the leadership of the uprising passed to the militants . . ." observes Joan Connelly Ullman in her detailed study of the insurrection. "They were anarchist by conviction, although nominally members of the Radical party or Solidaridad Obrera." Their efforts were never coordinated by the Committee, which stonily refused to issue any directives and wasted much of its time trying to coax the Radical *jefe*, Iglesias, into joining it. Iglesias, now concerned only with his personal safety, refused. Thus from the outset the insurrection followed its own course. The crowds roaming the main street were careful to distinguish between police and soldiers. The latter were wooed with cheers and antiwar appeals whenever they appeared; the police stations, on the other hand, were attacked with ferocity. This canny approach proved to be highly successful. The police made themselves scarce while at the Paseo del Colon, a group of dragoons refused to obey an order to open fire on the crowd. Railroad lines leading into the city were blown up, temporarily isolating Barcelona from garrisons outside the city. Barricades were thrown up in the working-class districts and arms distributed. Women played a very important role in the revolt, often joining the men in the actual fighting. The struggle aroused not only the workers and *Murcianos* but also elements of Barcelona's *déclassés*, especially prostitutes.

Nor was it for want of leadership that the insurrection was suppressed, all myths about the limits of popular spontaneity notwithstanding. The crucial problem was the lack of support outside Catalonia. The breakdown in communications between Barcelona and the rest of Spain worked to the full advantage of the government, which misrepresented the uprising as an exclusively autonomist movement. The non-Catalan working class and peasantry, lulled by a false picture of the events, made no effort to aid the revolutionaries. Except for workers in a number of industrial towns nearby, the Barcelona proletariat fought alone. And it fought with great courage and initiative. By Wednesday, July 28, large troop detachments had reached the city and were deployed against the insurrectionaries. Intense fighting continued well into the next day. In the Clot and Pueblo Nueva districts, the resistance of the workers was so furious that artillery was needed to clear the barricades. Even after the barricades were demolished, dogged fighting was carried on in buildings and from rooftops.

Elsewhere, the fighting was sporadic. The morale of the workers had been shaken by the news that their revolt was an isolated one. For instance, the UGT, the only national labor federation in Spain at the time, did not issue an appeal for a general strike until Tuesday night, July 27, two days after Barcelona had risen. Moreover, the appeal was not distributed until Wednesday, and it scheduled the strike for the following Monday, August 2—two days after the Barcelona insurrection had been suppressed.

There was little clarity about the aims of the insurrection. The Socialists, as we have noted, saw the uprising as an antiwar protest, the Anarchists as a social revolution, and the Republicans as a blow against the monarchy. By Tuesday the "Tragic Week" had developed a sharp anticlerical edge that was to characterize it almost to the very end. Before the week was over, an estimated eighty churches, monasteries, and Catholic welfare institutions were destroyed. It is fairly evident now that this widespread damage to clerical institutions was instigated by the Radical politicians who were eager to divert the workers from revolutionary paths into well-grooved anticlerical channels.

Very little was required to launch this effort: the church was thoroughly detested by the workers and middle-class radicals in Barcelona. The monasteries and nunneries were regarded as prisons in which recalcitrant novices were tortured into obedience or (as popular rumor had it) simply killed. The aura of torture and terror which suffused popular attitudes toward the church led to a number of macabre incidents. Having "liberated" the monks and nuns, the well-meaning attackers proceeded to exhume bodies in the monastic vaults and cemeteries, looking for evidence of ill-treatment before death. When some cadavers were found with bound limbs (a practice of the Hieronymite nuns), they were carried to the City Hall as evidence of torture. In one case, a number of bodies were deposited on the doorsteps of several prominent Catholic laymen. While this was going on, a young, simple-minded coalman, Ramon Clement Garcia did an obscene dance with one of the corpses as an "amusement." He was arrested by the Civil Guard and later shot, ostensibly for "building a barricade."[5]

The fighting in Barcelona came to an end on Saturday, July 31, when Horta, the last outpost of rebel resistance, was overcome. The rebels there had fought until further combat was impossible. They had insisted they were going to "carry out the revolution" despite the overwhelming odds against them. When the "Tragic Week" was over the police had lost a total of only eight dead and 142 wounded; the fatalities among the civilian population were officially reported as 104, but this figure is almost certainly an understatement and should be weighed against Buenacasa's claim of 600 dead (Buenacasa was one of the participants in the uprising and his figure, although almost six times the official one, should not be totally discounted). The number of wounded will never be known. Although the reactionary press bellowed about attacks on the clergy, only two monks had been deliberately killed. Clearly, in the assaults launched upon religious instituions, the objective was not to take life but, as Joan Connelly Ullman has noted, "to destroy the property—the wealth—of the clergy."

MANUEL BUENACASA (1886-1964). A dedicated Anarchist militant, he contributed significantly to the growth of the CNT and the early development of the FAI. Buenacasa strongly disagreed with the terroristic tactics of the Anarchist action groups although he remained a militant Anarchist throughout his life. His writings comprise a major internal source of data on the CNT and FAI.

No sooner was the revolt over when courts martial were established to punish the revolutionaries. According to official reports, 1,725 individuals were indicted by military courts in the ten-month period following August 1. Two hundred and fourteen had escaped the reach of the army and were never captured. On closer examination, the courts were obliged to dismiss the charges against 469 and acquit another 584. In the end, this left about 450 people to be tried and sentenced, mostly to varying terms of imprisonment. Seventeen were sentenced to death, but only five were executed in Montjuich prison. The remainder had their sentences commuted to life imprisonment.

In four of the five capital cases, the trials were almost completely without juridical foundation: the victims were executed not because they had committed the most serious offenses with which they were charged, but because the authorities wanted to make examples of them. The military had apparently decided to shoot at least one individual for each of the major acts committed in the insurrections. Thus its selection of victims was largely arbitrary. The fifth and last person to be executed was Francisco Ferrer. Ferrer had been abroad between March and June of 1909. He had returned to Barcelona in order to be at the sick bed of his sister-in-law and dying niece. During the uprising he had spent most of the time at his farm, some fifteen miles outside of Barcelona, and his movements had been watched closely by the police.

Ferrer had very little influence on rank-and-file revolutionaries and Radicals in the city. Although he had befriended such outstanding Anarchists as Anselmo Lorenzo and Federico Urales, the ordinary Anarchists and syndicalists had been scandalized by his financial activities and the publicity given to his relations with women. The Radicals were interested mainly in Ferrer's financial contributions to their cause. The Socialists, for their part, detested him. Nearly everyone regarded his political support as a liability. They were ready to take his money (*Solidaridad Obrera's* headquarters, for example had been rented with a loan from Ferrer) but few were willing to listen to his advice.

Yet this man was a sincere revolutionary. In contrast to Radical leaders like Iglesias, he devoutly hoped that the general strike would turn into a revolution. The government and clerics hated him and were intent on destroying him. When he was captured on August 31, after hiding for five weeks in caves on his farm, the prelates of Barcelona sent a letter to Maura openly demanding vigorous action against Ferrer and the *Escuela Moderna*. Maura publicly replied that the government "will act in the spirit of your letter and follow the line of conduct you indicate."

Accordingly, Francisco Ferrer was tried for his life by a military court that had arrived at its verdict well in advance. The proceedings lasted only one day. The prosecution was allowed liberties that scandalized world opinion: anonymous affidavits and hearsay accounts were admitted into evidence against the defendant; prisoners who were faced with serious punishment for their own offenses were evidently given the opportunity to trade heavy sentences for testimony against Ferrer. Evidence in Ferrer's favor was suppressed, and cross-examination by the defense circumscribed to a shocking extent, even by Spanish standards of the day. One witness claimed that Ferrer had participated in the burning of convents in a community where none in fact had been burned at all.

On the morning of October 13, 1909, Ferrer was executed by a firing squad in Montjuich prison. He is said to have died serenely and with great courage. As the men were aiming their weapons at him, he cried out: "Look well, my children! I am innocent. Long live the *Escuela Moderna!*"

The judicial murder of Ferrer was an act not only of gross injustice but political stupidity. The case led to demonstrations throughout Europe and contributed directly to the downfall of Maura's ministry. No less important were the long-run effects of the repression that followed the uprising. The government used the revolt as an excuse to suppress the Catalan unions, suspend the publication of opposition newspapers, and close virtually all private lay schools in the restive province. Although Spain had been placed under martial law directly after the outbreak of the insurrection, full civil rule was not restored in Catalonia until November 7, almost six weeks after its restoration in the rest of the country. As we shall see, these measures further radicalized the Catalan proletariat and increased the influence of the Anarchosyndicalists in the labor movement.

The "Tragic Week" rallied the manufacturers around Madrid and marked the first major step toward ending independent bourgeois politics in Catalonia. Indeed, almost everyone in Spain became mistrustful of electoral methods and drifted toward political subterfuge or the use of direct action. The industrial bourgeoisie returned to its old practice of making behind-the-scene deals. The Conservatives and Liberals, although falling out increasingly between themselves, became uneasy about calling elections. All the members of the privileged classes began to live under a single cloud: the danger of a mass uprising by the urban proletariat. The inner paralysis of these classses increasingly tended to paralyze the entire constitutional system, restricting political life to maneuvers within the government.

Ironically, the Barcelona uprising might have breathed some life into the dying system of *Turnismo*—just as the Federalist revolt of 1873 had evoked it—had it not been for the political machinations of the young king Alfonso XIII. His overt intervention in parliamentary affairs was to prove a fatal blow to electoral politics, leading directly to the Primo de Rivera dictatorship of the 1920s.

The first monarch of the Restoration, Alfonso XII, had accommodated himself to the constitutional regime of the 1870s and 1880s. The landowning oligarchy ruled, and the monarchy for the most part obeyed. The death of the king in November 1885 would have been greatly lamented had the oligarchs been able to foresee the role that his successor would play. They were to be spared this vision for two decades; the second Restoration monarch Alfonso XIII, was a posthumous child, born six months after his father's death. His mother, Dona Maria Cristina, did nothing to threaten Canovas's scheme for stability, and these decades were the most stable in modern Spanish history. Industrial developement proceeded at a fairly brisk pace. The army's role in politics was curbed, the Carlists were slowly assimilated into the established order, and the labor movement was periodically crushed when its growth became worrisome.

But while Canovas was building up this new political establishment, the young king was being taken over by the army. Educated in the fashion of a military prince, he lived amid parades, swords, uniforms, and officers who schooled him in the prerogatives of command. On ascending the throne in 1902, this half boy, half general began to exhibit an annoying interest in his kingly privileges. The Restoration Constitution of 1876 had given the monarch the right to appoint and dismiss the premiers of Spain and as 1909 drew to a close, Alfonso decided to exercise his royal authority in a more direct fashion. When Maura, confronted by Liberal obstruction in the Cortes, tried to bolster his position by asking the throne for a renewal of confidence, Alfonso astonished the Conservative premier by accepting his formal offer of resignation and replacing him with the Liberal, Moret. With this treacherous act, Alfonso virtually terminated the *Turnismo*, a system that had stabilized the Spanish government for a quarter of a century.

If Maura entertained any hope of using the repression to strengthen his own grip on the government, he was soon to be disenchanted. Although he had a majority in the Cortes, he was dropped because his handling of the "Tragic Week" and the Ferrer case had deepened the split within the country and turned world opinion against Spain. How long Maura could have survived had the king supported him is difficult to say. Obviously the whole structure created by Canovas was already disintegrating and Alfonso's intervention in the affairs of the oligarchy was doubtless an effect, not merely a contributory cause, of its decline. In any case, with the passing of the Maura ministry, the Canovite system of a disciplined alternation of parties began to give way to irresponsible infighting between unprincipled political factions, leading inevitably to the piecemeal crumbling of the constitutional structure.

Notes

1. Years earlier, Ferrer had broken off with his wife, Teresa Sanmarti, a woman of fairly orthodox views. In a rage she had tried to kill him and he took up relations with Leopoldina Bonald, a young woman who shared his radical ideas. Later Bonald and Ferrer parted on amicable terms, and he went to live with Soledad Villafranca, a teacher in his school who held Anarchist views. The Spanish church and the reactionary politicians of the day exploited to the hilt Ferrer's openness and freedom in his relations with women. In official Spanish society, it was perfectly acceptable to frequent brothels, support concubines, and carry on liaisons with the wives of other men—provided that all the public amenities of marriage were respected and love affairs kept discreet.

2. Toward the end of his life, Engels was to succumb with astonishing naivete to the political and parlimentary opportunities facing the Marxian parties of the late nineteenth century. In 1891, shortly before his death, the old barricade fighter of the 1840s was to write: "One can conceive that the old society can grow peacefully into the new in countries where popular representation concentrates all power in itself, where one can do constitutionally what one will as soon as one has the majority of the people behind one; in democratic republics like France and America, and in monarchies like England. . . ." The German Social Democrats were to use observations of this kind with great effect in order to block Socialist supporters of the general strike in the Second (Socialist) International.

3. Although Malatesta was to change his attitude toward syndicalism, he accepted the movement with many reservations and never ceased to emphasize that "trade unions are, by their very nature, reformist and never revolutionary." To this warning he added that the "revolutionary spirit must be introduced, developed and maintained by the constant actions of revolutionaries who work from within their ranks as well as from outside, but it cannot be the normal, natural definition of the Trade Union's function."

4. Henceforth, I will use the word "Anarchist" to describe Anarchosyndicalists and Anarchist Communists unless the difference between the two schools of Anarchism are relevant to the discussion. This is necessary because the two schools were soon to interpenetrate and for a time become indistinguishable.

5. This story has been told in some detail because it is an example of those wild inaccuracies that appear in many accounts of the Spanish Anarchists and the Civil War. In his brief account of the "Tragic Week," Gerald Brenan writes that "Monks were killed, tombs were desecrated and strange and macabre scenes took place, as when workmen danced in the street with

disinterred mummies of nuns." This lurid account may be excused by the fact that it was written nearly three decades ago in London, at a time when Brenan lacked adequate research material.

Hugh Thomas, on the other hand, writing in 1961, has less justification for repeating this account in his book on the Civil War. The story is not only repeated almost directly from Brenan but Mr. Thomas adds some sensational adjectives of his own. One now learns that "Drunken workers danced maniacally in the streets with the disinterred bodies of nuns."

Chapter Eight:
The CNT

The Early Years

The decade following the "Tragic Week" opens the mature period of Spanish Anarchism, when the movement assumed massive dimensions and fully developed its tactics and organizational forms. At this time we also witness the emergence of the CNT, the largest of the libertarian organizations that were to play a role in the Spanish Civil War.

The maturing of Spanish Anarchism was a complex process of rounding out earlier methods of struggle which had been used too one-sidedly, almost to the exclusion of all others. During the period of the International, the Anarchists were trying to find their way to a coherent body of theory and practice, and their influence on the laboring classes of Spain was very limited. This was probably the most experimental period in the early history of the movement. Its methods—the general strike tactic combined with local insurrections—could be deployed only on a very small operational stage, against an historic back-drop dominated by Federalism. By the 1880s and early 1890s, Anarchist tactics had veered over to a policy (influenced largely by the Andalusians) of local insurrections, culminating in the Jerez uprising. Then another shift took place, this time to the *atentados* and conspiratorial activities of the 1890s. Throughout this period, moreover, there were always Anarchists who emphasized the less dramatic tasks of propaganda and union organization. In time, all of these tactics began to fall together and were no longer regarded as mutually exclusive. Having exhausted the possibilities of using any one method as a panacea, the Spanish Anarchists now began to unite them as diverse elements in the totality of Anarchosyndicalism. The general strike was combined with local uprisings, a steady barrage of propaganda, direct action by individuals or small groups, and dogged union organizing, each flexibly deployed to reinforce the others. It is this resilience, this uncomplicated, free-wheeling combination of tactics, that accounts in great part for the remarkable growth of the movement in the years to come. The main problem now was to evolve libertarian forms of organization capable of encompassing this wide range of tactics and of promoting their use on a national scale.

Such organizational forms ripened gradually, almost unconsciously, nourished by the disintegration of social and political institutions in Spain. After 1909, the constitutional system became so weakened by internal political divisions that neither effective repression nor satisfying reforms could be undertaken. Maura had genuinely tried to buttress the oligarchy and crush the labor movement. He had attempted in June 1907 to undermine popular suffrage and lessen the influence of the *caciques* by establishing "corporate" vote-granting electoral privileges to institutions and limiting those of individuals. The Liberals and Republicans were alienated by this policy; to them it seemed to portend a drift toward a monolithic Conservative regime. Seven months later, when Maura's minister of the interior, La Cierva, presented a "Terrorist Law" that gave special provincial juntas sweeping powers to suppress Anarchist "terrorists," suspend their periodicals and exile labor militants, almost all opposition opinion in Spain was aroused.

The Liberal Party, more mindful than the Conservatives of the need to neutralize revolutionary discontent with concessions, formed an alliance with the Republicans to unseat the ministry. When the Liberal Moret replaced Maura as premier on October 21, 1909, he was publicly committed to a less repressive program. In November, four Anarchists charged with rebellion in the "Tragic Week" were removed from military jurisdiction and turned over to civilian courts. A few days later, martial law was lifted in Catalonia. Finally, a general amnesty was declared for the imprisoned rebels of July. This less oppressive atmosphere continued into the following year, when Moret was replaced by the Liberal Jose Canalejas, whose ministry was avowedly oriented toward reform and greater political freedom.

The Catalan labor movement now began to reemerge. On December 18, 1909, Solidaridad Obrera held a special assembly to piece the organization back together. It was attended by delegates from only twenty-seven unions with pledges of adherence from an additional forty—a substantial decline from the 108 that were represented in its April assembly eight months earlier. The membership of the labor federation had dropped from 15,000 to about 4,500. A pathetically defensive atmosphere prevailed at this gathering. The delegates were at pains to disclaim any official connection with the general strike of the previous July or any ideological association with Ferrer. In June Solidaridad Obrera had entertained hopes of expanding the Catalan regional federation into a national organization; now, these optimistic plans seemed quite remote. "Without doubt," notes the Anarchist historian, Jose Peirats, "the tremendous repression culminating in the Montjuich shootings retarded the confederal crystallization."

Within months, however, the tide once more began to turn in favor of the formation of a national confederation. The decline of Solidaridad Obrera after the "Tragic Week" had at least one favorable aspect: the more moderate labor leaders had withdrawn for a time, giving freer play to Anarchist influence. This influence was strengthened by the rehabilitation of Ferrer's name. The injustice of the charges against him, followed by the drama of his martyrdom, produced (in Diaz del Moral's words) "an exaltation of syndicalism and of anarchism in the peninsula." Finally, strong sentiment for a national confederation began to build up within unions outside of Catalonia, where Maura's repression had been less severe.

On October 30, 1910, delegates from local confederations throughout Spain convened at the Palacio de Bellas Artes in Barcelona for an informal three-day exchange of views and experiences. It was at this gathering, called by the reconstituted Catalan Labor Confederation (the regional organization of Solidaridad Obrera), that a decision was finally made to establish a new national labor confederation: the National Confederation of Labor (*Confederacion Nacional del Trabajo*)—the famous CNT. The movement really got underway at the CNT's first congress, also held in the Bellas Artes, between September 8 and 11 of 1911. By this time a surprising unanimity of opinion in Anarchist ranks favored the establishment of the new organization. Owing largely to the efforts of Anselmo Lorenzo, many Anarchist Communists of *Tierra y Libertad* began to express the need to work in mass labor movements. The new Confederation, to be sure, was still very small: the delegates represented no more than 30,000 members in some 350 unions throughout Spain. But discussion was animated, and a lively spirit pervaded the proceedings.

We must pause here to examine how this new labor organization was structured. The CNT was built up organically, initially around the Catalan Regional Confederation (*Confederacion Regional del Trabajo de Cataluna*). Later, other regional confederations were established from local unions in each province until there were eight by the time of the Second Republic. The national organization was in effect a loose collection of regional confederations which were broken down into *comarcal* (local and district) confederations, and finally into *sindicatos*, or individual unions. These *sindicatos* (earlier known by the dramatic name of *sociedades de resistencia al capital*—societies of resistance to capital) were established on a vocational basis and in typical syndicalist fashion grouped into local and trade federations (*federaciones locales* and *sindicatos de oficio*). To coordinate this structure, the annual congresses of the CNT elected a National Committee whose primary functions were correspondence, the collection of statistics, and aid to prisoners.

The general secretary of the National Committee and the secretaries of the Regional Committees were the only paid officials in the Confederation. During the first few years, the post of general secretary was occupied by Jose Negre. In contrast to its Socialist rival, the CNT shunned any manifestation of bureaucracy and centralization. It relied primarily on the initiative of its local bodies, *comarca*, and regional confederations to carry out the work of the organization. No strike funds were established. Strikes were expected to be short, and if necessary, violent as befitted a revolutionary organization whose primary aim was the overthrow of capitalism. The purpose of the CNT—or so its Anarchist militants believed—was to keep alive the spirit of revolt, not to quench it with piecemeal reforms and long, attritive strikes. Regular funds were established, however, for aid to prisoners and their families, and to some degree for "rationalist schools." There have been few unions more concerned than the CNT with the defense of its imprisoned members and the cultural, spiritual, and moral elevation of the working class. The phrase *emancipacion integral de los trabajadores* (integral emancipation of the workers) recurs in all the leading documents of this extraordinary organization.

How did the CNT function? For part of the answer we may turn to the statutes of the Catalan Regional Confederation, which established the guidelines for the national movement as a whole. The organization was committed to "direct action." It rejected all "political and religious interference." Affiliated *comarcal* and local federations were to be "governed by the greatest autonomy possible, it being understood by this that they have complete freedom in all the professional matters relating to the individual trades which integrate them." Each member was expected to pay monthly dues of ten centimes (a very small sum), to be divided equally among the local organization, the Regional Confederation, the National Confederation itself, a special fund for "social prisoners," and the union newspaper, *Solidaridad Obrera*.

The Regional Committee—the regional equivalent of the CNT's National Committee—was an adminstrative body. Although it played a clearly directive role in coordinating action, it was bound by policies established by the annual regional congress. In unusual situations, the committee was obliged to consult local bodies, either by referendum or written queries. In addition to the annual congress of the national movement, a regional congress was to be held every year at which the Regional Committee was elected. The statutes contained no provision for the recall of the Committee members—a significant omission—but extraordinary congresses could be held at the request of the majority of local federations. Three months' notice was to be given to the local federations before a regular congress was held "so that they may prepare the themes for discussion." Within a month before the congress, the Regional Committee was obliged to publish the submitted themes in the union newspaper, leaving sufficient time for the workers to define other attitudes toward the topics to be discussed and instruct their delegations accordingly. The delegations to the congress, whose voting power was determined by the number of members they represented, were elected by general assemblies of workers convened by the local and *comarcal* federations.

In practice, the CNT was more democratic than these statutes would seem to indicate. There was a throbbing vitality at the base of the organization, a living control and initiative from below. The workers' centers (*centros obreros*) which the Anarchists had established in the days of the International were not merely the local offices of the union; they were also meeting places and cultural centers where members went to exchange ideas, read, and attend classes. All the affairs of the local CNT were managed by committees staffed entirely by ordinary workers. There were no paid officials, of course. Although the official union meeting was held only once every three months, there were "conferences of an instructive character" every Saturday night and Sunday afternoon. The junta of the local union characteristically included a president, several vice-presidents and secretaries, a small battery of "accountants" to keep a watchful eye on the funds, and a librarian.[1] The solidarity of the *sindicatos* was so intense that it was not always possible to maintain an isolated strike in a locality. There was always a tendency for one strike to trigger off others in its support or generate active aid by other *sindicatos*. This was especially true of strong Anarchist centers like Saragossa, where the movement had established deep and vital roots.

Obedience to the wishes of the membership was a cardinal rule. At the annual congresses, for example, many delegations arrived with mandatory instructions on how to vote on each major issue to be considered. If an action was decided upon, none of the delegations which disagreed with it or felt it was beyond the capacity of its membership was obliged to abide by the decision. Participation was entirely voluntary. Quite often this voluntaristic approach led to all the practical results imputed to centralization—but without the need for creating the same deadening structural forms. On other occasions, it led to sporadic, ill-timed outbursts, easily crushed by the government. But such outbursts were usually due to overconfidence on the part of the CNT's local unions, a zealousness that could only be corrected by experience.

In 1911, the CNT was still very immature, and its radiant optimism about its prospects very nearly had disastrous results. No sooner had the congress established a national confederation when it secretly decided to call a general strike in support of strikers in Bilbao and as a protest against the war in Morocco. The action was scheduled for September 16—only five days after the founding of the CNT. The general strike started in Saragossa and spread rapidly to Gijon, Valencia, and Seville. Partial strikes also broke out in Oviedo, La Coruna, Malaga, Santander, and other cities. In Cullera, a town near Valencia, the general strike exploded into full-scale insurrection. The workers took over the community for several hours and in the course of the uprising killed the mayor and a judge. In Madrid the movement was aborted by the Socialists, who used their influence in the capital to prevent a strike from getting underway. Surprisingly, no strike developed in Anarchosyndicalist Barcelona, where the CNT had held its congress only a few days earlier. There, the authorities had been alerted to the strike plans by Sanchez Villalobos Morena, the brother of Miguel, who had helped constitute the strike committee of July 1909. On the night of September 15, the Barcelona police rounded up five hundred CNT militants or *cenetistas* (as members of the organization were soon to be called) and, with the cooperation of Lerroux, who regarded the union as a rival of the Radicals, managed to stop the strike movement.

Canalejas, the Liberal premier, reacted energetically. Troops were moved into all the major cities and the entire country placed under martial law. The CNT's *centros obreros* were closed down, along with the *Casas del Pueblo* of the Socialists, whom the government suspected of planning to support the strike. The Anarchist press was suspended and a partial censorship imposed on other periodicals. Arrests of labor militants were made everywhere. Heavy sentences were meted out to those strike leaders who could be found. With this began the first flight (to be repeated many times) of *cenetista* militants to France. On January 10, 1912, five Anarchists were given death sentences for their part in the Cullera uprising, but these were commuted to life imprisonment. The last of the group, Juan Jover Ferrer ("Chato de Cuqueta"), was spared the garrot by Alfonso XIII who was now eager to curry favor with the left.

The CNT went underground. Its press disappeared and its membership dropped precipitously. Canalejas, who had been welcomed as a reform-oriented premier, began to curb the entire labor movement, even alienating the moderate Socialists and Republicans. To break a railway strike in 1912, Canalejas drafted 12,000 of the workers into the army. The Liberal premier was to pay dearly for his energy. He was shot to death in the Puerta del Sol, the main plaza of Madrid, by a young Aragonese Anarchist, Miguel Pardinas. Pardinas, whom Buenacasa knew personally as a mild-mannered, inoffensive boy, took his own life to escape capture. With the repression of the movement came a new wave of *atentados*. In April of the following year, another young Anarchist from Barcelona, Jose Sancho Alegre, tried to kill Alfonso XIII at a military parade in Madrid. Although the attempt failed, Sancho Alegre was condemned to death. Again the indulgent monarch commuted the sentence.

By degrees, the fortunes of the Anarchosyndicalist movement began to change, although it was to grow slowly in the next few years. In 1913, Canalejas's successor, the Liberal premier Romanones, declared an amnesty for all imprisoned offenders in the general strike of September 1911. The CNT still remained an illegal organization, however. It had originally been banned by the judiciary of Barcelona, and the courts refused to revoke their decision. But the intrepid union continued to function in the underground, still conducting strikes and carrying on agitation in the factories.

The outbreak of the First World War divided virtually all the working-class organizations north of the Pyrenees. The defection of outstanding Anarchist leaders like Kropotkin, Grave, and Malto to the Allied side, followed by a small number of Spanish Anarchists and their periodicals, shocked the movement, which came out overwhelmingly against the war. "Rather than war—revolution!" cried the Ateneo Sindicalista of Barcelona in a manifesto written by Antonio Loredo and signed by hundreds of organizations. *Tierra y Libertad* remained fervently internationalist, advocating an antiwar position from the very outset of the conflict.

Buenacasa was convinced that the defection of Kropotkin and other leading figures in the international Anarchist movement hastened the death of Anselmo Lorenzo. In any case this grand patriarch of Spanish Anarchism died on November 30, 1914, having devoted almost a half century to the libertarian movement. The CNT, whose formation had meant so much to Lorenzo, numbered no more than 15,000 members at the time. By 1916 the labor organization had recovered sufficiently to publish *Solidaridad Obrera* as a daily newspaper, but the movement was still subjected to severe harrassment. The Anarchists' militant antiwar position greatly displeased the authorities. Although Spain remained neutral, its ruling classes were emotionally committed to the belligerents and profited greatly by the continuation of the war.

In the spring of 1915, the Ateneo Sindicalista of Ferrol tried to hold an international antiwar congress, an event which attracted delegates from Portugal, Brazil, and other countries, including representatives of Socialist youth groups in France. Eduardo Dato, the Conservative premier, fearful of offending the warring powers in Europe, banned the meeting shortly after the delegates arrived, but the ban did not prevent the Catalan *cenetistas* from holding a clandestine conference of their own with a view toward rebuilding the badly fractured CNT.

To the Spanish masses, the war had brought jobs and a certain amount of economic improvement. But it had also brought a spectacular price inflation which outstripped the increases in wage earnings, particularly for unskilled and semiskilled workers. Once again a wave of dissatisfaction began to sweep the country. This time disaffection developed not only among the workers but also in the Spanish army, middle classes, and industrial bourgeoisie. The social situation in Spain began to take a very curious turn. The Conservative and Liberal parties had virtually dissolved into factions, making the old parliamentary system increasingly unmanageable. The army, riddled with dissatisfaction, had begun to form *Juntas de Defensa*. This was a system of councils which seemed to resemble the workers' syndicates, at least in their demands. They asked for seniority in promotions, pay increases, and the right to bargain with the government for overall improvements in the military service. Their chief, Colonel Marquez, was regarded as a simple, honest soldier with Republican sympathies who desired not merely army reforms but an end to oligarchic rule and *caciquismo*.

By 1917 a strange spectacle was unfolding: the army, banished decades earlier from politics to almost everyone's relief, was now being wooed as the hope for political regeneration. The industrial bourgeoisie, irked by economic restrictions and high taxes, began to see the military as a possible lever for overthrowing the landowning oligarchy and taking political power for itself. Francisco de Asis Cambo, the Catalan industrialist and leader of the Lliga, established contact with Colonel Marquez, to be joined by Lerroux and a variety of Republicans, Radicals, and Catalan Conservatives. The linkage extended to the labor movement by means of alliances that had been cultivated between the Socialists and Republicans. For the first time, Spain seemed to be working toward a loose coalition of conservative industrialists, middle-class Republicans, petty-bourgeois democrats, and, through the Socialists, a major labor federation. This agglomeration of basically hostile elements was united by a fixed desire to overthrow the landowning rulers of the state and establish a freely elected Constituent Cortes that would write a new, enlightened Constitution for Spain.

To what extent was the CNT drawn into this curious bloc? The Anarchosyndicalist union found itself involved to the degree that it was committed to common action with the UGT. The CNT, it must be emphasized at this point, was not homogeneous in its outlook. It contained a strong syndicalist tendency, represented by Salvador Segui, the general secretary of the Catalan Regional Confederation, and later by Angel Pestaña, the editor of *Solidaridad Obrera*. Both men believed in Anarchism as a social ideal and were unquestionably individuals of great sincerity and capacity for sacrifice, but their practical views were shaped by day-to-day issues and organizational exigencies. They placed a strong emphasis on the need for immediate gains, often at the expense of their libertarian principles. Moving increasingly into opposition to them were the more principled Anarchists, who were concerned mainly with the revolutionary overthrow of capitalism and the establishment of a libertarian society.

Segui was eager to promote cooperation with the UGT. It is likely that he found practical Socialists like Pablo Iglesias and Largo Caballero more compatible than the "zealots" of *Tierra y Libertad*. By late 1916, the idea of establishing a working cooperation between the two great labor organizations seemed irresistible. The political parties were in shambles; the manufacturers and oligarchy were more deeply divided than ever; the unions were growing rapidly; and the army's loyalty to the crown seemed equivocal. Massive discontent existed among the workers over the soaring cost of living. What could be more natural than to establish a cooperative relationship within the union movement?

This prospect began to take on practical dimensions when an assembly of the CNT in Valencia decided formally to explore opportunities for joint action with the UGT. After an "exchange of impressions," the two organizations established a working agreement which came to be known as the "Pact of Saragossa." The agreement centered primarily around economic issues: the CNT and the UGT decided to call on the government to reduce the cost of living by curbing monopolists, speculators, and food exporters. A plan was drawn up to initiate a series of escalated actions to reinforce these demands. The movement reached its culmination when on December 16, 1916, the two labor organizations carried off an impressive twenty-four-hour general strike throughout Spain to protest rising prices.

By the summer of 1917, the link between the two unions was becoming increasingly political. The time had come for the manufacturers, the Republican middle-classes, and the *Lerrouxistas* to be catapulted into direct confrontation with the oligarchy. In June, Dato, the newly appointed premier, responded to the mounting revolutionary threat by dissolving the Cortes and suspending constitutional guarantees. The Catalan deputies, called back to Barcelona by the Lliga, thereupon declared themselves to be a National Assembly with the mission of renovating the entire political structure of Spain. The assembly managed to collect about seventy deputies out of 760 and hold two secret sessions before it was dispersed by the police.

At this point, the government shrewdly decided to provoke the labor movement into premature action. Dato's intention was fairly clear: to stampede the Lligistas back to the governmental camp and quell the maturing revolutionary unrest among the workers before it went too far. The occasion for this ploy arose when the railroad workers of the *Compania de Ferrocarriles del Norte* in Valencia decided to go out on strike. Why the strike occurred is unclear. It is quite possible that it was the work of an *agent provocateur*, although it may have also been the result of the hopes produced by the assembly of parlimentarians in Barcelona. In any case, the government counseled the company to take a firm stand against the railroad union, an affiliate of the UGT. Although the Socialists managed to get the workers to return to their jobs, the company provoked a crisis by refusing to take back forty-three militants. The railroad workers thereupon walked out again.

Feeling had now risen to a fever pitch in nearly all the working-class districts of Spain. In Vizcaya, 25,000 metallurgical workers had walked out, supported morally and materially by the miners of the region. The Socialists found themselves in a desperate position. Convinced that a general strike was doomed to failure owing to lack of sufficient preparation, they had managed to persuade the CNT to call off all strike actions in Barcelona. At the same time, grossly mistaking the intent of the governement, they had threatened it with a general strike if the forty-three railroad workers were not given back their jobs. This threat, which the Socialists were convinced would suffice to cow the government, was precisely what Madrid wanted. Moreover, it was generally regarded by the UGT rank and file as the opening shot in a social revolution. Everyone was straining at the leash, but this time the leash was held by the UGT leadership, and was rapidly slipping from their hands.

The general strike was called on August 13, and in most areas it was smashed within a few days. Heavy fighting had broken out in a number of cities, particularly in Barcelona, where the CNT reluctantly honored its agreement with its Socialist allies. Barricades went up in the Atarazanas district and the sharpest encounters occurred when the strikers tried to keep the trolleys from operating. Significantly, the troops came out on the side of the government, raking the streets with machine guns and artillery. They even accepted Civil Guard officers as commanders. Officially, the fighting left seventy persons killed, hundreds wounded, and some two thousand arrested. Martial law was declared throughout Spain. But this time, the main burden of the repression fell on the Socialists: Largo Caballero, Anguiano, Besteiro, and Saborit were arrested and received life sentences. In the following year, however, they were elected to the Cortes by working-class majorities and freed in the general amnesty that followed the period of repression. On the whole, Dato had shown more determination in quelling the labor movement than Canalejas—and several years later he was to pay the same price as his Liberal predecessor.

The strike proved to be entirely political, its demands influenced not by Anarchist ideas but by those of the Socialists. The CNT program in Barcelona for example, went no further politically than a demand for a republic, a militia to replace the professional army, the right of labor unions to veto (not enact) laws, divorce legislation, the separation of church and state, and the closing of churches "for a certain period." Economically, the union asked for a seven-hour day, a minimum wage of four pesetas daily, the nationalization of the land, the abolition of piecework, stronger child labor regulation, and so forth. In demanding a plebiscite for declarations of war, the program ironically stipulated that "those who voted for it . . . be enlisted first." However moderate these demands, at least by Anarchist standards, they did not placate the bourgeois parliamentarians in Barcelona. Predictably, the Lliga and its allies completely deserted the labor movement.

The general strike of August 1917, however, marks a turning point in the modern history of Spain. It finally sealed the alliance of the Catalan bourgeoisie with Madrid: henceforth, the Lliga and its wealthy industrial supporters were to openly subordinate all their autonomist visions to brute class interests. To the Catalan bourgeoisie, the main enemy was to be the Catalan proletariat, not the landowners of Castile and Andalusia. Thus was created the social setting that eventually would lead the manufacturers of Barcelona into the arms of General Franco.

The Postwar Years

The end of the European conflict brought an economic crisis to Spain—and nearly four years of bitter social war. The contraction of the wartime market, together with the closing down of shipyards, steel plants, mines, and the withdrawal of land from cultivation, produced widespread unemployment in the cities and countryside. Intent on reducing wages, the manufacturers began to gird themselves for a struggle with the unions. To this end they were prepared to use lockouts, the black-listing of union militants, the *sindicatos libres* (the so-called "free unions," many of which the employers promoted as substitutes for the CNT) and, as we shall see later, private gangs of gunmen—the *pistoleros*—to intimidate and kill union leaders.

The main target of this offensive was the CNT. The labor organization had emerged from the war years and the general strike stronger than ever: by 1919, the CNT numbered from 600,000 to a million members. It had absorbed nearly all the older and established unions in Catalonia whose prudence led them to resist entry into Solidaridad Obrera and its predecessors. This expansion of the Anarchosyndicalist union after the failure of the August general strike is highly significant. In the past, Anarchist-influenced unions were easily repressed. After each defeat, they either emerged weaker than before or disappeared entirely. Now the CNT had not only survived major government attacks but had grown into a formidable revolutionary force in Spain.

To a large extent, the growth of the union can be attributed to the intransigence of the Catalan bourgeoisie. The militancy of the manufacturers evoked a corresponding militancy in the working-class; the failure of political methods promoted antipoliticism and direct action. Certainly this had occurred before, but in the past it had always left the effectiveness of repressive measures undiminished. Obviously other factors had now emerged which promoted the growth of the union despite vigorous efforts to destroy it.

The most important of these was the postwar revolutionary crisis of 1918-20. The Spanish laboring classes shared the sense of exhilaration that swept over the world with the success of the Russian Revolution. The fact that the Czar had been overthrown, followed by the Bolshevik takeover—an insurrection that proclaimed Socialist ideals—produced wild enthusiasm in every corner of the peninsula. The ruling classes were terrified. "The imminence of a political revolution," writes Diaz del Moral, who lived through those upheavals, "worried even the most optimistic. . . . The clear vision of these events and the examples of eastern Europe animated all of the proletarian strata with hopes of victory. At this point, the most potent labor agitation in the history of our country was initiated."

This agitation reveals the considerable role Anarchist militants played in fostering the CNT's growth and giving it a revolutionary direction. In the winter of 1918 a national Anarchist conference was held in Barcelona to define a common policy toward the CNT. The union, it was agreed, could not be regarded as an Anarchist organization in the strict sense of the word. But it was decided that the CNT should be a major arena of Anarchist activity. Anarchists throughout Spain were urged to enter the union and proselytize it. "The results of the conference in Barcelona could not have been better," observes Buenacasa. "Within a few months, all the entities of the CNT were perfectly penetrated by the Anarchist spirit and idea."

Buenacasa's conclusion, however, should not be too hastily accepted, as witness the results of the congress of the Catalan Regional

ORGANIZATIONAL STRUCTURE OF
THE NATIONAL CONFEDERATION OF LABOR OF SPAIN (CNT)

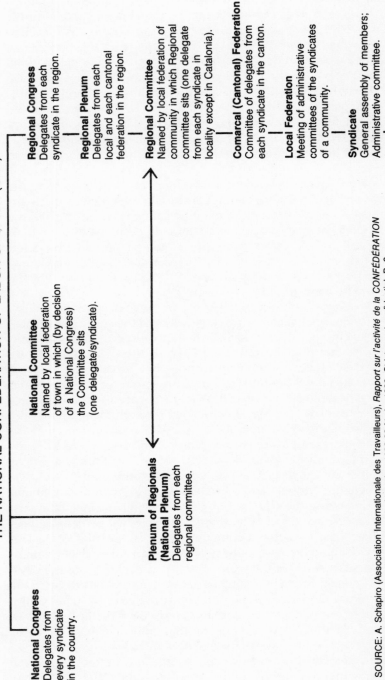

National Congress
Delegates from every syndicate in the country.

National Committee
Named by local federation of town in which (by decision of a National Congress) the Committee sits (one delegate/syndicate).

Plenum of Regionals (National Plenum)
Delegates from each regional committee.

Regional Congress
Delegates from each syndicate in the region.

Regional Plenum
Delegates from each local and each cantonal federation in the region.

Regional Committee
Named by local federation of community in which Regional committee sits (one delegate from each syndicate in locality except in Catalonia).

Comarcal (Cantonal) Federation
Committee of delegates from each syndicate in the canton.

Local Federation
Meeting of administrative committees of the syndicates of a community.

Syndicate
General assembly of members; Administrative committee.

Section of a Syndicate
General Assembly of the section; Administrative committee.

SOURCE: A. Schapiro (Association Internationale des Travailleurs), *Rapport sur l'activité de la CONFÉDÉRATION NATIONALE DU TRAVAIL d'Espagne*, 16 décembre 1932-26 février 1933. Strictement confidentiel. P. 2.

The author wishes to express his appreciation to Martha Ann Ackelsberg for drawing the Schapiro source to his attention. See M.A. Ackelsberg: *The Possibilities of Anarchism: The Theory of Non-Authoritarian Organization* (Princeton University Doctoral Dissertation, September, 1976).

Confederation (the famous "congress of Sans") convened in Barcelona on June 28, 1918. This four-day assembly was attended by 164 delegates, representing some 73,860 members in twenty-seven local federations. So important were the decisions of the congress to the future development of the CNT that they must be examined in some detail.

The syndicates were completely restructured on what, in the United States, would be called an "industrial basis." Until the congress of Sans, the workers in the same factory had been divided among separate, independent craft syndicates, based on trades; now they were to be organized as a *sindicato unico*, uniting all the workers of the same enterprise in a single union. This reorganization did not eliminate all of the established craft unions in the CNT, a number of which still persisted in areas dominated by the craft-oriented UGT, nor did it eliminate representation by trades within the *sindicato unico* itself. Workers of different skills were grouped into trade "sections," then united in a common industrial union.[2] In an industrial dispute, all the sections acted as a single entity. The *sindicato unico* formed the basis of the Catalan Regional Confederation and of the unions that were to enter the CNT in the future. By uniting the skilled and unskilled in a single enterprise, the unions not only increased their fighting power but also made it possible for the poorly paid, unskilled workers to exert a radicalizing influence on the better-paid craft elite.

To further stiffen the militancy of the union, the congress reaffirmed its opposition to *cajas de resistencia*, or strike funds. This stand met with general approval. As Pestana declared, the "Catalan worker from time immemorial has always resisted the *cajas de resistencia* because he felt that this dulled his desire to struggle. . . . " At the same time, Pestana recognized that many employed members would probably want to levy a contribution on themselves—as they had done in the past—to aid strikers in major labor conflicts. Such arrangements, however, had to be made privately, not within the union structure. And if there were to be no *cajas de resistencia*, militant tactics would be necessary to settle strikes. At the same time, however, the congress of Sans articulated its commitment to direct action with prudence— merely as a "preferred means"—and only indirectly expressed its opposition to political methods. It refrained from declaring its support for *comunismo libertario*. As Buenacasa disapprovingly noted, the congress "did not endorse a frank declaration of libertarian principles."

Yet suprisingly, when the delegates took it upon themselves to elect a new National Committee (at least until the next national congress) they chose Buenacasa as secretary general and Anarchists such as Evelio Boal and Vincente Gil as secretaries, Jose Ripoll as auditor, and Andres Miguel as treasurer. "These five," notes Buenacasa, "constituted themselves into an Anarchist group and, in line with their ideas, they oriented the Confederation until the Congress of Madrid" (the second national congress of the CNT in 1919).

The regional congress of Sans, in effect, regarded itself as an interim national body. Its authority to do this, and its choice of a temporary National Committee composed exclusively of Anarchists, may seem as questionable as it was ambiguous. But the Catalan gathering had been inspired in great measure by Anarchist Andalusia, where a regional confederation had been established on May 1st in a congress at Seville. It was at this Seville congress, in fact, that the *sindicatos unicos* were adopted for the first time by a Spanish syndicalist union, paving the way for their acceptance in Catalonia and finally by the CNT as a whole. Since Catalonia and Andalusia were now in close contact, the Catalans were doubtless confident that their actions reflected the wishes of the labor federation as a whole.

At this time the south was in a fever of expectation. Gone were the memories of the defeats suffered at the turn of the century, of the 1905 famine that had starved out the very spirit of agrarian rebellion. Signs of a recovery were already evident in the spring of 1913, when a congress at Cordoba had led to the founding of the *Federacion Nacional de Agricultores* (FNA). Generally, the success of this new organization had been modest although it succeeded in holding regular annual congresses up to 1919, when it dissolved into the CNT. Most important of all, it had won the greater part of Murcia and Valencia to the libertarian fold and provided a springboard for steady agitation to promote the simple demand of the *reparto*: "The land for those who work it!"

With the outbreak of general strikes in the north and the success of the Russian Revolution, an intoxicating wave of hope swept through the south initiating the *Trieno Bolchevista* or "Bolshevik Triennium" of 1918-20. The popular writings of Sanchez Rosa, Kropotkin's famous *Conquest of Bread*, Medico's *To the People!* together with periodicals like *Accion* of Seville, *La Voz del Campesino* of Jerez, and *Solidaridad Obrera* of Valencia, began to inundate the countryside. Sanchez Rosa personally conducted a propaganda tour of the region, followed by Diego Alonso, Higinio Noja, and Francisco Cabello, to mention only a few of the popular Anarchist speakers of the time. By December 1919, a major campaign had been launched to sweep Andalusia into the CNT. Local newspapers were started up in dozens of towns, and a stream of Anarchist speakers, pamphlets, and leaflets flowed through the south.

Diaz del Moral, who witnessed the effects of this Anarchist propaganda at first hand, describes it with great verve and color:

Those who were present at the time in 1918-19 will never forget the astonishing spectacle. In the fields, in the shelters, and in the courtyards, wherever peasants gathered to talk, to everyone's recurring delight there was one topic of conversation that was discussed seriously and fervently: the social question. During the smoking breaks during the day and at night after supper, the most educated would read the leaflets aloud while others listened with great attention. Then came the prerorations, corroborating what had been read and followed by unending praise. They did not understand everything; some words they did not know; some interpretations were childish, others malicious, depending upon the personalities involved; and basically all agreed with each other. How could it be otherwise? For they had all heard the pure truth that they had experienced all their lives, even though they had never been able to express it! Everyone read continually; curiousity and thirst for learning was insatiable; even along the roads, the horseback riders read on their animals leaving reins and halters trailing; when they packed their food, they always put a pamphlet into their sacks.

The account, written after the upsurge had subsided, is inadvertently patronizing. Similar descriptions can be found in the writings of travelers to Paris on the eve of the Great Revolution: the cab driver holding slackened reins while his eyes devour a seditious pamphlet; the soldier on guard duty avidly poring over a radical newspaper; the heated discussions in the Palais Royal, in the narrow streets, and in the cafes. In the case of France, however, this was taken as evidence of the harvest produced by the "Enlightenment" and as testimony to Gallic *civilisation*; in the case of Spain, it was regarded as "fanaticism" and "infantile millenarianism." The point is that Andalusia in 1918-19, like France in the 1780s, was teetering on the brink of revolution. The prudent Cordobese lawyer had come face to face with the insurgent Cordobese peasant—and he was frightened.

In all revolutionary situations, the sedition spreads rapidly. So it had been in France, and so it was in Andalusia. In Diaz del Moral's account, we get not only the facts but also the fears of the privileged classes, who saw this movement only as a terrible contagion spreading across the land:

Within a few weeks, the original nucleus of ten or twelve adepts expanded into one or two hundred; in a few months, almost the total working population, captured by ardent prosleytism, frantically propagated the flaming ideal. The obstinate few who resisted either for reasons of discretion, passivity, or for fear of losing their status, would be harassed on the hillsides as they plowed the furrow, in the cottage, in the tavern, in the streets and squares by committed groups with reasons, with imprecations, with scorn, with irony, until they agreed, for resistance was impossible. Once the village was converted, the agitation spread to those nearby; it sufficed for a worker of one pueblo to speak to a comrade of another. In all cases, the effect was successful; with more or less ability, all were agitators. Thus the fire spread rapidly to all 'combustible' villages. The propagandist's task was easy; it sufficed that he read an article from *Tierra y Libertad* or *El Productor* for the hearers, like those of Fanelli in Rubau Donadeu's guest room, to feel themselves suddenly illuminated by the new faith.

Then would come the strikes. Many of them exploded spontaneously, sweeping in everyone from day laborers and craftsmen to the house servants and wet nurses of the privileged classes. Stores would close, the cafes would empty, and the fields would go untended. If provoked by the *Guardia* there might be violence—rioting, acts of incendiarism, the killing of watch dogs and cattle. Quite often, however, nothing would stir; an eerie silence would descend upon the entire town. Although many of these strikes would raise specific demands (and in 1918, Diaz del Moral tells us, the majority of them were successful), others were strictly revolutionary. The strikers would pose no demands. Their purpose was to achieve *comunismo libertario*. When at last it was clear that this was not to come, the strikes would end as suddenly as they had begun, and everyone would quietly return to work. Then the town would wait for the next opportunity. The swollen groups would shrivel back to a small nucleus of devoted revolutionaries until another upsurge swept across the land.

The coming of the CNT gave these agrarian movements greater cohesion. The union established a *centro obrero* in each town and created permanent organizational forms with regular meetings and experienced organizers. In time, even the most isolated towns developed large, reliable memberships and became linked to other communities by regional conferences and newspapers. This was a vitally important advance. In the past, strikes had been sporadic, often doomed to failure by isolation. In later years, they were to be linked together into great provincial movements, sometimes leading the way for the cities, sometimes reinforcing urban struggles. Speakers from the large cities and occasional visitors from abroad would tour the *centros obreros*, bringing the culturally starved country people into living contact with the most talented individuals in the movement. Here would come the theoreticians of Anarchism, its most capable organizers, its most renowned journalists. These would be great moments, like important holidays, when enraptured audiences would listen to the newest ideas or heatedly debate the most objectionable policies. Then there would be periods when the local speakers, each in turn, would expound "the Idea" in all its nuances to neighbors and friends.

Local newspapers played a major role in this development, not only by informing and coordinating the agrarian movement, but also by providing the *braceros* and peasants with a source of expression. CNT and Anarchist periodicals were remarkable human documents. They were filled with letters—some barely literate—from all parts of the district. The *sindicatos unicos* would post notices of their activities; individual *braceros* and peasants would discuss a host of issues ranging from politics to morality; experiences would be exchanged, and, of course, there would be news of all important events that concerned the interests of the laboring classes. The periodicals, in short, were living organs; their readers devoured them avidly and wrote to them frequently. Devoted Anarchists might subscribe to a number of papers: usually *Tierra y Libertad* or one of the *Solidaridad Obreras*, several of which were published in the large cities. In addition there were scores of local newspapers to choose from in Andalusia alone. These periodicals were supplemented by pamphlets and books on geography, history, science, and agronomy, as well as social issues, and included morally elevating dialogues, poems, and novels. Many of them were printed in very large editions on cheap paper and usually sold for a fraction of a peseta.

In Andalusia and the Levant the *sindicato unico* usually embraced the entire town, bringing together workers, craftsmen, peasants, *braceros*, and even shopkeepers in a single union. Thus any strike involved everyone to some degree and usually took on the proportions of a general strike. In small communities, the Sunday meetings of the *sindicato* were simply village assemblies. Anyone was free to attend, to speak and vote on the topics at issue, which often included not only union business but all the affairs of the community. Women participated as freely as men. Between the weekly assemblies, the adminstration of the community's affairs was vested in the *Junta del Sindicato* and its committees. The assemblies made all decisions of policy and the committees executed them, imposing fines if necessary. Any action of the committees, however, could be challenged and revoked at weekly assemblies. During periods of upheaval, the *sindicato* as a whole became a "dual power" in the full sense of the word, often completely undercutting the authority of the official municipality.

Although recent evidence suggests that the *braceros* were already organized in quasi-syndicalist unions as early as the 1880s and were hardly the amorphous mass described by Brenan and Hobsbawm, the richly articulated forms described above did not fully emerge until the Second Republic. In 1918 the CNT was still a new organization in the south and the *sindicato unico*, although initiated by Andalusia, had yet to develop stable roots. In any case, time was working against the rebellion in the countryside. For years the ruling classes of the south had answered the demands of their laborers with an arrogant indifference, safe in the knowledge that they wielded complete power over their domains. With the upsurge of 1918, they panicked completely. The early concessions to the rural strikes were made as a result of fear, not in a spirit of compromise. Many landowners responded to the demands of their laborers by packing off to the provincial cities, in some cases leaving Spain altogether. Those who remained behind—the more determined proprietors, the *caciques* and their ruffians, the conservative middle classes—mobilized into armed groups. Every *cortijo* became an armory bristling with weapons.

Finally, in May 1919, the new Maura ministry sent General La Berrera into the south with a division of troops. The soldiers, divided into small detachments, occupied vitually all the restive towns and villages. With the declaration of martial law that accompanied this invasion, workers' centers were closed down, radical newspapers suppressed, and thousands arrested. Those who were not confined to jail were simply expelled from the region. The rural movement now began to roll back. The ebbing of the tide was hastened by demoralizing quarrels between the Socialists and Anarchists and by bitter infighting between the Anarchists and syndicalists in the local federations of the CNT.[3] Finally, where all repressive measures had failed, the strikes were literally starved out by the deepening economic crisis that followed the war. A quiet once more descended upon the south, not to be broken until the 1930s.

In the north, repression had started even earlier, under the Liberal premier Romanones, but its effects were to backfire completely on the government. During the summer of 1918, the CNT launched a massive propaganda campaign throughout most of Spain to win over the working class. Within six months, the labor organization had increased its Catalan membership nearly fivefold, leaping from 75,000 in June to 350,000 by the end of the year. CNT speakers crisscrossed the country addressing large meetings and winning adherents by the thousands. In some cases, the gains were utterly spectacular: in December, for example, while stopping at Valencia, Buenacasa and his comrades won over to the CNT the entire *Federacion Nacional de Agricultores*, which was then holding its fifth national congress. In addition, the CNT gained the adherence of the Regional Workers' Federation of Andalusia, bringing two of the largest rural unions into its fold.

As the agitation continued to mount, the government became increasingly alarmed. Finally, on January 16, 1919, Romanones decreed the suspension of all constitutional guarantees in Catalonia. Nearly all the top CNT officials, including Buenacasa, Segui, Herreros, and Negre, were rounded up and imprisoned in the battleship "Pelayo" lying at anchor in Barcelona. Pestana managed to escape arrest, but *Solidaridad Obrera*, on which he served as editor, was suppressed.

These arrests produced an uproar in Catalonia. Although the labor organization had been driven underground, it continued to grow. In fact, it was at this point in the CNT's fortunes—when it was technically an illegal organization, its top officials in jail and its newspaper suppressed—that Barcelona was rocked by one of the most memorable general strikes in the history of the Spanish labor movement.

The strike began with a minor dispute in the "Canadiense," the popular name for an Anglo-Canadian hydroelectric company (*Reigo y Fuerza del Ebro*) that furnished Barcelona with power and light. Here the CNT had organized one of its strongest *sindicatos unicos*. However, it was not with the well-organized utility workers that the strike of the "Canadiense" began, but with the office employees. Toward the end of January, a number of clerks had received wage-cuts, and they turned to the *sindicato* for assistance. The union made an attempt to negotiate the dispute, but the English director of the firm, Peter Lawton, though at first disposed to deal with the workers, finally responded by discharging eight of them. Three days later, on February 5, the entire clerical staff declared a sit-in strike and sent a committee to the highest public officials of Catalonia requesting their intervention in the conflict. They were answered by the arrival of the police, precipitating a strike by the majority of the workers in the plant.

The intransigence of the "Canadiense" director requires an explanation. At this time in Barcelona, a policy conflict existed between the civil and military authorities. Reflecting the state of mind in Madrid, the civil governor Gonzalez Rothwos was inclined to deal amicably with the moderate officials in the CNT. He sensed that a policy of brute repression strengthened the Anarchist militants in the union, undercutting the position of Segui. On the other hand, the captain general Milans del Bosch was a harsh reactionary of the old school who had only one answer to labor unrest: *dar la batalla*—"to give battle." In this stance he was completely supported by the newly organized Employers' Federation, which sought to establish an anti-labor, militaristic regime in open defiance of the civil authorities in Barcelona and Madrid. As Brenan notes, the paradoxical union of the "nationalistic" Catalan manufacturers with the anti-Catalan army had turned Milans del Bosch into "a sort of Viceroy," clearly demonstrating that "for the Lliga, the social question took precedence over the Catalan one." Apparently, it was the captain general and the

Employers' Federation which stiffened Lawton's attitude in the dispute with the *sindicato*.

Before Milans del Bosch could "do battle," however, the strike began to spread—and to the most strategic sectors of the economy. On the same day that the "Canadiense" went on strike (February 8), the workers of the *Energia Electrica de Cataluna* followed them in an act of solidarity, sitting-in in their own plant. Nine days later, on February 17, the textile workers walked out. They were followed by a nearly complete strike by all the electrical workers of Barcelona. The city was plunged into darkness. The government, faced with a desperate crisis in Spain's leading industrial region, brought in the army to restore electrical service, but it could do so only partially, and 70 percent of the factories in the area were paralyzed.

The conflict between civil and military authorities now came into the open. While Gonzalez Rothwos was trying to restore negotiations, Milans del Bosch placed the entire province of Barcelona under martial law. For its part, the "Canadiense" issued a proclamation warning that any worker who failed to return to his job by March 6 could consider himself fired. At this point, an extraordinary thing occurred: the *Sindicato Unico de Artes Graficas* informed the Barcelona newspaper publishers that they would refuse to print anything that was prejudicial to the interests of the strikers. When Romanones in Madrid tried to break the strike by calling up the workers for military service, the printers kept the proclamation out of the newspapers. At length, this document found its way into print, only to be answered by a strike of all the railway and trolley workers. The majority of the mobilized strikers refused to answer the call-up, and those who reluctantly did so refused to act as strikebreakers. Some 3,000 of them were packed off to the Montjuich Fortress. By March 13, the frantic Romanones, pursuing a policy of negotiation with the strikers, installed Carlos Montanes as civil governor and Gerardo Doval as Barcelona police chief—both well-known for their liberal views. By now, the "Canadiense" equipment was suffering from major deterioration; the company, in fact, was facing bankruptcy.

A settlement was finally negotiated by Jose Morote, an official in the Catalan government. Although the strikers had been motivated largely by solidarity for their fellow unionists, most of them asked for wage increases, an eight-hour day, recognition of the *sindicatos* by management, and the reinstatement of discharged personnel. All of these demands were granted. In addition, the workers compelled the employers to reimburse them for the earnings they had lost while striking. As for the government, it was required to release all those imprisoned for "social questions," including the CNT officials who had been arrested in January. There remained one qualification: the authorities refused to release anyone who was currently on trial.

On the night of March 16, the settlement was submitted for approval to a huge mass meeting of strikers at Barcelona's *plaza de toros de Las Arenas*. The workers agreed to everything except the qualification on the "social prisoners." A cry went up over the entire *plaza*: "Free everybody!" Indeed, feeling ran so high that the settlement was nearly rejected; but Segui, by arguing that nothing short of an insurrection could free those prisoners, gained the provisional approval of the audience. It was agreed to return to work for now, but to resume the strike if the government failed to release all the prisoners in seventy-two hours.

This general strike had lasted forty-four days, paralyzing virtually the entire economy of Barcelona and the towns in the surrounding area. The strikers had resisted a military call-up, thus risking imprisonment for four years. Not only workers in industry and transportation but shop clerks and civil servants had walked off their jobs. Thousands had been packed off to the Montjuich Fortress. Finally, on March 11, Romanones had tried to curry favor with the strikers by decreeing an eight-hour day for the construction workers, which was to be extended to all trades on April 3. The decree made Spain the first country in the world to enact the eight-hour day into law.

The workers knew that they had won an historic victory—but so did the employers. Now the hand of Milans del Bosch began to be felt, and it tightened into a fist. Despite pleas by union officials, the government let the seventy-two hours pass without releasing the remaining prisoners. There was no way to avoid this challenge, and on March 24, wisely or not, the strike was resumed in full force.[4] This time the captain general acted with energy and decisiveness. Troops were stationed at all strategic points in the city with machine guns and artillery. To reinforce the soldiers, Milans del Bosch called up 8,000 men of the archaic Civic Guard, a volunteer militia recruited overwhelmingly from the bourgeois classes. Stores were forced open with rifle butts, even though the clerks were still on strike. Members of the Civic Guard transported supplies into the city, and armed troops patrolled the streets.

The government flatly refused to make any compromises with the strikers. To the contrary: the police launched a massive roundup of all the CNT officials, strike committees, and union militants they could find. By March 28, the strike had begun to follow a noticeable downward trend. First the store clerks and office workers returned to their jobs, followed by workers in light industry, transportation, and utilities. The metallurgical workers held out to the last, but by April 7 the general strike had essentially come to an end. A key factor in bringing about the resumption of work in an enterprise was the arrest of the strike committee and the demoralization that ensued. Although workers remained out well into April (partly because of lockouts) and the conflict lingered on in outlying industrial communities, the backbone of the strike had been decisively broken. Milans del Bosch, acting for the army and the arrogant Employers' Federation, capped his victory with an act of defiance that virtually shaded into a *pronunciamiento*: he removed Montanes and Doval from office, packing off the civil governor to Madrid. This action toppled the Liberal government, and Romanones was replaced by Maura.

Milans del Bosch, whatever may have been his expectations, did not smash the CNT. The union was evidently a formidable power in Catalonia, and in the following year its strikes were to increase in number. The captain general, however, succeeded in realizing all the fears of his former civil governor, Gonzalez Rothwos: the violent tactics advocated by Anarchist militants were to replace the moderate methods of the syndicalists. *Pistoleros*, or gunmen, would soon begin to operate more frequently on behalf of both the union and the employers.

The last serious attempt to resolve the bitter conflict in Barcelona was made in the latter half of 1919, when Maura, repudiated by the electorate, was replaced by Sanchez de Toca. The new ministry, composed entirely of Conservatives, made a last ditch effort to reconcile the two classes. That the ministry was formed at all is almost miraculous; the king had begun to meddle in parliamentary affairs in a manner that verged on the erratic. The military juntas, now extremely reactionary, supported the employers in their policy of *dar la batalla*. Despite these formidable obstacles, Sanchez de Toca made an unusual effort to arrive at a *modus vivendi* with the labor movement. His cool and conciliatory behavior in the great strikes that swept Malaga, Valencia, and Saragossa in 1919 stand out in sharp contrast to the mindless repression initiated by Maura and his aide La Cierva.

Barcelona was dealt with cautiously. The new civil governor, Julio Amado, tried to create a stable system of labor arbitration by establishing a Mixed Commission of Labor *(Comision Mixta de Trabajo)*, on which sat an equal number of employer and union representatives.[5] For a while, it almost seemed that Amado's policy of conciliation might succeed: the number of *atentados* fell off sharply, and an agreement was reached in September for the return of 70,000 workers (many of them lockouts as well as strikers) to their jobs.

But this period of conciliation was to be very shortlived. In October 1919, a congress of the Employers' Federations in Barcelona secretly voted to initiate a general lockout in Catalonia and, if necessary, throughout Spain, in the event that the government should fail to end the "present situation of social disorganization." The decision

SALVADOR SEGUI (1890-1923), the most prominent figure in the Catalan Regional Confederation of the CNT during the post World War I era. Although Segui led the reformist wing of the CNT and might well have earned the opprobrium of the militant Spanish Anarchists had he lived in the 1930s, he is remembered today for his personal courage, earthiness, and ideological commitment to a libertarian society.

ANGEL PESTAÑA (1889-1937), variously editor of *Solidaridad Obrera* and secretary general of the CNT, essentially agreed with Segui's reformist policies. Expelled from the CNT in the 1930s as a leading spokesman of the Trientistas, he went on to found a Syndicalist Party and entered the Popular Front. Pestaña was readmitted to the CNT during the Civil War but never regained the stature he enjoyed in earlier years.

was followed by a month of maneuvering between the union and the manufacturers, in which the latter tried to create the very "social disorganization" they had been complaining about.[6] When, on November 25, some 25,000 construction workers went on strike, the employers apparently decided that the opportune moment for their offensive had arrived. The lockout began on the very same day, throwing 200,000 out of work. The action lasted well into January of the following year—a period of ten bitter weeks during which virtually all industry in Barcelona was brought to a standstill.

It was in the midst of the lockout—indeed, during one of its worst phases—that the CNT decided to hold its second national congress. Since Barcelona was no longer safe for such a gathering, it was to take place in the Socialist stronghold of Madrid.[7] On the morning of December 10, 1919, 437 delegates gathered in the aristocratic Teatro de la Comedia, filling most of the orchestra seats and boxes. The remaining sections of the Teatro were occupied by a large assortment of artists, writers, poets, and academicians; in short, that unique peripheral group of intellectuals that had collected around the Madrid Anarchist organizations from the days of the First Republic. It was truly a people's congress, with each delegation wearing its own regional garb: the Basques in their berets, the Andalusians in their large Cordobese hats and peasant blouses, and so forth. The delegates represented over 700,000 members. The overwhelming majority—427,000—were located in Catalonia, while the Levant claimed 132,000. The Andalusian delegation—"the most anarchist delegation," according to Buenacasa—represented less than 90,000, a reflection of the harsh repression Maura had inflicted on the region.

Although somewhat formally structured, with a credentials committee and special committees to report on important issues, the congress was highly democratic. From the outset it was decided to grant everyone present the right to speak, although many individuals in the Teatro were not members of the CNT. Voting privileges, of course, were reserved for the authorized delegates. From beginning to end, it was a stormy congress. For eight years, repression had prevented a representative, national assembly of this kind from convening. Passions and ideas were pent up in all of the delegates. No sooner had the lean figure of Boal called the crowded meeting to order than scores of delegates sprang to their feet, demanding the floor. Later, an extremely able chairman, Jose Maria Martinez of the Asturian delegation, managed in an affable but decisive manner to keep the proceedings orderly, but "vivas" to Anarchism and to the CNT exploded throughout the sessions.

The congress unequivocally declared its belief in *comunismo anarquico*. It adopted the *Sindicato Unico de Ramos e Industrias* (single union of branches and industries) for large cities and the more encompassing *Sindicatos Unicos de Trabajadores* (single union of workers) for the smaller towns and villages. This merely acknowledged the fact that craft sections within the *sindicato unico* were not feasible for unions in small or rural communities.

With the adoption of the *sindicato unico*, the congress annulled the *Federaciones de oficio* (the federations organized by trade and industry), replacing them by simple *Comites de relacion profesional* (committees of professional relations). No longer was the labor organization to have the dual aspects advocated by traditional syndicalism: there were to be *sindicatos unicos*, grouped into local or territorial federations. Craft problems were to be handled by the trade sections within each *sindicato unico* and, on a larger scale, by simple, loosely organized committees of professional relations. "The National Confederation will be composed basically of its Regional Federations," declares the resolution adopted on this issue, "these by the Local and Comarcal Federations and these by the Sindicatos." With this structural change, the CNT was now essentially decentralized and its internal relations made entirely organic. Although a National Commitee continued to exist, the autonomy of the local and regional federations was no longer abridged by the existence of parallel, separately organized craft bodies.

The congress called upon the printers' *sindicatos* to refuse to publish any periodicals in localities where authorities had suspended the CNT press. Furthermore, the printers were asked to exercise a "red" censorship in direct proportion to the censorship imposed on labor periodicals. The delegates affirmed their commitment to *accion directa* and declared their support for the "intelligent," "opportune" use of sabotage. They condemned any participation by the CNT unions in the Mixed Commissions. By this time, the Catalan Regional Confederation had acknowledged its error in joining the Mixed Commissions organized under the Sanchez ministry, an act of self-criticism that the delegates accepted without reproaches.

The biggest problem facing the congress was its attitude toward other movements, notably the UGT and the Communist International. A strong sentiment for fusion with the Socialist union existed among delegates from Asturias and Castile, the two areas where the UGT had deep roots in the working class. The Saragossa delegate supported fusion, reminding the congress that workers from his area were not yet aligned with either labor organization. On the other hand, the Andalusians as a bloc and Anarchist militants from other regions opposed it furiously. The ill-feeling of many *cenetistas* toward the Socialist union can best be conveyed by referrring directly to one of the resolutions condeming fusion. The *ugetistas* (UGT members) were described as *"amarillos y al margen del movimiento obrero"*: "yellows and on the margin of the labor movement." Nourishing this sharp language were bitter memories of strikes in which *ugetista* workers had scabbed against their brothers in the CNT and the cynical advantage the Socialist leadership had taken of Anarchist defeats. Yet the use of these words produced a sensation at the congress, and for three days the delegates heatedly debated the issue. When it finally came to a vote, the fusionists were defeated by 324,000 to 170,000. The number of abstentions was fairly large and, unaccountably, delegates representing some 200,000 members did not participate in the voting at all.

By contrast, the Bolshevik Revolution was greeted with unrestrained enthusiasm. The congress called upon all Spanish armament workers not to produce any weapons destined for use against the Red Army and threatened to call a general strike if Spain sent troops to Russia. After avowing their support of Bakunin's principles in the First International, the delegates voted for provisional adherence to the Communist International.

"In spite of the fact that not one of the four hundred anarchist delegates of the Spanish organization in Madrid was disposed to cede a single point of our ideological convictions," observes Buenacasa, "the truth is that the immense majority behaved like perfect Bolsheviks. This was in spite of the great love we felt toward the libertarian ideal. It had an explanation: the Russian Revolution impressed us to the extreme that we saw in it the revolution we dreamed of." The Asturian delegate, Quintanilla, warned against this naivete: "The Russian Revolution does not embrace our ideals; it is a socialist type of revolution, common to all the revolutionary socialist tendencies started in Europe. Its direction and organization does not correspond to our concept of workers' intervention, but to that of political parties." While calling upon the delegates to oppose European intervention in the Russian Civil War, the Asturian urged them not to join the Communist International.

The relationship of the CNT to the Russian Bolsheviks was to follow a strange trajectory. In June 1920, Angel Pestana was sent to Moscow to represent the labor organization at the Second Congress of the Communist International. In Moscow he was courted by Zinoviev and Losovsky, but he soon began to sense the enormous gap that existed between the libertarian ideals of his movement and the authoritarian practices of the Bolsheviks. The Russians tried to be accommodating; to lure Anarchosyndicalist unions into the Communist fold, they established the International of Red Trade Unions ("Profintern"), presumably an independent body that accepted all revolutionary unions irrespective of their political views.

These flirtations did not last long. In March 1921, the Soviet regime harshly suppressed the Kronstadt sailors uprising. The Kronstadt issue, coupled with a mounting campaign against Russian Anarchists, began to alienate the libertarian movement throughout the world. The relations between the CNT and Moscow became increasingly taut. Pestana, returning to Spain, reported on his bleak experiences. His account was corroborated by Gaston Leval, who had gone to Russia separately as a representative of the Catalan Anarchists. On June 11, 1922, a conference of the CNT at Saragossa rejected affiliation with the Bolshevik movement, and the CNT together with other independent syndicalist unions in Europe, began to explore the possibility of forming a new international. Bearing the traditional name of "International Workingmen's Association," the syndicalist international was founded at a congress held in Berlin from Decemeber 26, 1922, to January 3, 1923. The adherence of the CNT to the new body finally ruptured all ties between the Spanish labor organization and Moscow.

The Bolsheviks, however, did not suffer a complete loss in Spain. In April 1921, a group headed by Andres Nin and Joaquin Maurin surfaced in Moscow, professing to represent the CNT. Actually, Nin and Maurin represented virtually no one but the Lerida local federation (their stronghold), which they had persuaded to send them to Russia.[8] Both men were deeply enamored of the Bolsheviks and, without consulting the movement they professed to represent, proceeded to affiliate it to the Communist International. Their actions and claims were disavowed by a plenum of the CNT at Logrono the following August. After a futile attempt to return to Spain, Nin went back to Moscow to become head of the "Profintern." Maurin managed to reach Spain and together with Anarchosyndicalist and Socialist dissidents, established a Communist-syndicalist group of his own, largely independent of the newly founded Spanish Communist Party. In later years, both he and Nin were to combine and establish the semi-Trotskyist *Partido Obrera de Unificacion Marxista* (Workers' Party of Marxist Unification): the ill-fated POUM.

The Madrid congress of the CNT in December 1919 marks the high point in the postwar development of Spanish Anarchosyndicalism. The movement had taken on a more national character, expanding beyond the confines of Catalonia and Andalusia. It had become a serious competitor of the UGT in the mining districts of Oviedo and had established roots in the steel plants of Gijon and La Felguera. Saragossa was a center of "pure" Anarchism—a "Jerez of the north"—with tendrils extending into the estates of the steppe country and the vineyards of Rioja. A strong Anarchosyndicalist movement existed in La Coruna, particularly among the dock workers, as well as in the surrounding rural districts. In most Spanish ports the majority of sailors and stevedors favored the CNT. The union had wide support among the mountain peasants of the Levant and strong *sindicatos* in the Rio Tinto mining district.

Anarchist groups, as distinguished from Anarchosyndicalist unions, were forming into regional federations after having existed for years in relative isolation from each other. An Andalusian Anarchist Federation had been established in 1917, and now there was one in Catalonia as well as other provinces. These finally collected into a loosely organized National Federation of Anarchist Groups, later establishing an exile offshoot in France called the Federation of Anarchist Groups of the Spanish Language. In the late 1920s, the two federations were to form the basis of the *Federacion Anarquista Iberica*, the redoubtable FAI of the Republican years and the Civil War.

In Catalonia, however, the CNT had entered a period of deep crisis. The lockout was to completely exhaust the labor organization and the *pistolero* war was to claim a disastrous toll in dead and wounded among its most capable militants. Indeed, this savage duel between armed Anarchists and employer-hired thugs was to cost many lives not only among the unionists but also among public officials, manufacturers, and the highest echelons of the state.

No less important than the claim it made in human life was the atmsophere of illegality it generated. After the street war, the country would never again be the same. Everyone, from Cortes deputies to Anarchist militants, pocketed revolvers, and almost every large organization had some kind of paramilitary force at its disposal. On an ever-increasing scale, political disputes involved a recourse to arms. The return of the "permanent guerrilla" to Spanish society is vitally important in understanding the social atmosphere that produced the Civil War.

The Pistoleros

In 1916 Angel Pestana, who at that time was editor of *Solidaridad Obrera*, was privately approached by two young workers who, without any preliminaries, declared:

> We are going to pose a question to you. We belong to an Anarchist action group and are disposed to continue the work already started. We come to propose that you be our spokesman in the confederal committees, especially in the Regional Committee. Our proposal is as follows: we are willing to make an *atentado* against any employer or factory director the organization considers it advisable to eliminate. In exchange for this sacrifice, which we are willing to make for the organization, we only ask that you pay us the expenses which we incur and the wages of the days

lost from work. Furthermore, that there be a reserve fund of two or three thousand pesetas so that in case of the necessity for flight, if our identity is discovered, we can put our hands on it immediately. And if anyone is imprisoned, as you can understand, we want you to help us. What we ask of you, as you will see, is very little; what we offer, on the other hand, is a great deal.

Pestana, who knew the young men, tried to dissuade them. They were wasting their time, he warned, for he was unalterably opposed to such methods. Later he learned that they had made the same offer to the organization through one of its committees and that it had been accepted. These young Anarchists, Pestana goes on to say, did not decide which of the employers and their factory directors were to be assassinated. The decision was made by the men who accepted their services. The *atentados* were entirely impersonal and were performed without expectation of financial reward or desire for personal vengeance. At that time, according to Pestana, two or three Anarchist action groups were operating in Barcelona. "Let us state that those who took advantage of this and paid the young men for their work," he adds, "were some elements, very few, among the leaders of the textile unions. When this was done, the first step had been taken."

If this was the "first step," however, it was not a major one. Sastre y Sama's study of *atentados* performed against Barcelona employers shows that they were not greater in number between 1916 and 1919 than they had been in 1914.[9] It was not until late 1919 that the number of Anarchist *atentados* began to rise significantly, paralleled by increasing assassinations of CNT militants and officials. The year was a particularly bitter one for the labor federation. It was the year of the February-March general strike, Maura's campaign of persecution, and the long lockout from November until January of the following year. Except for a brief truce initiated by the Sanchez ministry, the government had been especially provocative: constitutional guarantees in Catalonia were suspended between late January and mid-March, and again in late March, by which time some 40,000 workers had seen the inside of jails. The *sindicatos* had been attacked repeatedly, their records seized and the *centros obreros* closed down. Finally, to cap these provocations, one of the most outstanding CNT officials was cut down by the bullets of assassins. On the night of July 19, two men in police uniforms drove up to the home of Pablo Sabater, the president of the textile union, and shot him to death. Perhaps more than any other event up to that point, the murder of a revered union militant increased *pistolerismo* in the Catalan seaport to uncontrollable proportions.

The disease was endemic in Barcelona. Even in the prewar years *agents provocateurs*, either hired or encouraged by the police and civil governors, planted bombs in Barcelona to provide an excuse for crackdowns on the union movement. A network of informers extended through the city, parasitizing the labor movement like lice. In unruly periods, of course, they had their work cut out for them; in lean periods, these elements learned to create their own "incidents" and generate a demand for their services. One of the most notorious examples in its day was the Rull family—Juan Rull, his brothers, and his mother—who for years had set off bombs in Barcelona and collected fees from the police for spurious information on the "perpetrators" of these "Anarchist outrages." As an informer, Juan Rull had access to the ears of three civil governors; indeed, there is compelling evidence that he was in the pay of high clerical politicians like Eusebio Guell. Rull's arrest in July 1907 produced a scandal that lingered beyond his execution in August, a year later. On that day, a bomb went off on a main boulevard of Barcelona. Nearby, a note was found declaring that Rull was innocent and that the bombings would continue despite his death—which, to many, meant that it was not one man or his family but an entire syndrome that lay at the root of Barcelona's *atentados*.

The outbreak of the First World War found neutral Spain—and particularly Barcelona—infested by adventurers, criminals, and mercenaries. At first living on opportunities for espionage, these elements soon began to thrive on the frayed nerves of the Catalan bourgeoisie and on the Barcelona police department's growing demand for hired assassins. Perhaps the most sensational example of these sinister connections was revealed in the pages of *Solidaridad Obrera* on June 8, 1918, when Pestana published evidence that a district police chief, Manuel Bravo Portillo, was operating a German espionage ring in the port area. Although Pestana's charges were to cost Bravo his job, the captain general, Milans del Bosch, recruited his services in the early street war with the CNT.

During his years in the police department, Bravo had served in the volatile Atarazanas quarter of the city, where the brutality of his methods had made him a particular object of detestation among the Barcelona workers. With the outbreak of the February-March general strike the ex-police officer and his cronies, in close association with a self-styled "Baron Koenig," were given a monthly stipend of about $6,000 to perform special services for the employers. Their jobs included *atentados* against CNT officials and union activists. There seems to be little doubt that men from Bravo's gang murdered Sabater. Bravo, in turn, did not survive the summer. On September 15, at noon, he was shot down in the Calle de Santa Tecla. Two days afterward, one of his most detested agents, Eduardo Ferrer, a former leader in the metallurgical union, was killed. News of Bravo's assassination produced a carnival atmosphere in Barcelona. Buenacasa tells us that "thousands of workers celebrated the event with banquets, singing, and speeches on the subject."

The gang, however, did not disappear. It was taken over by the "Baron," a foreign adventurer who lacked even the residual social and national loyalties Bravo had possessed. "Koenig" (his real name may have been Coleman) was simply out for what he could get. He extorted "protection" money from the individual employers; those who refused to pay became victims of "Anarchist outrages," whether they had particularly outraged the Anarchists or not. The situation began to get out of hand when the "Baron" became involved in disputes within the Employers' Federation itself. Accordingly, in the late spring of 1920, he was quietly expelled from Spain and his gang dissolved.

The work of the Bravo-Koenig gang had already been taken up on a broader scale before the "Baron" disappeared. In December 1919, the Carlist Ramon Sales founded the *sindicato libre* (free union) at the Ateneo Legitimista in Barcelona. Patronized by the church and employers, the new body—whatever the sincerity of many of its founders and followers, who may have been "pure-and-simple" trade unionists—was used to divide the labor movement. Recruiting its membership from the more religious, more conservative, or simply more opportunistic strata of the working class, it made very little headway against the CNT. But it provided a new reservoir of *pistoleros* and an ideological covering for professional gunmen in the union's cadres. Superficially, the battle in Barcelona now took on the appearance of an inter-union rivalry waged with revolvers in hand.

To worsen a rapidly deteriorating situation, in November 1920 the captain general of Catalonia, Severino Martinez Anido, was appointed civil governor, replacing Carlos Bas. This appointment, as Brenan notes,

> was an act of defiance to all moderate and humane opinion in the country. His disagreement with Bas was due to the fact that he had supported extra-legal means for dealing with terrorism: he is said to have shown Bas a list of 675 syndicalists whom, he declared, ought to be shot outright. Unamuno describes him as follows: "The man is a pure brute—he can't even talk, he can only roar and bray, though his roars and brays always mean something."

The Anarchists, in turn, attempted to regroup their own forces. There can be little doubt that increasingly violent elements began to influence the direction of the CNT, although professional gunmen were rarely to be found in an organization whose resources were slim and whose members were bitterly persecuted.[10] The remarks of

Buenacasa on this state of affairs convey the disgust that the more staid Anarchists felt over their inability to arrest the trend toward *atentados*. Buenacasa complains that few of the *atentados* were revolutionary acts. "The unions," he concludes, "were unable to shake off these *pistoleros* who were acting on their own and who in a few cases were able to seize the leadership of important committees of the organization."

Yet by this time, the Anarchists may very well have had no choice: with Martinez Anido at the helm, any failure to resist might have been more demoralizing than the rampant gunplay. To all appearances the new civil governor and the Employers' Federation were waging a war of extermination against the CNT. A distinguished conservative politician, Burgos y Mazo, leaves no doubt that the blame for the crisis in Barcelona belonged to the ruling classes. "It must be said in all clarity," he emphasizes, "without fear, and in due tribute to truth: the employer class and other leading elements in Barcelona were the principle culprits of this horrible social state today."

An incredible situation now began to unfold in Barcelona: the *atentados* of the employers' *pistoleros* were matched, almost victim for victim, by the *atentados* of the Anarchists. Nothing quite like this macabre bookkeeping had occurred before. Following an attempt on Segui's life on January 4, 1920, the Anarchists responded with *atentados* against the president of the Employers' Federation, one of its directors, and two police agents. *Atentados* now began to occur almost regularly, alternating between the two sides like the movement of a pendulum. By the autumn of 1920, there was one nearly every day. One of the most senseless atrocities occurred on the night of September 12, when a bomb exploded in a working-class dance hall on the Paralelo, killing three and wounding twenty. A month later, the head of a metallurgical firm, E. Tarrida, was assassinated. This was followed two weeks later by the death of Jaime Pujal, president of the Association of Electrical Employers.

The arrest of sixty-four CNT officials on November 20 led to a general protest strike. On November 23, Martinez Anido responded by outlawing the labor federation and reestablishing censorship. Three days later, the president of the *sindicato libre* of Reus was killed. His death was followed the very next day by the assassination of Jose Canela, an important member of the Regional Committee of the CNT. The authorities and *pistoleros* did not spare even the attorneys of the labor federation: the lawyer Luis Companys was arrested and shortly afterward his colleague, the popular Republican deputy Francisco Layret, was murdered.

The pistol war claimed victims not only from the Employers' Federation, the unions, and the police, but from the highest summits of the government. In 1920, the civil governor of Catalonia, the Conde de Salvatierra, who had presided over the lockout of late 1919 and early 1920, fell before the guns of Anarchist *pistoleros*. On March 8, 1921, the Conservative premier, Eduardo Dato, was killed by three Catalan Anarchists in reprisal for restoring the *Ley de fugas* (Law of Flight), a disgusting practice in which the police killed arrested syndicalists, claiming they were shot while "trying to escape." For its part, the CNT paid a corresponding price with the death of Evelio Baal, the general secretary of the National Committee, killed at dawn on June 15, minutes after having been released by the police. His companion, Antonio Feliu, another National Committee member, managed to escape this attempt, but was shot down two weeks later.

Between 1918 and 1923, this systematic slaughter claimed about nine hundred lives in Barcelona alone and about 1,500 throughout Spain. A premier, two former civil governors, an Archbishop, nearly 300 employers, factory directors, foremen, and police, and many workers and their leaders in the *sindicato libre*, fell before the bullets and bombs of Anarchist action groups. The CNT, in turn, lost many outstanding members of its national, regional, and local committees. In the end, the labor organization paid a heavier price than its opponents. "Assassinations in the public streets," writes Buenacasa, "followed the authoritarian persecution of the state; the very best of our cadre was threatened with this dilemma: die, kill, flee or fall in prison. The violent ones defended and killed; the stoic died and also the brave . . . the cowards or prudent fled or hid; the most active wound up in prison."

A failure of nerve was already evident in the late summer of 1920, when the CNT leadership began one of those curious flirtations with the bureacracy of the UGT from which the Anarchosyndicalist union invariably emerged with bitter misgivings. Pressured to the point of near-panic by the employer offensive in Barcelona, the moderates of the National Committee and Catalan Regional Committee decided to solicit the UGT for a common defense pact.

In itself, such a pact would have been a meaningless achievement for the CNT unless it opened the way to a joint general strike. The UGT had no resources in Catalonia and was faced with very little prospect of repression in its own strongholds, despite the increasingly reactionary policies of the Dato ministry in Madrid. Indeed the Socialists had everything to gain by a pact with the CNT: the Russian Revolution had deeply divided their party. A large percentage of the Socialist membership had veered to the left, committing the party to adherence to the Communist International. The reformists in the party and the UGT needed all the revolutionary camouflage they could acquire, and nothing seemed better, at this point, than the prestige of a pact with the militant Anarchosyndicalist union.

Having received a favorable nod from the Madrid Socialists, Segui, Boal, and Quemades hastened to the Spanish capital and conferred with Largo Caballero, Cordero, Fernandez, de los Toyos, and Martinez Gil. On September 3, 1920, these moderates signed a pact which advanced a demand for the restoration of constitutional guarantees. The defensivness of the wording is astonishing: "We, the declared enemies of bourgeois society constitute ourselves as the defenders of its laws." From this coterie, the Spanish bourgeoisie had little to fear, and it is testimony to the stupidity of the ruling classes that they made little effort to coopt the ready and waiting reformist leaders in both labor organizations. Rather, the Conservative government of Eduardo Dato hardened its attitude and prepared to do battle, if any was really necessary.

The pact produced an angry uproar in the CNT Regional Committees outside of Catalonia, all the more because the National Committee and the Catalan leadership had consulted with no one in undertaking it. Under pressure from the regions, a plenum was held in October, where the agreement was roundly attacked. It was decided to withhold public criticism of the pact owing to a strike of the Rio Tinto miners, where CNT-UGT collaboration was desperately needed.

But the strike was to gain absolutely nothing from the pact. The conflict in the Rio Tinto, a rich copper district in Andalusia, was one of the most bitter, and certainly one of the most poignant disputes in the history of the Spanish labor movement. The mines were owned by British interests. They had been acquired for a preposterously low sum decades earlier, when the national wealth of Spain had been placed on the open market for foreign exploitation. The strike, which began in June 1920, was led by the CNT. Although strong UGT unions existed in the area, the Anarchosyndicalists and Socialists regarded each other with deep suspicion. But this infighting was overshadowed by the desperate lengths to which the miners had gone to win their struggle; at the time of the pact, the majority of them had sold all their personal possessions and gone to live in the towns rather than yield to the employers. There was talk among the strikers of seizing the mines and the offices of the mine owners. The dramatic features of this struggle aroused the working class throughout Spain. Andalusia was on the brink of a general strike in sympathy with the miners, a move that would have gained wide support in the north had the two labor organizations been prepared for militant action.

But this movement came to nothing. A delegation of CNT and UGT leaders went to the Rio Tinto to examine the problem at first hand. On their return, the UGT leaders could suggest little more than an assessment of one peseta per week on the membership of the two organizations in support of the miners. An earlier CNT proposal for a joint general strike, to be initiated by UGT miners and railway workers, had been rejected by the Madrid Socialists. The problem was resolved for the moderates in both unions when the miners, after striking for four months, returned to work in defeat.

By now the pact was in shreds. It was to be eliminated completely when a general strike broke out in Barcelona over the arrests of the CNT leaders and the assassination of Layret. Once again the CNT called upon the UGT for support. Not only was aid refused but it was denied with an arrogance that clearly indicated the Socialists had lost all interest in future collaboration with the CNT. The responsibility for making this evident was left to Largo Caballero, who, when he asked why the UGT workers in the Basque province of Vizcaya had not been called out to aid the Catalans, answered: "Because we are not obliged to do so." As Buenacasa tells the story, the Anarchosyndicalists of Bilbao, the great Basque industrial city, on leaving Largo Caballero, "told him energetically: 'In spite of this there will be a strike in Vizcaya.' But Largo Caballero, top representative of the UGT, sent dispatches to Bilbao telling his followers that if the anarchists and syndicalists try to paralyze the work in the factories, mines, etc., they should be beaten with cudgels."

The strike in Catalonia collapsed and, with it, any prospect of collaboration between the two unions for years to come.

The CNT at this time was plagued not only by bitter harassment at the hands of the authorities but also by the divisive activities of the Communists, who were determined either to control the labor organization or to split it. In Catalonia, Andalusia, and other regions, sharp infighting between Communists and Anarchists dissipated much of the union's energies. The Communists were defeated not merely by the weight of Anarchist influence in the CNT, but by a general revival of the labor movement, which temporarily lifted the heavy atmosphere of defeat and isolation that nourished internecine fighting. In April 1922, constitutional guarantees were restored for the first time in nearly a year and a half. A walkout of the teamsters in Barcelona turned into a general strike of nearly all the transport workers of Catalonia. The CNT, reemerging from a harassed clandestinity, managed to hold a successful national conference on June 11 in Saragossa. The forty-two delegates who attended the conference broke all ties with the Communist International. Dominated largely by the moderates in the CNT, the conference expressed its support of Segui's participation in the mixed commission and passed a resolution favoring salaries for union officials. To still further exacerbate the differences between the Anarchist and Syndicalist tendencies within the confederation, the conference approved a vaguely phrased "political" resolution, largely conciliatory in tone towards the Socialists and liberals, that implied the possibility of CNT electoral blocks with parties that favored the restoration and extension of civil liberties. As it turned out, this was to be the last major national gathering of the union in Spain until the declaration of the Second Republic. Already Primo de Rivera stood in the wings, and events were moving the scenery into place for a dictatorship that would last more than six years.

As if to symbolize the end of the postwar era, on March 10, 1923, Salvador Segui and a companion, Francisco Comas, were shot down in Barcelona's Calle de la Cadena. The assassination occurred during the busiest part of the day, when the street was filled with people. Segui's death, at the age of thirty-three, removed the most important and influential spokesman for "restraint" in the CNT. The syndicalists in the great labor organization, producing no worthy successor to Segui, were for some time relegated to a secondary role. But with the disarray produced in Anarchist groups by the dictatorship, they returned to the foreground.

Although Segui ranks high in the pantheon of Anarchosyndicalist martyrs, his contribution to the CNT is difficult to evaluate. He was born of working-class parents in industrial Lerida on December 23, 1890. The family moved to Barcelona while he was still a child, and here, in the streets of the proletarian quarters, he formed the earthy competence and aggressive temperament that were to make him one of the CNT's most capable organizers. This *"instinctivo"* of the streets, whose employment in a sugar refinery earned him the life-long nickname of *"Noi del Sucre"* ("Sugar-boy"), was also an admirer of Nietzschean individualism, of the *superhombre* to whom "all is permitted." At an early age, Segui was sent off to work as a house painter and was drawn into the labor movement. He took an active part in the "Tragic Week" and became a refugee from the repression that followed. His life thereafter centered almost entirely around the movement—a sequence of meetings, propaganda tours, negotiations, conferences, and hard committee work in preparing strikes.

Although Segui was familiar with Anarchist and Socialist writings, he remained above all a practical organizer to whom *comunismo libertario* (he regarded himself as an Anarchosyndicalist) remained a distant ideal. Revolution, in his eyes, seemed primarily a matter of organization. A moderate who consistently favored collaboration with the UGT, he became a target of bitter criticism by Anarchist militants, who detested his policies while admiring his administrative talents. In turn, he regarded them as "doctrinaires" whose lack of "realism" endangered the development of a mass, united labor movement. Accordingly, Segui always came to the fore whenever balm was needed to quiet the restive ranks of the CNT. He was one of the architects of the Pact of Saragossa; a proponent of the Mixed Commission (in which he participated with great earnestness); the ideal negotiator in agreements with employers and with UGT bureaucrats.

It was Segui who, almost single-handedly, persuaded the Barcelona workers to return to their jobs during the general strike of 1919, when the "Canadiense" was facing bankruptcy and the manufacturers were in full retreat. As it turned out, he was wrong in much of the advice he offered. Although words like "compromise," "restraint," and "moderation" evoke a certain reverence in many quarters, they never truly belonged to the vocabulary of the Spanish bourgeoisie. For his attempt to promote compromise and restrain violence, Segui was humiliated by the intransigence of the Catalan manufacturers—and probably murdered by their *pistoleros*.

Ironically, the men who were to avenge Segui's assassination were the very human types he fought so vigorously in the CNT. On May 17, 1923, Anarchist *pistoleros* from Barcelona assassinated Fernando Gonzalez Regueral, the former governor of Vizcaya. Three weeks later, on June 11, they killed Cardinal Juan Soldevila y Romero, the Archbishop of Saragossa. Both men were notorious reactionaries who bitterly opposed the unions. They were killed by members of the "Solidarios," a group of young Anarchists whose practices and outlook were antithetical in almost every respect to those of the man they avenged.

We must pause here to look closely at this Anarchist action group, for in many ways it typifies the *grupo de afinidad* that was later to exercise so much influence in the FAI. Many such small Anarchist groups had been in existence as far back as the 1890s. The "Solidarios," and others like "El Crisol," which acquired a certain fame, were formed late in 1920 or early in 1921, when the Syndicalist Youth was established for the purpose of dealing with the *pistoleros* of the *sindicato libre*. Ricardo Sanz, who belonged to the "Solidarios," tells us that they were young people, the majority under twenty-five years of age, who had been drawn to Barcelona from different regions of Spain. These youths, "spontaneous in principle, felt themselves ever more tied morally to the group," writes Sanz,

> and there were many of them, those who might be called direct collaborators, who felt themselves by right, not only in fact as components of the group.
>
> All the components of the group were workers and, therefore, lived on their daily wages. The group had no other income in any sense, but it

also had no other expenditures; this was covered by arrangements according to the capabilities of each one of its members. Thine and mine hardly existed among the members of this group—in any case, not when it was a matter of activities related to the collective plan. Individually, each member of the group was free to do what he felt convenient, it being well understood that the activity was not in contradiction with the purity of the ideas.[11]

The "Solidarios" included a famous threesome—Buenaventura Durruti, his close friend Francisco Ascaso, and Juan Garcia Oliver—whose collaboration as "Los Tres Mosqueteros" was to acquire almost legendary proportions. In time, the group came to be known as much by Durruti's name as by the one it originally adopted. According to Sanz, however, neither Durruti, Ascaso, nor Garcia Oliver were regarded as leaders. The "Solidarios" were a "group of individuals," he emphasizes, among whom "no one was more or less important than any other."

Accordingly, the "Solidarios" resembled a community rather than a conventional political organization. To fully understand the close personal relationships within this typical *grupo de afinidad*, we must ʌ·y to compare it with the type of organization favored by the Socialists and Communists. A Marxian party consisted of a hierarchical cadre—a bureaucracy composed of paid officials—forming a distinct, clearly defined chain of command. The Communists, and to a lesser extent the Socialists, demanded obedience from those below. Authority was vested in a supreme executive body which made all decisions of policy and administration in the interims between party congresses.

The party's complex cadre was fleshed out by a well-disciplined membership, each individual marching in step with the others in accordance with the decisions of the party congresses and leading committees. The preferred type of relationship within this political army verged on the impersonal. Although it would have been impossible for individuals in any group exposed to some degree of persecution not to feel a kinship for each other, Marxists tended to stress the value of morally and emotionally neutral ties within their organizations. Today's comrade might well be tomorrow's political foe or factional opponent. "Scientific socialism" demanded a certain detachment toward people and ideas, a severe rationalism that could prevail over passions, impulses, and personal intimacy. One owed one's primary loyalties to the party, that is to say, to its apparatus, not to those who shared one's struggles, risks, and responsibilities.

The Anarchists were genuinely horrified by this arrangement. They regarded it as passionless, soulless, even morally indecent. The revolution for them was, above all, a great moral transformation which was expected to liberate individuals, to restore their freedom and spontaneity of development. Individuals had to be remade, not merely as producers of goods but as new totalities, free to take full command of their destiny and daily life. Any lesser goal was not worth fighting for. Accordingly, the Anarchists regarded the Marxist party as another statist form, a hierarchy that, if it succeeded in "seizing power," would preserve the power of one human being over another, the authority of the leader over the led. The Marxist party, in their eyes, was a mirror image of the very society it professed to oppose, an invasion of the camp of the revolution by bourgeois values, methods, and structures.

The Marxists argued that their organizational forms gave them greater efficiency and effectiveness, a claim the Anarchists emphatically denied. To the contrary, they insisted that the most efficient and effective organization was ultimately based on voluntarism, not on coercion or formal obedience. A movement that sought to promote a liberatory revolution had to develop liberatory and revolutionary forms. This meant, as we already have noted, that it had to mirror the free society it was trying to achieve, not the repressive one it was trying to overthrow. If a movement sought to achieve a world united by solidarity and mutual aid, it had to be guided by these precepts; if it sought a decentralized, stateless, nonauthoritarian society, it had to be structured in accordance with these goals. With voluntaristic aims in mind, the Anarchists tried to build an organic movement in which individuals were drawn to each other by a sense of "affinity," by like interests and proclivities, not held together by bureaucratic tendons and ideological abstractions. And just as individual revolutionaries were drawn together into groups freely, by "affinity," so too the individual groups federated by voluntary agreement, never impairing the exercise of initiative and independence of will.

It will be recalled that the Anarchists continually stressed the importance of education and the need to live by Anarchist precepts—the need, indeed, to create a countersociety that could provide the space for people to begin to remake themselves. Accordingly, they placed a great deal of emphasis on leisure and moral excellence. The Socialists were despised because their demands focused primarily on wage increases and material improvements. Far more important, in the Anarchists eyes, was the need to shorten working hours so that, as Anselmo Lorenzo argued, people "would have the liberty in which to think, to study . . . to satisfy their moral instincts." This type of language—words like "liberty" and "moral instincts"—was alien to the Socialist and Communist parties. In Saragossa, the Anarchists developed a proletarian following that was unique in the history of revolutionary movements. These Aragonese workers began to emphasize moral, political, humanistic struggles over economic ones. As E.H. Carr has observed, their strikes "were characterized by their scorn for economic demands and the toughness of their revolutionary solidarity: strikes for comrades in prison were more popular than strikes for better conditions.

The "Solidarios" were to stand out among other *grupos de afinidad* by virtue of the scope and boldness of their escapades. In other respects, however, they were typical of the Anarchist action groups operating in Spain at the time . There can be little doubt that they— and others like them—terrified many men in the government who were guilty of major crimes against the labor movement. On this score, the case of Martinez Anido is revealing. After ruling Barcelona for two years in a manner that had completely shocked public opinion throughout Spain, this brutal soldier was finally dismissed in 1922. One of the immediate causes of his departure was characteristic of his administration as a whole: it had been found that while Angel Pestana was recovering from wounds inflicted by the civil governor's *pistoleros*, another group of Anido's gunmen was stationed outside the hospital with orders to shoot the Anarchist as soon as he emerged. The story was given wide publicity. By now, a more moderate Conservative government, again headed by Sanchez de Toca, had come into office, intent on achieving political reforms. With Martinez Anido's dismissal there now began a remarkable pursuit in which the "Solidarios" tried to track down this man in order, as Sanz puts it, to "settle accounts."

Anido simply went underground. In May 1923, the "Solidarios," armed with submachine guns and bombs, tracked him to San Sebastian, but he had fled to La Coruna, where they pursued him again. Martinez Anido then disappeared completely. Although a general in the army and ex-governor of Catalonia, this worthy was forced to remain underground until the *pistolero* threat had been largely removed by repression.

While the hunt was going on, the "Solidarios" succeeded in locating Ramon Laguia, one of the chief *pistoleros* of the *sindicato libre*, whom they severely wounded in a cafe in Manresa. It was around this period that they also assassinated the ex-governor of Vizcaya and the Archbishop-Cardinal of Saragossa. The *atentados* against these dignitaries were followed by several daring robberies, the most famous of which occurred on September 1, 1923, when a group of "Solidarios" held up the Bank of Gijon, making off with over 600,000 pesetas. The raid produced a sensation throughout Spain and ranks as one of the largest "expropriations" of its day.

In the meantime, the Anarchist action groups were preparing an insurrection against the newly installed Primo de Rivera dictatorship.

Arms were desperately needed. There now began a series of fantastic escapades in which tons of weapons were manufactured or shunted around under the very eyes of the police with a courage and bravado that would have seemed possible only in Spain of that time—and perhaps only among the Spanish Anarchists. The "Solidarios" bought an iron foundry in the Pueblo Nuevo district of Barcelona and put it to work manufacturing grenades and bombs. Some six thousand of these weapons were cached away in the Pueblo Seco district before they were discovered by the police—who must have been astonished by the group's audacity. In addition, the group deposited caches of rifles and pistols in almost every neighborhood of Barcelona. A regular arms traffic was organized in which weapons bought in Belgium and France were transported clandestinely into Spain through the frontier town of Puigcerda or shipped in by sea.[12]

In October 1923, as the day of the uprising approached, the group managed to buy 1,000 rifles and 200,000 cartridges from the firm of Garate y Anitua in the town of Eibar. The insurrection never came off, at least not in October, and the weapons remained in the firm's warehouse. Later, the "Solidarios" shunted them to a warehouse in Barcelona, where they lay for months while Anarchists in the city negotiated with Catalan nationalists over how to use this deadly largesse. When the two groups fell out, the weapons were sent back to Eibar where the manufacturer accepted them as "returned merchandise." It is testimony to the astonishing effectiveness of the Anarchist action group that the purchase, movement, and storage of 1,000 rifles and 200,000 cartridges during a period of military dictatorship was never discovered by the police.

The "Solidarios," in fact, had by this time developed into a far-flung libertarian enterprise. A partial list shows that there were at least thirty members, many of whom were prepared to leave Barcelona at a moment's notice for an "action" elsewhere in Spain. Besides trafficking in thousands of weapons, operating a grenade foundry, and staging carefully planned "actions," they were a source of considerable funds for various libertarian projects. Their "expropriations" sustained Ferrer-type schools, Anarchist printing presses, and a large publishing enterprise in Paris which produced the *Anarchist Encyclopedia*, as well as many books, pamphlets, and periodicals. The group included men like Durruti, whose prestige by now was enormous, but if we are to believe Sanz, it had no leaders and no hierarchy.

Durruti earned his prestige; it was entirely the result of his personal courage and obvious ability. There was nothing in his background that made him distinctive: like everyone else in the group, he was a worker, perhaps with a slightly better than average education. Born in the city of Leon in July 1896, of working-class parents, Durruti became an apprentice in a machine shop at the age of fourteen. Four years later he began work as a motor mechanic in a railway shop, where he joined the UGT and became active in the labor movement. His father had been a Socialist and Durruti seemed at first to be following the same political path. But he was a combative young man, attracted by the militancy of the CNT, and at the time of the August 1917 general strike he shifted his allegiance to the Anarchosyndicalist union. With the repression and black-listing of union militants that followed the defeat, Durruti left Leon to seek work further north on the Atlantic coast in Gijon. There he was befriended by Buenacasa and instructed in Anarchist ideas by the older, more experienced revolutionary.

By this time Durruti had reached twenty-one, the age of obligatory military service. He left Spain for Paris, where he met the Anarchist luminaries of the French capital and became increasingly involved in the libertarian movement. The upsurge of revolutionary activity below the Pyrenees brought him back to Spain after a three-year stay in France. He settled in San Sebastian, reestablished his contact with Buenacasa, and joined the "Justicieros," a newly established Anarchist group. Looking for a more combative arena in which to work, Durruti then decided to move on to Barcelona. On his way to the Catalan seaport he stopped at Saragossa, where he picked up Francisco Ascaso, the man who was to be his alter ego in the years to come.

With Durruti's arrival in Barcelona in January 1922, the "Solidarios" began to take form as an action group. A prime suspect, Durruti was obliged to use an alias and to operate in the twilight zone of the underground. The sheer nerve of the man is shown by the fact that, while in Madrid at an Anarchist conference, he paid a visit to the imprisoned assassins of Dato, an act which led to arrest and months of detention. The police were eventually obliged to release him for lack of adequate evidence although he was involved in almost all the plans—and, when he was not being detained, all the actions—of the group he helped to form. By December 1923 Durruti's position had become so precarious that it was necessary for him to leave Spain and take refuge in France.

In fact, the "Solidarios" as a group was faced with dissolution. The *atentados*, bank robberies, and arms traffic had claimed a heavy toll of its most militant and active members. Ascaso was in prison for the assassination of Soledevila, although he soon made a daring escape, returning by rail to Barcelona disguised as a train conductor and then making his way to Durruti in Paris. Eusebio Brau had been killed in the aftermath of the Gijon robbery and Rafael Torres Escartin was jailed and also accused of participating in the *atentado* against the

Cardinal. In February 1924, the secret police (according to Sanz) had murdered Gregorio Suberbiela and Manuel Campos, two members of the "Solidarios." Garcia Oliver and Figueras were imprisoned; Sanz and Alfonso, although still in Barcelona, were in and out of jail. The high point of the *atentados* and "expropriations" had passed and a new period was emerging, defined increasingly by the military dictatorship of Primo de Rivera.

What had the Anarchist *pistoleros* achieved? Were the *atentados* simply futile gestures, blind provocations that played into the hands of the authorities, who wanted nothing more than excuses to crack down on the CNT? This is the prevailing opinion among contemporary historians, while even most Spanish Anarchists today deal with the subject defensively and touch upon Durruti's illegal activities with the utmost reticence. Yet this approach, like so much that is written about Spain, must be regarded as an oversimplification. However one chooses to assess the political consequences of the assassinations of Canovas in 1897 and of Canalejas in 1912, the fact remains that these *atentados* removed two of the shrewdest premiers in the modern history of Spain. They occurred in critical times—the period leading into the Spanish-American War and the exhaustion of *Turnismo* before the First World War—when decisive statecraft was needed to deal with a disintegrating political situation. The deaths of Canovas and Canalejas produced a serious vacuum in the leadership of the Spanish state. Most of the premiers who followed them were utterly incapable of dealing with the crisis and antagonisms that developed in Spanish society.

When the Catalan manufacturers turned to *pistolerismo* after the First World War, there could be no other answer than the counter-*pistolerismo* of the Anarchists. This macabre interplay becomes evident from an examination of Segui's attempt to promote a moderate trade-union approach within the CNT. Segui's approach clearly prevailed for a time: the union cut short the general strike of 1919; it joined the Mixed Commission, participating in it with the utmost seriousness; it followed a policy of collaborating with the UGT, even subordinating itself to Socialist policy in the August general strike. The employers, on the other hand, merely used the truce in the general strike of 1919 to mobilize their forces and launch a fierce counteroffensive against the union; they made a mockery of the Mixed Commission; and the Socialists turned their backs on the Anarchosyndicalists as soon as they were called upon to act resolutely.

For all its shortcomings, *pistolerismo* and a militant Anarchist policy in the CNT emerged as a result of defeats suffered by the moderate trade-union wing. A policy based on acquiescence would have demoralized the labor organization completely. The Anarchist *pis-*

toleros showed the more militant workers in Barcelona that in a period when the employers seemed to have a completely free hand, a force on their behalf was still alive, effectively answering blow for blow.

Finally, the Anarchist militants were not interested in "social peace" or in a restful period of trade-union growth. They regarded bourgeois society as incurably diseased. In their view, the opportunism of Largo Caballero and the reforms of Sanchez de Toca were simply half-hearted efforts to preserve a fundamentally sick society. Better to reveal the disease, to use the scalpel in removing the spreading infection, than to conceal the sores of the social system. The terrorism of the Spanish Anarchists was designed not only to keep alive the spirit of revolt and to provoke the Spanish bourgeoisie, but to undermine the stability of the social system. Thus emerged a policy of "destabilizing" capitalism which, as the 1930s were to show, catapulted Spain into social revolution. As we shall see, the Anarchists actually succeeded in getting the revolution they wanted. Without them, it is very doubtful if there would have been one in 1936. If their revolution failed, it was not for want of any effort to produce one.

Notes

1. The reader should be alerted to the fact that the Spanish workers' movement was very officious, abounding in high-sounding titles for officers and "commissions." Even to this day, the meetings of exiles' union and radical organizations are formal, at least among the older people. The Spanish workers, like all pariahs in a highly stratified society, took the prestige of their organizations and the conduct of their business very seriously. To underscore this, alas, they could think of nothing better than to copy the ruling classes.

2. Alberto Balcells gives a succinct description of how the new *sindicatos* were structured: "Each trade would form a section of the *Sindicator* and name a *Junta de Seccion* of two or three members and a permanent commission of seven affiliates, changeable every six months, which in addition to directing the section, named the representatives of the section to the *Junta del Sindicato*. All of the sections would be represented equally on the *Junta del Sindicato*. Only the president of the *Sindicato* would be elected by the general assembly. The *Sindicato* would be represented in the Local Federation and these in the Regional Confederation."

3. It was at this time that the National Committee of the CNT expelled the venerable Andalusian Anarchist Sanchez Rosa, who had been engaged in a bitter fight with the Regional Committee of the Andalusian Confederation. The expulsion created such acrimonious feelings between Anarchists and syndicalists that it nearly split the entire labor organization. The Anarchists

now excoriated the *sindicatos unicos* and syndicalism generally, demanding a return to the old trade sections and a more libertarian type of organization. Although a peace of sorts was established between the two wings, the wounds never fully healed and were to reopen in later years.

4. I do not believe this strike—which in retrospect has been regarded as a grave error—could have been prevented. That the workers were to lose their victory could only have been seen afterwards. Milans del Bosch plainly meant to provoke them and it is doubtful if the greatest prudence by the CNT could have avoided an eventual clash on terms unfavorable to the workers.

5. The extent to which coercion was used in establishing the Mixed Commission is difficult to judge. At any rate, Amado offered an amnesty to the syndicalists of the CNT in return for their temporary renunciation of direct action and their participation in the commission.

6. Despite continual efforts by CNT moderates to come to terms with the manufacturers, the goading of the union reached scandalous proportions. So eager were the employers to initiate their planned lockout that they began one prematurely, on November 3. Compelled to allow the workers to return, the employers thereupon refused to take back any union activists. This provocation finally forced the CNT to withdraw from the Commissions.

7. The Socialists were furious. Quite conveniently for the UGT, a newspaper strike broke out in the capital, threatening to blanket all press coverage of the CNT's congress. The *cenetistas*, however, persuaded the publisher of Madrid's popular Republican daily, *Espana Nueva*, to accede to the grievances of the typographers and the paper began to appear a few days before the opening of the congress. The agreement broke the unity of the publishers, who hastened to end the strike on terms favorable to the workers.

8. Their delegation included Gaston Leval, who represented the newly created Catalan Federation of Anarchist Groups. Apparently Leval had been "integrated" into the delegation as camouflage, but he later separated from it.

9. In the 1914 there were nine *atentados* against employers in the Barcelona area. In 1916 there were only eight; the next year, five; then nine again and in 1919, eight.

10. The extent to which the CNT hired professional *pistoleros* has been greatly overemphasized. As a result of lengthy personal interviews with former Spanish Anarchists, particularly Gaston Leval, I am quite persuaded that the CNT's resources at this time were woefully limited and that the great majority of *pistoleros* were ordinary workmen whose activities were mainly defensive. The "hired" *pistoleros*, while not entirely a myth, have been given undue importance by most historians of the period and the "income" they acquired from their "actions" has been exaggerated to absurd proportions.

11. By "activity" that is not in "contradiction with the purity of the ideas," Sanz simply means a moral integrity consistent with Anarchism, not blind obedience to a political "line." This moral integrity, as has already been pointed out, was a matter of great importance to the Spanish Anarchists, who otherwise always accepted complete independence of behavior and ideas.

12. One of the most daring of the "Solidarios," Antonio Martin, handled the transit of arms through Puigcerda. In 1937, Martin was shot down by gunmen of the Spanish Communist Party.

Chapter Nine:

From Dictatorship
to Republic

The Primo de Rivera Dictatorship

On September 13, 1923, General Miguel Primo de Rivera, the captain general of Catalonia (a post to which he had been appointed during the previous year), proclaimed himself military dictator of Spain, bringing to an end the parliamentary oligarchy Sagasta had labored to create in the 1870s.

The dictatorship was the culmination of a period of growing disenchantment with the army and with the role of the monarchy in the country's political affairs. The army had proven itself grossly incompetent. Two years earlier, in June 1921, a large column in Spanish Morocco, advancing under the command of General Silvestre from Melilla to Alhucemas, was ambushed at Annual and virtually destroyed by a smaller force of Riff tribesmen. Ten thousand were killed, four thousand captured, and all the column's equipment lost to the Riffs. In the following two weeks the Riffs took the Spanish-fortified posts at Monte Arrut, reaching the outskirts of Medilla before they were stopped. Silvestre's advance, at first widely touted as a bold stroke against the Riffs, turned into a nightmarish route that threatened the Spanish presence in North Africa.

The entire country knew that the king was deeply implicated in these disasters. Silvestre, who perished in the Riff ambush, had been a protege of Alfonso. The king encouraged the advance in the hope that bold military successes in Morocco would strengthen his position against the Cortes. A damning dispatch from the monarch to Silvestre advised the ill-fated commander to "do as I tell you and pay no attention to the Minister of War, who is an imbecile." Despite the lapse of two years between the Annual disaster and Primo's *pronunciamiento*, the out-cry over the affair continued unabated. Fed by rumors of corruption in the army, the public had become so uneasy that Sanchez de Toca, the Conservative premier, was replaced by a Liberal, Garcia Prieto, ending the reactionary politcal pattern that had been foisted on Spain since 1919. A new government of "liberal concentration" threatened to initiate sweeping reforms, including the democratization of the army and monarchy. While the Cortes was on summer vacation, a parliamentary commission of inquiry into the Moroccan defeats was sifting the details of army corruption, low troop morale, and the complicity of the king in the Annual defeat. Everyone recognized that when the Cortes reconvened in the autumn, the commission's conclusions would essentially place the king and army on trial before public opinion.

Primo's dictatorship brought this crisis to an end and deflected public attention from the corruption of the army and the ambitions of the monarchy to the "irresponsibility" of parlimentary government. A state of martial law was declared, suspending the Cortes and invoking censorship of the press. Political parties that continued to criticize the dictatorship were suppressed. By offering the promise of "social peace" to a public weary of social instability, the dictator started his rule with a certain amount of political capital. To a Spain overfed with parlimentary crisis and corrupt politicians, Primo's simple patriotism and amateurism became attractive qualities. A pleasure-loving Andalusian rake, Primo functioned by "intuition"; his speeches, gestures, and public behavior were marked by an embarrassing frankness which often mixed maudlin effusiveness with provincial canniness. "I have no experience in government," he declared, not without honesty. "Our methods are as simple as they are ingenuous." And he proved this by working at fits and starts at the most irregular hours, lecturing the Spaniards endlessly on a motley assortment of personal matters, and correcting social abuses suffered by "little people" when they came under his purview. This paternalistic style was displayed at the very outset of his regime when, in a grand gesture, he redeemed the pawn shop receipts of the Madrid poor with surpluses from his first budget.

To organize mass support for the dictatorship, Primo established a loose, rambling organization, the Patriotic Union (UP), which attacked individualism, democracy, and intellectualism, stressing obedience to social institutions and a pragmatic political philosophy. In the mid-1920s this program seemed like nothing less than fascism. Primo, in fact, expressed an admiration for Mussolini and adopted the external trappings and verbal style of the Italian dictator. His bluff soldierly traits and his regime's denial of democratic process alienated Liberal opinion. Driven into exile more by disgust than by physical violence, Liberal and Republican dissidents slowly collected on the French side of the frontier and occupied themselves with plots against the dictatorship. But Primo de Rivera was not a fascist and his UP was not a fascist movement. The dictatorship existed by sufferance of the monarchy and the army, which supported it as a last ditch alternative to the democratization of both institutions. The destiny of the monarchy was now tied to that of the dictatorship, for Alfonso would never be forgiven by Liberal opinion for validating Primo's *pronunciamiento* by making the general into a premier. Ultimately, virtually all sections of the ruling class came to despise the new regime. Having assented to its establishment only in desperation, the more sophisticated reactionaries and monarchists were repelled by Primo's naivete, exasperated by his eccentricities, and humiliated by his crudeness.

More significant evidence of the regime's nature is provided by its social policy—a policy that fixes it more in the Bonapartist than the fascist tradition. Primo had no objection to an organized labor movement, provided it posed no political challenges to his regime. His despotic benevolence allowed room for material concessions to the working class, including government-sponsored medical services, modest wage increases, cheap housing, and a bureaucratic apparatus for labor arbitration. These policies found willing collaboration from the Spanish Socialist Party and the UGT. Following the logic of its reformist and opportunist traditions, Spanish Socialism, almost alone among the older political movements, worked with the dictatorship. The UGT leaders entered the *comites paritarios*—the parity committees—in which labor, government, and employer representatives decided wage disputes. As salaried bureaucrats of the union, they found no difficulty in becoming salaried bureaucrats of the state. Largo Caballero, muting even his democratic scruples, acquiesced to the regime and became a councillor of state. The Socialist Party (which Primo genuinely admired) preserved it bureaucratic apparatus or, as Carr observes, its "modern organization with typewriters, secretaries, burial insurance, and the Madrid cooperative. . . ." The UGT even enjoyed a modest increase in membership, from 208,170 in December 1922 to 228,501 in December 1929, shortly before the fall of the dictatorship.

The Anarchists and the CNT were suppressed. Primo may have entertained some hope of splitting moderates from militants in the CNT; at any rate he waited for nearly a half year before suppressing the syndicalist labor union. Although moderate syndicalists such as Angel Pestana tried in various ways to accommodate themselves to the new state of affairs, the union's implacable hostility to the dictatorship had been fixed at the very outset of Primo's regime. On September 14, a day after Primo's *pronunciamiento*, the CNT declared a general strike. In the absence of Socialist support and sufficient time for adequate preparation, the strike was easily suppressed by the military. Remarkably, despite this gesture, the union was still permitted to function openly.[1] On December 30, 1923, the Catalan Regional Confederation held a plenum at Granollers which attracted hundreds of workers; this was followed on May 4, 1924, by another plenum at Sabadell. On both occasions the union reaffirmed its commitment to Anarchist principles. But time, now, was running out. Three days after the Sabadell plenum, Anarchist terrorists assassinated an onerous Barcelona police official, one Rogelio Perez Cicario ("el ejecutor de la justicia"), whereupon the government immediately cracked down on the syndicalist labor union, rounding up all the CNT committee members and members of Anarchist groups it could find. Driven underground, the CNT was to disappear from the public arena for the remainder of the decade.

Yet the middle and late 1920s were not a period of total quiescence. Many *cenetistas* simply drifted into the *sindicatos libres* (which Primo perpetuated during the dictatorship), where they formed underground antidictatorial syndicalist nuclei. Despite the arrests of May 7, which netted many leading *cenetistas*, a National Committee of the CNT managed for a time to carry on a clandestine existence in Saragossa, while a Catalan Regional Committee survived in Mataro. Anarchist action groups, turning to more spectacular actions, attempted several heroic, if foolhardy, armed assaults on the dictatorship. These actions, almost foredoomed to failure, were largely symbolic. On November 6, 1924, small groups of militants attacked the Atarazanas barracks in Barcelona, apparently assured that the fortress gates would be opened by supporters within. At the same time, a small armed band of Anarchist exiles in France, led by Durruti, crossed the frontier and invaded Vera de Bidasoa, clashing with the Civil Guard. Both attempts miscarried completely. In Barcelona, two captured Anarchists, Juan Montijo Aranz and Jose Llacer Bertran, were executed by order of a summary court martial. The Vera de Bidasoa episode claimed the lives of three: Juan Santillan and Enrique Gil, who were executed, and another condemned participant, Pablo Martin, who leaped to his death from the prison gallery.

Perhaps the most renowned of the Anarchist conspiracies during the dictatorship was an audacious plot hatched by Durruti, Ascaso, and Grigorio Jover to kidnap the king during a state visit to Paris in the summer of 1924. Arrested by the French police, the three "Solidarios" made no attempt to deny their plot; yes, they declared emphatically, they planned to hold Alfonso in return for the dissolution of the dictatorship. Durruti and Ascaso, who had been in Latin America before arriving in France, were also charged with holding up the Banca San Martin in Argentina. The Argentine government demanded that they be extradited, while the Spanish government placed its own bid for their extradition, citing the Gijon holdup and additionally singling out Ascaso for his role in the assassination of Cardinal Soldevila. The case became a *cause celebre*. A wave of protests from French intellectuals and workers finally succeeded in quashing the extradition proceedings. Freed a year later, the Anarchists were expelled from the country, later to be expelled from Germany at the request of the Social Democratic minister of interior of Prussia. Their attempts to find refuge in Russia became untenable when the Soviet government imposed ideological conditions upon them which, as Anarchists, they could not accept. Thereafter, the exiles returned to France under aliases, were rearrested and held in prison for six months, and eventually made their way back to Germany under false identities.

It should not be supposed that Anarchist activities during this period were limited only to desperate acts by a few bold militants. In May 1925, Primo lifted the state of martial law, and social life in Spain began to ease considerably. During the period that followed, Anarchist and syndicalist periodicals began to appear in a number of cities, particularly in the north. The most notable of these, ¡*Despertad*!, was published in Vigo and edited by the Galician Jose Villaverde. The paper, serving as a major link for *cenetistas* in the north, enjoyed a considerable reputation for its vigorous writing and high theoretical level. In addition, the CNT published *Accion Social Obrera* in Gerona, *El Productor* in Blanes, *Redencion* in Alcoy, and *Horizontes* in Elda. Even *La Revista Blanca*, which had enjoyed such a distinguished reputation in the previous century, was revived. In Valencia, where Anarchism was known for its artistic interests, *Estudios* devoted itself, in Jose Peirats' words, to "themes on physical and human regeneration." The individualist Anarchists, in collaboration with vegetarians, naturalists, hedonists, and anarcho-mystics, published *Iniciales*. In a delightful passage, Peirats tells us that these

> extreme tendencies flourished in the anarchism of those times—stormy for some and times of hibernation for the majority. Secret meetings in the mountains were disguised as the excursions of ingenuous nudists, devotees of pure air, and sunbathers. All of this forms a picturesque contrast if one bears in mind that a sincere return to nature was perfectly compatible with conspiratorial planning, the chemistry of explosives, pistol practice, the interchange or periodicals and underground leaflets, and campaigns against tobacco and alcohol.

These preoccupations aside, the closing period of Primo's regime was marked by mounting conflicts within the CNT. By throwing the

A demonstration of CNT workers in 1931. The stencilled placard reads: "The unemployed are starving. Bread for our children."

union back upon itself, the dictatorship compelled moderates and militants to face the differences that had long divided them— differences that had often been obscured in the past by strikes and mass actions. Exile and life in the underground brought these differ- ences increasingly to the fore. Theoretically, virtually every tendency in the CNT professed to accept Anarchist principles of one sort or another. Segui, despite his obvious reformist proclivities, had consis- tently declared his commitment to libertarian ideals; so, too, did Pes- taña, the major spokesman for the moderate tendency after Segui's death. The moderates, however, regarded the realization of these ideals as a problem of the distant future. To Pestaña and his suppor- ters, Spain was not ready for an Anarchist revolution. Rarely invok- ing Marxist arguments, which would have stressed Spain's economic backwardness, the moderates shrewdly threw basic libertarian prin- ciples in the teeth of their militant opponents. Not only did the CNT lack the support of a majority of the Spanish people, they argued, but it lacked the support of the majority of the Spanish working class. Anarchosyndicalists were a minority within a minority. Even within the CNT membership, a large number of workers and peasants shared only a nominal allegiance to libertarian ideals. They were members of the CNT because the union was strong in their localities and work places. If these people, and Spaniards generally, were not educated in Anarchist principles, warned the moderates, the revolu- tion would simply degenerate into an abhorrent dictatorship of ideologues. Later, in a manifesto that was to split the CNT into two syndicalist movements, the moderates declared that the revolution must not rely exclusively on the "audacity of minorities, more or less brave; we want to see a mass movement of the people unfold, of the working class traveling toward definitive liberation." As Jose Vil- laverde declared: "A libertarian communist economy can be estab- lished today. But in the political and moral sphere the Confederation will have to establish a dictatorship that is in contrast with its funda- mental principles because the working class is not in the CNT."

This argument would have been incontrovertible had it remained a strategy for revolutionary education. But the moderates used it as a springboard for opportunistic politics. As early as 1924, the moderate-dominated National Committee of the CNT had flirted with a Catalan separatist conspiracy by Colonel Francisco Macia, founder of the Liberal *Estat Catala*. Two years later, in June 1926, it had become involved in an abortive conspiracy known as the "Night of St. John," a plot which may have been conceived by the monarchy itself in order to rescue its waning reputation by unseating Primo and reestablishing a constitutional government. Once revealed by the dic- tatorship, the plot found such reactionary generals as Weyler and

Aguilera, demagogues like Lerroux, and venal sycophants like Barriobera in the same conspiratorial bed with Anarchists like Amalio Quilez.

The years 1928 and 1929 mark the period of Primo's decline and removal from office. Although the dictatorship, sharing in the international economic boom of the 1920s, had materially improved living standards and profits, it had antagonized virtually all sectors of Spanish society. Proposed structural reforms, such as the Municipal Statute of March 1924, which promised to give extensive autonomy to the municipalities, were stillborn, leaving the restive towns in the hands of government appointees. The plan of Calvo Sotelo, Primo's finance minister, to introduce an effective income tax antagonized the financially irresponsible. The dictatorship's rural policy was confined largely to road-building, irrigation, and electrification projects, leaving the vital issue of land reform untouched; and despite the collaboration of the Socialists with the government, the Spanish working class did not have to be told that its legal organizations were the supine tools of the regime. But Primo made his greatest miscalculation when he alienated the most important pillar of his regime—the army—by challenging the seniority prerogatives of the artillery corps. Even Alfonso became a victim of this error. By failing to back the protesting officers, the king turned the artillery commanders into a corps of Republicans.

Having antagonized leading financiers as well as peasants, officers as well as workers, local town officials, as well as Madrid constitutionalists, Primo proceeded to lose whatever political support he might have gathered from the conservative middle classes and intellectuals. A respectable opposition within the towns and universities began to emerge, openly raising the cry for constitutional legality. Primo's attempt to create a constitution, based on a sharp separation between elective and corporative powers, merely widened this opposition to include the Monarchists, for the constitution barred the king from appointing and dismissing ministries. In the spring of 1928, widespread student protests presented the dictatorship with its first overt opposition since 1924. Under the relaxation of censorship introduced by the regime, the Liberal Madrid journal *El Sol*, commenting on the constitution, bluntly "advised" Primo "to abandon his post." Not to be denied a claim to the "exalted defenders . . . of Parliament and of public liberties," Sanchez Guerra, the seventy-year-old leader of the Conservative Party, crossed the frontier into Spain and offered his person as an umbrella of respectability for a prearranged *pronunciamiento* by General Castro Girona, the captain general of Valencia. But the general reneged on the old man and arrested him. The plot ended in a fiasco; only the artillery officers at Ciudad Real revolted.

Despite the failure of the "Valencia Conspiracy," as this narrow-based abortion by old Conservative politicians was called, the dictatorship was on its last legs. On January 26, Primo, agonized by growing internal opposition and fiscal difficulties, circulated a query to the captain generals, asking if the army supported him. If it did not, averred the dictator, he would resign immediately. Not only were the replies less than enthusiastic, but it was evident to Primo that the king was determined to remove him from office. On January 28, 1929, two days after his query, Primo de Rivera resigned and departed for the fleshpots of Paris, where he died a few months later. His place was taken by General Damaso Berenguer, a highly respected but ailing officer who could hardly be regarded as a permanent fixture in Spanish politics. Berenguer was entrusted with the impossible task of restoring a constitutional government without jeopardizing the future of the monarchy.

The CNT did not remain aloof from the antidictatorial conspiracies that marked the closing period of Primo's regime. In the course of organizing the "Valencia Conspiracy," Sanchez Guerra had approached a CNT contact committee in Paris, soliciting the union's cooperation. The moderates were determined not to be found lagging in the antidictatorial movement, despite a decision by a previous plenum forbidding the CNT's National Committee from negotiating with political parties. On July 28, 1928, the National Committee convoked a clandestine plenum in Barcelona, including delegates from all the regions except for the volatile Levant, with the purpose of authorizing negotiations with antidictatorial politicians and military leaders. Having pocketed the plenum's authority, the National Committee joined in the "Valencia Conspiracy." If we are to believe Comin Colomer, a police official turned historian, whose rather unreliable historiography draws lavishly on police files, several syndicates supported the conspiracy with strikes. By and large, however, the CNT's role seems to have been as stillborn as the conspiracy itself.

Actually, the CNT contributed very little to Primo's downfall. Its attempts to formulate a consistent policy in the struggle against the dictatorship are interesting primarily as evidence of a bitter tug-of-war between militant Anarchist revolutionaries and cautious syndicalist moderates. Cushioning this conflict was a centrist tendency, perhaps best represented by Manuel Buenacasa, which tried guardedly to achieve a compromise between the two wings. By controlling the National Committee, the moderates had only to work through the CNT's structure to achieve a sense of unity. The union's apparatus held them together. By contrast, the Anarchists were dispersed in small groups. The National Federation of Anarchist Groups (FNGA), founded in the stormy postwar years, was virtually defunct. On the initiative of Catalan Anarchist groups and the Federation of Anarchist Groups of the Spanish Language, a Marseilles-based organization of exiles, serious attempts were made to revive a national movement. On July 24 and 25, 1927, a clandestine conference of Spanish and Portuguese Anarchists was held at Valencia. To guard the delegates from Primo's watchful police agents, the dates for the conference were selected to coincide with a fiesta that brought thousands of visitors into the Mediterranean city. Peirats gives us an amusing picture of the delegates disporting themselves at the seashore as vacationers:

> A group of well-bronzed bathers, stretching out on the golden beach by the surface of the Latin sea under the benevolent and warm caress of the sun—men, women, young, old, and children, some of them gathered in arms, others occupied with diversions and games, the classic "paella" bubbling and boiling . . . —this gathering formed the birth of one of the revolutionary organizations which very soon was to express its romantic dreams, its virility and its heroism: the FAI.

The FAI, or *Federacion Anarquista Iberica* (Iberian Anarchist Federation), occupies a unique and fascinating place in the history of classical workers' and peasants' movements. Organized primarily to assure the CNT's commitment to Anarchist principles, the FAI acquired a reputation as one of the most dreaded and admired organizations of revolutionaries to emerge in Spain. The term "Iberian" had been chosen to express the organization's peninsular scope; the FAI originally intended to include Portuguese as well as Spanish Anarchists. In reality, it remained Spanish, acquiring its own distinctive forms and ambience. The new organization based itself on the traditional nuclear groups so ardently favored by Spanish Anarchists since the days of the First International. The "affinity group" (*grupo de afinidad*), a term officially adopted by the FAI, accurately denotes the early Spanish Anarchist concept that true revolutionary groups must be kept small in order to foster a sense of deep intimacy between members. An affinity group rarely numbered more than a dozen people. Each member was drawn to others not only by common social principles but also by common personal proclivities, or "affinities." The group, in effect, was an extended family—with the added feature that the Spanish Anarchists placed an immensely high premium on personal initiative and independence of spirit. Owing to this intimacy, a *faista* affinity group was not easily penetrated by police agents. The FAI continued to be a secret organization, highly selective in its choice of members, up to the Civil War, although it easily could have acquired legal status after the founding of the republic.

Like the CNT, the FAI was structured along confederal lines: the affinity groups in a locality were linked together in a Local Federation and the Local Federations in District and Regional Federations. A Local Federation was administered by an ongoing secretariat, usually of three persons, and a committee composed of one mandated delegate from each affinity group. This body comprised a sort of local executive committee. To allow for a full expression of rank-and-file views, the Local Federation was obliged to convene assemblies of all the *faistas* in its area. The District and Regional Federations, in turn were simply the Local Federation writ large, replicating the structure of the lower body. All the Local Districts and Regional Federations were linked together by a Peninsular Committee whose tasks, at least theoretically, were administrative. The Peninsular Committee was responsible for handling correspondence, for dealing with practical organizational details, and (in the words of Ildefonso Gonzalez, an FAI secretary) for "executing any general agreements of the organization."

Gonzalez frankly admits that the FAI "exhibited a tendency toward centralism." That a Peninsular Committee with aggressive members walked a very thin line between a Bolshevik-type Central Committee and a mere administrative body is not hard to believe. And the FAI contained very agressive, indeed charismatic leaders, such as Garcia Oliver, the Ascaso brothers, and Durruti. The major policy declarations of the FAI were more commonly presented in the name of the Peninsular Committee than of *faista* plenums. This accustomed readers of FAI documents to regard the Peninsular Committee as an oracular body. Shielded by secrecy, the Peninsular Committee might well have enjoyed a wider latitude in the formulation of policy than would have been consistant with its expressed libertarian principles.

Yet it must also be emphasized that the affinity groups were far more independant than any comparable bodies in the Socialist Party, much less the Communist. We have only to read Ramon Sender's *Seven Red Sundays*, a novel based on a detailed knowledge of the Madrid FAI organization, to gain a feeling for the high degree of initiative that marked the typical *faista's* behavior. In later years, all the non-Anarchist organizations of the Spanish left were to declaim against Anarchist *"incontrolados"* or "uncontrollables" who persistently acted on their own in terrorist acts, defying governmental and even FAI policies. The very atmosphere of the organization spawned such people. We shall also see that the FAI was not an internally repressive organization, even after it began to decay as a libertarian movement. Almost as a matter of second nature, dissidents were permitted a considerable amount of freedom in voicing and publishing material against the leadership and established policies.

Every member of the FAI was expected to join a CNT syndicate. That the FAI tried to bypass the CNT membership, as Comin Colomer asserts, and take over the union indirectly by implanting nuclei of Anarchists in every Local and Regional Committee of the CNT, is not clear from the available facts. It was no secret, to be sure, that the Spanish Anarchists hoped to guide CNT policy. Even centrists such as Buenacasa, who became one of the earliest secretaries of the Peninsular Committee, may have joined the FAI mainly to dislodge the CNT's moderate leadership. If so, his motives were not exceptional; quite a few centrists, who like Buenacasa abhorred violent tactics, seem to have occupied key positions in the FAI at various times, probably with the same goals in mind. But this much is evident: by far the greater number of *faistas* were young, highly volatile men and women whose real preoccupation was not with the CNT apparatus but rather with direct, often violent action against the established social order. These "young eagles of the FAI" and their more "technical" affinity groups were responsible for the recurrent insurrections, the "forced appropriations" of banks and jewelry stores and the terrorist actions that marked *faista* activity in the stormy Republican period before the Civil War.

Owing to the FAI's passion for secrecy, we know very little about its membership figures. Judging by data published by Diego Abad de Santillan, a leading *faista*, the figure on the eve of the Civil War may have been close to 39,000. In any case, so carefully did the organization guard its clandestinity that it made no attempt to reveal its existence publicly until 1929, more than two years after it had been founded. In December of that year, the Peninsular Committee issued its first public statement as an organization—a manifesto that sharply denounced the moderate tendency in the CNT.

The events leading up to the FAI's manifesto reveal the sharp differences that were rending the CNT. The fact that the FAI was created in the summer of 1927 is probably not accidental; it was around this that Pestana, addressing members of the Barcelona textile syndicate, suggested that the dictatorship's *comites paritarios* were compatible with the CNT's principles. Pestana was prudent enough not to call for the entry of CNT delegates into the *comites*, but his views raised a furor among militant and centrist Anarchists. Yet these views were mild compared with Pestana's frontal demands two years later. In a series of articles titled "Situemonos," published in ¡*Despertad!*, Pestana called for entirely new principles for the CNT and, in a particularly cutting play on words, described the organization as "moderate" (*contenido*), not as "abstinent" (*continente*). This word play could be taken as a snide attack on Anarchist puritanism as well as purism. Peiro, replying on behalf of the centrists, acknowledged that while "confederal congresses could modify all the principles of the CNT," they could not challenge the organization's "reason for being: antiparliamentarism and direct action." Peiro's views had the support of other leading centrists, notably Buenacasa and Eusebio Carbo, both of whom enjoyed immense prestige among all syndicalist tendencies. Evidently, a great deal of counterpressure from left and centrist Anarchists began to build up against the moderates, for in the autumn of 1929 the moderate-controlled National Committee suddenly submitted its resignation in ¡*Despertad*! and intoned the "organic demise" (Peirats) of the CNT.

It is within this context of growing conflict that we must examine the FAI's first public statement. The manifesto reads more like an ultimatum than an argument. In a brief, almost ponderously legalistic document, the secretariat of the Peninsular Committee declares that to believe the workers' movement can be ideologically neutral is an error. Although material gains and improved working conditions are worthwhile goals, the workers' movement must seek the "absolute cauterization of all the prevalent wounds and the complete disappearance of economic and political privileges." To this end, the CNT must establish a "connection" with the organism that adheres to these revolutionary tactics and postulates—namely, the FAI. "If the CNT, on the contrary, does not accept the propositions made by the FAI's secretariat," the statement concludes, "it very possibly risks a very pernicious deviation from the cause of integral demands and the destruction of the moral and revolutionary values which alone distinguishes it. . . ."

It is plain that Pestana and the moderates had at least one strategic goal in mind—the legalization of the CNT. And they sought this goal even if it meant major concessions to the dictatorship. By offering to resign, the National Committee may well have been trying, in dramatic fashion, to force the issue. In any event, the entire question of legality soon became academic. The replacement of Primo by Berenguer in January 1930 completely altered the *de facto* status of the CNT and many syndicates began to function openly even before they acquired official legality.

The conflict between the moderates and Anarchist militants, however, did not disappear. On the contrary, it now settled down to basic differences in revolutionary strategy—differences that were to reach truly schismatic proportions in the early years of the republic. In the course of a broad statement on CNT goals, the moderate-controlled National Committee had managed to note its "concern over national problems" and more specifically its willingness "to intervene using its own methods with their ideology and history in the process of constitutional revion. . . ." With this formulation as an anchor, the

National Committee proceeded to declare, in effect, that it welcomed a republic as the most congenial framework in which to work for libertarian goals. The statement thus visualized a Spanish revolution as divided into two stages: the first (and more immediate one), a bourgeois democracy; the second (and more visionary one), a libertarian communist society. If one removes the National Committee's usual obeisances to broad Anarchosyndicalist ideals, its perspective could hardly be distinguished from that of the much-despised UGT. Needless to say, the National Committee's "scandalous" statement (as Peirats calls it) produced another uproar among Anarchist militants and further polarized the CNT.

Convoluted as these details may seem, they are vitally important to an understanding of the CNT's later development. The moderates were not merely willing to collaborate with bourgeois groups in order to establish a republic; they were also willing to follow a prudent and accommodating strategy *within* a republican framework. The Anarchist militants, on the other hand, were advocating a policy of unrelenting opposition to the state, be it dictatorial, monarchical, or republican. Much of the CNT's history in the years to follow was to turn around conflicts and compromises between these positions.

Even under the Berenguer regime, events were to show that the two policies were not mutually exclusive. Moderates were to take seemingly intransigent stands when it suited their purposes and the FAI to make concessions of its own when they furthered its short-term ends. It is interesting to note that in the *sub rosa* negotiations that led to the CNT's legalization, Pestana, representing the union, assumed an unrelenting Anarchosyndicalist position even to the point of dismissing the *comites paritarios* as a "monstrosity." Whether this firmness was the result of newly acquired convictions under changed political conditions or merely a shrewd accommodation to rank-and-file militancy is difficult to judge. Angel Pestana was not a demagogue; indeed, it is only fair to say that he was a man of great integrity and exceptional courage. General Mola, who represented the government in the negotiations, was obviously impressed by the dignity of this intensely moral labor leader—tall, lean, dressed in rough clothing, with an "inquisitive" demeanor. Although Pestana may have been willing to enter the *comites paritarios* three years earlier, when harsh conditions seemed to warrant this approach, Mola notes that he expressed genuine outrage over the fact that the labor delegates to the *comites* received salaries and were thus separated from their fellow wage-earners.

By the same token, the FAI did not always behave as a pure flame of Anarchist consistency; on the contrary, it was ready to bend its antiparliamentary principles almost to the breaking point when crucial situations arose. Thus, in the municipal elections of 1931, *faista* delegates joined their moderate opponents in supporting a Republican-Socialist coalition that packed the king off to exile. And although the FAI did not participate in the electoral coalitions of 1936, it "released" Anarchist workers from their no-voting scruples and contributed decisively to bringing the Popular Front to power.

The most serious inconsistencies of the FAI were to become painfully evident later—and in a more crucial context in the development of the Spanish labor movement. For the present, Primo's departure had opened a period of rebuilding for the scattered forces of Anarchosyndicalism. On April 30, 1930, the CNT was granted a form of "conditional" legality by the governor of Barcelona, followed by legalization in other provinces.[3] Although many syndicates were still illegal elsewhere in the country and thousands of *cenetistas* filled the jails of the Berenguer regime, Spanish Anarchosyndicalism began to pick up the threads that had been broken by the dictatorship in 1924. In little more than a year, the CNT membership numbered close to a half million. This figure, to be sure, is much lower than the CNT's peak membership of 700,000 in 1919, but it is quite substantial if one bears in mind that the organization was virtually nonexistent during the seven years of Primo's rule. In a series of conferences, plenums, and organizing drives, the CNT recouped the greater part of its losses and suceeded rapidly in restoring most of its contacts with other areas of the country. *Solidaridad Obrera* in Barcelona began to appear as a daily shortly after it was legalized on August 30 and, following the custom of the predictatorial years, sister publications with the same name began to spring up in other cities of Spain.

But the CNT of 1930 was no longer the same organization Primo had suppressed in 1924, nor was the FAI the same as the FNGA. The bloody *pistolero* period of 1919-23, the acrimonious years of introversion which brought latent differences to the surface, and the harsh experiences of repression by the dictatorship had altered greatly the atmosphere in the CNT and in Anarchist groups. The moderate, almost ecumenical outlook that had prevailed in the old CNT and even in the FNGA, had been invaded by an increasingly intractable spirit. The *pistolero* conflicts had produced a new kind of Anarchist—young, grim, prone to violence, and impatient with temporizing measures and compromises. These young Anarchists, typified by Durruti, Garcia Oliver, Ascaso, and Sanz, were accustomed to bold escapades. They were *ilegales* in the full sense of the term. Even the "pure-and-simple" unionists were shaken in their moderate views particularly after 1929, when the world economic crisis began to nourish a new spirit of militancy in the working class. Slowly, the bulk of rank-and-file members in the CNT came to favor the FAI over the moderates, the militants over the temporizers, the high-spirited young Anarchists over the older, more prudent, union-oriented leadership of an earlier generation.

In 1930 and 1931, however, the moderates still controlled the CNT and centrists like Buenacasa apparently continued to hold the young *faistas* in rein. The National Committee and the editorial staff of *Solidaridad Obrera* were in the hands of moderates and centrists. Nor was this control likely to be shaken without changes in the outlook of the Catalan *cenetistas*. Following the tradition of the old International, the CNT gave the responsibility of selecting the entire National Committee to the region which congresses had assigned as the national center of the union. Until the 1930s, the repeated choice of Catalonia and specifically Barcelona as the CNT's national office almost guaranteed moderate control over the National Committee and *Solidaridad Obrera*.

The weight of Catalonian influence reveals still another change that had occurred in the fortunes of Spanish Anarchosyndicalism—the eclipse of Andalusia as a decisive area of the movement. Contrary to the usual accounts of Spanish Anarchism, the CNT was largely composed of workers rather than peasants and its focus was primarily on the culturally advanced north rather than the backward south. The myth that Spanish Anarchism remained little more than an inchoate, village-based movement with peripheral working-class support has been refuted tellingly by Malefakis's recent study of peasant unrest in Spain. In 1873, when Spanish Anarchism exercised a considerable influence in the countryside, Andalusia (both urban and rural) provided nearly two thirds of the old International's membership. By 1936, this proportion had declined to about a fifth. As Malefakis observes:

The predominance of Andalusia in the Anarchist federations of the 1870s and 1880s had disappeared after the turn of the century and was but a distant memory. The two ancient centers of Spanish anarchism Catalonia and Andalusia were no longer in any sense equal. Urban anarchosyndicalism had far outdistanced rural; Catalonia far overshadowed Andalusia. This was especially true because Catalonia was now flanked by a new Anarchosyndicalist stronghold in Saragossa. The ties between these two regions were so much more intimate than those maintained by either with any other part of Spain that one may safely speak of a new geographical bloc within the CNT. The FAI leaders—Durruti, the Ascasos, and Garcia Oliver—were all from Barcelona and Saragossa. The major insurrections of the CNT-FAI originated and found most of their response within these two regions. And it was this bloc, with some assistance from the neighboring Levante, that was to carry on the Civil War for the Anarchosyndicalists after Andalusia had fallen to the Nationalists.

Attempts were made to revive the peasant movement, but they were half-hearted. The old Anarchosyndicalist FNAE (*Federacion Nacional de Agricultores de Espania*) had been swallowed up the repressive dictatorship; its newspaper, *La Voz del Campesino*, was revived in 1932 in Jerez de la Frontera, only to disappear later the same year. In 1931, at the CNT Extraordinary Congress of Madrid, a proposal was adopted to call a peasant congress and create a rural federation. The congress never came off. The CNT, to be sure, still had considerable strength in the cities of the south—especially in Cadiz, Malaga, Cordoba, and Seville—and in a number of Andalusian villages. But ties between the cities and villages were extremely weak. "Little effective cooperation," observes Malefakis, "existed between the Anarchosyndicalist unions of the major Andalusian cities and their rural counterparts."

The authentic peasant base of the CNT now lay in Aragon. The conversion of Saragossa during the early 1920s to a brand of Anarchism more "black" and resolute than that of Barcelona provided a springboard for a highly effective libertarian agitation in lower Aragon, particularly among the impoverished laborers and debt-ridden peasantry of the dry steppe region. Aside from the *Union de Rabassaires* in the vine-growing region, the Catalan countryside too had been infected by Anarchist agitation emanating from Barcelona. The CNT still preserved its strength in the mountain villages of the Levant and the Galician countryside around Coruna. Most of these rural areas were quiescent during the dictatorship. Not until the proclamation of the republic, with its promise of land reform and its new political possibilities, did the Spanish countryside spring to life again as a social force.

With Primo's departure, Spain began to settle its accounts with the monarchy. Alfonso, tainted by his role in establishing the dictatorship, tried desperately to retain the throne as a quasi-constitutional monarch. But the monarchy—both in the person of Alfonso and as an institution—had discredited itself completely. Berenguer's delays in assembling the Cortes and Alfonso's obvious maneuvers to retain his royal prerogatives eroded the confidence even of conservative politicians. "I am not a Republican," declared the old conservative wheelhorse Sanchez Guerra, "but I recognize that Spain has a right to be a Republic." Conspiracies against the dictatorship were now replaced by conspiracies against the monarchy, and they included not only Republicans and Socialists, but Liberal *caciques* like Alcala Zamora and army officers such as Queipo de Llano and Ramon Franco, the brother of the future *caudillo*. The gnawing conflicts over Catalan autonomy, which divided Republican ranks between Catalans and Spaniards, were resolved in August

1930, when both wings signed the famous Pact of San Sebastian. Catalonia was promised far-reaching autonomy in her internal affairs. The Pact was signed by a widely disparate group of politicians including Alcala Zamora, Manuel Azana (a Republican *litterateur* whose roots lay in the fashionable Ateneo, a Liberal Madrid literary and political club), and the inevitable Alejandro Lerroux. The San Sebastian crowd, from which Republican Spain was to recruit several of its presidents and prime ministers, was pledged to "revolutionary action" against the monarchy—an excursion into militant rhetoric that the Pact's signers were to modify considerably with *mea culpas* and appeals to nonviolence.

Two uncertainties confronted the National Revolutionary Committee which had emerged from the Pact: the role of the army and the workers in the overthrow of the king. The army, to be sure, would not shoot down Republicans, but would it join actively in a Republican rising? The only reliable mass following the Republicans could rely on were the workers but the Committee balked at giving them arms. Hateful as the monarchy was to the Ateneo Liberals, the specter of an armed working class terrified them. To keep the CNT from participating in the San Sebastian cabal without offending its sensibilities, the Republicans tactfully invited neither of the two labor organizations to the signing of the Pact.

How, then, could the CNT's aid be deployed against the monarchy without risking an authentic social revolution? Taking the Anarchosyndicalist bit in its teeth, the National Revolutionary Committee dispatched Miguel Maura and Angel Galarza to Barcelona to enlist the CNT's participation in a "peaceful" general strike against the monarchy. The strike, to be ignited by the UGT's railway workers, was to climax in a general rising of the military. There is no evidence that the CNT had any second thoughts about this plan. According to the moderate *cenetista*, Juan Peiro, the CNT at a national plenum of its regional delegates "agreed to establish an exchange of information among the political elements with the object of forming a revolutionary committee." Stated more bluntly, the CNT gave its assent to the plan. The plenum's delegates, to assure their independence, decided to prepare a manifesto that affirmed the CNT's commitment to apolitical principles and its adherence to libertarian forms of organization.

The general strike turned out to be a shabby failure, snarled by changes in dates, poor communications, and a gross miscalculation of the army's attitude. The uprising was scheduled for December 15. According to the Republican version, it was unexpectedly pushed back to December 12 by a premature revolt of the Jaca garrison in Aragon. The rebellious troops were quickly subdued and their two

commanders, Captains Fermin Galan and Garcia Hernandez, executed by firing squads. Alcala Zamora, Miguel Maura, and their
Socialist collaborators, Largo Caballero and Fernando de los Rios,
were arrested without difficulty in Madrid. The CNT issued a call for
a general strike and attempted armed attacks on strategic installations, but all its efforts came to grief.

Peirats, taking issue with the Republican version of the Jaca rebellion, gives us an entirely different account. Apparently this rebellion
had indeed been planned for the 12th, but the National Revolutionary
Committee had decided upon a delay. Casares Quiroga was sent off
as an emissary to forestall the rising, but "on arriving in Jaca at
night," notes Peirats, "he had preferred to sleep instead of complying
instantly with his urgent mission." If Peirats's version is true, Galan
and Garcia Hernandez were the needless victims of Republican
slovenliness. Since everyone in Spain knew that the declaration of a
republic was merely a matter of time (everyone, that is, except the
monarchy), the arrested Madrid conspirators were treated leniently—
indeed with deference, as the future leaders of the state. They spent
only a few months in prison and received provisional liberties. "One
could hope for no more from that so-called Revolutionary Committee," concludes Peirats acidly, "which had its social seat in the Madrid Ateneo and which later, when it was put in prison, was equipped
with telephone service and silk pajamas."

The CNT can hardly be reproached for its role in these events. Left
to its own devices, the union had functioned more creditably than all
of its Republican and Socialist "allies." CNT strikes, both before and
after the "rising" of December 12, were almost uniformly impressive
and the union's efforts to reknit its forces generally met with success.
The first plenum of the Catalan Regional Federation, held on May 17,
1930, initiated a drive to publish *Solidaridad Obrera* as a daily. This was
followed by a public plenary meeting on July 6. Shortly after the
second Catalan regional plenum, on October 5 and 6, the National
Committee suggested that a National Conference of Syndicates be
convened two weeks later, but the conference was suspended owing
to the heated political situation in Spain. Taking advantage of a general strike in Madrid that had broken out in reaction to police brutality, the CNT decided to present a show of force of its own. The
union's purpose, explains Peirats,

> was to show that a general strike was possible in Barcelona even though
> the transport syndicate had been closed down by the governor. The
> governor, Despujols, was obliged to admit the obvious—that his refusal
> to accede to the legalization of this syndicate had served for nothing. The
> work stoppage was total. . . . The end of the strike was fixed for

November 20 (it had started on the 17th) but the workers had continued it to the 24th. It had spread to various important townships in the region and the jails were so full that a number of ships anchored in the harbor had to be used to supplement them.

The Republican fiasco of December 12, 1930, had not resolved the problems of the CNT's relationship to bourgeois political movements. In theory, at least, the CNT adhered to antistatist principles. Rejecting political methods for social change, it advocated direct action by the oppressed against any system of political authority. The more intransigent Anarchists in the union carried these principles one step further and argued that every state was bad, be it monarchial, dictatorial, or republican, and could not be supported. But were these different state forms *equally* bad? Were no distinctions to be drawn between them in terms of Anarchist *tactics?* The CNT could hardly ignore the fact that significant differences existed between a dictatorship and a republic, indeed, between a monarchy and a republic. Primo's regime had virtually smashed any form of overt syndicalist activity in Spain, whereas a republic would clearly open new opportunities for syndicalist growth. Indeed, however much the Spanish Anarchists had denied the importance of distinctions in state forms, in practice they had reacted to these differences from the very inception of their movement. They had joined with radical Federalists in the early 1870s to create a cantonal republic. During the general strike of 1917, the CNT had proclaimed a minimum program which declared for a republic, the separation of church and state, divorce laws, and the right of unions to veto legislation passed by the Cortes. In March 1930, Peiro and three of his centrist comrades had added their names to a Republican manifesto that raised even milder demands than the CNT's earlier minimum program. Writing in *Accion Social Obrera*, Peiro, despite much breast-beating about the inviolability of his conscience, frankly admitted that his gesture stood in "contradiction" with his libertarian principles.

The FAI, although it had been led by its centrist members into shadowy violations of Anarchist principles, decried these contradictions vigorously. *Faistas* like Buenacasa had muted the voices of the young militants but had not silenced them. The failure of the Republican "rising" in December merely reinforced the intransigent position of the "young eagles of the FAI" toward the Republicans; indeed, even the centrists had begun to waver, some turning to a hard, noncollaborative stand and others to a moderate one.

How would the CNT deal with the republic once it emerged? This annoying question came increasingly to the fore as the monarchy began to totter. In February 1931, Berenguer, faced by massive public hostility, resigned his office. The king, forced to make meaningful concessions, had finally decided to remove the government-appointed municipalities that existed under Primo and to allow unfettered municipal elections. A nonpolitical government, headed by Admiral Aznar, took over Berenguer's vacant place. Even the king recognized that the destiny of the monarchy now depended upon the outcome of the municipal elections. On April 12, 1931, Spain went to the polls. By evening, the earliest returns left no doubt that the Republican-Socialist coalition had won a stunning victory. Two days later, Alfonso departed hastily for Marseilles while the avenues of Spain's major cities were swollen with jubilant crowds waving Republican flags.

The Azana Coalition

The Second Republic began its career in an atmosphere of public elation. Spain, swept up as by a national festival, flocked into the streets, hailed the new regime, and decorated itself in the Republican tricolor. Self-discipline became the maxim of the day. To protect the queen mother and her children from unruly crowds, Socialists from the *Casa del Pueblo* of Madrid provided them with a guard of young workers in red armbands. A hastily improvised citizens' police force guarded the doors of banks to prevent looting. Every effort was made to avoid dishonoring the new regime with acts of vandalism and destruction. In the words of Ramos Oliveira, "Both Spaniards and foreigners commented on the magnanimity and discipline of the people who, on recognizing liberty and power, made no use of their conquest to destroy or humiliate their erstwhile oppressors."

Yet within a year of this generous outburst of popular goodwill, the republic was to be torn by bitter political conflicts and bloody strike waves—and two years later it was to fall into the hands of rabid political opponents. The steady decline in the republic's prestige was virtually inevitable. The Second Republic, precisely because of its goodwill, had brought to power the most disparate group of politicians and labor leaders ever to adorn a Spanish cabinet. The new prime minister, Alcala Zamora, presided over a government that included Miguel Maura, an ex-Monarchist and ardent Catholic; Casares Quiroga, a wealthy Galician Liberal who, with Manuel Azana, later formed the Left Republicans; Martinez Barrio and Alejandro Lerroux, both luminaries of the venal Radical Party; and three Socialists: Largo Caballero, Fernando de los Rios, and Indalecio Prieto, the latter a spokesman for the party's right wing. For the most part, the new cabinet consisted of the men of San Sebastian. And once Alfonso had been removed, nearly all of them—singly or in pairs—were poised to desert each other with alacrity.

Alcala Zamora and Maura had entered the cabinet to make sure that the republic did not become too republican, i.e., that it left the landed estates, the church, and the army largely intact. Azana and Casares Quiroga, as spokesman for the lower middle classes and intellectuals, recognized the need for reforms; but how much reform was possible in the face of an anti-republican oligarchy, a covertly reactionary army, an overtly reactionary church, and a revolutionary working class remained an imponderable. Martinez Barrio and Lerroux made a career of vacillation between the anti-republican oligarchy and the Ateneo Liberals. Later, they parted ways when Martinez broke from Lerroux and drifted toward the Liberals. The Socialists, committed to a bourgeois republic, provided Azana and Casares Quiroga with a "responsible" left wing. Deployed by the Republicans to keep the proletariat in rein, they remained the beggars of Liberalism, pressing for reforms that invariably ended in shabby compromises.

The primary tasks of the new government were sternly Jacobin: to expropriate the great landed magnates, adopt effective measures against the deepening economic crisis, curb the army's role in political life, and weaken the church's hold on Spanish society. Had such a program been resolutely carried out in the opening months of the republic, when popular enthusiasm was still running high, the Liberals might have raised Spain to the level of a European bourgeois nation. But the government delayed, fearful of alienating the very classes it was obliged to oppose, while a Constituent Cortes occupied itself with writing a constitution. Although humane and brightly liberal in spirit, the constitution became a mechanism for placing legal formalities before social activism. In the end, nobody took this document very seriously. The constitution, however, served to reveal the patchwork nature of the new cabinet. When the Cortes adopted Article 26—a constitutional provision aimed at the enormous power of the Spanish church—Alcala Zamora and Maura resigned, the former to be reincorporated into the republic as its president. Azana, whose well-reasoned defense of Article 26 placed him in the limelight, became the prime minister and the spokesman for Republican virtue. These opening months, however, were not entirely wasted. Largely on the initiative of Largo Caballero, the new minister of labor, the government rapidly passed a series of laws that protected small tenants from arbitrary expulsion from their land and extended the eight-hour working day to the agrarian proletariat. Priority was granted to rural workers' societies in subleasing large tracts of land. To prevent migrant workers from claiming the jobs of locals, the Cortes, in a Socialist-sponsored Law of Municipal Boundaries, established rural frontiers around some 9,000 municipalities. No outsider could be hired by a landowner within these municipalities until the local labor force had found employment. Another law denied landowners the right to withdraw from cultivation land that had hitherto been farmed according to the "uses and customs" of the region; otherwise, the uncultivated land could be taken over for cultivation by local workers' organizations.

None of these measures was particularly radical. Although Malefakis describes the laws as "a revolution without precedent in Spanish rural life," the reasons he adduces for this conclusion are essentially juridical. The laws shifted "the balance of legal rights" from the landowners to the rural masses. But they provided no solution to the endemic unemployment that paralyzed the Spanish countryside and they left the key problem of land ownership unsolved. The republic's famous Agrarian Statute of September 1932, ostensibly designed to initiate a sweeping land redistribution program, hardly rates serious attention. Lacking adequate funds, hedged by legal stipulations, and burdened by administrative procrastination, the statute hobbled along without changing the status of the rural poor and landless. By late 1934, two years after the statute's passage, little more than 12,000 families had received land. The countryside, its hopes deflated by bitter disappointment, became more surly and finally more rebellious than it had been in the stormy years after the war.

Niggardly in its treatment of rural reform, the government swelled with generosity in its dealings with the army. In 1931 the Spanish army could claim the unique distinction of containing more majors and captains than sergeants; its 16 skeletal divisions, which normally required 80 general officers, were serviced by nearly 800. The republic's law on military reform was modest. The measure reduced the 16 existing divisions to 8, limited compulsory military service to one year, and abolished the rank of captain general, a position that had given the army jurisdiction over the civil government in periods of social unrest. To mollify the officer corps, the governement offered full pay to officers who elected to retire, based on the highest rank they would have achieved in the normal course of military service. The army reacted to this decree "with mixed emotions," observes Gabriel Jackson. "Almost everyone acknowledged that the Army was top heavy with brass, but many a proud career officer felt that Azana simply wished to destroy the officer corps by buying it off." As if to feed this suspicion, the government closed down the general military academy at Saragossa, an act which many officers viewed as a "blow to the *esprit de corps* of the Army, since this was the only institution in which officers of different branches of service trained together."

In the long run, the government's reforms left the country profoundly dissatisfied. The republic had awakened suspicion among the conservative classes without diminishing their power; it had also aroused hope among the oppressed without satisfying their needs. The republic, in fact, had hardly been in power more than a month before it suffered its first serious blow. Early in May 1931, Cardinal Segura, the primate of Spain, issued a pastoral letter sharply denouncing the "anarchy" and "grave commotion" that the new regime had introduced. Provocatively, the letter thanked the king for having preserved the piety and cherished traditions of Spain. As luck would have it, three days later scuffles broke out between Monarchists and anti-Monarchists in Madrid; a crowd, angered by anti-Monarchist rumors, gathered before the Ministry of Interior and in the morning hours six convents in the capital were set aflame. The convent burnings spread from Madrid to Malaga, Seville, Alicante, and other cities. The cabinet, fearful of staining the new regime with "Republican blood," delayed taking action for two days before calling out the army. Although the burnings were rapidly quelled, the damage had already been done; reaction found its issue in the status of the church, and the republic had tarnished its virtue with violence.

The middle classes were duly shocked by these events. Thereafter, right-wing hotheads were to make repeated assaults on the regime, riding on a growing wave of popular disillusionment. By 1932, monarchist and reactionary conspiracies against the republic had graduated to the level of a military coup. On August 10, General Sanjurjo, the erstwhile commander of the Civil Guard, declared against the "illegitimate Cortes" in a poorly planned, indecisive rising in Seville. Sanjurjo was easily defeated and the Azana regime emerged from the event with considerable prestige. But its victory was shortlived. This government of middle-class Liberals and Socialists had little more than a year of life before it was brought down—and ironically, its fall came not from an assault by the right but rather by the left.

Perhaps the most telling blow came from the Anarchists. The CNT had actually welcomed the republic. In April 1931 many syndicalist workers joined with Socialist workers in voting for the Republican bloc. "The vote of the working class was divided," notes Madariaga.

The workers affiliated to the UGT (Socialists) voted for their men; but the Anarcho-Syndicalists, whose numbers were about as numerous, voted for the middle-class liberals. There were two reasons for this: the first was the unbridgeable enmity which separates socialists and syndicalists, due to their rival bid for the leadership of the working classes; the second was that as the Anarcho-Syndicalists had always preached contempt for the suffrage, they had no political machinery of their own; so that, when it came to voting, which they did this time to help oust the Monarchy, they preferred to vote for the middle-class Republicans whose liberal views were more in harmony with the anti-Marxist ideas of the Spanish Syndicalists than with the orthodox and dogmatic tenets of the Socialists.[5]

The day after the republic was proclaimed, *Solidaridad Obrera* ventured a view that was hardly a clarion call to battle against the new state: "We have no enthusiasm for a bourgeois republic but we shall not give our consent to a new Dictatorship. . . ." The newspaper went on to remind its readers that many CNT members still languished in jail and demanded their immediate release. To give muscle to this demand, the Catalan Regional Confederation called a one-day general strike, whereupon the Generalitat (the Catalan provincial government) shrewdly declared the day a national holiday.

Having made these token gestures, the union settled down to a period of watchful waiting. Apart from sporadic violence in which CNT militants settled long-standing accounts with chiefs of the hated *libres*, Barcelona was comparatively peaceful. The city was still in a festive mood. Catalonia, ignoring the old and discredited Lliga, had cast its vote overwhelmingly for the *Esquerra* (Catalan Left), a new middle-class party headed by the aging Colonel Macia and a clever young lawyer, Luis Companys. Companys, it will be recalled, had defended *cenetistas* in the political trials of the 1920s; he knew the union's moderate leaders personally and was regarded by some of them as a "friend." Pledged to Catalan autonomy, the *Esquerra* was linked closely, by both personal ties and common outlook, to the Azana Republicans. Buoyed by the certainty that autonomy was now within its reach, the public was in no mood to challenge the new republic.

The CNT was wary of the new regime in Madrid. Indeed, it is highly doubtful that any prolonged truce could have existed between the respectable Liberals who headed the republican government and the Anarchist *ilegales* who were coming to the fore in the CNT. As it turned out, the Azana coalition did very little to allay the CNT's suspicions; the Anarchists, stoking the disappointment of the working class into anger, raised demands for a complete break with the republic. Events were soon to unfold that justified the mutual suspicions and hatreds of both sides, escalating government repression and Anarchist assaults into a condition of virtual civil war.

The Socialist Party, it must be added here, played a critical role in exacerbating this conflict. That the UGT and CNT were bitter rivals has already been emphasized by Madariaga and other writers; for decades the two labor organizations had contested each other for every jurisdiction where they overlapped. Rarely did they cooperate, and the few pacts they signed for common action usually degener-

Arrested CNT workers, during an Anarchist-inspired strike in Saragossa in the early 1930s. These were the workers who disdained strikes merely for economic gain and conducted walkouts primarily for "social reasons."

ated into a welter of mutual recriminations. With the establishment of the republic, Socialist attitudes toward the CNT became unconscionably venomous. "There is a great deal of confusion in the minds of many comrades," warned a Socialist leader in 1932. "They consider Anarchist Syndicalism as an ideal which runs parallel with our own, when it is its absolute antithesis, and that the Anarchists and Syndicalists are comrades when they are our greatest enemies."

This statement should not be dismissed as mere rhetoric. It bluntly expresses what many Socialist leaders practiced daily in their relations with the rival union. UGT bureaucrats often provided scabs to break up CNT strikes (and replace the striking syndicates by their own unions)—only to accuse the Anarchosyndicalists of *pistolerismo* when they defended themselves.[6] Ruthless in the exercise of his powers, Largo Caballero used the immense apparatus of the Ministry of Labor to undermine CNT influence wherever he could. It would be difficult, in fact, to clearly understand the labor legislation of the early republic without bearing in mind this aim of the Socialists. As if to confirm the harshest anti-republican verdict of the Anarchists, the new government passed a law to establish a system of "mixed juries" for dealing with labor disputes. The law made it illegal to strike without first bringing grievances before a "jury" composed equally of labor and employer representatives, with a government representative to break voting deadlocks. Although the jury's decision was not mandatory, there can be little doubt that it strongly influenced the outcome of many labor disputes by its moral authority. It need hardly be emphasized that the mixed jury system made it possible for Largo Caballero to give UGT representatives easy majorities by appointing Socialists as government representatives. Other legislation specified the conditions labor-management contracts had to fulfill in order to be valid and established a mandatory eight-day "cooling-off" period before workers could go on strike.

To the CNT this corpus of labor legislation was nothing less than a dagger aimed at its most treasured Anarchosyndicalist principles. As Brenan observes,

> Apart from the fact that these laws ran contrary to the Anarcho-Syndicalist principles of negotiating directly with the employers and interfered with the practice of lightning strikes, it was clear that they represented an immense increase in the power of the State in industrial matters. A whole army of Government officials, mostly Socialists, made their appearance to enforce the new laws and saw to it that, whenever possible, they should be used to extend the influence of the UGT at the expense of the CNT. This had of course been the intention of those who drew them up. In fact the UGT was rapidly becoming an organ of the state itself and using its new powers to reduce its rival. The Anarcho-

Syndicalists could have no illusions as to what would happen to them if a purely Socialist government should come into power.

That the UGT reaped enormous advantages from Socialist collaboration with the government (past as well as present) can be demonstrated with statistical precision. The Socialist labor federation, thanks to its "cooperative" attitude toward the dictatorship, had retained its apparatus intact throughout the 1920s, even increasing its membership slightly. In December 1929, shortly before Primo's fall, it could claim 1,511 local sections with about 230,000 members. With the establishment of the republic, the UGT enjoyed a phenomenal growth. By December 1931, eight months after the republic was proclaimed, the union could boast of 4,041 local sections and nearly 960,000 members, a tripling of membership in only two years. In July 1932, these figures had soared to almost 5,107 and 1,050,000 respectively.

Most of this expansion occurred in the countryside. In the hectic period directly following the war, the UGT, shaken by the Russian Revolution and Anarchist insurrections in Andalusia, began to discard some of its Marxian shibboleths and direct its energies toward winning the rural poor. Led by Luis Martinez Gil, a follower of Julian Besteiro, Socialists tried to use Primo's *comites paritarios* to extend the UGT's rather limited roots in southern Spain. In April 1930, the UGT established a separate rural federation, the FNTT or *Federacion Nacional de Trabajadores de la Tierra* (National Federation of Land Workers). It began with a membership of only 27,000, but by June 1933 this figure had soared to 451,000, accounting for 40 percent of the UGT's total membership.

The CNT watched this increase with alarm. To the Anarchosyndicalists, the growth of Socialist-controlled unions meant nothing less than the bureaucratic corruption of the Spanish masses. They earnestly believed that a UGT worker or peasant was virtually lost to the revolution. What was even more appalling, the UGT, aided by the Ministry of Labor and the mixed juries, began to make serious inroads into traditionally Anarchist areas. Not only were Estremadura and La Mancha Socialist strongholds, but sizeable FNTT unions now existed in Malaga, Seville, and Valencia.

Ironically, both labor organizations failed to anticipate the radicalizing impact this massive influx of rural poor would have on Spanish Socialism. The countryside was in the midst of revolutionary ferment. The new Republican agrarian laws had opened the sluice gates of rural discontent without satisfying the peasant's hunger for land. Thousands of tenants flocked to the courts and to their unions to demand the settlement of grievances under the new laws; strikes and demonstrations swept the countryside, locking the new FNTT in bitter struggles with the civil authorities. The pressure of the impetuous Spanish peasantry and rural proletariat on the UGT bureaucracy began to produce major fissures in the once-solid edifice of Socialist reformism. Although the FNTT's militancy fell far short of the CNT's, it is significant that Martinez Gil and Besteiro were strongly opposed to the entry of Socialists into the Republican government. The Socialist left wing, so hopelessly isolated after the Russian Revolution, began to increase its influence in party ranks. Within a few years, it would become the most important tendency in the Socialist Party.

Although the UGT remained the CNT's main rival, the small Spanish Communist Party began to take up its own cudgels and enter the battle between the two unions. Until the early Republican period, the Communist Party was little more than an interloper in the Spanish labor movement. From a sizeable organization at its founding, the party in 1931 had dwindled to little more than a thousand members. Primo had all but ignored its existence. The dictatorship did not even bother to suppress the party's newspaper, *Mundo Obrero*. The split between the Communist syndicalists like Nin and Maurin and the traditional Leninists had left the party in the hands of docile mediocrities whose principal qualification for leadership seems to have been their subservience to the Stalinist Comintern. During this period, virtually all Catalan Communists, following the tendency represented by Maurin, had formed the BOC, the *Bloc Obrer i Camperol* (Worker-Peasant Bloc), a revolutionary organization which stressed the need for cooperation between working-class and left middle-class groups. Others, mainly intellectuals, collected around Nin and established the *Izquierda Communista* or Left Communists, an avowedly Trotskyist organization, also rooted primarily in Catalonia. Together, the BOC and *Izquierda Communista* virtually supplanted the Communist Party in Catalonia and for many years may have outnumbered it in Spain as a whole. In 1936, the two organizations merged to form the POUM—the *Partido Obrero de Unificacion Marxista* (Workers' Party of Marxist Unification)—a sizeable organization which became the principal target of Stalinist abuse and repression during the Civil War years.

Generally, the Communist Party exercised very little influence on the Spanish working class. Apart from some nuclei in Asturias and Madrid, the party could boast of only one major achievement: in 1927 it had managed to win control over a considerable number of underground CNT syndicates in Seville—principally in the dock area—which it began to use as a base for duels with rival Anarchosyndicalist and Socialist unions. During the early 1930s, the Andalusian capital became the arena for a three-way conflict between the CNT, the UGT, and the Stalinist-manipulated "Committee of Reconstruction,"[6] so named because of a conference on Syndicalist Reconstruction which the party had convened in the spring of 1930. According to Gabriel Jackson, who made a recent on-site study of the conflict:

> Most of the urban workers belonged to CNT unions. The communists were strongest among the port workers. The UGT Federation of Land Workers had been growing in the villages, and the UGT was challenging the communists for control of the stevedores. Each of these groups, plus the employer organization, the Economic Federation of Andalusia, hired pistoleros on occasion. There were perhaps a dozen clashes leading to death or serious injury during the course of the year 1933. . . . The pistoleros were hired at a rate of ten pesetas per day, at a time when the average daily wage in unionized factories was about twelve. Each organization reduced the individual risk to its strong-arm men by maintaining hideouts, supplying false papers, and forming prisoner welfare committees to aid those unfortunate enough to see the inside of a jail. The occasional violence was localized in the port area, and if cases came to court, they usually led to acquittal, since none of the witnesses could remember anything.

Such struggles were to be waged with increasing frequency as Spain began to slip into civil war. The Anarchists were not the only source of social violence; employers, Socialists, and Communists hired *pistoleros* against each other when the need arose—only to unite in accusing the Anarchists of their own crimes. Of course with the FAI at its disposal, the CNT had very little need for professional gunmen. That *faistas* were prepared to use weapons more readily than the Socialists and Communists at this time is quite true; but they were not cynical paid killers who threatened to corrupt the organizations for which they worked. Reactionary newspapers, like the monarchist *ABC*, picked up the most trifling altercations in Seville and magnified them enormously in order to terrify the middle-classes. "If a CNT worker punched a communist in a waterfront bar," notes Jackson, "the Seville edition of *ABC* reported an outbreak of lawlessness. If one of the syndicates called a general strike, and a few prudent shopkeepers pulled down their shutters in case anyone might throw a rock, *ABC* had the city paralyzed. Actually, life was normal outside the port area, and the harbor districts of all the world's seaports were the scenes of union rivalry and sporadic violence in the 1930s."

But the period of greatest violence still lay ahead; in 1931 the CNT was largely occupied with internal organizational problems and with defining its strategy toward the republic. An Extraordinary National

Congress was planned for mid-June in which these problems were to be thrashed out. This was to be the first national congress of the CNT since 1919. As it turned out, it was to be the last one the Confederation would hold until the eve of the Civil War.[7] When the 418 delegates to the congress convened at the Madrid Conservatory on June 11, the CNT could claim a membership of over a half million, organized into 511 syndicates. If this seems like an inflated figure, as some writers have suggested, it should be added that many syndicates, particularly in the south, were too poor to send delegates. According to the congress's statistics, the key Catalan Regional Confederation had no more than 240,000 affiliates, most of whom worked in Barcelona, a membership decline in Catalonia of nearly 40 percent since 1919.

The agenda for the congress had been prepared by the National Committee and approved by a plenum of regional delegates. Thus, it was possible for a number of the syndicates to debate the agenda in advance and adopt positions on the issues to be discussed. All this was normative CNT procedure, although in the past, owing to repression and the need for haste, the Confederation had not always adhered to it. At the congress, discussion centered around four issues: the National Committee's policies during the dictatorship, the all-important question of the present situation in Spain, the need for changes in the CNT's organizational structure, and, permeating all the issues discussed, the conflicts between the FAI and the moderates. This congress was a crucial one for the CNT, for it paved the way for the defeat of the moderates by the more radical tendencies inside the Confederation. Indeed, the growth of the FAI's influence on the syndicates was to affect the future not only of the CNT but also of the Second Republic.

The 14-man National Committee, composed entirely of Catalans, fell under attack from the outset of the congress and its members responded with vigor. The give-and-take between individual members of the National Committee and the delegates was a temporary departure from the practice followed by previous CNT congresses. Ordinarily, the National Committee was expected to stand apart from debates between delegates in order to give the latter the widest latitude in discussion. The National Committee's views were usually voiced in its reports. To *cenetistas*, every labor leader (even an unpaid one who professed to hold Anarchist views) was a potential bureaucrat who required continual watching. As an argument for removing Pestana from the editorship of *Solidaridad Obrera*, Buenacasa, for example, noted that the moderate spokesman had not engaged in his profession as a watchmaker for more than five years—a clear sign that he had become too entrenched in the CNT apparatus. It might also be recalled that Pestana, in his talk with Mola, voiced his outrage that the labor delegates to the *comites paritarios* were paid officials.

The rules of the congress caused great consternation among delegates. Radicals complained that the rules were visibly biased against the FAI; the more moderate delegates, in turn, were outraged that official representatives of the FAI (an "outside organization") had been admitted to the congress at all. Finally, when a FAI spokesman rose to express his organization's view on an issue, mayhem broke loose. The FAI could have expressed its views through sympathetic delegates (Garcia Oliver, for example, was an authorized delegate from Reus), but its right to participate in the congress in an official capacity was a matter of prestige. Although most of the delegates would not have denied the FAI a voice in the congress, its spokesman withdrew his request to speak, leaving the onus of suppression on the National Committee and the moderates.

This sparring formed the backdrop to serious discussions on the past and future policies of the Confederation. Perhaps the most breathtaking session occurred when Juan Peiro rose to give an account of the National Committee's links with the antidictatorial conspiracies of the late 1920s. Very few of the details had been known before, and many delegates, hearing of past negotiations with Liberals who were now among their most bitter enemies, were obviously shocked. Peiro's report, moreover, was not a *mea culpa*. He had supported the negotiations then and he supported Pestana's attempts to accommodate the CNT to the republic now. A number of speakers rose to denounce the National Committee and the delegates passed a resolution that rejected all responsibility for its past actions.

The congress decided that the next region to select the National Committee should be Madrid, thereby breaking Catalonia's longtime grip on the national organization. The wind, clearly, was blowing against the moderates.

The centrist tendency in the congress, which probably included most of the delegates, was moving toward the left. But this should not be taken to mean that the FAI had gained control of the congress. True, the FAI was making inroads into the Catalan Regional Confederation, to which it owed its invitation to attend the congress. In Barcelona the FAI had planted firm roots in the construction syndicate and probably in the barbers' syndicate as well. And when the moderates presented a minimum program for the CNT not unlike the reformist demands earlier congress had adopted, the Badalona chemical syndicate and the Barcelona light and power, chemical, and automobile syndicates joined the construction and barbers' delegates in protest. But the minimum program was accepted by the congress nonetheless. Moreover, despite vigorous FAI opposition, the congress adopted the moderates' reorganization plan. Essentially, the plan restored the national industrial craft federations which had existed in the old International. The committee report which proposed the plan agreed that the greater concentration of capital required a concomitant structural concentration of the CNT in the form of national federations. While the report, prepared primarily by Juan Peiro, did not urge any diminution in the role and authority of the local geographic federations, it distinctly superimposed a quasi-centralistic industrial structure on the CNT. Ensuing events were to largely nullify the decision to establish the national industrial craft federations—indeed, they were not fully established until the civil war was well underway—but the heated debate which followed the presentation of the plan should not be underestimated.

The significance of this reorganization plan, and of the debate which followed its presentation, can hardly be underestimated. The plan was classical syndicalist doctrine and the FAI, in objecting to it, unknowingly recapitulated the historic battle that had divided Anarchists from syndicalists at the turn of the century. Garcia Oliver, speaking for the FAI, warned that the plan would result in the centralization of the CNT and denounced it as a corrupting "German invention" that reeked of beer. (The double meaning of Garcia Oliver's metaphor should be noted. The FAI leader was alluding not only to the "Marxist" thrust of the proposal but also to the support it had received by German syndicalists in the IWMA.) Another delegate rose to warn the congress that the plan would lead to a salaried CNT officialdom. A generation earlier, the Italian Anarchist Errico Malatesta had voiced similar objections in more sophisticated and elegant terms. The objections had lost none of their validity over the passing years.

Although the plan was not really applied until the Civil War it almost certainly reinforced the tendency toward centralization and bureaucratization that had existed in the CNT by identifying *comunismo libertario* with a potentially centralized economy. Depending upon how decisions flowed between the center and base of the economy, a fragile barrier separated the economic structure advocated in the plan from the nationalized, bureaucratic economic order advocated by the Socialists. Without complete control of the decision-making process by assemblies of the factory workers, the two "visions" would be virtually indistinguishable. Tragically, the Confederation did not occupy itself with this crucial problem. On the contrary, the moderates' argument that the CNT had to adapt itself to the centralist economy created by modern capitalism seemed highly plausible. It was to be echoed five years alter by Diego de Santillan, a very influential *faista* theoretician whose writings in economic recon-

struction provided the CNT with a rationale for accepting a centralized, highly bureaucratic economy during the Civil War.

Why, after voting for the moderates' reorganization plan and
minimum program, did the congress select Madrid as the next center
of the CNT? This patent defeat for the moderates would be difficult to
explain merely in terms of factional voting patterns. Revolutionary
fervor was welling up in the CNT ranks. The rapid collapse of the
dictatorship and monarchy, the deepening economic crisis, and the
restlessness of the Spanish people after a longer period of torpor
combined to create the belief among the Anarchosyndicalists that a
libertarian revolution was drawing near. Apparently, many delegates
to the congress saw no contradiction between preparing for a revolution and voting for a minimum program that proclaimed the need for
democratic rights, secular schools, and the right to strike. The reorganization plan of the moderates must have seemed all the more
valuable as a concrete, practical, and eminently constructive alternative to capitalism which Anarchosyndicalists could advance in the
event of a revolution.

The FAI spoke to this vision without supporting the moderates'
plans and programs. It favored immediate revolution. The moderates, while offering a concrete alternative to capitalism, denied that
Spain was faced with revolution as an imminent prospect. Villaverde,
a centrist turned moderate, pointedly warned the delegates: "The
Confederation is in no condition to be able to revolt in the historic
moment in which are living." Like all the moderates he reminded the
congress that Anarchosyndicalism had influence only over a small
minority of the working class. The delegates, however, seem to have
used the moderates' proposals to give reality to the FAI's revolutionary perspective. Although the FAI's specific proposals were defeated by the congress, its revolutionary spirit almost certainly infected the majority of the delegates.

The government did not have to wait long to feel the impact of this
growing revolutionary elan. A few weeks after the delegates dispersed, the CNT threw down the gauntlet. On July 4, thousands of
CNT telephone workers walked off their jobs, confronting the government with what Peirats calls *"un 'test' "* of the republic's intentions. The strike achieved its greatest successes in Barcelona and
Seville, where telephone service was cut off completely, but it also
affected Madrid, Valencia, and other key communications center in
the country. Although the leaders of the telephone syndicate tried to
conduct the strike peacefully, serious fighting broke out when armed
workers, probably spearheaded by *faistas*, tried to attack the telephone buildings. The strike quickly "degenerated into guerrilla actions" (to use Peirats's words) between commando squads of CNT

The bodies of Anarchist peasant insurrectionaries displayed at the Casas Viejas cemetery. It was photographs of such "displays" published in the press that shocked the Spanish public and helped bring down the Azaña government in 1933.

saboteurs and government forces. Before it tapered off, some 2,000 strikers had been arrested.

This was no ordinary strike. Peirats correctly describes it as a " *'huelga de la Canadiense' en miniatura.''* To clearly understand its implications, the strike must be placed in the context of the period. The *Compania Telefonica Nacional de Espana* was not merely a strategic communications network but a huge monopoly owned by American capital. Under the dictatorship a subsidiary of the International Telephone and Telegraph Corporation, the *Compania Telefonica*, had been granted a twenty-year monopoly over all telephonic communications in Spain. After this period, the installations owned by the company could revert to the government, provided that the ITTC was compensated for all the capital it had expended plus 15 percent interest. This staggering compensation had to be paid in gold. To most Spaniards, the *Compania Telefonica* was a monstrous symbol of foreign imperialism. As recently as 1930 the right-wing Socialist Indalecio Prieto had publicly denounced the contract between the company and the government, calling it systematic robbery and promising that the future republic would cancel its terms. Now Prieto was the republic's minister of finance and Socialists dominated the Ministry of Labor. If the CNT was seeking to embarrass the republic, particularly the Socialists, it had chosen its target well.

That the government would spare no effort to resist the strike was a certainty. Spain had just gone to the polls to elect the Constituent Cortes, and Azana was eager to show that the republic was a mature, orderly democracy. Prieto, who was "bending every effort to assure Spain's [foreign] creditors, stem the export of wealth, and arrest the downward trend of the peseta" (Gabriel Jackson), was more than disposed to forget his militant pledges of a year earlier. Thus the strike was an acute embarrassment to the government. The UGT, meanwhile, had its own bone to pick with the CNT. The telephone syndicate, which the CNT had established in 1918, was a constant challenge to the Socialists' grip of the Madrid labor movement. Like the construction workers' syndicate, it was a CNT enclave in a solidly UGT center. Accordingly, the government and the Socialist Party found no difficulty in forming a common front to break the strike and weaken CNT influence.

The Ministry of Labor declared the strike illegal and the Ministry of the Interior called out the Civil Guard to intimidate the strikers, many of whom were women telephone operators. Shedding all pretense of labor solidarity, the UGT provided the *Compania Telefonica* with scabs while *El Socialista*, the Socialist Party organ, accused the CNT of being run by *pistoleros*. Those tactics were successful in Madrid, where the defeated strikers were obliged to enroll in the UGT in order to retain their jobs. So far as the Socialists were concerned, the CNT's appeals for solidarity had fallen on deaf ears, although elsewhere workers responded with funds and sympathetic, if ineffective, strikes.

In Seville, however, the strike began to take on very serious dimensions. Late in June, even before the telephone workers walked out, the government had gotten wind of an insurrectionary plot by Anarchists and disaffected air force personnel. According to the government's account, the purpose of the insurrection was to prevent the forthcoming elections for the Constituent Cortes. This incredible conspiracy apparently included the future *caudillo's* volatile brother, Major Ramon Franco, who had moved steadily to the left since his Republican days. General Sanjurjo and "loyal aviators" were dispatched to Seville to abort the conspiracy. Franco was arrested and the local commander of the aerodrome relieved of his duties. In nearby villages the government claimed to have found arms that Anarchists had distributed among the peasants.

Scarcely had this conspiracy faded from public attention when, on July 20, a general strike broke out in Seville and serious fighting erupted in the streets. This strike, which also had Communist support, stemmed from the walkout of the telephone workers. It is hard to judge whether the CNT, the FAI, or the Communists (who were following an ultrarevolutionary line in 1931) hoped to turn the strike into an insurrection. There are very few accounts of the Seville strike to be found in Anarchist sources. Again, the government professed to find "evidence" that arms had been distributed to the peasants and, indeed, pitched battles took place in the countryside around the city between the Civil Guard and the agricultural workers. Maura, as minister of interior, decided to crush the "insurrection" ruthlessly. Martial law was declared and the CNT's headquarters was reduced to shambles by artillery fire. After nine days, during which heavily armed police detachments patrolled the streets, the Seville general strike came to an end. The struggle in the Andalusian capital left 40 dead and some 200 wounded.

These events polarized the CNT as never before. To the moderates, the violent tactics of the previous weeks had produced a needless cleavage between the CNT and the republic—a political system which in their view had opened new possibilites for Anarchosyndicalist propaganda and the Confederation's growth. To the FAI, and perhaps the majority of CNT militants, the government's ruthlessness in dealing with the telephone strikers and the Seville workers was proof that the republic was no better than the monarchy and the dictatorship. The FAI called for all-out social war against the government.

The moderates' efforts to win the CNT away from the FAI influence became increasingly desperate. The tensions within the organization finally came to a head when in August 1931, thirty moderates signed a vigorous statement denouncing the conspiratorial, ultrarevolutionary policies of the FAI. Although the FAI was not mentioned by name, *"El Manifiesto de los 'Treinta' "* ("Manifesto of the 'Thirty' "), as the document came to be known, denounced the Anarchist organization's "simplistic" concept of revolution, warning that it would lead to "a Republican fascism." The republic, said the *Treintistas*, still enjoyed considerable moral authority as well as armed power, and until that moral authority was destroyed by the government's own corrupt and repressive practices, any attempted revolution if it succeeded, would lead to a dictatorship by ideologues. "Yes, we are revolutionaries, but not cultivators of the myth of revolution," declaimed the statement.

> We want capitalism and the State, be it red, white or black, to disappear; but we do not want it to be replaced by another. . . . We want a revolution that is born of the profound sentiment of the people, not a revolution that is offered to us. . . . The Confederation is a revolutionary organization and not an organization which propagates abuse and riots, which propagates the cult of violence for the sake of violence, revolution for the sake of revolution. . . .

The statement did not alter the course of the CNT. On the contrary, it produced widespread anger which the FAI skillfully used to isolate the moderate wing. The statement, in fact, was the most crucial factor in the downfall of Pestana, Peiro, and their followers. For years the moderates had obscured their skepticism toward demands for immediate revolution in vague generalities on their adherence to Anarchist ideals, thereby leaving the CNT membership unclear about the differences between the moderate wing of the union and the FAI. The Manifesto dispelled this obscurity completely. The *Treintistas*, it was clear, were opposed to the revolutionary tactics promoted by the FAI, indeed, to any CNT policy that favorably acknowledged such tactics. The camaraderie of common membership in the Confederation had been totally subordinated to visible policy differences—one moderate the other extremist. Mere membership in the CNT could no longer blanket such profound disparities in program and approach and, as Buenacasa was to point out by the 1930's, it was the FAI's adherence to a policy of immediate revolution that accounted for its popularity among most Anarchosyndicalist workers.

An outright physical split within the CNT was now merely a matter of time. By September 1931 the FAI, riding on a rank-and-file wave of revolutionary enthusiasm, had gained control of Barcelona's key syndicates; a month later, in October, *faistas* and hard-line Anarchosyndicalists unseated the moderate editorial board of *Solidaridad Obrera* and assumed control of the newspaper. The two wings began to trade vituperative insults—the moderates decrying *"la dictatura de la FAI,"* and the *faistas* sneering at the moderates as *"traidores"* and *"renegados."* The following year, Pestaña was to be expelled by his own syndicate for attacking a CNT uprising in the Llobregat valley. He was to be accompanied by his *Treintista* comrades and by several syndicates—a miners' syndicate in Asturias, virtually all the syndicates of Tarassa and Sabadell, and about half of the syndicates in Valencia. Led by moderates, these syndicates were to group together to form a separate federation of their own—*Los Sindicatos de Oposicion* (Opposition Syndicates)—whose membership probably rarely exceeded 60,000. Finally, in April 1932, Pestana, parting even from his moderate comrades, was to found his own Syndicalist Party, which actually sent two deputies to the Cortes in the elections of 1936.[8]

Most writers on the Spanish labor movement seem to concur in the view that, with the departure of the moderates, the CNT was to fall under the complete domination of the FAI. Cesar M. Lorenzo, in a highly informative work on Spanish Anarchism, speaks of the FAI as the "masters" of the CNT. But is this appraisal really correct? The FAI, as we have already seen, was more loosely jointed as an organization than many of its admirers and critics seem to recognize. It had no bureaucratic apparatus, no membership cards or dues, and no headquarters with paid officials, secretaries, and clerks. According to Brenan, most of its uprisings at this time were hatched in the *Cafe Tranquilidad* on Barcelona's main working-class thoroughfare, although it seems more likely that *faistas* preferred to use their apartments for serious conspiracies. This informality is significant as a reflections of the *faistas'* state of mind. However much they behaved as an elite in the CNT, they genuinely dreaded bureaucracy. They jealously guarded the independence of their affinity groups from the authority of higher organizational bodies—a state of mind hardly conducive to the development of tightly knit, vanguard organization.

The FAI, moreover, was not a politcally homogeneous organization which followed a fixed "line" like the Communists and many Socialists. It had no official program by which all *faistas* could mechanically guide their actions. Its views were usually expressed in statements by the Peninsular Committee. These "communiques" were highly respected by most *faistas*, but at least in the early 1930s, they made very limited demands upon the independence of the affinity groups. Despite their hortatory accolades to Anarchist ideals and principles, they were usually calls to action. The FAI was not oriented toward theory; in fact, it produced few theoreticians of any ability. Overwhelmingly working class in composition and youthful in age, the organization had its fair share of the shortcomings as well as the admirable qualities of the proletariat everywhere. It placed action above ideas, courage above circumspection, impulse above reason and experience. Gaston Leval has described the FAI as the "passion of the CNT," and Peirats, in earthier terms, as its "testicles," but no one, to the knowledge of this writer, has called it the "brain" of the Confederation. And in the early 1930s, as Spain drifted toward civil war, what the FAI needed desperately was theoretical insight and understanding into its situation.

Finally, in the FAI there was no consensus about how to proceed in a revolutionary situation. On this critical issue it contained sharply divided tendencies whose basic disagreements were never fully resolved. Addressing herself to the major tendencies within Spanish Anarchosyndicalism, Federica Montseny, one of the FAI's luminaries during the Republican period and a scion of the Urales, a famous Anarchist family, notes three currents: "Those known as Treintistas, who formed the right-wing, the anarchists who formed the left-wing, and a third current, the 'anarcho-Bolsheviks,' embodied by the group of Garcia Oliver and the playful partisans of 'one for all,' who made glancing contact with the theories of the Russian revolutionaries." His statement, in fact, is rather restrained. The "partisans of 'one for all' " were the *Solidarios* of the 1920s who had renamed themselves *Nosotros* (literally, "we") in the 1930s and included not only Garcia Oliver but Durruti, the Ascaso brothers, and Ricardo Sanz. If we are to accept Peirats's account of their views, their "contact" with Bolshevism was more than "glancing." "It was Garcia Oliver who declared himself for the taking of power (*prise de pouvoir*) in a public lecture which he gave to the woodworkers' syndicate of Barcelona in January or February, 1936. He had also made this affirmation beforehand at the very restrained meeting of notables in the editorial board of *Solidaridad Obrera*."[9]

This trend, to be sure, did not go unchallenged. Some of the most theoretically gifted and highly respected figures of the FAI sharply opposed Garcia Oliver's approach. The "A" affinity group, which included such prominent *faistas* as Jacinte Toryho, Alberdo Iglesias, and Ricardo Mestre, called for the expulsion of the *Nosotros* group. The *Nervo* group, led by Pedro Herrara and the Anarchist theorist Abad de Santillan, shared this hostility. It was joined by the "Z" group, a particularly significant affinity group because of its considerable influence over the libertarian youth movement of Catalonia.

Yet if Garcia Oliver's theory of "seizing power" was not acceptable to the FAI as a whole, there seems little doubt that the putschism implicit in this approach prevailed in practice from the early 1930's onward. It is not unfair to say that from January 1932 to the beginning of 1933, various FAI groups and eventually the FAI as a whole launched a "cycle of insurrections" that, more than any other single factor, brought down the Azana coalition.

The first of these insurrections began on January 18, 1932, in the Catalan mining *comarcal* of the Alto Llobregat. In Figols, Manresa, Berga, Sallent, and other towns, miners and other workers seized town halls, raised the black-and-red flags of the CNT, and declared *comunismo libertario*. After five days, the revolt had been all but crushed, with surprisingly little bloodshed. According to Peirats, Azana, in a rare spasm of determinaton, gave the commanding general "fifteen minutes to eliminate them [the *cenetista* workers] after the troops arrived." Fortunately for the workers, the government forces in the Alto Llobregat were commanded by one Humberto Gil Cabrera, who did not share Azana's bloodthirsty aversion for the CNT. In this region, at least, the army's repression was not notable for its severity. In Barcelona, however, the authorities used a sympathy strike as an excuse to round up hundreds of militants. The repression carried out by the Republican government extended well beyond Catalonia to include the Levant, Aragon, and Andalusia. Thousands of workers were thrown into jails and prison ships in the coastal cities. A month later, over a hundred militants, including Durruti and Francisco Ascaso, were deported to Spanish West Africa and the Canary Islands. Durruti was not to be released until the following autumn.

The deportations were followed by an explosion of protest strikes, some of which lasted well into the spring and escalated the severity of the government's repression. In Tarassa, the workers staged a small-scale replay of the Alto Llobregat uprisings, seizing the town hall and raising the CNT's black-and-red flags. The town was swept by street fighting and inevitably by severe repression. The January uprising in the Alto Llobregat was not quite the monumentally revolutionary action it seems to be in the descriptive rhetoric of Federica Montseney. Although highly localized and poorly planned, it was partly a calculated effort by the FAI to enhance its revolutionary reputation among Spanish workers generally and *cenetista* workers in particular. Peirats leaves us with very little doubt on this score—and not only in the case of the Alto Llobregat insurrections but also in those which were to follow. "The extremists [one should read *faistas* here—M.B.] who expelled the moderates felt an obligation to be revolutionary," Peirats observes.

In the debates preceding the expulsions, a polarization took place: the revolution was considered to be either near or distant. The pessimism of some led to a kind of optimism in others, just as the cowardice of one who flees increases the bravery of one who pursues. To prove the validity of their accusations of impotence, defeatism or treason on the part of the moderates, the extremists had to prove their own virility. In the big meetings, where up to 100,000 people gathered, libertarian communism was declared to be within everyone's grasp. Not to believe in the imminence of libertarian communism was grounds for suspicion.

In the harsh light of the January events, Pestana's failure to support the FAI's tactics, indeed his unequivocal opposition to them, was characterized as nothing less than treachery. It was in the aftermath of these events that he was replaced by the *faista* Manuel Rivas as secretary of the National Committee and finally expelled from his own union. At the Catalan regional plenum of Sabadell in April 1932, the walkout of *treintista*-influenced syndicates initiated an outright split that extended from Catalonia, through the Levant, to Andalusia and Asturias. As we have already seen, the *treintista*-influenced syndicates thereupon formed their own confederation, *Los Sindicatos de Oposicion*, with centers in Sabadell, Valencia, and Asturias. Despite their opposition to the FAI, the *Sindicatos de Oposicion* did not follow Pestana's trajectory into "syndicalist" politics. In the years ahead they functioned primarily as an oppositional tendency on the periphery of the CNT.

Far from cooling the FAI's insurrectionary fever, the split that began at Sabadell seemed to heighten it by removing the restraining hands of the moderates. In January 1933, almost a year to the day after the Alto Llobregat events, the FAI dragged the CNT into another insurrectionary adventure. This insurrection was to be initiated by a railway strike of the CNT's *Federacion Nacional de la Industria Ferroviaria* (FNIF). But the FNIF, riddled with uncertainty and organizationally uncoordinated, kept delaying its decision on a strike date. The FAI, eager to initiate an insurrection, became increasingly impatient. As for the CNT's leadership, it simply drifted along with events. Virtually all insurrectionary initiatives were left to the FAI-controlled Committees of Defense, a euphemism for the elaborate committee structure composed of Cadres of Defense at local, *comarcal*, and national levels which Anarchist action groups had created under the umbrella of the CNT and FAI to conduct miltary operations. Indeed, so closely wedded had the CNT and FAI become after the split within the Confederation that Manuel Rivas, the secretary of the CNT's National Committee, was also secretary of the *faista*-controlled National Committee of Defense.

Throughout, the police were completely informed about the FAI's plans and prepared meticulously to counter them. The insurrection began on January 8 with assaults by Anarchist action groups and

Cadres of Defense on Barcelona's military barracks. The Anarchists had expected support from segments of the army rank and file, but the attacks had been anticipated by the authorities and they were repelled with bloodshed and arrests. Serious fighting occurred in working-class *barrios* and outlying areas of Barcelona, but the struggle was doomed to defeat. Uprisings occurred in Tarassa, Sardanola-Ripollet, Lerida, in several *pueblos* in Valencia province, and in Andalusia. They too were crushed without difficulty. In Catalonia, virtually every leading *faista*, including Garcia Oliver and most members of the FAI's Peninsular Committee, were arrested. The event was a total calamity. With a certain measure of justice, the CNT denied any part in the insurrection, implicitly blaming the FAI for the disaster. Even the old Anarchist Buenacasa bluntly dissociated Anarchism itself from the FAI's tactics by angrily declaring: "*El faismo* and not anarchism provoked the happenings of last January 8 in Barcelona. . . ." In any case, whether or not one regards the FAI's insurrectionary fever as creditable, the organization made no attempt to deny its responsibility for the January events.

Despite the defeat, the FAI's insurrectionary mood had slowly percolated into some of the most remote *pueblos* of Andalusia where a millenarian ambience, dating back to a bygone age in the history of Spanish Anarchism, still existed among a number of the peasants. Here, another uprising inadvertently had a profound impact on the destiny of the Azana coalition. In Casas Viejas, a small, impoverished *pueblo* not far from Jerez de la Frontera, there still existed an Anarchist "dynasty" headed by a venerable old man in his sixties nicknamed *Seisdedos*, or "Six Fingers," who had heard of the uprisings elsewhere in Spain. Inspired by these events, *Seisdedos* decided that the time had finally arrived to proclaim *comunismo libertario*. The old man, his friends, and his relatives—in all a party of little more than thirty—proceeded to arm themselves with cudgels and shotguns and take over the village. Accounts vary from this point onward. According to Brenan, *Seisdedos* and his party naively marched to the Civil Guard barracks to proclaim the glad tidings. The *Guardia*, more alarmed than elated by this party of armed peasants, proceeded to exchange shots with *Seisdedos*, who accordingly besieged them. Eventually, *Seisdedos* and his group were turned from besiegers into besieged when troops and even airplanes attacked the *pueblo*, brutally exterminating most of them.

Peirats presents a different account. After *Seisdedos* and his party had proclaimed *comunismo libertario* (presumably to the village at large) all "was peace and order until the police arrived."

They came into the village shooting. Several were left dead in the streets.

Then they went into the houses and began to line up prisoners. In the process they came to a hut with a roof of straw and dry branches. They break in. A shot is heard, and a soldier spins. Another shot and another soldier falls. Another is wounded as he attempts to sneak in through the yard. The rest retreat. Who is inside? Old 'Sixfingers,' a sixty year old with a tribe of children and grandchildren. The old man will not give up. The others cannot leave without getting hurt. The guards take their positions and receive reinforcements. They use their machine guns and hand grenades. Sixfingers does not give in. He saves his shots and uses them well. Two more guards fall. The struggle lasts all night. Two of the children escape, covered in their retreat by someone who dies riddled with bullets. Dawn is coming and they want to end it once and for all. The hand grenades bounce back, or their impact is cushioned by the thatched roof. The bullets are blocked by the stones. Somebody has an idea. They gather rags, handfuls of cotton, and make balls with them, which they dip in gasoline. Red flashes break the darkness like meteors. The roof crackles and turns into a torch. Soon flames envelop the hut. The machine guns smell blood. Someone comes out, a burning girl. The machine guns leap and leave little fires burning on the ground that smell of burnt flesh. The hut, like an enormous pyre, soon collapses. A sinister cry, a mixture of pain, anger, and sarcasm, echos through the night. And afterwards the quiet silence of the coals. It was over.

The Casas Viejas affair stirred the country to its depths.[10] The image of heavily armed Civil Guards and contingents of the newly formed Assault Guards—the latter ostensibly paragons of Republican legality—wantonly murdering simple, impoverished peasants in a grossly unequal struggle aroused indignation in almost every sector of Spanish society. Initially the government had tried to palm off the event as a mere episode in its chronic war against the lawless Anarchists, but word had spread that no quarter was given to prisoners captured by the Guards. Some fourteen such prisoners had been shot in cold blood by a platoon of Assault Guards under the command of a Captain Rojas. The right gleefully joined the left in condemning the Casas Viejas event and the government, its back to the wall, was obliged to investigate the affair. Captain Rojas was tried and his statements implicated the director general of security in a series of unsavory orders that were directly traceable to Azana. The orders "from above," a subject that was treated rather evasively, called upon Rojas to take no wounded and no prisoners. The Guards were ordered to "shoot for the belly."

Although the Casas Viejas affair did not in itself bring down the Azana coalition, it crystallized all the frustrations, resentments, and barbarities that finally caused the government to resign nine months later. The Liberal republic which had begun so brightly and enthusiastically a few years earlier, had satisfied nobody precisely because it followed the path of least resistance—a path which, as Brenan astutely observes, proved to be the path of greatest resistance. The government's dilemma was obvious almost from the start of its career: it depended on the middle classes and working classes to maintain the facade of Republican virtue, but it could gain the support of one class only at the expense of the other. In time, the republic lost the support of both classes simply by trying to steer a course between them.

Lacking satisfaction in the Azana coalition, the Spanish middle classes moved increasingly to the right in the hope that Anarchist violence and labor disorders generally would be definitely repressed. Translated into crass economic terms, this meant that the Spanish bourgeoisie and petty bourgeoisie, victimized by the world depression of the 1930s, saw its only hope for economic respite in a disciplined, well-mannered, and obedient proletariat whose economic needs would not be too demanding, or impose too grave a strain upon profit. Azana tried to demonstrate to the bourgeoisie that working-class collaboration could be achieved by means of political, religious, and trifling economic reforms. Ultimately, despite Socialist support, his "New Deal" for Spain failed miserably and the middle classes veered rightward toward parties that promised a stern government that could safeguard property and provide safety to the propertied classes.

It may well have been that Azana himself entertained precisely such a stern perspective in the closing months of his stewardship. As Gabriel Jackson points out, "he confided to his diary that deputies of three different parties were proposing a dictatorship as the only solution to continued anarchist risings, and that friends as well as enemies of the Republic were saying that things could not go on this way indefinitely." One might even suspect that the Socialist bureaucrats on whom Azana relied as perhaps the firmest pillar of the liberal republic would learn to adapt themselves to such a dictatorship, for they had proved themselves remarkably supple under Primo de Rivera. But the same economic and political forces that were pushing the Spanish middle classes to the right were also pushing the Socialist rank and file to the left. This single fact was crucial. Pressured by Anarchist militancy, by the newly recruited rural masses, and by the underlying instability of the economy, even such tried reformists as Largo Caballero began to veer to the left, if only to retain their influence over their own parties. To this growing radical constituency, the Azana coalition was a pathetic anachronism, a ruin from a more romantic era when social harmony seemed to be a greater desideratum than class war.

Finally, the most conspicuous weakness of the Azana coalition was its inability to resolve Spain's historic agrarian problem. Obsessed with legality and prudence, the *reparto* had been slowed to a snail's pace. Casas Viejas summed up what every Republican knew with aching intensity: the peninsula was on the brink of a peasant war. What must have struck home almost as poignantly as the barbarities of the Guards was the desperation of the peasants. No less sensational than newspaper photographs of strewn bodies was the evidence of the misery that had driven these peasants to sacrifice their lives in so uneven and hopeless a struggle. At Casas Viejas, the Azana coalition had shown that it could neither produce order without barbarity nor accept barbarity as a means of producing order. Extravagant in repressing rebellious villages, it foundered before a country that was swelling with revolution.

The Spanish Anarchists for their part not only dramatically exposed the Azana coalition's vulnerabilities at Casas Viejas; they continued their pressure against the republic through more conventional methods. Although the CNT had been declared an illegal organization after the events of January 1932, the Confederation regained sufficient strength in the spring of 1933 to launch on the most massive strike waves in its history. A plenum of regional Confederations at Madrid in late January and early February resolved to launch a general strike on behalf of amnesty for prisoners and freedom for closed-down and outlawed syndicates and periodicals, and against compulsory arbitration of labor disputes. It can hardly be emphasized too strongly that to a considerable extent, what has so facilely been described as FAI and CNT "adventurism" was a struggle for survival against the republic's favored treatment of the Socialists.

The UGT, openly abetted by Socialist ministers, civil servants, and their arbitration juries, had made serious inroads into traditional Anarchosyndicalist areas. The CNT had no choice but to reveal the Socialists, not only the *Treintistas*, as reformists, a task which was largely spearheaded by the much-maligned FAI. The popularity the FAI enjoyed among the more militant *cenetistas* in the early 1930s was not merely the product of social and economic instability in Spain, but stemmed in no small measure from the FAI's willingness to do many of the risky and thankless tasks which the staid CNT leaders were reluctant to undertake on behalf of their own syndicates. Mistaken as it surely was in so many of its tactics, the FAI was often more ill-served by CNT leaders (and by recent historians of Spanish Anarchism) than was the CNT by *faista* "adventurism."

CNT strikes now swept through Catalonia. In mid-April the potash miners walked out in Cardona, followed a few days later by the building workers in Barcelona. Shortly afterward, the dock workers went on strike. Before the spring was out, the city and eventually the country had been rocked by a general strike of nearly all CNT syndicates. Together with these strikes, the CNT launched a massive campaign to release imprisoned CNT-FAI militants whose numbers had now soared to about 9,000. The campaign was marked by immense demonstrations and rallies. In September, this movement reached its peak with a monster rally of 60,000 *cenetistas* in Barcelona's huge bull ring. The word "amnesty" appeared everywhere—on posters, as headlines in CNT-FAI periodicals, and on banners in the hands of demonstrators, although no amnesty was declared up to the last days of the Azana coalition. Although there was little doubt that the right would win the forthcoming elections, Azana was vindictive enough to turn these immense numbers of Anarchosyndicalist prisoners over to his reactionary opponents.

Ultimately, far more telling in its effect than the strikes was the *"No Votad"* campaign that the Confederation launched as the November elections drew near. From its printing presses, *centros obreras*, and syndicate offices, the CNT, eagerly assisted by the FAI, initiated an anti-electoral campaign unprecedented in the history of both organizations. On November 5, at an immense anti-electoral rally of 75,000 workers in the Barcelona bull ring, Durruti shouted: "Workers, you who voted yesterday without considering the consequences: if they told you that the Republic was going to jail 9,000 working men, would you have voted?" The question, by this time, was almost rhetorical; the crowd roared back a vigorous "No!"

This meeting was merely the culmination of months of smaller rallies in almost every city, town, and *pueblo* within the reach of the CNT; it represented the high point of a poster and press campaign whose essential message, besides "amnesty," was *"No Votad."* The Socialists, who had turned against Azana by now and decided to launch their own independent electoral campaign, were bluntly rebuffed in their efforts to gain Anarchosyndicalist votes. Warnings that a rightist victory would be followed by a fascist regime evoked a fairly characteristic (and, to this day, alluringly simplistic) reply: fascism would at least compel the proletariat to rise in revolution, whereas a reformist victory would simply lead to a piecemeal but ultimately more debilitating repression. A victory by the right was, in fact, now guaranteed not only by Azana's unpopularity but by the stormy anti-electoral campaign of the Anarchosyndicalists. At a FAI plenum held in Madrid during the last days of October, the delegates pressed the need to prepare for an uprising after the elections. The Peninsular Committee warned that "If the [anti-electoral] campaign yields practical results, the FAI must throw itself into the struggle that would follow a rightist victory." Accordingly, the delegates at the plenum resolved that "the upsurge of all our effectives into Social

Revolution must be our answer to any possible reactionary outbreak." Around the same time, a CNT plenum of Regional Confederations, also held in Madrid, adopted a similar resolution: "That if the fascist tendencies win in the elections, and for this or some other reason, the people become impassioned, the CNT has the responsibility of pushing on this popular desire in order to forge its goal of libertarian communism."

Notes

1. All the more remarkable, it should be added, because it was during this period that the *Solidarios* and other Anarchist action groups staged the series of spectacular bank holdups at Tarrasa, Manresa, at the "Fonda de Francia" opposite the civil government building in Barcelona, and, most notably, at the Banco de Espana in Gijon.

It is also worth noting how Arthur Landis, the "chronicler of the Abraham Lincoln Brigade" (as one admirer designates him) treats this sequence of events. "In 1923" writes Landis, "the CNT, under Anarchist direction dissolved itself," whereas the Socialist, "UGT did *not* do this; stayed alive, and helped lay the groundwork for the demise of the dictatorship and the overthrow of Alfonso XIII." Such distortions are not uncommon from historians of virtually all political connections.

2. The word "conditional" is used here to denote the fact that the CNT's statutes had to be approved by the provincial governor. The union's legality was still somewhat precarious in 1930. It is remarkable testimony to the influence of the CNT over the Barcelona proletariat that the government, despite Pestana's strong stand in his negotiations with Mola, was obliged to legalize the union.

3. Madariaga greatly exaggerates the ideological affinity of the Anarchosyndicalists for the Liberals. As we shall see, the animosity between the Socialists and the Anarchosyndicalists was so intense during the closing years of the dictatorship that the CNT workers voted for the Liberals out of sheer spitefulness.

4. Throughout the latter part of 1931, almost endemic violence engulfed the Barcelona port area for example, where the UGT tried to undermine the traditional hold of the CNT on the dock workers.

5. The long lapse between national congresses of the CNT should not be seen as evidence that the union was lacking in democracy. On the contrary, between national congresses the formulation of policy and initiative in action fell back to Regional, District, and even Local Federations. The need for coordinating or establishing policy on a national scale was usually effected through plenums of delegates from Regional Federations, but the regions and

districts usually did what they wanted anyway, even plunging into near-insurrections without gaining consent from national bodies.

6. The program of the Syndicalist Party is worth noting. The party called for a Socialist society based on economic self-management and federalism, the collectivization of land into free rural communes, and the coordination of industrial and commercial activities by the unions. The Cortes, in Pestaña's vision, would be replaced by a "National Chamber of Labor" in which the unions and rural communes would be fully represented. Pestaña, although advocating a highly flexible strategy which included electoral politics as well as direct action, did not renounce his Anarchist beliefs. He regarded Anarchism as a moral philosophy which played a key role in educating and improving people until such time as they could establish a fully libertarian society.

7. In all fairness to other members of *Nosotros* I have found no evidence that Durruti or the Ascaso brothers supported Garcia Oliver's authoritarian views. If they did, it would have been more out of personal loyalty (a very important factor within FAI affinity groups) than a matter of considered political conviction or programatic agreement. *"Los Tres Mosqueteros,"* as Garcia Oliver, Durruti, and Francisco Ascaso were called, were by no means the same personalities. Brenan, in an excellent discussion of the matter, draws important distinctions between Durruti and Francisco Ascaso on the one hand and Garcia Oliver on the other, which I have confirmed through personal contact with Spanish Anarchists who knew all of them:

> Durruti was a powerful man with brown eyes and an innocent expression and Ascaso a little dark man of insignificant appearance. Inseparable friends, they had together robbed banks, assassinated enemies of the cause and been in the forefront of innumerable strikes and acts of violence. Most of their lives had been spent in prison: as soon as they came out they returned to their humble work in the factory, for, naturally, none of the money they acquired by their forcible expropriations (on one occasion they opened and emptied a safe in the Bank of Spain) was kept for themselves. . . . Garcia Oliver, on the other hand, belonged rather to the type of Irish revolutionary of 1919. Though a workman by origin and only partly educated, his political instincts were well developed. He was credited with a special flair for the revolutionary feeling of the masses and for the right moment for action. He thus became the leading tactician of this period and the organizer of its various revolutionary strikes and insurrections. Only, being an Anarchist, he did not remain like a general in the background, but led his men with bomb and revolver in his hand himself.

The simplicity of Durruti and Ascaso should be contrasted with the "political instincts" and "flair" of Garcia Oliver. These different traits guided Durruti and Garcia Oliver in two contrasting directions: Durruti became the head of a militia column and was killed in Madrid; Garcia Oliver became—a minister of justice in the Popular Front government.

8. Brenan's account, although scanty, seems to be accurate enough with respect to the opening phase of the event. Peirat's account is more detailed on its closing phase. Among the more grotesque features of the story, mentioned by neither Brenan nor Peirats, is that the partially burnt corpses were left on display as warnings to the villagers. According to press accounts of the event, the Guards were reported to have rounded up innocent villagers at Casas Viejas and forced them into the pyre that consumed *Seisdedos* and his party.

Chapter Ten:
The Road to Revolution

El Bienio Negro

The parliamentary elections of November 19, 1933, brought an overwhelming victory to the right and ushered in what the Spanish labor movement was to call *el bienio negro*—the two black years. Yet despite this harsh characterization, the period generally fell far short of the fearful prognoses advanced by the labor movement. Newly organized fascist groups such as the JONS and the Falange, the latter led by Jose Antonio Primo de Rivera, the dictator's charismatic son, had supported the right. They supplied it with a sufficient amount of street thuggery to arouse fears that Spain was following the same path that had just brought the Nazis to power in Germany. But the Falange, even after it had absorbed the fascistic JONS, (*Juntas de Ofensiva Nacional Sindicalista*), barely numbered 3,000 members. Despite the adulation the young Primo de Rivera aroused among reactionary university students and aristocratic youth, his influence on larger sections of the Spanish population was negligible.

The real victors of November consisted largely of indecisive coalitions of the center as well as the right, notably Alejandro Lerroux's opportunistic Radicals and Jose Maria Gil Robles's CEDA (*Confederacion Espanola de Derechos Autonomos,* or Confederation of Autonomous Right Parties), a coalition of Catholic and Monarchist groups that mouthed the reactionary platitudes of "Religion," "Family," "Fatherland," "Work," "Order," and "Property" against secularism, labor "disorders," and "anarchy." The CEDA, with 110 seats, became the largest single party in the Cortes, followed by the Radicals with 100 seats. Gil Robles's coalition acquired its support primarily from industrialists, landowners, Carlist peasants, clerics, and devout Catholics, no small number of whom were newly enfranchised women who voted according to the dictates of their local priests. The Radical Party mustered most of its votes from anti-Socialist urban middle classes. The greatest parliamentary problem facing the CEDA and the Radicals was the need, first, to allay the fears of troubled Liberals who, while drifting to the right, were deeply mistrustful of Gil Robles's reactionary and military connections, and second, perhaps more seriously, to reconcile the devoutly Catholic CEDA with the traditionally anticlerical Radicals.

The new regime began by trying to keep Gil Robles in the background and thrusting Lerroux forward as prime minister. Lerroux, a pure adventurer, occupied himself by replacing one demogogic personality with another. The anticleric of yesteryear became a guardian of the church. In fairly rapid order the Lerroux ministry restored most of the clerical salaries which the Constituent Cortes guided by Azana had abolished, also returning substantial church properties which that Cortes had confiscated. Church schools were reopened and any objectionable anticlerical legislation which was not directly repealed was simply ignored.

Having made its peace with the church, the new ministry began an unconscionable assault upon the meager social legislation enacted by the Constituent Cortes. Agrarian reform, limited as it was, came to a dead halt. Pro-industry chairmen replaced Largo Caballero's pro-labor (more precisely, pro-Socialist) appointees. Agricultural wage increases achieved under the Azana coalition were rolled back 40-50 percent and, as if to warn the peasants and workers of the futility of resistance, the number of Civil Guards was increased by a thousand. The cabinet even tried to restore the death penalty, but its efforts were frustrated by the Cortes.

Despite the harshness of the Lerroux program, it failed miserably. Like the Azana coalition, the new ministry satisfied no one on the right and served only to increase the militancy of the left. Lerroux became snarled in sharp disputes over attempts to grant amnesty to the Sanjurjo military conspirators who had risen earlier in Seville. He was replaced by another Radical, Ricardo Samper, who, in turn, found himself beleaguered by the problems of Basque and Catalan nationalism, by contraband arms that were flowing into the country and reaching the left as well as the right (even the old Socialist right-winger, Indalecio Prieto, was involved in smuggling arms into Asturias), by gunplay between Falangists, Socialists, and Anarchists, and finally by the CEDA's threat to deny the Radical ministry its vote of confidence if it was denied posts in the cabinet.

Whether or not right and center parties on their own could have won the November elections, this much is certain: the Anarchosyndicalist anti-electoral campaign had contributed decisively to the magnitude of their victory. The abstentionist propaganda of the CNT and FAI had been conducted under the slogan: "*Frente a las urnas, la revolucion social*"—"Before ballot boxes, social revolution."

Having advanced revolution as the alternative to parliamentary reform, the Anarchosyndicalists now had to deliver the goods. But
could they do so? The January insurrections of 1932 and 1933 had
taken their toll in thousands of imprisoned militants, depleted resources, and lowered morale. At a plenum of regional confederations
held in October, most of the delegates probably opposed an uprising,
"but not openly," as A.M. Lehning reported. Only a few delegations,
most notably the Aragonese, pressed for an uprising. The other delegations merely promised to give what aid they could. This lagging of
enthusiasm was portentous. Failure was being built into the insurrection well in advance of its occurrence and, given the lack of any
tactical sense of timing and resources, rhetoric was being offered as a
substitute for even the most remote possibility of success. It is
noteworthy that Garcia Oliver, who had been so instrumental in
fomenting earlier *faista* uprisings, broke openly with Durruti for the
first time by attacking an insurrection as absurd.

The uprising was timed for December 8, 1933, the opening day of
the new Cortes. In Barcelona, it began with a spectacular prison break
in which many militants who had been imprisoned for participating
in the Tarassa events tunnelled their way to freedom. The government, alert to the Anarchosyndicalist plans, headed off strikes by
declaring a state of emergency, arresting leading *cenetistas* and *faistas*,
imposing press censorship, and closing down the syndicates. Similar
steps were taken in Madrid and other possible insurrectionary centers. In Valencia, where the Opposition Syndicates exercised considerable influence, the strike orders of the CNT's National Committee
were largely ignored.

Only Aragon rose on any significant scale, particularly Saragossa,
where *faista* notables such as Durruti, Isaac Puente, and Cipriano
Mera had gone to organize the insurrection. Again, the government
acted decisively to forestall an uprising; on the night of the eighth,
nearly a hundred militants (including Durruti, Puente, and Mera)
were arrested. Deprived of their ablest people, the workers nevertheless reared barricades, attacked public buildings, and engaged in
heavy street fighting. But the uprising was disorganized and quickly
subdued. Following the pattern of previous insurrections, many villages declared libertarian communism and perhaps the heaviest fighting took place between the vineyard workers in Rioja and the authorities. Within four days, the entire insurrectionary movement was
crushed. Perhaps the most noteworthy break in the *faista* pattern of
ill-prepared rising, sporadic conflicts, shortlived localized victories,
and swift triumphs by the army occurred in Villanueva de Serena,
where a group of soldiers under a Sergeant Sopena joined the insurrection. For the rest, Anarchosyndicalist militants were arrested in

the thousands, their presses stopped, and their syndicates closed down.

According to Brenan, "What was remarkable about this rising was that for the first time in Spain clear instructions were issued for a social revolution. Mills and factories were taken over by the workers, and factory committees set up. Other committees for food, transport and so on were organized on the lines set down by Kropotkin. The rising was regarded as a rehearsal for the coming revolution, if not as the actual beginning of it." Perhaps—but I have found nothing exceptional about the December uprising as compared with its predecessors. Wherever possible, earlier insurrections had carried out industrial and agrarian takeovers and established committees for workers' and peasants' control, libertarian systems of logistics and distribution—in short, a miniature society "organized on the lines set down by Kropotkin." Indeed, what is perhaps most striking about the December uprising is the extent to which it was localized in Aragon, the palpable lack of enthusiasm for it, and the opposition it encountered from flagging militants like Garcia Oliver.

In any case, with the December uprising, the Anarchist-led "cycle of insurrections" had come to its end. Azana himself virtually admitted that these insurrections contributed to his downfall. The electoral abstentionist campaign had also contributed to the victory of the Radicals and the CEDA. For better or worse, Anarchosyndicalism had proven itself the force most like to exacerbate polarization, labor unrest, and social disequilibrium in Spain. To condemn the Anarchists for producing "anarchy" is simply silly; for the more idealistic Anarchists not to foment unrest, revolutionary upheavals, and ultimately social revolution would have been completely out of character. One can snicker at their tactics, naivete, and recklessness but more than any other single force in Spain they had shattered the facade of liberalism and paved the way for an historic confrontation between the great contending social classes in the peninsula.

As for the December revolt, far from being "a rehearsal for the coming revolution," it was the most destructive exercise in futility ever undertaken by the CNT and FAI. Indeed, it significantly eroded the fighting power of the two organizations. Perhaps the example set by the uprising succeeded in fostering the militancy of the growing left factions in the Socialist Party, but apart from strike actions and terrorism, it completely exhausted the movement. Henceforth, the Spanish Anarchists were to occupy themselves primarliy with recovering their forces and uniting their ranks. The initiative for revolutionary action in Spain was to pass to the Socialist left, particularly to the Asturian miners and the newly converted peasants of the south. The great October Insurrection in the mining districts of Asturias was

GARCIA VIVANCOS, GARCIA OLIVER, LOUIS LECOIN, PIERRE FRANCISCO ASCASO and BUENAVENTURA DURRUTI. Garcia Oliver (1901-), Ascaso (1890?-1936), and Durruti (1896-1936), the most well-known of the *Nosotros*, an FAI action group, were to gain national reputation for their courage and daring in bank robberies, atentados, and insurrections.

FRANCISCO ASCASO and BUENAVENTURA DURRUTI
with their wives in Brussels.

drawing near—and with it, the real "rehearsal for the coming revolution. . . ." But in this "rehearsal," the institutions of neither the UGT nor the CNT played a significant role as such; rather, the workers were the principal sources of revolutionary initiative. In this respect these workers behaved as Anarchists even when they were avowedly committed to Socialism.

The CNT and FAI, to be sure, were still intact, despite the arrests, losses, and disorganization they had suffered over the previous two years. Even Saragossa, which had suffered the heaviest casualties in the December uprising, had not lost its celebrated fervor and militancy. In April the Aragonese city was paralyzed by one of the most extraordinary general strikes to occur in the stormy history of the Spanish labor movement—a strike lasting nearly five weeks whose spirit of self-sacrifice, solidarity, and tenacity reached heroic proportions. The strike was occasioned by acts of police brutality which followed the explosion of a bomb in front of the police headquarters. The two-day protest strike which followed the mistreatment of arrested workers was extended into a 36-day general strike when several bus and tram drivers who refused to return to work were deprived of their licenses. Before the week was out, industry, transportation, and nearly all services in Saragossa were at a complete standstill.

Typically, the civil governor compounded the crisis by declaring the strike illegal and calling out the troops. The workers, more determined than ever, doggedly continued to stay out despite enormous material sacrifices. The entire CNT, particularly the Catalan Regional Confederation, now rallied behind its Saragossa comrades. To lighten the burden of the Saragossa workers, the Barcelona proletariat under Durruti organized a spectacular caravan to bring the children of the strikers to Catalonia. Fleets of taxis were mobilized to convey 13,000 children to the thousands of *cenetista* families which had pledged to care for them. Here, as Brenan observes, the *cenetistas* revealed where their real strength lay: "not in their armed revolts, but in their powers of syndical resistance. . . . When one remembers that the CNT had no strike funds, one can appreciate the courage and endurance required in these contests. If the Anarcho-Syndicalists could not bring off their revolution, they aat all events knew how to keep a revolutionary situation alive."

By now a new issue began to come to the fore. The Socialists, pressured by the example of Anarchist intransigence, by hundreds of thousands of newly recruited, often feverishly militant rural workers, disillusioned by their alliance with the Liberals, and fearful of what seemed like a drift toward fascism in the government, began to raise the cry for an *Alianza Obrera*—for a "united front" of all the labor organizations in Spain. This *Alianza*, so characteristic of policies that began to prevail among leftist political groups in Europe and America during the mid-1930s, particularly after a bitterly conflicted German left had capitulated to Hitler, was to be advanced by Largo Caballero. The slogan, in fact, had been raised as early as October 1933, when Pestana, on behalf of the *Treintistas*, spelled out the need for an "entente," a "coalition" of the UGT and CNT to stop fascism in Spain. Peiro, in elucidating this position, emphasized that the *Alianza Obrera* was not to be conceived as an electoral pact, indeed, that it implied direct action in opposition to fascism and on behalf of a "Federalist Social Republic." A pact between factions of the Catalan left had, in fact, come into existence shortly after the December uprising of the Anarchists, but it did not include the CNT or the FAI who were wary of the new "allies." Experience had nurtured a deep mistrust among the Anarchists toward the UGT, the Opposition Syndicates, the Socialist Party affiliates of Barcelona, Maurin's Worker-Peasant Bloc, Nin's Left Communists, and the union of the vineyard workers in Catalonia, the *Rabassaires*, who were under the control Luis Companys's liberal nationalist party, the *Esquerra*. To the degree that these disparate, generally authoritarian groups formed an alliance, the Anarchists could regard it only as a mischievous one which had to be shunned.

Not unexpectedly, the *Alianza* received considerable support from the moderate CNT in Asturias. Largo Caballero's drift to the left after the elections of 1933 had made a pact with the UGT more seductive than ever. Although the CNT as a whole retained its hostility toward the alliance, at a June plenum of regional confederations its opposition was modified to allow for agreements with the UGT on a local level. This qualification simply ratified an independent alliance which the Asturian CNT had made four months earlier with the local UGT, thereby setting the stage for the forthcoming October uprising of the Asturian miners. Officially, however, and to a large degree in practice, the CNT preserved its aloofness toward the *Alianza*. In early autumn, the CNT, apart from its Asturian confederation, responded to a spate of *Alianza*-inspired strikes with qualified support at best or with total indifference. The *Alianza Obrera* had much less magnetism than has been imputed to it in many discussions of the Spanish labor movement. Even Maurin of the Worker-Peasant Bloc failed to "recall the enthusiasm attributed to him in Brenan's account" observes Gabriel Jackson in a note based on an interview with Maurin. "He spoke of the Alianza as having been crippled from the start by antipathy between Caballero and the Catalans, nor does *El Socialista* [the organ of the Spanish Socialist Party—M.B.] for the spring and summer of 1934 give the impression that the new movement was very important."

The status of the *Alianza Obrera*, however, was to change significantly in October 1934. As autumn approached a heightened sense of militancy, paralleling the trajectory of the Spanish labor movement, began to sweep over the right. Internal pressures on Gil Robles to stake out the CEDA's ministerial claims on the Ricardo Semper government, which had resisted the entry of the CEDA into the cabinet, mounted steadily. With the convening of the Cortes on October 1, the CEDA, demanding seats in the cabinet, dramatically toppled the Radical government. Despite his profound hostility to Gil Robles, President Alcala Zamora had no choice but to accede to the CEDA's demands. Shortly after the cabinet crisis, the president called upon Lerroux to form a second cabinet, this time one in which the CEDA would be granted three ministries.

Today, looking back after more than forty years, it is difficult to convey the impact this concession had on the Spanish left. The CEDA, a Catholic party supported largely by funds from rabidly reactionary Monarchist contributors, seemed to be the exact Spanish counterpart of the Austrian Catholics who had raised Dollfuss to power in the early 1930s. Only shortly before the CEDA had received seats in the cabinet, Dollfuss had proclaimed himself virtual dictator of Austria and his ascent to power had been marked by the harsh suppression of a Socialist uprising in Vienna after a week of severe street fighting. Artillery had been callously turned on the Karl Marx houses, a cooperative complex of workers' dwellings in the Austrian capital. Among the Socialists the cry quickly went up, "Better Vienna than Berlin," an unmistakable allusion to the fact that the hopeless but courageous resistance of the Austrian proletariat to fascism was better than the supine acquiescence of the German left to Hitler.

The crisis triggered by the CEDA's entry into the cabinet was not limited to the Socialists. It also had its echo among the Catalan autonomists. Despite the large Lliga delegation in the Cortes, representing the victory of the conservative Catalan industrialists in the 1933 elections, the Catalan Generalitat which governed the province on a local level was controlled by Luis Companys's *Esquerra* (the Catalan Left), an autonomist middle-class movement whose views, under Companys's influence, were more closely wedded to Azana's Republicans than to the separatist tendencies within Catalan nationalism. The *Esquerra* had come to power in the local elections that followed the 1933 fiasco, after many Catalan *cenetistas* had second thoughts about the impact of their anti-electoral campaign and had voted, at least locally, for Liberal groups. Under Companys, the *Esquerra* had begun to abandon the unequivocally separatist policies of its founder, Colonel Macia (who died in December 1933) and was in the process of orienting itself toward autonomy within the Spanish republic. Companys, a shrewd politician, had acquired a certain status as a crypto-radical. At considerable personal risk, he had used his legal talents to defend many *cenetista* militants in the trials of the 1920s. Perhaps more than any republican politician in Spain, he retained important connections and undeservedly high credibility with the CNT leadership long after liberals of his breed were to be completely discredited with the Spanish working class.

In Catalonia, Companys was also a major rival of the CNT. He competed with the Anarchosyndicalists by organizing tenant farmers of the vineyards into the *Union de Rabassaires*, an *Esquerra*-controlled trade union. The *Esquerra*, to retain its influence in the rural areas of the province, had promoted and passed a *ley de cultivos* in the Generalitat empowering vineyard tenants whose leases were expiring to acquire title to land they had cultivated for fifteen years or more. Completely regional in character, this law was confined exclusively to Catalonia; it had been passed by a provincial authority whose political interests were limited to local concerns. Yet in June 1933, even this circumscribed piece of legislation was so antithetical to Madrid's conservative agrarian policies that it was overturned by the Tribunal of Constitutional Guarantees, the Spanish equivalent of the American Supreme Court. By voting against the *ley de cultivos* the court upheld not only the landlords against the tenants, but the power of Madrid to curb regionalist legislation. Even the conservative, strongly Catholic Basque deputies to the Cortes protested, all the more because they had been repaid for their support of Lerroux and the CEDA with frustrating indifference toward a proposed Basque autonomy statute.

The Basques now threw their support to the Catalan Left on the *Rabassaires* law. Their action was a portent of the future Popular Front alignment of 1936, which was to unite Basque conservatives, the Catalan Left, the Azana Republicans, the Socialists, and the Communists in an ill-fitting electoral bloc against reaction and the threat of fascism. The CEDA's ministerial demands had divided even the Radicals. Samper, the out-going Radical prime minister, warned darkly on October 1: "Confronted by a period of oppression and shame, no way out remains except for a revolutionary outbreak. If Gil Robles' forces of the Right do not evince any understanding [of the emerging situation], the road to legality will be removed."

This verbal saber-rattling should not be taken too seriously. As events were to show, for most Radicals, indeed even for Companys, it was mere rhetoric. Companys, urged by his followers to pursue an insurrectionary course after the *ley de cultivos* had been overturned by the courts, was more the victim of a crisis within the *Esquerra* than within the Cortes. Sections of the *Esquerra*, itself a bloc of disparate elements, had been moving toward their own version of militancy.

The *escamots* (or squads), a quasi-fascistic, paramilitary youth group of the *Esquerra*, exerted mounting pressure on Companys and his moderates to seize power and declare an independent Catalan republic. Led by Jose Dencas, a councilor of public order who detested the CNT and FAI, the *escamots* had begun to occupy portions of Barcelona in open defiance of the vacillating Companys. Together with other separatists, they demanded a clear-cut separation of Catalonia from Madrid.

Companys, in the meantime, was secretly making frantic telephone calls to the president of the republic in Madrid (who did not respond to them personally), warning Alcala Zamora's secretary that he could not contain the *Rabassaires* on the left and the *escamots* on the right. Huge crowds collected before the building that housed the Generalitat, demanding decisive action; indeed, Barcelona was placarded with demands for an independent Catalonia. The situation had degenerated to *opera bouffe*. Companys, his back to the wall, went through the public motions of declaring a "Catalan State within the Federal Spanish Republic" (a far cry from the outright independence the crowds were clamoring for) and quickly barricaded himself inside the Generalitat building, awaiting rescue by the central government's troops. A "surrender" with "dignity" was arranged at dawn and Companys was provided with the safety of a prison cell on charges of "rebellion." Dencas, whether because he scented failure, as Jackson observes, or because he had been a CEDA *agent provocateur*, as Brenan argues, took to his heels across the frontier and finally found political asylum in Mussolini's Italy.

It is important to stress these events because they exercised a profound influence on Anarchist policy during the October Insurrection of the Asturian miners. As a scenario of things to come, they provide a remarkable image of how the Liberals, whether in Madrid or Catalonia, were to respond to the more serious military rebellion of July 1936. Irresolution, paralyzing panic, and above all, a greater fear of the working classes than of any threat posed by reaction, had been the ingrained traits of Liberal behavior. As for the Catalan autonomists and separatists, they had hoped to achieve their goals by riding on the crest of a general strike initiated by the Socialists. This strike, called officially in the name of the *Alianza Obrera*, formed the UGT's strategic response to the second Lerroux ministry with its three CEDA members.

In Catalonia, no such strike could possibly hope to succeed without CNT support. The CNT, which had been left to its own devices in the December uprising against the first Lerroux cabinet, was in no mood to respond to Socialist appeals of an ill-defined programmatic character. In Anarchist eyes the *Alianza* had fallen far short of a serious revolutionary force. Toward the *Esquerra* the CNT had good reasons to nourish the strongest feelings of antipathy: the night before the outbreak of the *Alianza* strike, the Generalitat's police had arrested scores of Anarchist militants, including Durruti, and closed down *Solidaridad Obrera*. Attempts by *cenetistas* to reopen syndicate headquarters that had been closed since the December rising encountered armed resistance from the *escamots*, who fired directly on the workers. Dencas took to the radio and denounced *faistas* as "anarchist provocateurs in the pay of reaction," calling upon his *escamots* and the police to take firm measures against them. The Generalitat, more fearful of the workers than the CEDA ministers, had even alienated the *Alianza Obrera*. Although Companys was quite willing to declare a "Catalan State" in complicity with the *Alianza* by inviting it in to his "new" government, the *Esquerra*-controlled Generalitat flatly refused to arm the workers. Bitterness and disillusionment infected the Catalan labor movement. The CNT, which participated half-heartedly in the *Alianza* strike, ordered its members back to work, dissociating itself from the entire adventure. With the surrender of the Generalitat, the autonomist movement collapsed throughout Catalonia.

Elsewhere, the general strike called by the *Alianza Obrera* had mixed consequences, indeed, in some areas highly dramatic and historic ones. Suprisingly, in Socialist Madrid, the strike almost assumed the comic opera forms it had acquired in Barcelona. Although the Socialists had presumably been planning the strike in the Spanish capital since the summer, almost every aspect of the plan went awry. The police were well-informed about the Socialists' intentions and arrested the Socialist-contolled Revolutionary Government before it could be installed. The arrests netted Largo Caballero, who was in charge of the strike and the rising. A curious listlessness seemed to afflict the Madrid leadership. The writing of the *Alianza's* program had been left to the right-wing Socialist Indalecio Prieto, who listed a series of demands hardly differing from those that would have been prepared by Liberal Republicans. Coordination between the striking groups in the *Alianza* proved to be incredibly shabby and amateurish. A massive strike in Madrid, which was supported by the entire left, foundered for want of arms and a revolutionary sense of direction.

As usual, the Socialists emerged as unreliable allies of the Anarchists. A revolutionary committee, established by the CNT and FAI to coordinate their own operations, was denied direly needed weapons by the UGT. The arms, as it turned out, had been conveniently intercepted by government troops. But even if they had been available, it is almost certain that the Socialists would not have shared them with the Anarchists. Indeed, relationships between the two major sectors of the labor movement had already been poisoned by the failure of the Socialist Youth and the UGT to keep the CNT adequately informed of their plans or to confer with Anarchosyndicalist delegates. Despite heavy fighting in Madrid, the CNT and FAI were obliged to function largely on their own. When, at length, a UGT delegate informed the revolutionary committee that Largo Caballero was not interested in common action with the CNT, the committee disbanded. Later, Abad de Santillan was to observe with ample justification that Socialist attempts to blame the failure of the October Insurrection on Anarchist abstention was a shabby falsehood:

> Can there be talk of abstention of the CNT and censure of it by those who go on strike without warning our organization about it, who refuse to meet with the delegates of the National Committee [of the CNT], who consent to let the Lerroux-Gil Robles Government take possession of the arms deposits and let them go unused before handing them over to the Confederation and the FAI?

Alvarez del Vayo, one of Largo Caballero's most trusted colleagues, gives us a remarkably candid insight into Socialist policy during the opening days of the uprising. Nearly all the adverse circumstances that ensnarled the insurrection "could have been partly offset if there had not been too much delay about the order to start," he observes.

> The twenty-four hours during which the government was being formed [by Lerroux and Alcala Zamora] were decisive. To the very last, Caballero, to say nothing of Prieto, nursed the hope that President Alcala Zamora would not take into the cabinet known enemies of the Republic. When the news came that the coalition government had been completed, Caballero was with Prieto and a couple of other leaders of the movement. Caballero's comment revealed his stubborn desire to trust Alcala Zamora: "Until I see it in the *Official Gazette*, I won't believe it." Caballero's closest associates, including myself, earnestly insisted that the rising should begin that same night, October 4. In the end Caballero gave in, but by then it was too late. It had to be postponed until the next night. During those twenty-four hours martial law was declared, and this meant the collapse by its own weight of the plan for military cooperation. Under martial law all officers, pro and anti-republican, were confined to barracks. Thus, when the rising finally got under way, its chances were much diminished. We found ourselves lacking the military support on which we had counted; the Socialist militias were in the street but were unable by themselves to carry out the crucial missions assigned to them.

What is absent in Alvarez del Vayo's account is that, military support

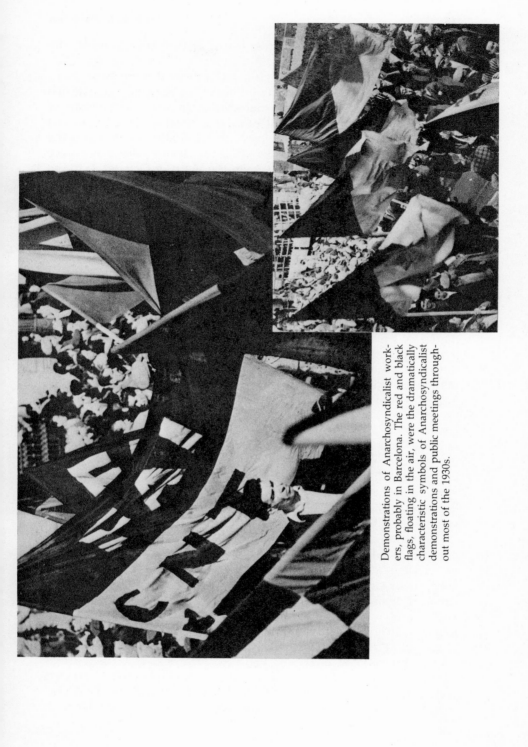

Demonstrations of Anarchosyndicalist workers, probably in Barcelona. The red and black
flags, floating in the air, were the dramatically
characteristic symbols of Anarchosyndicalist
demonstrations and public meetings throughout most of the 1930s.

or not, the considerable Anarchist forces in the capital were coldly rebuffed.

Almost unknown to Madrid, indeed to the rest of Spain, a major rising was launched in the mining districts of Asturias—one which was to add a haunting sense of tragedy and grandeur to the October events.[1] The miners, irrespective of their political affiliation, took the call for a general strike very seriously. As S.J. Brademas observes, the Asturian miners of all unions regarded the *Alianza Obrera* as "more than pious revolutionary jargon." On the night of October 4, to the sound of sirens in the valley towns along the Aller and Nalon rivers, the miners began their strike with attacks on Civil Guard and Assault Guard barracks. The great majority of the Asturian miners belonged to the UGT, although the CNT enjoyed a considerable influence of its own. In recent years, the Communists had assumed control of several union locals and presumably it was in the Communist-controlled town of Mieres that the most dramatic initiatives were reported.[2] There, some 200 militants besieged the police barracks and town hall with about 30 rifles, firing the same rifles from different positions to create an exaggerated impression of their stength. Following the surrender of the Civil and Assault Guards, they proceeded to occupy towns along the route to Oviedo, the provincial capital of Asturias, until on October 6 they attacked the city itself. In fact at this time a miners' column of 8,000, a force well beyond the numbers the Communists could have mobilized, began to occupy all of Oviedo with the exception of the Pelago and Santa Clara barracks, where sizeable government troops continued to hold out. For the first time, the famous Asturian *dinamiteros* appeared in force: the recklessly bold miners who were to compensate for their lack of guns and artillery with sticks of dynamite. The Asturians had learned to do more than mine coal; they were also skilled blasters who were to gain an awesome reputation in October 1934 and later in the Civil War for their skill with explosives and their unsurpassable courage.

Within a matter of days, the miners had occupied most of the Aller and Nalon valley towns, nearly all of Oviedo, and the industrial city of La Felguera. Attempts were also being made to seize the strategic seaports of Gijon and Aviles, and it was here that the insurrection came up against its gravest political obstacles. The workers of Aviles and Gijon were largely under Anarchist influence. They too had joined the uprising under the local *Alianza* slogan of *"Union, Hermanos Proletarias"* ("Unity, Proletarian Brothers"), the famous "UHP" which was to be initialed on walls, vehicles, factories, and troop trains throughout the Civil War. So far as the Aviles and Gijon Anarchists were concerned, however, their Socialist and Communist "brothers" were to honor the slogan only in the breach. When Anarchist delegates from the seaports arrived in Oviedo on October 7, pleading for arms to resist the imminent landings of government troops, their requests were totally ignored by Socialists and Communists who, as Jackson notes, "clearly mistrusted them. . . ." The Oviedo Committee was to pay a bitter price for its refusal. The next day, when Anarchist resistance, hampered by the pitiful supply of weapons, failed to prevent the government from landing its troops, the way into Asturias lay open. The two seaports became the principal military bases for launching the savage repression of the Asturian insurrection that occupied so much of October and claimed thousands of lives.

The Asturian insurrection lasted some two weeks, roughly from October 5 to October 18. During this brief period, the miners had behaved with exemplary dignity and moral rectitude. "For the best of the militant elements," observes Jackson, "the revolutionary regime was to be a demonstration of proletarian morality. Bourgeois received the same food rations as did workers. In the hospital, doctors were instructed to treat equally the government wounded and the revolutionary wounded. Non-political middle-class and professional people were to be protected, even at the risk of life, by the revolutionary militia." Anarchists, far from running "amuck" (as so often predicted by their opponents on the left as well as the right), were perhaps even more exemplary in their behavior than the dour Communists and many Socialists, whose authoritarian tendencies fostered a repressive atmosphere in the areas under their control. Peirats, in fact, regarded the Asturian Anarchists as excessively naive owing to the feelings of reconciliation and good-naturedness that marked their behavior toward erstwhile social enemies. In any case, when military repression by the government replaced proletarian dignity, "many a surviving soldier and priest testified to the efforts of the [revolutionary] committee leaders to prevent the assassination of priests and prisoners, intervention which had saved dozen of lives."

Notwithstanding the propaganda of the period—a propaganda inspired as much by the Communists as by the government—the Asturian insurrection made no attempt to establish soviets, much less a "soviet republic." Structurally, the insurrection was managed by hundreds of small revolutionary committees whose delegates were drawn from unions, parties, the FAI, and even anti-Stalinist Communist groups. Rarely, if at all, were there large councils (or "soviets") composed of delegates from factories. Indeed, the notion of councils, on the Russian models of 1905 and 1917, was alien to the Spanish labor movement. The Socialists generally functioned through tightly knit committees, commonly highly centralized and with strong bureaucratic proclivities. In Asturias, the UGT tried to perpetuate this form wherever possible, at most admitting Communists and moderate *cenetistas* into their "revolutionary committees." But the mountainous terrain of Asturias made such committees difficult to coordinate, so that each one became an isolated miniature central committee of its own, often retaining its traditional authoritarian character. The Anarchists, on the other hand, favored looser structures, often quasi-councils composed of factory workers and assemblies composed of peasants. The ambience of these fairly decentralized structures, their improvisatory character and libertarian spirit, fostered an almost festive atmosphere in Anarchist-held areas.

This difference is vividly conveyed by Avelino Gonzalez Mellada, who compares Anarchist-controlled La Felguera with Marxist-controlled Sama. Both towns, he observes, were of equal size and were separated from each other only by the Nalon river. They were linked to each other by two bridges. The October Insurrection,

> triumphed immediately in the metallurgical and in the mining town. . . . Sama was organized along military lines. Dictatorship of the proletariat, red army, Central Committee, discipline, authority. . . . La Felguera opted for *comunismo libertario*: the people in arms, liberty to come and go, respect for the technicians of the Duro-Felguera metallurgical plant, public deliberations of all issues, abolition of money, the rational distribution of food and clothing. Enthusiasm and gaiety in La Felguera; the sullenness of the barracks in Sama. The bridges [of Sama] were held by a corp of guards complete with officers and all. No one could enter or leave Sama without a safe-conduct pass, or walk through the streets without passwords. All of this was ridiculously useless, because the government troops were far away and the Sama bourgeoisie was disarmed and neutralized. . . . The workers of Sama who did not adhere to the Marxist religion preferred to go to La Felguera, where at least they could breathe. Side by side there were two concepts of socialism: the authoritarian and the libertarian; on each bank of the Nalon, two populations of brothers began a new life: with a dictatorship in Sama; with liberty in La Felgeura. . . .

In contrast to the severely delimited Marxist committee in Sama, La Felguera workers met in popular assembly, where they socialized the industrial city's economy. The population was divided into wards, each of which elected delegates to supply and distribution committees. The committees determined the consumption needs of the wards, managed transport facilities, and assumed responsibility for the medical and sanitary needs of the city. The La Felguera commune, so rarely mentioned in most accounts of the Spanish labor movement, proved to be so successful, indeed so admirable, that surrounding communities invited the La Felguera Anarchists to advise them on reorganizing their own social order. Rarely were comparable institutions created by the Socialists and, where they did emerge, it was on the insistence of the rank-and-file workers. At Mieres, by contrast, the Communists established a crassly authoritarian *comite de guerra*, which even preempted the rights of the town's revolutionary committee. So preoccupied were the Socialists and Communists with asserting their sectarian control over Asturian towns that Marxist militias which should have been fighting in desperately beleaguered Oviedo were kept at home for strictly political purposes.

Every one of these situations was to reappear in the Civil War two years later, and on a larger, more terrifying scale. Anarchist militias were to be denied arms and support in desperate military situations while the choicest weapons were to be reserved for Communist and Republican police detachments behind the front lines. These detachments were to serve more as forces to subvert social revolution than to ferret out Franco supporters. The CNT and FAI were to experience the full gamut of treachery at the hands of every group in the Popular Front—from the Caballero "left" Socialists to the openly counter-revolutionary Communists. Almost alone, the Anarchists were to create viable revolutionary institutions structured around workers' control of industry and peasants' control of the land. That these institutions were to be duplicated by Socialist workers and peasants was to be due in no small measure to Anarchist example rather than Socialist precept. To the degree that the Asturian miners and industrial workers in various communities established direct control over the local economy and structured their committees along libertarian lines, these achievements were due to Anarchist precedents and long years of propaganda and education.

The Asturian insurrection revealed not only the deep-seated divisions that permeated the left but the capacity for savage repression that was to mark the right in later years. Lerroux, distrustful of Spanish troops on the peninsula, dispatched the Foreign Legion (*Tercio*) and mercenary Moorish troops (*Regulares*) to Aviles and Gijon, mercilessly unleashing them on the Asturian insurrectionists. The job of commanding the campaign was assigned to a General Francisco Franco, who had earned a reputation for molding the *Tercio* into the most effective fighting force in the Spanish army. This use of the *Regulares* and *Tercio* was without precedent in the history of Spain. The irony of using the Foreign Legion and the Moslem *Regulares* on the sacred Christian soil of Asturias is conveyed with telling effect by Brenan:

In 1931, just before the fall of the monarchy, a regiment of the *Tercio* had been brought over from Africa on the King's express wish to put down the expected republican rising. They had broken out and committed their usual depredations and Major [Ramon] Franco, the famous cross-Atlantic flyer, had protested over the barbarity of their being used on Spanish soil. Now it was Major Franco's brother, General Francisco Franco, who had ordered their despatch and employment. . . . But if the despatch of the Foreign Legion to fight the miners shocked public opinion, what is one to say of that of the Moors? For eight hundred years the Crusade against the Moors had been the central theme of Spanish history: they still continued to be the hereditary enemy—the only enemy, in fact, against which the Spanish armies had ever fought. Their savagery in war was well known—only a dozen years before these same tribesmen had surrounded a Spanish army and massacred every man of them except the officers, whom they held for ransom. Yet they were now being brought to fight in Asturias, that one sacred corner of Spain where the Crescent had never flown. By this single act the Spanish Right had shown that neither tradition nor religion—the two things for which they professed to stand—had any meaning for them. In the terror produced in them by the rebellion of 40,000 miners, they showed that they were ready to sacrifice all their principles.

The repression of the miners was marked by wanton carnage in battle; later, by the torturing and horrible mutilation of captured miners, many of whom were shot in batches without trial or owing to the slightest whim and provocation. Estimates of these executions numbered in the thousands. After the executions came the torture squads, which by every disinterested account matched the savagery of the Nazi torturers in Germany's concentration camps. In all, apart from the thousands of dead, 30-40,000 prisoners filled Spanish jails. Despite attempts by the right to depict the Asturian miners as killers of priests, nuns, and members of the possessing classes, the very extravagance of the charges, coupled with acknowledgements by the alleged victims that the miners had behaved with remarkable moral probity, proved to be self-defeating. One investigating group after another revealed that most of the government's charges were false; that it was the *Tercio, Regulares,* and police which engaged in unspeakable acts of barbarity. As the facts slowly filtered out, the country was overwhelmed with shock and revulsion: the right was to pay dearly for its savagery.

The crises which had been shaking Spain for years came to a head when the right overreached itself by seeking not only to undermine the left and the Republicans, but also to subvert its centrist allies. Vengeful to the point of blindness, Gil Robles had sought to convict several leading Asturian Socialists—one of them a moderate who had opposed the rising. Although Alcala Zamora and Lerroux had accepted with equanimity the executions of proven Asturian militants, they balked at the victimization of innocent or harmless Socialists who scarcely deserved the death penalty even by rightist standards. Their sentences were commuted, whereupon the CEDA at the end of March withdrew from the government, provoking another ministerial crisis. But no government could be formed without the CEDA. Gil Robles, feeling power within his grasp, pressed his advantage unrelentingly. A new cabinet was formed in which most of the seats were occupied either by the CEDA or by CEDA-controlled ministers of the Agrarian Party, the organization of Spain's major landowners. But it was not stability under the aegis of a center-right coalition that Gil Robles was seeking. Exuberant over the influx of reactionaries into the CEDA, Gil Robles had overtly begun to fulfill the bleakest predictions of the left. It required no politcal astuteness to see that he envisaged himself as Spain's Dollfuss. Abandoning virtually all prospects of economic and social reform, Gil Robles began to direct his energies toward constitutional changes that would have ultimately replaced Spanish republican institutions by quasi-fascistic corporative forms. At the same time, as minister of war, he began to reorganize the army, removing officers whom he suspected of leftist or Republican sympathies. Despite the odium that surrounded the *Tercio*, he appointed Franco as Chief of Staff of the Spanish army.

The center-right coalition, limping through 1935, began to lose its support among the inchoate middle-classes of Spain. It had rejected land reform, restored Jesuit properties, and starved laic education. Its tax policies brazenly favored the wealthy over other classes in the country. It had shaken what little popular confidence the army enjoyed as a protector of the republic by advancing fascistic-minded officers to key positions at almost every echelon. Finally, the CEDA completely abandoned its alliance with the Radicals when Lerroux and his associates became involved in several shady scandals around gambling licenses and army supply contracts. By December, Lerroux was forced to step down; indeed, the entire Radical Party had become a useless and discredited anachronism. "The only party in Republican Spain to have no political ideals," observes Brenan, "all [the Radicals] wanted was that the country should jog along quietly." But Spain was polarizing sharply. Neither the left nor right appeared willing to give quarter, least of all to an archaic party whose leaders seemed to be lining their own pockets. Ironically, what finally finished Lerroux's ministerial career were not the scandals that gathered around him but his efforts to tax the landowners by raising inheritance taxes from 1 to 3½ percent. Consistent with its intransigent reactionism, the CEDA withdrew from the cabinet over this issue, finally terminating the two-years of center-right rule.

Clearly, Gil Robles was convinced that, with the Radicals discredited, the time had arrived for the CEDA to take full control of the government. The way, it appeared, was now open for an authoritarian regime. But the rightist leader had totally misjudged the integrity of the president. Alcala Zamora's ministerial aim was to restore the power of the center, not to deliver Spain into the hands of a quasi-fascist right. Despite his own conservative outlook, he was a defender of parliamentary government. On December 14, to the utter astonishment of the right, Alcala Zamora turned the government over to a caretaker prime minister, Manuel Portela Valladares, formerly Lerroux's minister of interior and an opponent of Gil Robles's attempts to transfer the Civil Guards to the Ministry of War. Within three weeks, Portela lifted the press censorship which had existed since the Asturian uprising and had virtually stifled any discussion in Spain for over a year. At the same time, he dissolved the Cortes and announced national elections for February 16, 1936. *El bienio negro*, the two black years of reactionary rule, repression, and the drift toward a corporative state, had come to an end.

From February to July

We may ignore any account of Gil Robles's fury at this course of events. His plan to use republican institutions to undo the republic had reached an historic impasse. Throughout 1935, the left and the Republicans had also undergone their own series of crises. In trying to involve Azana in the *Esquerra* debacle of October, the right had totally alienated the Republicans and driven them toward the left. Azana, who had gone to Barcelona solely to prevent the *Esquerra* from rising against Madrid, had been placed in the dock by the right and accused of engineering the entire October revolt. The charges were too preposterous to be taken seriously and served only to discredit the right. Indeed, to the Spanish Republicans of almost every variety, the vindictivness of the CEDA meant that all its verbal commitments to a stable Republican order were meaningless. Uniting around Azana, the Liberals formed a new coalition, the *Izquierda Republicana* or "Left Republicans," using a political nomenclature that would have been difficult to conceive three years earlier. The conditions were fully ripe for a coalition between the Liberals and the leftist parties—a coalition that would shortly take the historic form of the "Popular Front."

The Socialists too had responded to the CEDA's vindictiveness by veering further to the left. Right-wing Socialists like Besteiro, who had opposed the October rising, or Prieto, who had fled to France after its failure, had lost virtually all prestige with the party except for its hardened bureaucracy. Caballero, at least, had remained behind. By merely sitting in prison (where he read Marx for the first time), he had become the idol of the Socialist Youth and the party's growing left wing. No matter that he had shrewdly ensconced himself in his apartment after the start of the October events to guard himself against legal accusations; the "Spanish Lenin," as he was soon to be called, became intoxicated by a messianic sense of his historic mission. If Spain was to move toward revolution, he had been chosen by history to lead it—or, as events were to show, to subvert it. For the present, as Jackson notes, he found himself in prison "in the company of ardent young intellectuals who regretted their own bourgeois background and who idolized him doubly, as an authentic proletarian, and as the spiritual successor *'el abuelo'*—the equally proletarian, equally austere, equally honorable Pablo Iglesias." Soon to be released from prison, he became the indubitable leader of the Socialist left and another architect of the "Popular Front" coalition that was to take power in February 1936.

The Anarchists, despite their comparative inactivity during the October events, had suffered no less heavily than the Socialists. Unjustly accused of abstentionism by Socialists and Communists alike, the CNT had lost a measure of its revolutionary prestige while its most able militants had been packed off to prison by the thousands. In proportion to their strength in Asturias, perhaps as many Anarchosyndicalists had perished in the uprising as Socialists, yet they received little credit for their sacrifices. What was even more galling, the treachery they had suffered at the hands of the Socialists and Communists had gone virtually unnoticed. The coming elections in February offered them no consolation. The Socialists had shown that they were no more capable of honorable or comradely behavior in 1934 than they had been in 1932, when Caballero had tried to smash the CNT syndicates. Could the Anarchists expect any better from Azana's Liberals who, in 1932, had favored the UGT over the CNT, censored the libertarian press, and imprisoned them by the thousands? With this grim record, the CNT had no cause to be elated over a Liberal or Socialist victory in the forthcoming elections. But it had more reason to be alarmed over a rightist one. Caught in the old dilemma of "lesser evils," the CNT began to seek a regroupment of its own, perhaps a new entente of all libertarian forces, however disparate their tactical and strategic viewpoints. The days of the *faista* insurrections were now over for good. The dire prospects opened by a rightist victory in the February elections made it difficult to fall back on traditional methods of Anarchosyndicalist action; such a victory would almost certainly lead to a Dollfuss-type of reaction, followed by the brutal suppression of the left. It is not surprising, then, that despite its militant rhetoric between December and February, the CNT began to turn to its own version of *realpolitik*.

Erecting barricades on the university campus in Barcelona,
in preparation for the 19th of July.

Barcelona, July 19-20, 1936.

The CNT's first steps toward a libertarian regroupment were taken by establishing cordial relations with the *Sindicatos de Oposicion*, the once-detested *Treintistas*, led by Pestana, Peiro, Lopez, and the so-called "simple syndicalists" who favored pragmatic trade unionism. This was no mere organizational maneuver to infuse the Confederation with additional forces; it was a significant poltical act which led toward collaboration first with the UGT, eventually with the Socialists, and finally with the Popular Front. The basis for unity between the CNT and the Opposition Syndicates had been cleared in great part when Pestana, striking out on his own, broke with the people of his own faction and moved toward direct political activity, forming his own Syndicalist Party. The new party soon joined the Popular Front and acquired two seats in the Cortes after the February elections. Despite Catalan opposition, the movement for uniting the CNT with the Opposition Syndicates grew steadily. As early as May 1935, a national plenum of Regional Confederations had invited the Opposition Syndicates to participate in the next national congress of the CNT, albeit with a voice and not a vote.

Despite many vacillations on both sides in the ensuing months, contacts between Anarchists and syndicalists became increasingly cordial. Both libertarian tendencies had suffered heavily from the *bienio negro* repression and each had tended to support the other at the level of practical activity in periods of acute crisis. The problem of confederal unity came to a head in March 1936, when the National Committee of the CNT invited former *Treintistas* to attend the forthcoming congress of the Confederation at Saragossa on May 1st. It was here that the Opposition Syndicates were officially readmitted to the CNT. Fusion meetings held in all localities where duplicate syndicates existed integrated the two organizations completely. Some 70,000 oppositionists rejoined the parent organization. The unification had brought Peiro, Lopez, and other syndicalist right-wingers back to positions of confederal power, a situation that was to reinforce the growing orientation of the CNT's leadership toward political action. Despite its militant rhetoric after the February elections, the organization was to become more syndicalist than Anarchist, while towing the Anarchist tendencies behind it. As many Anarchist leaders were later to complain, it was not the FAI that changed the CNT but rather the CNT that began to change the FAI.

But most of these changes still lay in the future. Between December 1935 and February 1936, Anarchosyndicalist policies seemed to move at curious cross-purposes to each other. The CNT, although bitterly hostile to the "political" Socialist Party, seemed rather naively to be highly receptive to common action with the UGT, as though the leadership of the UGT were not staffed by Socialists. Having initiated the concept of an *Alianza Obrera*, the Socialists and the UGT, in turn, seemed receptive only to local alliances and resisted attempts to raise the *Alianza* to the dimensions of a national movement. The "UHP" slogan had yet to extend itself beyond Asturias. By December, in fact, the Socialist Party had moved toward an electoral bloc with Azana's Republicans, largely ignoring the CNT's efforts to foster trade-union collaboration on a more radical basis.

In mid-January 1936, a pact to form a Popular Front was finally established by the Socialist Party, the UGT, the Left Republicans and their allies of the Republican Union, the Socialist Youth, Pestaña's Syndicalist Party, the Communist Party, and suprisingly, the newly formed POUM (composed largely of Nin's Left Communists, formely a Trotskyist organization, and Maurin's Worker-Peasant Bloc). The pact was limited almost exclusively to practical collaboration in the coming elections. Its program was strictly middle-class—designed, in Portela's words, not to frighten its moderate constituency. It threatened no nationalization of property, no workers' control of industry, not even unemployment compensation. To the left, it merely offered the promise of amnesty for its thousands of jailed workers and a liberal parliamentary shield against authoritarian reaction. Although the Popular Front pact reinforced demands within the CNT to press the UGT for an alliance based on a revolutionary program, presumably in order to rescue the Spanish working class from reformism, these demands, whether sincere or not, were essentially meaningless. The "Spanish Lenin," Largo Caballero, had committed the UGT to political collaboration with the Republicans; the CNT promptly denounced this as class collaboration. Any unity between the two major labor organizations in Spain was thus almost indefinitely precluded.

Which is not to say that the CNT was entirely hostile to the Popular Front. As the elections drew near, the CNT began to reveal a disconcerting loosening of its former antipolitical stance. On January 25, 1936, at a conference of the Catalan Regional Committee, angry delegates bluntly charged the Regional Committee with a temporizing attitude toward the forthcoming elections. The CNT, in contrast to its vigorous abstentionist campaign of 1933, refused to urge its members to stay home. While reiterating its traditional opposition to electoral policies, the organization maintained a discreet silence in the face of demands to boycott the polls. Indeed, the prominent Anarchist dynast Urales had already admitted quite bluntly "I would consider it a great error on the part of the anarchists if, as a consequence of their action during the electoral period, the rightists triumphed over the leftists."

This statement by perhaps the most venerated Anarchist of his day, the founder of a distinguished family that included the best-known woman *faista*, Federica Montseny, unquestionably affected the strategy of the CNT and FAI for the February elections. A peninsular plenum of the FAI, held in Barcelona on January 30 and February 1, ratified the electoral position of the Catalan regional conference. *"Para salvar las apariencias"* (to save appearances), the FAI reaffirmed its "complete abstention from all direct and indirect collaboration with the policy of the State," but this almost legalistic verbiage was far removed in spirit and emphasis from an active policy of abstention.

Brademas gives a devastating description of the CNT-FAI policy toward the elections.

> During these last days of January and the first two weeks of February 1933 the CNT boomed to the surface all over Spain with meetings protesting against fascism, against the death penalty (restored in October 1934) and . . . in favor of the revolutionary union of the UGT and the CNT and—of course—amnesty for the prisoners. But there were no anti-electoral campaigns. The words "Don't vote!" and "Abstention!" were not to be found in pre-election manifestos. "Durruti," said Santillan, "was not given to subtleties and he, as did some others, began openly to advise attendance at the polls."

The CNT's and FAI's attitude toward the Popular Front was no mere issue of episodic abstention or participation in a specific electoral campaign (as some Anarchists were to claim), nor was the Popular Front an indigenous product of Spanish political conditions. The strategy, formulated by the Communist International after the signing of the Franco-Soviet nonaggression pact of 1934, was a barely disguised diplomatic response to the threat Hitler seemed to pose to Stalinist Russia. From a policy of mindless insurrectionary rhetoric, in which the entire Social Democratic movement had been designated as "social fascists—indeed, as greater enemies than the fascists themselves—the Communist parties of the world veered over to a policy of outright class collaboration. So completely was the cry of "social revolution" subordinated to one of defending bourgeois democracy at all costs against "fascism," that even mild conservative opponents provided an excuse for Communist parties to foster blocs with the most venal and discredited liberal parties of Europe. By 1936 the Spanish Socialist left with considerable justification could mock the Communists with the cry: "To save Spain from Marxism, vote Communist!"

The Popular Front, in effect, was no tentative act of collaboration between the growing left and the declining center to obstruct the CEDA and its allies. It reflected a far-reaching shift in policy which

A militiawoman raising the banner of victory.

Stalinist Russia imposed on the Communist parties of the worlds so that joint nonaggression or defense pacts against Nazi Germany might be signed with the western democracies. The policy had its origin in strictly Russian national interests and, perhaps more significantly, in the identification of these interests not with the world labor movement and cause of Socialism, but with the liberal bourgeoisie and the perpetuation of liberal capitalism. Stalinist Russia had dropped any pretense that the word "socialism" had any viable meaning in international policy or, for that matter, in the execution of internal policy. Even the memory of the October Revolution, for all its limitations, was to be drowned in the blood of the Old Bolsheviks, nearly all of whom were to be purged secretly or, in show trials, during the Popular Front years.

The Communist parties, in turn, were to try to foist the Popular Front policy on the left in the most shamelessly deceptive and manipulative manner with the goal of strengthening their control over the international working class. As in the case of Russian diplomatic policy, to the extent that this control was achieved, the Communist parties were concerned not to advance social revolution but to prevent it. Indeed, the Popular Front was consciously designed to demonstrate to the full satisfaction of the liberal bourgeoisie that the Communist parties, like Stalinist Russia, could be counted upon to promote class collaboration, to neutralize any revolutionary tendencies within the labor movement, and if necessary, to assassinate revolutionary spokesmen and suppress revolutionary movements. Knowingly or not, the CNT and FAI were riding the back of a tiger. From a policy of "nonabstention" in February, they were to be led into a policy of participation in September, and ultimately, in the later years of the Civil War, into a policy of collaboration with their most dangerous opponents. These opponents were not simply the right-wing Socialists, who at least had some sense of responsibility to the Spanish working class, but the Communists, a small group whose growth and influence depended upon the impact of Stalinist Russia on Spanish events. Apart from the mythology of the Bolshevik Revolution, which seemed to validate the Spanish Communist Party as a "revolutionary" organization, the conditional military aid which Russia spoon-fed to Spain during the Civil War was to give the Communists immense control over the course of events.

The elections of February 1936 brought the Popular Front parties to power by a margin of some 700,000 votes. Of 271 seats acquired by the coalition, a number which constituted an absolute majority in the Cortes, the Republicans (including Martinez Barrio's Republican Union as well as Azana's *Izquierda*) were given 117 seats, the Socialists 90, and the Communists 16.[3] The electoral victory of the Popular

Front had been much narrower than the 700,000 received out of the million votes cast. "In the first round of voting," observes Stanley G. Payne, referring to February 16,

> the left [that is, the left-liberal colaition of the Popular Front—M.B.] won altogether slightly more than 200 seats out of the total of 473 that made up the Cortes. The plurality was not due to an equivalent lead in the popular vote, for in the total balloting for the first round the popular vote for left and right was approximately equal. Under the complicated list-voting system, however, the decisive factor was not proportionate cumulative vote, but the concentration of ballots province by province. Popular Front votes were combined much more effectively for majority lists in the larger districts. The second runoff contests were held at the end of the month under leftist supervision and considerable pressure from the leftist street mob. In the runoffs the Popular Front increased its plurality further, though constitutional legality of the administration of the vote was dubious.

Payne neglects to tell us, that the same "complicated list voting system" had assured the right its own sweeping victory in 1933. What had favored the right three years earlier now favored the left. Nor does Payne give sufficient attention to the rightist "street mob," notably the hired *pistoleros* of the Falange who created so much bloody disorder during the first five months of the Popular Front regime, the reactionary students and *senoritos* who broke up meetings of the leftist groups, the rightist thugs who fired point-blank into crowds of workers' *barrios* from speeding motor vehicles, the police of Granada who kept workers and peasants from the polling places, the *caciques* who threatened punitive action against entire villages that failed to return rightist candidates, and the landlords' agents who threatened to discharge agricultural workers and tenants who failed to vote the reactionary ticket. These qualifications aside, Payne's factual conclusions are correct. What really emerges from the 700,000-vote plurality of the Popular Front was not so much the fact that the runoffs were conducted under "leftist supervision" or that the "leftist street mob" played any larger role in influencing the vote than the rightist thugs and *senoritos*, but that the Popular Front would not have come to power without Anarchosyndicalist electoral support.

Far from concealing this major departure from Anarchist precept, the leading *faista* Abad de Santillan was to emphasize it. In February, he observes, "participation in the elections was advisable. We gave power to the leftists, convinced under the circumstances they were the lesser evil." This could be construed as a reasonable and honest statement if action based on the "lesser evil" was seen for what it really was—a distinct departure from principle, openly admitted to be such, a bitter pill to be swallowed to deal with an acute illness. Given highly critical circumstances, the Bolsheviks had boycotted elections without becoming Anarchists and one could envision a situation where Anarchists would have voted in elections without becoming Bolsheviks. From hindsight, Vernon Richards's observation that a conservative victory in the February elections would have been far less of a setback for the Spanish labor movement than the slaughter that followed the generals' rebellion is a tempting conclusion which would have preserved Anarchist purism. But Gil Robles seemed definitely intent on becoming Spain's Dollfuss (his public speeches had acquired an unprecedentedly violent character) and the CEDA's electoral posters had a distinctly fascistic flavor, appealing for the "Ministry of War and all the power," "All power to the Leader," and the like.

In such ominous situations, who controls the state, with its arms and monopoly of violence, is not a matter of complete indifference. Boxed into an isolated land mass behind the Pyrenees and (as events were to show) lacking in significant support from the international proletariat, the Spanish Anarchists in 1936 did not have the revolutionary advantages enjoyed by the Russian Bolsheviks in 1917, notably international opponents bitterly divided by a world war, scattered domestic opponents also in conflict with each other, vast spaces into which to retreat, active aid from the international proletariat, and perhaps above all, the support of the Russian army, which not only failed to oppose the takeover of the Bolsheviks but which provided them with an enormous armamentorium of weapons inherited from the Czarist war effort and a reservoir of highly trained military manpower. If Gil Robles today seems like a mild figure beside Franco, much the same could have been said in comparing Dollfuss to Hitler. But all appearances aside, Dollfuss effectively smashed the Austrian labor movement long before the German army crossed his frontiers. That history never tested Gil Robles's capacity to do the same in Spain is due, ironically, to the fact that Liberals controlled the Spanish state throughout 1936, not the CEDA. This was no trifling factor in the sweeping libertarian revolution that occurred in July 1936, however much Anarchists prefer to deny the importance of who controls the state and under what circumstances they control it. It took considerable courage for a moderate Anarchosyndicalist such as Juan Peiro to write in September 1935: "I have said, and I repeat it here, that if an electoral class front should appear against the fascists who now govern us, I, for the first time in my life, would vote. . . ."

But after this has been said, one must emphasize that it would have been preposterous to expect a "lesser evil" to behave with noble virtue. Having voted in a bourgeois election, it was necessary to acknowledge the limitations of the act and to recognize that political maneuvering on the part of libertarians could develop into a bad habit. In fact, the gravest obstacle to social revolution in Spain was not the generals alone but forces within the Popular Front itself, notably an increasingly powerful Communist Party which employed duplicity and finally open violence to suppress revolutionary tendencies. The best the CNT and FAI could have hoped for from the newly elected state would have been neutrality; to base one iota of their policy on active state support was not only absurd, but marked the initial steps toward the "politicization" of the Spanish Anarchist movement and its eventual conversion into a political party. Yet so oblivious were many of the Anarchist leaders to this possibility that when the newly elected Generalitat, overwhelmingly *Esquerra* in character, failed to act decisively enough in resolving two CNT strikes in Barcelona, Durruti could peevishly complain: "We didn't come here to celebrate the arrival of a group of men. We came to tell the Left that we were the ones who decided your triumph and we are the ones who are maintaining two conflicts [the strikes in question—M.B.] which must be solved immediately. It was our generosity that decided the reconquest of February 16th."

The statement was remarkable as evidence of the trend it seemed to reveal. The Anarchists, even militants such as Durruti, were slowly becoming clients of the creature they most professed to oppose: the state power itself. Two bitter years of repression and, by contrast, the obvious power they felt (and enjoyed) in tipping the Popular Front to the side of victory, served not to render their thinking more guarded, subtle, and flexible, but rather more naive, crude, and complacently rigid. Having taken to the vote, they began to take to politics. This tendency, which the FAI had originally been created to block, was reinforced by the increasing bureaucratization of the CNT. As Richards notes,

> there can be no doubt that whilst paying lip-service to the principle of abstention in the February elections, the leadership of the CNT was working behind the scenes, offering the Left politicians the *potential* vote of the Confederation represented in return perhaps for guarantees that the political prisoners would be released in the event of a Popular Front victory. These are far from being wild speculations. What is certain is that within the CNT there have always been strong personalities who, as is always the case with those who would ride roughshod over basic principles, declared themselves to be the practical men, the realists of the movement.

The union with the Opposition Syndicates which later was to occur increased the number of these "strong personalities" in the leadership of the Anarchosyndicalist movement. The problem of how to deal with them had not been adequately worked out in the Spanish libertarian movement, any more than it has in movements for human freedom generally, a failure for which all have paid dearly.

But February 1936 and the following spring did not seem like a time for deep reflection and critical self-analysis, but an occasion for exaltation, hope, and direct action. Within a week after Azana formed the first Popular Front cabinet, crowds of workers opened the jails and released their comrades; in the case of Burgos, the prisoners literally took over the jail themselves. General strikes were declared by the UGT and CNT demanding a broad and immediate amnesty, a demand which Azana was obliged to satisfy if he hoped to preserve any penal system at all. In the five-month period that followed, Spain was to be convulsed by strikes, massive demonstrations, street battles between contending crowds, repeated shoot-outs between *pistolero* groups, land seizures, factional maneuvers within and between Popular Front parties, accusations of conspiracy, and finally, assassinations and near-rebellions that were to exceed the unrest that marked the Azana coalition of the early 1930s. Polarizing almost savagely to the extremes of right and left, the peninsula had entered into a prerevolutionary crisis that could be resolved only by armed confrontation between the two sides.

To unravel this complex skein of events, in which years of social unrest seemed to be compressed into a few months, would require a work of its own. Only the broadest trends and most significant occurrences can be cited here. The first trend that requires consideration is the unabated strike wave that exploded across Spain shortly after the Popular Front victory. Although both the UGT and CNT launched so-called "lightning" strike actions throughout the spring, it is generally agreed that the CNT established the pace and remained almost continually in the forefront of the movement. Hardly a week passed without syndicates in one of the two unions calling out workers, at times in general strikes that paralyzed major cities. In late March, both UGT and CNT steel workers left their foundries; in mid-April the CNT initiated a general strike in Madrid that gained the support of the UGT workers, to be followed in early June by still another strike, this time of construction and elevator workers. Salvos of strikes swept the country, involving nearly every sector of the Spanish working class. According to data gathered by Gil Robles and accepted as fact by Peirats, there were about 113 strikes involving an entire branch of an industry, and nearly 230 partial strikes. The movement, mainly CNT-inspired, reached such acuity that Largo Caballero's newly established left Socialist periodical, *Claridad*, joined *El Socialista* in counseling moderation and restraint. But the CNT, or at least its rank and file, continued the pressure right up to the military rebellion in July.

In the countryside the popular movement was perhaps less sensational but no less significant. The rural poor of western and southern Spain were now largely organized in the Socialist-controlled Federation of Land Workers (*Federacion Espanola de Trabajadores de la Tierra* or FETT), but the Federation's leadership had been so leftist politically from the very start of the FETT in 1931 and it was so oriented toward direct action as to be virtually indistinguishable from the CNT, which still retained its traditional strongholds in the south and east. After the victory of the Popular Front, both organizations began to encourage the outright occupancy of the land. In March, some 250,000 hectares were taken over by squatters, about 150,000 in April, and more than 90,000 in May and June together. Despite this decline in figures, possibly reflecting both government measures to accelerate the passage of land reform legislation and the restraining hand of diehard Socialists in Madrid, the countryside was seething with peasant revolt. Thousands of peasant families had taken to roads and were looking for work; others, under Anarchist influence, seized the land and claimed it as their own irrespective of any pending or existing legislation. In most cases, when Civil Guards reoccupied expropriated land, the peasants left temporarily, only to return when the *Guardia* had departed. The landlords were in a panic. Recalling the uprisings and barn-burnings of earlier times, they and their families fled to the safety of the cities, leaving entire plantations deserted. The peasant seizures were no longer the episodic flare-ups of the past, rising and subsiding from village to village, nor could they be contained by sending a division or two into the countryside to pacify a string of isolated *pueblos*. Spain was in the throes of a full-scale revolution in the countryside, comparable in every way to the great land revolts of Mexico and Russia.

The Popular Front government flailed out helplessly in all directions and failed miserably wherever it struck. To the largely CNT-inspired strike wave, it responded with severely repressive measures while it tried to placate the left's anger over rightist terrorism by arresting the Falangist leadership, including Jose Antonio Primo de Rivera. *Solidaridad Obrera* was censored so systematically and stringently that many Anarchosyndicalists could claim with some justice that their press had enjoyed more freedom under the *bienio negro* than the Popular Front. The government closed down syndicate headquarters and arrested Anarchist militants in sizeable numbers, even detaining the National Committee of the CNT in Saragossa. But the inefficacy of these measures soon became obvious. Madrid had plainly lost control over events and the syndicates, in flagrant disregard of official authority, reopened their headquarters almost as rapidly as they had been closed. The struggle was passing from the Cortes and the bureaucratic offices of the state into the streets where massive demonstrations, clashes between crowds, and shootings of political opponents seemed to reveal even more dramatically than the strikes and land seizures the breakdown of traditional authority.

Everyone sensed the impending explosion. The Socialist Youth and the Falange had formed their own paramilitary forces and were training almost within sight of each other in Madrid. Falangist terrorism began to reach menacing proportions almost directly after the Popular Front victory, when a group of Falangist students tried to assassinate the Socialist deputy Jimenez de Ascia.[4] The "leftist street mob" responded by partially burning two churches and the printing plant of *La Nacion*, a particularly reactionary periodical. Scarcely four days later, shots were fired at Largo Caballero's home. The period of assassinations by both sides now began in earnest. Within a week after the attack on Caballero's home, the rightist deputy Alfredo Martinez was killed in Oviedo; in April, a bomb was found in the home of the Liberal deputy Ortega y Gasset, followed by further assassination attempts against Republican civil governors, mayors from all parts of the political spectrum, journalists, and the murder of Judge Manuel Pedregal, who had sentenced a Falangist thug to a long prison term for killing a newsboy who sold leftist papers. Armed clashes broke out between Falangists and leftists, police and peasants; even CNT and UGT workers disputed union rivalries and strike issues gun in hand.

The rivalries within the left were paralleled by rivalries within the right. Falangists were now attacking leaders and supporters of the CEDA for temporizing and behaving too moderately by fascistic standards. Gil Robles may not have been wrong when he listed nearly 270 deaths and more than 1,200 wounded as a result of street fighting and assassinations in the months following the Popular Front victory. In most of these cases the initiative probably came from the right, but they invariably called forth violent reactions from the left. "Ideologically speaking," observes Jackson, "heroic violence belonged more to the fascist spirit than to the Left, but the Socialist Youth, meditating the fate of the German Socialists in 1933 and the Austrians in 1934, chose to fight fire with fire." Certainly the Anarchists were as sensitive to the fate of the German and Austrian labor movements as the Socialists, although they seemed to engage in less violence during that spring than other groups on the left and right.

In fact the Socialists were undergoing the most tumultuous changes in their history since the period following the Russian

Revolution. Largo Caballero's conversion to revolution had produced—and revealed—a crisis within the party. With the victory of the Popular front, an unavoidable question emerged: should the Socialists form another coalition with the Republicans? Four years earlier this question would have raised no serious factional disputes within the party; indeed, Caballero had occupied the post of minister of labor with telling effect upon the CNT. Now the reformist of yesteryear who had willingly collaborated with the Primo de Rivera dictatorship had become the "Spanish Lenin." He had a highly influential paper of his own, *Claridad*; he was the adored Achilles of the Socialist Youth and spokesman for growing leftist tendencies within the Socialist Party and the UGT. As the "Spanish Lenin," he opposed the entry of any Socialists into the Popular Front cabinet. Indalecio Prieto, on the other hand, had emerged as the spokeman for the party bureaucracy, which preached the verities of moderation, and for many Asturian miners who had paid dearly for the revolutionary adventures of 1934. Prieto charted a distictly reformist path for the party and favored ministerial collaboration with the Republicans. Although nominally in control of the party, his influence with the rank and file seemed to be dwindling rapidly. The struggle between the Caballerists and Prietists reached acute form in mid-Spring when both sides did not hesitate to use physical violence against each other at party meetings.

But Caballero's influence was tentative at best and turned out to be largely illusory so far as the party's diehards were concerned. At the party elections of June 30, Prieto's supporters received a larger proportion of the votes than Caballero's. The fact is that the stalwarts within the Socialist Party were really moderates after all; to the degree that Caballero continued to beat the drums of revolution, the membership gradually backed off. Perhaps even more significantly, Caballero had lost his hard-core support when he permitted the Socialist Youth to combine organically with the Communist Youth in a single organization. Grossly ill-advised by his close friend Julio Alvarez del Vayo, who had just returned from a dazzling trip to Stalinist Russia, he had been led to believe that a fusion between the 200,000 young Socialists and some 50,000 Communist Youth would permit the assimilation of the Communists by the Socialists, thereby strengthening his hand in the struggle with Prieto. A similar ploy was later planned for Catalonia, where the Socialists and Communists fused under Juan Comorera to found the Unified Socialist Party of Catalonia (PSUC). But this strategy backfired, producing the very reverse of what had been intended. By 1936 it required exceptional political myopia not to see that the Communists had become masters at swallowing up independent organizations under the cry of "unity." For the Spanish

Communist Party, as for Communist parties everywhere, "unity" had become the talisman for cannibalizing the entire left and making it over into a merchandisable instrument for Russian foreign policy in general and local Stalinist movements in particular. Accordingly, it was the Communists who acquired control over the Socialist Youth and the Catalan Socialists, depriving Caballero of his most important supporters. Neither the Caballerist policy of "revolution" nor the Prietist policy of collaboration won out. The Socialist Party merely stumbled through the spring of 1936, lacking a policy that would have unified either the forces for revolution or those for moderation.

The trajectory of the CNT and the FAI seemed to follow a diametrically opposite course. While the Socialist Party was torn by divisions, the CNT was uniting with the Opposition Syndicates. Theoretically, the CNT favored unity with the UGT but on terms so revolutionary that they made collaboration on a national scale virtually impossible. Caballero had counted heavily on gaining wide support not only from the left of his own party, but from the Anarchosydicalists as well. The latter, however, mistrusted him completely. His appeals for UGT-CNT unity failed to evoke a positive reaction within Anarchosyndicalist ranks, which had stored up gnawing recollections of treachery and betrayal at his hands. His appearance of the CNT's national congress in May at Saragossa yielded no decisive results. The test of Caballero's intentions came in June 1936, when 40,000 construction workers and 30,000 electricians and elevator repairmen, both groups drawn from the CNT and UGT, went out on strike in Madrid. The strike unnerved the Socialists completely. Even many Caballerists proved reluctant to match their revolutionary rhetoric with revolutionary action. The Socialists wanted to conclude the strike as quickly as possible, hopefully by arbitration and conventional negotiating methods. The CNT, on the other hand, openly pressured the workers for a revolutionary type of conflict. When their funds ran out *cenetista* strikers were encouraged to live according to the principles of *comunismo libertario*: they simply took their meals at restaurants and collected their groceries without paying for them. Embarrassed by such tactics, the UGT leaders vacillated over the question of a continuation of the strike. Finally, they withdrew. The CNT, however, carried it forward, and clashes between returning *ugetistas* and striking *cenetistas* resulted in several deaths.

Caballero was totally discredited. His policy of UGT-CNT collaboration had been reduced to a shambles. The militancy of the CNT had not only frightened off many of his left-wing supporters but had corroborated the worst suspicions of the Anarchosyndicalists about the sincerity of his new revolutionary stance. No less significantly, the strike itself, with its revolutionary connotations, thoroughly alarmed the middle class throughout Spain. If the strike was in any way a harbinger of the "Spanish Lenin's" policies and his declamations in favor of a proletarian dictatorship, the middle class plainly wanted no part of them.

Perhaps the alarm was greatest within the Popular Front government itself. If Prieto's policy was to strengthen the Republicans with a Socialist coalition, Caballero's was to weaken that coalition by abstaining from any ministerial support. The Caballerists, in effect, were waiting for Azana to discredit himself, after which the Socialist left would take over the government completely. The description of Caballero as the "Spanish Lenin" carried the unmistakable implication that Azana was the "Spanish Kerensky." This was a position Azana would have never permitted himself to occupy. By 1936, both men had to come to detest each other, but personal considerations aside, Azana was in an excellent position to block the left Socialist strategy. Although his popularity was waning rapidly among every sector of the Spanish population, in May he had changed the robes of prime minister of a Popular Front cabinet for that of president of the republic, thereby freeing himself from the vicissitudes of an uneasy ministerial alliance and parliamentary votes of confidence. He was now in a position to select the appropriate prime minister for the coalition and he had chosen as his substitute one of his closest friends and collaborators, Casares Quiroga, a consumptive who, in Brenan's words, "reacted to the danger of the situation by an optimism that would have been considered insane if it were not a symptom of his disease." Azana himself had grown listless, almost indifferent; his dream of a stable republic seemed to be turning into a nightmare whose course he could no longer control and whose destiny imbued him with the darkest pessimism. But if he was certain of anything, it was that Caballero would not play "Lenin" to his "Kerensky." Thus on the eve of the most fateful military *pronunciamiento* in Spanish history, Republican policy, however much it vacillated, was consistent in at least one respect: the Socialist Party, especially its Caballerist faction, would not be permitted to acquire power. Stated in broader social terms, the Popular Front cabinet was committed above all else to preventing the working class from taking over Spain. The very class that had contributed most materially to the Popular Front victory was viewed by the leaders of that government as its most formidable and dangerous enemy.

While Spain drifted toward civil war, the Anarchosyndicalists were occupied with cementing their own ranks at the famous national congress of the CNT in May 1936 at Saragossa. On the first day of the month, nearly 650 delegates, representing 982 syndicates with a membership of 550,000, convened at the Iris Park. This congress, lasting ten days, was to become known as one of the most memorable meetings in the history of the CNT. It not only brought the Opposition Syndicates back to their parent organization but opened the most important discussion on the nature of a libertarian communist society to ever occupy a major working-class organization.

Virtually all the speakers at the congress seemed to feel that Spain was entering into a revolutionary situation. Their seemingly utopian discussions of how the future society that followed that revolution would be organized thus had practical, indeed, immediate significance. Amidst the welter of petty squabbles over delegate credentials, personalities, and the fate of the Opposition Syndicates, the congress found time to discuss problems as far-ranging as sexual rights and communal organization. Perhaps the most fascinating of the Saragossa congress's resolutions dealt with "The Confederal Conception of Libertarian Communism." Although this resolution received far less conventional newspaper coverage (the bourgeois press liked to titillate its readers with reports of discussions of "free love"), it became one of the most important statements of libertarian principles by the CNT.

The resolution was careful to deny that it sought "to predict the structure of the future society . . . since there is often a great chasm between theory and practice." Nor was the revolution which ushered in that future society to be regarded as a sudden act of violence, for much depended upon revolutionary action as "a psychological phenomenon in opposition to the state of things that oppresses the aspirations and needs of the individual." Violence was not the totality of the revolution but merely the first step which abolishes "private property, the State, the principle of authority, and consequently, the class division of men into exploiters and exploited, oppressors and oppressed." Its emphasis on revolution as a psychological phenomenon and its abhorrence of authority marks the resolution as a strictly Anarchist document. Indeed, such an orientation would have seemed out of place amid the "scientific," "objective," depersonalized rhetoric of a Marxist document.

The resolution went on to describe the structural details of communal organizations and their federation. Economic planning had its base in "the producer, the individual as the cell, as the cornerstone of all social, economic and moral creation," who functions through the work place, the syndicate, and the geographic commune. No contradiction need exist between the individual and free communal entities. "In accordance with the fundamental principles of libertarian communism, as we have stated above, all men will hasten to fulfill the voluntary duty—which will be converted into a true right when

The people in arms. A truckload of armed CNT workers in Barcelona during the July, 1936 fighting against the insurgent garrison.

FRANCISCO ASCASO (left) a few minutes before he was
killed in the assault on the Altarazonas Fortress in Barcelona,
July 19, 1936.

men work freely—of giving his assistance to the collective, according to his strength and capabilities, and the commune will accept the obligation of satisfying his needs." The famous Communist slogan, "From each according to his ability, to each according to his need," was to guide the commune in its allocation of resources and its claims on human labor.

The resolution did not try to argue "that the early days of the revolution" would be easy ones. "Any constructive period calls for sacrifice and individual problems and of not creating difficulties for the work of social reconstruction which we will all be realizing in agreement." But the National Confederation of Communes which the new society would establish would allow for many variegated forms. "Naturists and nudists" (*naturistas-desnudistas*) or opponents of industrial technology, as well as traditional Anarchosyndicalists, would be free to create their own communal organizations. Amusing as this might have seemed to bourgeois journalists more than forty years ago, today, when our puritanical distance from the natural world may well lie at the root at the modern ecological crisis, the liberatory spirit of these lines seems almost prophetic. In time, "the new society should assure each commune of all the agricultural and industrial elements necessary for its autonomy, in accordance with the biological principle which affirms that the man, and in this case, the commune, is most free, who has least need of others."

The resolution exuded a liberty-loving generosity toward the capacity of people to manage society freely and directly. "All of these functions will have no bureaucratic or executive character. Apart from those who work as technicians or simply statisticians, the rest will simply be carrying out their job as producers, gathered together at the end of the working day to discuss questions of detail which do not call for reference to a general assembly." No systems of hierarchy here; no representatives invested with the power to make policy decisions; no organization of the division of labor into a system of authority. Indeed, according to the resolution, even the social enemies of today would be won over eventually to the Anarchist ideals of love, liberty, and education. "Libertarian communism is incompatible with any punitive regime,which implies the disappearance of the present system of punitive justice and all its instruments, such as prisons." For "man is not bad by nature, and that deliquency is the logical result of the state of social injustice in which we live." Clearly, "when his needs are satisfied and he is given rational and humane education, [the causes of social injustice] will disappear."

The revolution would not try to destroy the family, which, at its best, had played a solidarizing role in society. Libertarian communism, however, "proclaims free love, with no more regulation than the the free will of the men and women concerned, guaranteeing the children with the security of the community." This resolution was carried unanimously by the delegates of the congress. It was written, discussed, and adopted not in the "enlightened" 1960s and 1970s, but in the severely patriarchal Catholic Spain of 1936. Today, it is impossible for an urbane and modernistic generation to realize how far these Anarchosynidcalist workingmen and workingwomen were in advance of their time. The tragedy of the movement they represented is that their dream was to be drowned in blood and washed away into the most remote corridors of history. Other people, living in another age, would be obliged to rediscover it without any knowledge that it had articulated the dreams and hopes of innumerable workers and peasants.

When the delegates finally dispersed—many to die a few months later in the Civil War—the vision of this society seemed to override many practical problems. If there was anything "utopian" about the Saragossa congress, it was not its resolution on a libertarian communist society but (as Vernon Richards points out) "the lack of any discussion of the problems that might face the organization during the revolutionary period." More specifically,

> what was to be the attitude of the organization on the morrow of the defeat of the military putsch when it found itself suddenly at the head of the revolutionary movement. Such a possibility could easily be envisaged in Catalonia, if not in the provinces under the Central Government. Perhaps for the rank and file the answer was a simple one: the social revolution. But in the light of subsequent actions, for the leadership of the CNT it was not as simple as all that. Yet these problems and doubts were not faced at the Congress, and for these serious omissions of foresight, or perhaps of revolutionary democracy in the organization, the revolutionary workers paid dearly in the months that followed.

As early as March, scarcely more than a few weeks after the Popular Front had come to power, the generals and politicans who were to stage the military uprising of July 17 met secretly in Madrid to formulate their plans. The natural leader for the revolt seemed to be General Jose Sanjurjo, organizer of the aborted *pronunciamiento* of August 1932, who lived in Portugal but kept himself intimately informed of events across the frontier. A military conspiracy alone, however, hardly seemed tenable. Political support was needed. Sanjurjo was a Monarchist and so too were an appreciable number of officers involved in the conspiracy. No one seemed more suitable to advance their cause among civilian Monarchists than Jose Calvo Sotelo, the former minister of finance in Primo de Rivera's government, who enjoyed a reputation as a formidable orator and a shrewd politician.

Calvo Sotelo had traveled widely through Europe, where he became enamored of corporative and fascist ideologies. In the Cortes he was the avowed spokeman of the Monarchists, perhaps of the entire militant right. By June, his speeches had virtually disrupted parliamentary debates: he avowed fascistic beliefs, attacked the "antimilitary" policies of the government, and freely delivered himself of insulting personal remarks to Republican officials. The left saw him as a continual provocation and viewed him as the very incarnation of fascism in Spain.

More symbolic than real at these conspiratorial meetings was the figure of Jose Antonio Primo de Rivera. While in prison the son of the former dictator had become the hero of the extreme right. From the welter of Carlist, conservative, and clerical groups, the Falange was to eventually emerge as the political backbone of what was later to be called the "Nationalist" cause and Jose Antonio was to become its martyr after his execution during the Civil War. Behind the parties and generals stood the entrenched wealth and power of Spain's great land magnates, industrialists, aristocrats, clergy, and sectors of the petty bourgeoisie.

But the real responsibility for the revolt rested in the hands of the generals and their success required careful planning. Colonel Valentin Galarza represented Sanjurjo. He was joined by the presumably liberal General Mola, Colonel Yague of the Foreign Legion, the moderate Republican General Gonzalo Queipo de Llano, who had abandoned his slender loyalties to the government with the victory of the Popular Front, Generals Villegas and Fanjul, who had the misfortune of being stationed in Madrid, General Goded, and only later, by General Francisco Franco. The government was not unmindful of the potential for a military *pronunciamiento*. It had been quietly shifting reactionary officers to remote posts—Franco had been packed off to the Canary Islands, Goded to the Balearics. The minister of war, authorized to ignore rules of seniority in appointing commands, filled key vacancies with officers known to be sympathetic to the republic. Unluckily, Mola, who held the main threads of the conspiracy in his hands, had been assigned to the Pamplona military district in the heart of Navarre, where he could count on Carlist support.

The rising was scheduled to occur between July 10 and 20, at which time Sanjurjo was to return to Spain by airplane and take over command of the rebel forces. Mola was to lead the garrisons of Pamplona and Burgos; Villegas, the Madrid garrison. Cabanellas was to seize Anarchist Saragossa; Goded, Barcelona; and Queipo de Llano, Seville. Trusted junior officers were to lead out their garrisons in other cities. Franco was to fly to Spanish Morocco, where he would take command of the army of Africa. It was generally agreed that the leading military conspirators would form a Directory with the power to issue laws, later to be ratified by a Constituent Assembly elected under an implicitly restricted suffrage. The *pronunciamiento* seemed, as yet, to be inspired more by the precendent of Primo de Rivera than by Hitler's, although it was slowly to acquire many fascistic features. The bloody Civil War, the Falange, and perhaps the vindictive personality of Franco, who was destined to replace Sanjurjo after the latter was accidently killed in the flight to Spain, would give the movement the most vicious thrust of any modern civil war in western Europe.

The uprising of the generals had been predicted by left-wing spokesmen months before it occurred. As early as February 14, the CNT had issued a prophetic manifesto warning that day by day, "the suspicion grows that right-wing elements are ready to provoke a military coup. Morocco appears to be the focal point of the conspiracy. The insurrection is subject to the outcome of the elections. The plan will be put into effect if the Left wins. We do not support the Republic, but we will contribute all our efforts to an all-out fight against fascism in order to defeat the traditional oppressors of the proletariat." This, of course, was mere guesswork. It tells us more about the course the CNT was to follow in the Civil War and its inability to formulate a policy to deal with the consequences of its electoral support of the Popular Front than it does about the actual behavior of the right on the eve of the elections. Republican officers with more substantial facts had informed the government in April that military conspiracies were underway. On May 1st, Prieto with uncanny prescience not only had warned of a military revolt but had singled out Franco as the most likely candidate for the dictator of Spain. The government was well aware of Fanjul's operations in Madrid. Even conservative deputies whom Calvo Sotelo had tried to enlist in the conspiracy reported his efforts to the cabinet.

As the evidence increased, so did the government's paralysis in the face of the impending crisis. Indeed, shortly before the rebellion, Azana publicly assured journalists and political colleagues that the current unrest was temporary and would soon be followed by a more tranquil atmosphere. But tension continued to mount. On July 11, a group of Falangists briefly seized the radio station of Valencia and broadcast the following message: "Radio Valencia. The Spanish Falange has taken possession of the transmitter by force of arms. Tomorrow the same thing will happen at all the radio stations in Spain." This event followed by only a few hours a confidential warning to Casares Quiroga that a military uprising was imminent, to which the prime minister flippantly replied: "So you are assuring me that the officers are going to rise! Very well, gentlemen, let them rise.

I, in contrast, am going to lie down." The next day, on July 12, a Socialist lieutenant of the Assault Guards was shot to death by a group of Falangist gunmen. Within hours of the assassination, the victim's angry comrades had decided upon a dramatic act of revenge. Arriving at Calvo Sotelo's home in a police car, they "arrested" the right-wing parliamentary leader, drove off with him in their vehicle, and shot him, dumping his body in the Madrid cemetery. The generals had found their martyr. The day of the uprising was pushed forward to July 17 to take advantage of the sensation produced by the assassinations and the commanders were placed in a state of readiness.

In Madrid the leftist parties, headed by Caballero requested arms but the government coldly refused. Up to the very point of rebellion, when transmitters seized by the army in Morocco were broadcasting the news of the *pronunciamiento*, the government of Liberal Republicans was to speak out "again to confirm the absolute tranquility of the whole Peninsula" and inform the workers' organizations that they should "guarantee the normality of daily life, in order to set a high example of serenity and of confidence in the means of the military strength of the government"—a "military strength" the Popular Front government no longer enjoyed. While the government enjoined the workers' parties to passivity and "serenity," the National Committees of the Socialist and Communist parties in Madrid obligingly issued a joint declaration of their own opining that the "moment is a difficult one but by no means desperate." The declaration concluded with the stirring injunction: "The Government commands and the Popular Front obeys." The workers of Madrid were assured that the "Government is certain that it has sufficient resources to overcome the criminal attempt." In response to Calvo Sotelo's assassination, the government in fact had closed down not only the Monarchist and Carlist headquarters in the capital (presumably to prevent disorders) but also the Anarchist centers. This attempt to neutralize the most militant elements in the labor movement all but assured that Madrid would remain "serene." A confused situation emerged in the capital: the CNT, "on war footing ever since the building strike," observe Pierre Broue and Emile Temime in their perceptive account of the Spanish Revolution and Civil War, "decided to use force to reopen its offices closed by the police and began to requisition cars and search for arms. David Antona, secretary of its National Committee, was freed [from prison] on the morning of 19 July; he went to the Ministry of the Interior and threatened to send his men to attack the prisons and release the militants who were still imprisoned there." The left Socialists unearthed and distributed the arms they had concealed since the October events of 1934. Workers' patrols began to appear on the streets. Yet Madrid, on the whole, was strangely guarded in its actions. No assaults were made on the barracks; indeed, one rebel regiment made its way out of the capital, apparently without opposition, to join forces with Mola in the north. UGT construction workers, dutifully obeying the Ministry of Labor's strike awards, returned to their jobs. The CNT continued its strike, although by now both unions had given orders for a general strike. No decisive fighting occurred on either side in Madrid until two days after the *pronunciamiento* when loudspeakers in the streets broadcast the news that the Barcelona proletariat had been victorious in an open struggle with Goded's troops.

It was in Anarchosyndicalist Barcelona—and virtually in that city alone—that serious preparations and the most effective efforts were undertaken to cope with the military rebellion. Instead of issuing reassuring statements after the fashion of the Socialist and Communist parties in Madrid, the CNT and FAI placed the entire working class of the city on the alert. *Cenetista* workers filled their syndicate halls clamoring for arms. Although the CNT and FAI had formed a liason committee with the Generalitat to cope with the military uprising in a united manner, Companys responded to these demands by declaring that no weapons were available. But this was Barcelona, not Madrid, where "The Government commands and the Popular Front obeys." With characteristic independence, a group of Anarchosyndicalist dock workers led by Juan Yague secretly boarded ships in the harbor, stripped them of weapons, and deposited the arms in a syndicate headquarters. The headquarters was soon surrounded by police and after delicate negotiations some of the weapons were returned to avoid a conflict with the police, many of whom were sympathetic to the workers' cause and were later to aid them in fighting the rebel troops. During the afternoon of the 18th, *cenetistas* raided sporting goods stores and whatever arms depots they could find; they also seized dynamite from the dockyards. Sympathetic Assault Guards distributed arms from their barracks. From the building syndicate, which had now become a sort of "war" headquarters for the CNT, plans were drawn up for resistance. Private cars, splashed with the letters "CNT-FAI," prowled the streets as a warning that the Anarchosyndicalists were prepared for battle in the event of any uprising. Workers, often acting largely on their own, began to arrest known Falangists and rightists, stopping all suspicious passersby near government buildings and barracks. CNT workers mounted a 24-hour guard on their headquarters while all over town their comrades, armed with makeshift weapons, lay in wait for any suspicious action by the troops.

On July 18, the generals declared their *pronunciamiento* and, in the morning hours of the next day, solidiers of the Barcelona garrison, perhaps the largest in Spain, began to leave their quarters to occupy strategic centers of the city. Almost everywhere they encountered workers massed behind barricades, snipers from rooftops, and immense crowds walking toward them with their few weapons raised over their heads, pleading with the soldiers not to shoot their proletarian brother and sisters. Where these pleas were disregarded, the troops encountered furious resistance by armed workers or, to their utter amazement, were simply overwhelmed by crowds that surged forward in total disregard of the military's superior fire-power. The generals' uprising had begun—but so too had the libertarian social revolution.

Notes

1. To a great extent, the October events in Asturias are still little known to us. Gabriel Jackson quite rightly observes that, in addition to the political biases aroused by the events themselves, the Spanish press was censored until early 1936 and the electoral campaign of February in that year completely subserved the facts to party interest. "Since the Civil War, only the victors' version has been documented in Spain. Needless to say, the thousands of knowledgeable leftists who fled Spain at the close of the Civil War did not carry documents in their baggage." After sifting many accounts of the Asturian revolt, I have settled on three: Brademas's brief but excellent summary, Jackson's apparently on-site study (an account which suffers from an inadequate discussion of the Anarchosyndicalists' role, particularly in Gijon and La Felguera), and Peirats's splendid account. In my personal contact with Peirats I have been struck by his independence of mind and guileless candor—qualities which have greatly enhanced his credibility in my eyes—and I have drawn much of my material from his *Los anarquistas en la crisis politica espanola*.

2. The reader would be well-advised to take such reports with reservations. It does not deprecate the role of the Mieres miners to emphasize that the Communists staked out a claim to nearly all the dramatic initiatives in the Asturian insurrection, although the union locals they actually controlled probably commanded little more than 3,000 members. Indeed, on the basis of my own researches and personal recollection of this period, I can say that the Communists in America as well as in Spain described the entire insurrection as Communist-led and depicted its goal as the establishment of a "soviet republic." As the reader will see, none of these claims even remotely corresponded to the facts.

3. I say "given" because these seats did not reflect the popular vote received by the parties but the number of seats they were allocated by agreement between the Popular Front coalition. I share Brenan's view that the

Republicans and Communists were probably given more seats by the coalition than they would have acquired had each party run independently. I would also accept his view that the Communists may well have received four times as many seats as they would have gained on their own; in addition to the 16 mentioned above, they received five from Catalan Socialists, who were now virtually under Communist control due largely to Stalinist infiltration tactics and the manipulations of Juan Comorera, one of the most sinister politicians of the left. Comorera was to engineer the Stalinist counterrevolution in Catalonia during the Civil War and eventually find a welcome home in Franco Spain.

4. It is interesting to note that Payne makes no mention of this assassination attempt when he accuses the Popular Front government of showing bias in suppressing the Falange shortly afterward. One would think from Payne's account that the government was merely making "symbolic concessions" to the left, when in fact the Falange behaved with conscious provocation in its terrorist acts. Brenan not unfairly points out that in 1936 the Falange may have exceeded the much-maligned Anarchists in the number of *atentados* it attempted.

Chapter Eleven:
Concluding Remarks

We must leave the details of that revolution—its astonishing achievements and its tragic subversion—to another volume. That Sanjurjo was to perish in a plane crash on his way to Spain, leaving Franco commander of the entire military uprising; that the war on the peninsula was to become inextricably tied to European power politics; that Spain was to endure three tormenting years of internecine conflict—all of these events belong to the conventional histories of the Spanish Civil War. Without entering into a discussion at this time of the Anarchist collectives and the experiments in workers' control of industry that developed in the latter half of 1936, we must try to assess the meaning of the events recounted in this volume. What was the place of the Spanish Anarchist movement in the larger history of proletarian socialism? What were its possibilities—and its limits? Are the organizational forms developed by the CNT and FAI relevant to radical movements in our own time? Today, long after the Spanish Anarchist movement was destroyed by Franco, these beguiling questions linger on. The movement still haunts us—not only as a noble dream or perhaps a tragic memory, but as a fascinating test of libertarian theory and practice.

Although Spanish Anarchism was virtually unknown to radicals abroad during the "heroic years" of its development, it could be argued in all earnestness that it marked the most magnificent flowering and, in the curious dialectic of such processes, the definitive end, of the century-long history of proletarian Socialism.

The emergence of the working class, specifically of the Parisian proletariat, as a revolutionary force on the June barricades of 1848 had totally changed the landscape of earlier radical theory. Until that event, critical views of society had been shaped by the notion of a broad populist conflict between an entrenched minority of oppressors and a dominated mass of oppressed. Radicals generally conceived of these polarized segments of society in very ill-defined terms. Under the rubric of the "people" (le peuple), they fashioned a broad constituency in which highly variegated, later historically hostile, strata such as craftsmen, factory workers, peasants, professionals, petty merchants, and entrepreneurs of small industrial installations were cemented by a common oppression at the hands of monarchs, aristocrats, and the wealthiest sectors of commercial, financial, and industrial classes. Accordingly, the "people" were united more by the social elements they opposed than by an authentic community of shared economic interests.

In the opening years of the Great French Revolution of 1789, the "people" was actually a coalition rather than a class. As the revolution unfolded, this coalition began to disintegrate. Lofty utopian ideals based on liberty and equality could not suppress the antagonisms that craftsmen felt for their erstwhile merchant allies or factory workers for their employers. Nor were these ideals sufficient to temper the narrow parochialism of the peasantry and the egotistical aspirations for advancement on the part of the professionals. "Nationhood," "patriotism," and the republican virtues that inhered in the concept of "citizenship" barely concealed the widening antagonisms and diverging interests that coexisted within the so-called "Third Estate,"—a term, it is worth noting, that was initially borrowed from feudalism in order to oppose feudalism.

The June 1848 rising of the Parisian proletariat replaced the populist struggle with the class struggle, dispelling the traditional mystique of the "people," the "nation," and the "citizen." It was now clear that the popular coalitions against pre-industrial elites embodied hostile classes. A "scientific" socialism, divested of any moral or ethical content, began to replace the ethically charged populist and utopian socialism that had been born in the late years of the Great French Revolution and its aftermath. "Surplus value" was an increment unique in form: the bourgeoisie acquired it not by the forcible appropriation of surplus labor and of the laborers themselves but by the seemingly fair exhange of labor power for wages on the open market. Workers were no longer slaves or serfs; they were juridically "free" and hence represented an historically unprecedented type of oppressed class. Lacking the industrial facilities which were owned by the bourgeoisie, they were free to work—or, of course, to starve. "Liberty" in becoming a political reality, had only been rendered even more of an economic fiction. By the mere possession of industrial facilities that were too large to belong to the tool kit of the traditional craftsmen, the bourgeoisie (itself a unique historical class) had emerged, and by the mere workings of the free market in labor power, this class was able to ensnare the proletariat in a skein of subservience, expropriation, and exploitation. Everyone in society was "free" and "equal"; indeed, this very "freedom" to own property without restriction and the "equality" of a fair exchange of labor power for wages concealed the enslavement of the workers to capital as an inevitable process.[1]

The "free market" also made inevitable the radicalization of the proletariat. The ongoing competition between "free entrepreneurs," each seeking to capture an increasing portion of the market, involved a ruthless process of price-cutting and capital accumulation, concomitantly leading to overall reductions in the wages of the working class. Eventually, the working class would become so impoverished that it would be driven to social revolution. Marx gave no credence to the notion that the proletariat would revolt under the impulse of high-minded ideals. "When socialist writers ascribe this revolutionary historic role to the proletariat," he observes,

> it is not . . . because they consider the proletarians as *gods*. Rather the contrary. Since the abstraction of all humanity, even of the *semblance* of humanity, is practically complete in the *full-grown proletariat* [my emphasis, here—M.B.] since all the conditions of life of the proletariat sum up all the conditions of life of society today in all their inhuman acuity; since man has lost himself in the proletariat, yet at the same time has not only gained theoretical consciousness of that loss, but through urgent, no longer disguisable, absolutely imperative *need*—that practical expression of *necessity*—is driven directly to revolt against that inhumanity. . . . Not in vain does it go through the stern but steeling school of *labour*. The question is not what this or that proletarian, or even the whole of the proletariat at the moment *considers* as its aim. The question is *what the proletariat is*, and what, consequent on that *being*, it will be compelled to do.[2]

Accordingly, socialism becomes "scientific" and develops as a science of "proletarian socialism" because of what the proletariat "will be compelled to do," not because it is composed of "gods." Marx, moreover, imparted this revolutionary function to the "full-grown proletariat," not to *déclassé* peasants who had been removed from the land or to impoverished craftsmen, the social strata with which the capitalist class was to man the factories and mills of industrial society. Unless events patently forced Marx to acknowledge the radical traits and insurrectionary volatility of these *déclassé* elements, he generally viewed such strata as the *alte scheisse* (the "old shit"), lingering over from the formative era of industrial capitalism. The hopes of "proletarian socialism" lay primarily in the "full-grown" proletariat of modern industry, "a class always increasing in numbers, and disciplined, united, organized by the very mechanism of the process of capitalist production itself." Proletarian socialism, in effect, was meant to demystify the notion of the "people" as a homogeneous revolutionary mass and to demonstrate that beliefs such as "liberty" and "equality" could not be divorced from the material conditions of social life.

Yet within this very process of demystification, Marxism generated a number of highly misleading myths which were to show the limits of proletarian socialism itself. The June barricades of 1848 had in fact been manned not by an industrial proletariat "disciplined, united, and organized by the process of capitalist production," but by craftsmen, home-workers, nondescript laborers of every sort, porters, unemployed urban and rural poor, even tavern keepers, waiters, and prostitutes—in short, the flotsam and jetsam of French society which the ruling classes had habitually designated as *canaille*. These very same elements, nearly a quarter of a century later, were to man the barricades of the Paris Commune. It was precisely the industrialization of France after the Commune—and with this process, the emergence of a "full-grown" hereditary proletariat "disciplined, united, organized by the process of capitalist production"—that finally was to silence the "crowing" of the French "Red Cock" that had summoned Europe to revolution during the nineteenth century. Indeed, much the same could be said of the Russian proletariat of 1917, so recently recruited from the countryside that it was anything but a "full-grown" working class.

The great proletarian insurrections that seemed to lend such compelling support to the concept of proletarian socialism were fueled primarily by social strata that lived within neither industrial nor village society but in the tense, almost electrifying force-field of both. Proletarian socialism became a revolutionary force for nearly a century not because a well-organized, consolidated, hereditary proletariat had emerged with the factory system but because of the very *process* of proletarianization. Dispossessed rural people and craftsmen were being removed from a disintegrating preindustrial way of life and plunged into standardized, dehumanizing, and mechanized urban and industrial surroundings. Neither the village and small shop as such nor the factory as such predisposed them to the boldest kind of social action; rather, they were moved by the disintegration of the former and the shock of the latter. Demoralized to the point of recklessness, *déclassé* in spirit and often in fact, they became the adherents of the Paris Commune, the Petrograd soviets, and the Barcelona CNT.

The very "half-grown" quality of the early proletariat, formerly peasants and craftsmen or perhaps a generation removed from such status, produced a volatility, intractability, and boldness that the industrial system and factory hierarchy was to attenuate in their descendants—the hereditary proletariat of the 1940s and 1950s, a class that knew no other world but the industrial one. For this class, no tension was to exist between town and country, the anomie of the city and the sense of shared responsibility of the small community, the standardized rythmns of the factory and the physiological rhythms of the land. The premises of the proletariat in this later era were formed around the validity of the factory as an arena of productive activity, the industrial hierarchy as a system of technical authority, and the union bureaucracy as a structure of class command. The era of proletarian socialism came to an end in a step-by-step process during which the "half-grown," presumably "primitive," proletariat became "full-grown," "mature"—in short, fully proletarianized.

The proletariat, in effect, became psychologically and spiritually part of the very social system it had been destined, according to Marxian precept, to overthrow. Proletarian socialism, not surprisingly, became an institutionalized movement for the industrial mobilization of labor, largely economistic in its goals; it solidified into labor parties that articulated a pragmatic liberalism, thereby blunting even the intellectual susceptibility of the working class to revolutionary ideals. Finally and most disastrously, it fused with capitalism's inherent historic trend toward economic planning, centralized political and industrial control, hierarchical regulation, and economic nationalization. The socialist ideal of freedom, divested of its ethical content by "scientific socialism" and burdened with the pragmatic considerations of centralized planning and economic nationalization, became a mere ideological device for mobilizing popular support around state capitalism.

If only because of the element of time, Spanish Anarchism did not share the historic fate of proletarian socialism. Indeed, it may very well have formed the last step in the development of revolutionary proletarian socialism before the latter's destiny as a variant of state-capitalist ideology became evident. In any case, the libertarian revolution of July 1936 seemed to have gathered to itself many of the noble qualities that were only partially developed in earlier uprisings of the worker's movement. In July 1936, the CNT and FAI were sufficiently independent as a workers' movement, certainly by comparison with the Socialists and POUM, to make Barcelona the most revolutionary city in Spain. No other large urban area was to achieve the social goals of revolutionary syndicalism as fully, to collectivize industry as resolutely, and to foster communal forms of land management as extensively as Barcelona and its environs. Orwell's description of the city during this phase is still intoxicating: the squares and avenues bedecked with black-and-red flags, the armed people, the slogans, the stirring revolutionary songs, the feverish enthusiasm of creating a new world, the gleaming hope, and the inspired heroism.

Yet the limits of this development become painfully evident if one asks: could there have been an Anarchosyndicalist society even if the generals had been crushed in 1936? Apparently, very few serious Anarchist theoreticians seem to have believed this. A mixed economy, yes—although how long the revolutionary fervor of the more ascetic communistic collectives might have resisted the temptations and demands of a coexisting market economy is difficult to predict. Whether a communist revolution could occur in an industrially undeveloped country—indeed, whether such a revolution might even succeed temporarily under materially demanding conditions of life—has never been a matter of dispute between Marx and the Anarchists.[3] Whether such a revolution could permanently establish a communist society, however, is quite another matter. In a work called *After the Revolution*, written shortly before the military rebellion and widely discussed within the Spanish Anarchist movement, the distinguished Anarchist theorist Abad de Santillan shows a keen realization of the importance of this problem:

> We are cognizant of the fact that the grade of economic development and material conditions of life influence powerfully human psychology. Faced with starvation, the individual becomes an egoist; with abundance he may become generous , friendly and socially disposed. All periods of privation and penury produce brutality, moral regression and a fierce struggle of all against all for daily bread. Consequently, it is plain that economics influences seriously the spiritual life of the individual and his social relations. That is precisely why we are aiming to establish the best possible economic conditions, which will act as a guarantee of equal and solid relationships among men. We will not stop being anarchists, on an empty stomach, but we do not exactly like to have empty stomachs.

The problem of material scarcity is not merely that "Man pitted against man is a wolf and he can never become a real brother to man, unless he has material security," but perhaps more significantly that with material security, indeed, with abundance, human beings can also discover what they do *not* need. I refer not only to material needs but also to spiritual ones—notably competition, money, and even contracts and social institutions that underwrite strict systems of reciprocity based on equivalences. No longer driven by material insecurity, no longer a creature of brute necessity, the individual can advance from the realm of "fairness," equivalence, and justice to the much higher moral realm of freedom in which people work to the best of their abilities and receive according to their needs. Finally, in an abundant economy that can provide for personal needs with a minimum of toil, the individual can acquire the free time for self-cultivation and full participation in the direct management of social life.

Spanish Anarchism revealed how far proletarian socialism could press toward an ideal of freedom on moral premises alone. Given a favorable conjunction of events, a revolutionary workers' and peasants' movement had indeed been able to make a libertarian revolution, collectivize industry, and create historically unprecedented possibilities for the management of the factories and land by those who worked them. Indeed, the revolutionary act of crushing the military rebellion in key cities of Spain, of taking direct control of the economy, even if under the mere compulsion of external events, had acted as a powerful spiritual impulse in its own right, appreciably altering the attitudes and views of less committed sectors of the oppressed. Thus proletarian socialism had pushed Spanish society beyond any materially delimiting barriers into a utopian experiment of astonishing proportions—into what Burnett Bolloten has aptly described as a "far-reaching social revolution . . . more profound in some respects than the Bolshevik revolution in its early stages. . . ." Not only had workers established control over industry and peasants formed free collectives on the land, but in many instances even money had been abolished and the most radical communistic precepts had replaced bourgeois concepts of work, distribution, and administration.

But what would happen when everyday life began to feel the pinch of economic want—of the material problems imposed not only by the Civil War but by Spain's narrow technological base? "Communism will be the result of abundance," Santillan had warned in the spring of 1936, "without which it will remain only an ideal." Could the revolutionary ardor of the CNT and FAI surmount the obstacles of scarcity and material want in the basic necessities of life, obstacles that had limited the forward thrust of earlier revolutions? Could mutual aid and proletarian initiative survive the drift toward egotism and bureaucratization? The answers to these questions must be deferred to the next volume, together with an account of the impact of Stalinist counterrevolution, particularly in the Anarchist areas of Spain.

But the paradox confronting the classical doctrine of proletarian socialism must be seen clearly, if the Spanish Revolution is to have any meaning for our times. Proletarian socialism, as doctrine and historic movement, is trapped by its very premises. For workers to become revolutionary *as workers*—as a *class* of dispossessed wage earners engaged in an irreconcilable struggle with a *class* of capitalist property-owners—presupposes the very material want which in no small measure prevents the proletariat from directly organizing and controlling society. Material want, a product not only of exploitation but also of an inadequate technological base, denies workers the material security and free time to transform the totality of society—its economic, politcal, and spiritual conditions of life.

The relatively affluent decades that were to follow the Spanish Revolution—decades that were a product not only of economic rationalization and planning along state capitalist lines but also of extraordinary technological achievement—revealed that the proletariat could be absorbed into bourgeois society, that it could be turned into an adaptive rather than a revolutionary class. Organized and disciplined by the factory, it could in fact become an extension of the factory into society at large, a victim of the factory's narrow economistic functions and its system of standardization and hierarchy. I am not contending here that any social revolution in our time can be achieved without the active support of the proletariat but rather that any such revolution can no longer be cast in terms of "proletarian hegemony," of working-class leadership. A social revolution, at least in the advanced capitalist countries of the world, presupposes a wide-ranging discontent with every aspect of capitalist society: the anomie and atomization fostered by the bourgeois megalopolis, discontent with the quality of everyday life, an awareness of the meaninglessness of a life devoted to mindless toil, an acute consciousness of hierarchy and domination in all its forms. In the case of hierarchy and domination, a liberated society would be expected to feel the need to abolish not only class rule and economic exploitation, but the domination of women by men, of the young by the old, of one ethnic group by another. One can easily enumerate a host of such broader issues and these have increasingly supplanted, even within the working class itself, the traditional economic issues that emerged out of the struggle between wage labor and capital. The traditional issues of wages, hours, and working conditions remain, to be sure, and the traditional struggle continues, but they have lost their revolutionary thrust. History itself has turned them into routine problems of negotiation, to be dealt with through established mechanisms and institutions that function entirely within the system. The steady erosion of the trade-union movement and of labor parties from institutions with a larger social vision to a "loyal opposition" within the factory, office, and state is perhaps the most telling evidence of this degeneration.

The larger problems of abolishing hierarchy and domination, of achieving a spiritually nourishing daily life, of replacing mindless toil by meaningful work, of attaining the free time for the self-management of a truly solidarizing human community—all of these growing demands have emerged not from a perspective of mere survival in an economy of scarce means, but rather from the very opposite social constellation. They stem from a gnawing tension, the problem of new technological advances, between needless scarcity on the one hand and the promise of free time and the satisfaction of basic human wants on the other. This tension is felt by a much wider constituency than the industrial proletariat. It can be sensed in students, professionals, small proprietors, so-called "white-collar" workers, service and government employees, *déclassé* elements, and even sections of the bourgeoisie as well as in the "full-grown" proletariat—in short, in sectors of society that were never accorded serious consideration as forces for revolution within the framework of proletarian socialism. This tension centers not only on economic problems but spiritual ones as well. It fosters a unique commitment not so much to "socialism," with its highly centralized state institutions and hierarchically organized bureaucratic infrastructure, but to a vision of a nonhierarchical, libertarian society (often simplistically designated as "socialism") in which people in free communities administer society on the basis of direct democracy and exercise full control over their daily lives.

The genius of Spanish Anarchism stems from its ability to fuse the concerns of traditional proletarian socialism with broader, more contemporary aspirations. In the very act of criticizing one remarkable achievement of the Spanish Anarchist movement, the affinity group, Santillan inadvertently reveals its uniqueness. Moreover, he discloses the clash between tradition and dream that existed within Spanish Anarchism in the 1930s. "We believe there is a little confusion in some libertarian circles between social conviviality, group affinity and the economic function," he warns. "Visions of happy Arcadias or free communes were imagined by the poets of the past; for the future, conditions appear quite different. In the factory we do not seek the affinity of friendship but the affinity of work. It is not an affinity of character, except on the basis of professional capacity and quality of work, which is the basis of conviviality in the factory."

These are stern words. They emerge from the vocabulary of scarcity, the work ethic, toil, and Iberian puritanical mores. They would have been viewed as gravely realistic injunctions by the leaders of the Spanish Socialist Party. They reflect the harsh realities of proletarian socialism in the 1930s, not the sensibilities of the "future."

But the fact that for Santillan to enjoin his comrades in the spring of 1936 to reject "social conviviality" in the work process, to eliminate "group affinity" in productive activity as an archaic vision of "happy Arcadias," reveals the visionary form in which such groups were actually seen by many Spanish Anarchists. If we, today, increasingly see the need to turn work into a festive and "Arcadian" experience, if we address ourselves to a new sense of possibility that inheres in the work process, we would do well to recognize that it is only because of the technological opportunities created by our own time that we enjoy this privilege. Proletarian socialism in the 1930s had turned the factory not only into the locus of social change but into the reality principle of the socialist spirit. In a world of material scarcity and toil, this reality principle allowed for minimal "social conviviality." Santillan errs primarily in one respect: he speaks not for the "future" but for the "present," a "present" whose values were destined to undergo major transformation in the decades that lay ahead. A dedicated Anarchist of a distinct historical era, he reveals all its limitations even as he tries pragmatically to chart its future trajectory. Although he may have been correct for his time, it was a time that could scarcely yield a society of "happy Arcadias" in which the means of life would be freely available to all and work would be performed according to one's desire and ability.

How did it happen than, that the Spanish Anarchists in the 1930s formed such visions of "social conviviality," "group affinity," and "happy Arcadias"? On this score at least, Santillan, even as he voices his objections, is true to the locale as well as to the time of his movement. The Spanish Anarchists who held these Arcadian visions were, in fact, poets of the past. They had formed their dreams from the "social conviviality" of their *pueblos*, from their pre-industrial culture and spiritual heritage. To use our own terms, in their dreams the Spanish Anarchists perpetuated a sense of continuity with a "primitive communism" of the past, one which they doubtless idealized within the context of Spanish conditions. Yet this communism, despite its "primitiveness," possessed more elements of the sophisticated communism of the future than the factory socialism of the workers' movement. It should not be forgotten that the "happy Arcadias" and "free communes" which Spanish Anarchists had borrowed from visions of the past were often no less stern than Santillan's image of the factory. They too conceived their communal, free "Arcadias" in gravely puritanical terms. They believed in "free love" because they believed in the freedom to mate without political or religious sanction, but they shunned free sexuality and promiscuity. They envisioned conviviality at the work place, but they admired hard work and almost celebrated its purifying qualities. In their "Arcadian" society there could be "no rights without duties, no duties without rights." Although all these traits add a spiritual, ethical, and convivial dimension to the proletarian socialism of the factory, it is a socialism that is built no less around scarcity, denial, and toil than is Santillan's. Santillan merely tried to remind them of the contradiction that lurked in their vision, for there could be no real "Arcadias" unless the land flowed with milk and honey. If the paradisiacal poetry to which Santillan refers has any possibility of reality today, the puritanical Spanish Anarchist "Arcadia" of yesteryear was no less a vision, a "mere ideal," than Santillan's sterner vision of a future libertarian society based on "the affinity of work."

Yet the Spanish Anarchists left behind a tangible reality that has considerable relevance for social radicalism today.Their movement's "heroic years," 1868 to 1936, were marked by a fascinating process of experimentation in organizational forms, decision-making techniques, personal values, educational goals, and methods of struggle. From the days of the International and the Alliance of Social Democracy to those of the CNT and FAI, Spanish Anarchists of all varieties—collectivist, syndicalist, and communist—had evolved an astonishingly well-organized subculture within Spanish society that fostered enormous freedom of action by local syndicates and affinity groups. If the Spanish political sphere had denied the individual peasant and worker full participation in the management of social affairs, the Anarchist movement nourished their participation. Far more important than the episodic revolutionary uprisings, the individual *atentados*, or the daring escapades of small circles of comrades like the *Solidarios* was the ability of the Spanish Anarchists to patiently knit together highly independent groups (united by "social conviviality" as well as by social views) into sizable, coherent organizations, to coordinate them into effective social forces when crises emerged, and to develop an informed mode of spontaneity that fused the most valuable traits of group discipline with personal initiative. Out of this process emerged an organic community and a sense of mutual aid unequaled by any workers' movement of that era. Indeed, no less important as a subject of study than the workers' committees and agrarian collectives that were to follow the July revolution was the movement that created the ground work for libertarian social structures—the Spanish Anarchist movement itself.

Notes

1. It need hardly be pointed out at any great length that the workers' "labor power" was marked by their capacity not only to meet their survival needs, but to produce "surplus labor" over and beyond what was needed for the maintenance and reproduction of the working class. Hence "labor power" was also a unique commodity: it could be deployed not only to sustain the worker and his or her family (hence wages were seen as a "fair exchange" in the labor market at this level alone), but also to provide the capitalist with an increment, i.e., "surplus value" or "profit." A "fair exchange," however, presupposed that "labor power" would be conceived of as a commodity—a

product, as it were, to be traded on the market like a tangible commodity—not as the onerous duty of a slave or serf on behalf of a coercive master. Marx regarded this concept of "labor power" as one of his most vital contributions to politcal economy, and, one may add, as a cornerstone of "scientific socialism."

2. The last two lines of this passage were momentous. These lines and others like them in Marx's writings were to provide the rationale for asserting the authority of Marxist parties and their armed detachments over and even against the proletariat. Claiming a deeper and more informed comprehension of a situation than "even the whole of the proletariat at the given moment," Marxist parties went on to dissolve such revolutionary forms of proletarian organization as factory committees and ultimately to totally regiment the proletariat according to lines established by the party leadership.

3. Toward the end of his life, Marx in fact tended to accept the possibility that the European Socialist revolution would be initiated by industrially backward Russia rather than France or Germany. In his correspondence of 1881 with Vera Zasulitch, he entertains the possibility that a timely revolution in Russia would make it possible for the collectivistic peasant village or *mir* to bypass the capitalist development of the West and "gradually slough off its primitive characteristics and develop as the direct basis of collective production on a national scale." For an interesting discussion of this correspondence, see Martin Buber's *Paths in Utopia* (Boston: Beacon Press, pp. 90-94).

In a mass demonstration in Barcelona, workers hold a banner reading, "*Solidaridad Obrera,* the daily newspaper of the Revolution." The banner is inscribed with the initials CNT, FAI, and AIT (the International Workingman's Association).

Bibliographical Essay

1. General Works

Surprisingly few general histories of Spanish Anarchism exist in any language and those which are available, with a couple of exceptions, are too cursory to supply a very rewarding account of the movement. Juan Gomez Casa's *Historia del Anarcosindicalismo* (Madrid, 1968) is simply an outline of the major events in Spanish Anarchist history and does not live up to its grandiloquent title. Jean Becarud and Gilles Lapouge's *Anarchistes d'Espagne* (Paris, 1970) is even more abbreviated and offers only a glimpse of its subject matter. Eduardo Comin Colomer's two-volume *Historia del Anarquismo Espanol 1836–1948* (Barcelona, 1956) is a typical Francoist *historia secreta*, written from an internal knowledge of the police files. It contains a wealth of anecdotal material, but it is often impossible to determine where the serious historian ends and the Francoist official begins.

Despite the minor errors that scholars have cited, Gerald Brenan's *The Spanish Labyrinth* (London, 1943) still remains the finest and most moving account in English of the Spanish Anarchists to date. Brenan was never an Anarchist and less than half of his book deals with Anarchism as such, yet like so many non-Spaniards in Spain, he came to admire the Anarchist movement with a warmth that occasionally verges on enthusiasm. Perhaps the weakest aspect of his book might be called its "Andalusian" standpoint: the author's view of the movement was shaped by his experiences with rural rather than urban Anarchism and he tends to give too much weight to its quasi-religious agrarian "millenarianism." Admittedly this emphasis adds a great deal of color to his account, but it does not provide a satisfactory explanation of the CNT and FAI's development in the industrial centers of Spain. Franz Borkenau's *The Spanish Cockpit* (London, 1937), a very thoughtful book in its own right, also depicts Anarchism as a quasi-religious movement, one which, despite Borkenau's Socialist convictions, earns his esteem. To counterbalance Brenan and Borkenau's semi-mystical treatment of Spanish Anarchism, the reader might care to consult Diego Abad de Santillan's recent series, *Contribucion a la Historia del Movimiento Obrero Espanol*, the first volume of which was published in Madrid in 1968. The reader should expect a textbook-like survey of the workers' movement, however, which often lacks the color and drama that one would expect to find after reading Brenan.

Introductory surveys of the early history of Spanish Anarchism appear in many of the larger works cited below. They serve primarily to orient the reader toward the specific period under discussion and do not constitute substitutes for a history of the movement. The opening chapters of Cesar M. Lorenzo's *Les Anarchistes Espagnols et le Pouvoir* (Paris, 1969), Jose Peirats's *Los Anarquistas en la Crisis Politica Espanola* (Buenos Aires, 1964), and Manuel Buenacasa's *El Movimiento Obrero Espanol* (Paris, 1966) are the best I have found of such summaries. As for surveys of Spanish Anarchism included in general histories of the international Anarchist movement or histories of Spain (at least those of recent vintage), some of them tend merely to repeat Brenan; others adopt a tone that is patronizing, if not bitterly caustic.

2. Early History (Chapters I-III).

The period prior to Fanelli's arrival in Spain is admirably covered by Fernanco Garrido Tortosa's *Historia de las Asociaciones Obreras en Europa* (Madrid, 1870). This two-volume account is perhaps the most valuable available source on early Spanish working-class movements. Garrido was a friend of Reclus and toured Spain with him; his observations are based not merely on research into these movements but also on participation in them. In English, a splendid survey of early labor agitation appears in Bruce Levine's *Economic and Social Mobilization: Spain, 1830–1923* (Ann Arbor, unpublished), a sizable paper that correlates the activities of workers' and peasants' movements with Spanish industrial development and agrarian reform.

A great deal of material now exists on the period during which the First International was formed in Spain. Within a single year, two excellent studies have appeared: Joseph Termes's *Anarquismo y Sindicalismo en Espana: La Primera Internacional (1864–1881)* (Barcelona, 1972) and Clara E. Lida's *Anarquismo y Revolucion en la Espana del XIX* (Madrid, 1972). In the following year, Lida published an accompanying volume of texts and documents under the title, *Antecedentes y Desarrolla del Movimiento Obrero Espanol* (Madrid, 1973), which also throws considerable light on the period from 1835 to 1868.

On the formation and development of Spanish Anarchism, the

reader should consult Anselmo Lorenzo's *El Proletariado Militante* (originally published in Barcelona, Vol. I, 1901; Vol. II, 1903); Juan Diaz del Moral's *Historia de las Agitaciones Campesinas Andaluzas* (originally published in Madrid, 1929); Max Nettlau's *Miguel Bakunin, la Internacional y la Alianza en Espana* (originally published in Buenos Aires, 1925); and Casimiro Marti's *Origenes del Anarquismo en Barcelona* (Barcelona, 1959). Lorenzo and Diaz del Moral's works are the real classics on the development of early Spanish Anarchism and provide major sources of data for later, more scholarly studies. *El Proletariado Militante* is really a memoir by one of the founders and outstanding propagandists of Spanish Anarchism. Diaz del Moral was not merely a historian but also an observer of some of the events he describes. Nettlau and Casimiro Marti have produced two brief but masterful pieces of research.

Many other workers provided invaluable background material for an understanding of this period, notably Nettlau's *Documentos Ineditos sobre la Internacional y la Alianza en Espana* (Buenos Aires, 1930) and his highly informative articles in *La Revista Blanca* (September 1, 1928-May 1, 1929), published under the title, "Impresiones historicas sobre el desarrollo del Socialismo en Espana," a superb series that has yet to be compiled as a volume; Juan Jose Morato's *Historia de la Seccion Espanola de la Internacional, 1868-1874* (Madrid, 1930); James Guillame's excellent four-volume *L'Internationale, Documents et Souvenirs* (Paris, 1905-1910), in my view one of the most outstanding of the many histories that are available on the First International; Maximiano Garcia Venero's three-volume *Historia de las Internacionales en Espana* (Madrid, 1956-1958) and the same author's *Historias de los Movimientos Sindicalistas Espanoles (1840-1933)* (Madrid, 1961).

Of the social histories of Spain, Brenan's *The Spanish Labyrinth* is certainly one of the most outstanding. For a truly exhaustive history, the reader may care to consult the five-volume series *Historia Social y Economica de Espana y America*, edited by Jaime Vicens Vives (Barcelona, 1957-1959) and Vicens Vives's *An Economic History of Spain* (Princeton, 1969). One of the best sources for popular collectivism in Spain is Joaquin Costa's *Colectivismo Agrario en Espana* (orginally published in Madrid, 1898). Raymond Carr's *Spain, 1808-1939* (Oxford, 1966) is an eminently readable and highly informative work on political events. Apart from Brenan's account, I know of no book in English that is more deeply sympathetic to—or so ably conveys—the libertarian spirit of the Spanish people than Elena de La Souchere's *An Explanation of Spain* (New York, 1964). Perhaps the most perceptive analysis of Spanish society is to be found in Karl Marx's "Revolutionary Spain," a series of articles published by the *New York Daily Tribune* between September 9 and December 4, 1854. These articles are compiled in Marx and Engels's *Revolution in Spain* (New York, 1939), a book that is sadly marred not only by Stalinist editing but by Engels's vulgar interpretation of early syndicalism in a propaganda diatribe, "The Bakuninists at Work."

Perhaps the best work I can recommend on Spanish Federalism is C.A.M. Hennessy's *The Federal Rebublic in Spain* (Oxford, 1962). Hennessy has also compiled a very extensive bibliography on the subject. R. Coloma's widely cited *La Revolucion Internacionalista Alcoyana de 1873* (Alicante, 1959), a work which seems to have acquired the reputation of an authoritative account on the Alcoy uprising, seems in my view to be patently biased against the Internationalists and their working-class supporters. Accordingly, my account has been based on a sifting of the limited literature and the available press accounts of the event. Fortunately, Clara Lida, in her *Anarquismo y Revolucion en la Espana del XIX*, carefully examines material on the uprising (see pages 216-22) and has produced a long-needed balanced account.

Even more problematical is the figure of Mikhail Bakunin—both the man and his social views. At this writing, no worthwhile biography of Bakunin exists in English. E.H. Carr, in his *Michael Bakunin* (London, 1937), has brought painstaking scholarship to the service of what are often scandalously trivial goals, including Bakunin's impecuniosity and sex life. Carr's account is steeped in malice toward his subject. Of the published material available to the reader, H.E. Kaminski's *Bakounine–La Vie d'un Revolutionnaire* (Paris, 1938) is the best biography to consult on Bakunin's activities, but it still awaits translation into English. The quotations from Bakunin in the text were taken from Gregory Maximoff's very unsatisfactory mosaic of Bakunin's writings, *The Political Philosophy of Bakunin* (Glencoe, 1953), a work that has been superseded over the past few years by more representative selections, notably in *Bakunin on Anarchy*, edited by Sam Dolgoff (New York, 1972), and *Michael Bakunin's Selected Writings*, edited by Arthur Lehning (London, 1973). Dolgoff's book also contains a very extensive bibliography, including an account of the Steklov and Nettlau biographies of Bakunin, available only in special collections and archives.

3. From the International to the CNT (Chapters IV and VII).

Virtually every account of peasant Anarchism in Spain owes a great debt to Diaz del Moral, who also enjoys the distinction of fostering the "millenarian" orientation that characterizes so many English works on the subject. Joaquin Costa's *Oligarquia y Caciquismo como la Forma Actual de Gobierno en Espana* (orginally published in Madrid,

1902) provides indispensable material on the *cacique* system and Vicens Vives's *Historia Social y Economica* . . . is an invaluable source of data and insights on Spainish agrarian problems. In *Politics, Economics and Men of Modern Spain (1808-1946)* (London, 1946), the intertwining of agrarian with political interests is discussed with much verve by A. Ramos Oliveira, a writer who is not to be denied his strong political prejudices and his animosity toward the Anarchists.

One of the most definitive studies of Spanish agricultural and rural unrest appears in Edward E. Malefakis's *Agrarian Reform and Peasant Revolution in Spain* (New Haven, 1970). The book also has an excellent bibliography. Although Malefakis is not sympathetic to the Anarchists, he clearly delineates their options and dilemmas. His later chapters provide a valuable account of their duels with the Socialists during the 1930s. For an excellent account of the poverty endured by the *braceros*, see "Agrarian Problems in Spain" by E.H.G. Dobby, *Geographical Review of the American Geographical Society* April, 1936). To gain some sense of the atmosphere of *pueblo* life—its parochialism as well as its internal solidarity—the reader should consult Michael Kenny's *A Spanish Tapestry* (New York, 1961) and J.S. Pitt-Rivers's sensitive study of an Andalusian mountain village, *The People of the Sierra* (Chicago, 1961). E.J. Hobsbawm's essay on Anarchist "millenarianism" in *Primitive Rebels* (Manchester, 1959) is riddled by Marxian prejudgments on the "archaic" nature of Anarchism. Apart from useful information about the Casas Viejas uprising, he adds very little to what Diaz del Moral observes with greater sympathy for his subject.

Very little has been written about the trajectory of Spanish Anarchism from the decline of the International to the emergence of the *Solidaridad Obrera* federation after the turn of the century. To establish a reasonably detailed continuity of events, it was necessary to turn to biographies and newpaper accounts for inportant data. Nettlau's "Impresiones historicas sobre el desarrollo del Socialismo en Espana" in *La Revista Blanca* (Numero 140, 1929) is informative, as is Pedro Vallina's biography of Salvochea, *Cronica de un Revolucionario* (Paris, 1958). The reader may also care to consult the opening chapters of Buenacasa's *El Movimiento Obrero Espanol* and the larger histories of Spanish Anarchism. Clara E. Lida's book of documents contains valuable statements, appeals, and reports up to the late 1880s. On Salvochea's life, the reader should examine not only Vallina, but also Rudolph Rocker's *Fermin Salvochea* in the *Precursores de la Libertad* series (No. 1, 1945) and the few pages of vignettes of Salvochea which Buenacasa includes in his *El Movimiento Obrero Español*.

Recent research has reopened the *Mano Negra* period for reevaluation and fresh discussion. Iris Zavala's discovery in the Archivo de

Palacio in Madrid of a copy of a document purported to be the *Mano Negra's* "regulations," a document drawn up some five years before the *Mano Negra* trials of 1883, does not entirely dispel my doubts about the reality of the organization. A copy is not an original and, given the circumstances of the time, even an "original" document would warrant the most scrupulous authentication, in my opinion, before any question of police forgery could be removed. Clara E. Lida accepts this document as fact and discusses its social context in "Agrarian Anarchism in Andalusia," *International Review of Social History*, XIV, 3 (1969). Her review of the period makes the article well worth reading, quite aside from the dispute that may arise about the authenticity of the document itself. On the trials, Ediciones "CNT" has republished *El Proceso de "La Mano Negra"* (Toulouse, 1958), an old collection of excerpts from statements of the accused and critical comments of the charges and proceedings. See also Glenn Waggoner's article, "The Black Hand Mystery," in *Modern European Social History*, ed. Robert Becucha (London, 1972).

Lida's article contains many informative observations on the disputes between the traditional Anarcho-collectivists and the emerging Anarcho-communists. Brenan's *The Spanish Labyrinth* and Max Nomad's "The Anarchist Tradition" (*The Revolutionary Internationals*, ed. M.M. Drachkovitch [Stanford, 1966]) provide valuable accounts of this split. For a succinct statement of Anarcho-communist principles, the reader should go directly to Peter Kropotkin's early essay "Anarchist Communism: Its Basis and Principles" (*Revolutionary Pamphlets* [New York, 1928]) and to his *The Conquest of Bread* (London, 1906). Fortunately, both volumes have recently been published in the United States and are no longer difficult to acquire.

My account of the terrorist movement at the turn of the century is drawn from so many sources, including contemporary newspaper accounts, that a single work is difficult to cite. The already cited volumes by Brenan, Peirats, Buenacasa, and Abad de Santillan collectively provide a good overall picture of the incidents, the social context, and the motives of the terrorists. A dramatic, at times lurid, but not inaccurate account of Anarchist terrorism appears in Barbara W. Tuchman's *The Proud Tower* (New York, 1966). F. Tarrida del Marmol's *Les Inquisiteurs d'Espagne* (Paris, 1897), a work that aroused European public opinion against the barbarous methods of the Barcelona police, is still the best account of anti-Anarchist repression during this period.

The reawakening of the Spanish labor movement in the decade prior to the formation of the CNT is very well documented. Stanley G. Payne's *The Spanish Revolution* (New York, 1970) contains an excellent bibliography of contemporary works on the subject, many of which go beyond the scope of this volume. Abad de Santillan's history covers the period in some detail and Brenan's chapter on the "Catalan Question, 1898–1909" provides a good political background. The finest account of the Barcelona labor movement during this decade is Joan Connelly Ullman's *The Tragic Week* (Cambridge, 1968), a superbly researched and immensely informative work. The conventional attitude toward the "Tragic Week" appears in Augusto Riera's *La Semana Tragica* (Barcelona, 1909), complete with photographs and inventories of gutted churches, monasteries, and seminaries. Diaz del Moral provides a detailed account of the agrarian movement in Cordoba between 1900 and 1909 and Malefakis devotes several highly informative pages to the reemergence of rural Anarchist agitation in Andalusia generally during the upsurge of 1903–1904.

An ample literature exists on Francisco Ferrer's career and death, including highly informative material in Joan Connelly Ullman's book. Ferrer's *La Escuela Moderna* has been translated into English by Joseph McCabe under the title, *The Origin and Ideas of the Modern School* (London, 1913), a work that has apparently undergone many reprints although the translation does not have a publishing history. This small volume presents a comprehensive statement of Ferrer's pedagogic ideals and still deserves reading. A. and C. Orts-Ramos's *Francisco Ferrer—Apostal de la Razon* (Barcelona, 1932) is a highly informative personal and intellectual biography. The Spanish Anarchists published a fair amount of material on Ferrer of which Hem Day's *F. Ferrer—sa vie, son oeuvre* (Brussels, n.d.) is still available. English accounts of Ferrer include *Francisco Ferrer: His Life, Work, and Martyrdom*, edited by Leonard D. Abbott for the Francisco Ferrer Association (New York, n.d.), and McCabe's *The Martyrdom of Ferrer* (London, 1909), both of which appeared shortly after Ferrer's execution and reflect the worldwide impact of the Spanish educator.

To gain an insight into the cultural life fostered by Anarchist intellectuals during the closing decades of the last century, the reader must turn to periodicals such as *La Revista Blanca* (old series) and the earlier review, *La Revista Social*. Jose Peirats's "Para una Monografia de Escritores Anarquistas Espanoles" in *Ruta* (Vol. III, No. 7, 1972) is a good survey of Spanish Anarchist writers, their works, and the periodicals to which they contributed. The topical range of these intellectuals can be judged by examining Ricardo Mella's *Ideario* (Gijon, 1926) and *Ensayos y Conferencias* (Gijon, 1934), both of which constitute Volumes One and Two respectively of the *Obras Completas de Ricardo Mella*.

The emergence of Anarchosyndicalism is ably discussed by Brenan in his chapter on the subject. The impact of Georges Sorel's *Reflexions sur la Violence* (originally published in Paris, 1908, and easily available in English translation) has been greatly overrated, but the work should be read as a characteristic response of many radical French intellectuals to the new workers' movement. Despite its brevity, Daniel Guerin's *Anarchism* (New York, 1970) is, in my view, the most trustworthy and perceptive recent survey of Anarchist ideas and history. It contains a good account of the pedigree and history of Anarchosyndicalism. Guerin's compilation of Anarchist documents, *Ni Dieu, Ni Maitre* (Paris, n.d.), reproduces early anticipations of syndicalist organization such as James Guillaume's "Idees sur l'Organisation Sociale" (1876) and the explicitly end-of-the-century syndicalism reflected by Fernand Pelloutier's "L'Anarchisme et les Syndicat's Ouvriers" and Emile Pouget's "Le Syndicat." Roger Hagnauer's *L'Actualite de la Charte d'Amiens* (Paris, 1959) contains a succinct account of the emergence of the French CGT and its shift toward a Marxist-controlled labor union. Errico Malatesta's criticisms of syndicalism appear in the *Compte Rendu Analytique* of the *Congres Anarchiste Tenu a Amsterdam, Aout 24-31, 1907* (Paris, 1908). The most definitive biography of Malatesta and the finest selection of his writings in English has been prepared by Vernon Richards under the title, *Malatesta: His Life and Ideas* (London, 1965).

4. From the Early CNT to the Second Republic (Chapters VIII-IX)

The early history and structure of the CNT are discussed in detail in the historical works of Brenan, Buenacasa, Abad de Santillan, and Garcia Venero. Jose Peirats's *What is the CNT?* (London, 1972), the English translation of an article in *Ruta*, gives a description of the organization's structure and goals as well as general background material. A brief but useful account of the events leading to the formation of the CNT appears in Peirats's *Los Anarquistas en la Crisis Politica Espanola*. The greater part of this book deals with the confederation's activities under the Primo dictatorship, the formation and role of the FAI, and the conflicts within Spanish Anarchosyndicalism during the Second Republic. Cesar M. Lorenzo also provides a survey of Anarchosyndicalist activities during this period, although the book deals mainly with the Civil War.

The most informative English account of Anarchist activities between the World War I period and the Primo dictatorship is Gerald H. Meaker's *The Revolutionary Left in Spain, 1914–1923* (Stanford, 1974), a work that deals equally with the Socialists at this time and the Communist tendencies that emerged from the Russian Revolution. Meaker is not sympathetic to the Anarchists, but his study is meticulously researched and highly perceptive. Diaz del Moral and Malefakis's accounts are indispensable to an understanding of the rural movement. For a detailed account of the "Bellas Artes" congress of the CNT, see the *Congreso de Constitucion de la Confederacion Nacional del Trabajo (CNT)*, Ediciones "CNT" (Toulouse, 1959) and for the 1918 Barcelona congress see the *Memoria del Congreso celebrado en Barcelona los dias 28, 29 y 30 de Junio y 1 de Julio de 1918*, Ediciones "CNT" (Toulouse, 1957).

Detailed accounts of the strike movement during this period appear in Alberto Bacells's *El Sindicalismo en Barcelona (1916-1923)* (Barcelona, 1965), Jacinto Martin Maestre's *Huelga General de 1917* (Madrid, 1966), Garcia Venero's *Historia Movimientos Sindicalistas Espanoles (1840–1933)*, Angel Pestana's *Lo que Aprendi en la Vida* (Madrid, 1933), and Francisco Largo Caballero's *Mis Recuerdos* (Mexico, 1954). Most of the overall accounts of Spanish radicalism, such as Brenan's and Abad de Santillan's, contain valuable accounts of their own.

Bacells also provides a comprehensive survey of the *pistolerismo* tendency that plagued the postwar years. Buenacasa's account provides an example of the reaction of a distinguished Anarchist militant to the damage *pistolerismo* inflicted on the CNT. The reader who is interested in this phase of Spanish Anarchosyndicalism may care to consult Maria Farre Morego's *Los Atentados Sociales en Espana* (Madrid, 1922) and Miguel Sastre y Sama's *La Esclavitud Moderna* (Barcelona, 1921). The foregoing works represent only a fraction of the very considerable contemporary literature on the period, most notably on the strikes and the *pistoleros*.

Brenan, Raymond Carr, Buenacasa, Abad de Santillan, and Peirats's historical works provide highly informative accounts of the period leading into and including the Primo dictatorship. A laudatory compilation of material on Salvador Segui by a variety of libertarian writers has been prepared by Ediciones "*Solidaridad Obrera*" under the title *Salvador Segui: su vida, su obra* (Paris, 1960). Meaker also discusses Segui's policies in detail. An excellent account of the conflict between various tendencies within the CNT during this period appears in George Breitman's *Spanish Anarcho–Syndicalism, 1918–1931: Moderates vs. Extremists* (University of Michigan, unpublished paper, 1969). Ricardo Sanz provides a personal account of the *Solidarios* and *Nosotros* affinity groups in *El Sindicalismo y La Politica* (Toulouse, 1966), an account that is filled out by personal interviews with Anarchist *grupistas* and militants in Abel Paz's *Durruti: Le Peuple en Armes* (Paris, 1972). The Paz biography, perhaps the most informative account of Durruti's life available, has been translated into English by Nancy MacDonald and is scheduled for publication by Black Rose Books in Montreal in 1977.

Meaker's book and Peirats's *Los Anarquistas* . . . contain valuable accounts of the fortunes of Spanish Anarchism as the CNT slipped into illegality under the Primo dictatorship. Angel Pestana's report of his visit to Russia has been published in recent years as two pamphlets by Editorial ZYX under the titles, *Informe de mi Estancia en la U.R.S.S.* (Madrid, 1968) and *Consideraciones y Juicios Acerca de la Tercera Internacional* (Madrid, 1968). Breitman chronicles the disputes that emerged in the CNT during the dictatorship and up to the expulsion of the *Treintistas* with a great deal of understanding and perception. One of the most detailed accounts of these conflicts appears in John Brademas's *Anarcosindicalismo y Revolucion en Espana (1930–1937)* (Barcelona, 1974), a modified version of Brademas's highly informative doctoral dissertation, "Revolution and Social Revolution: A Contribution to the History of the Anarcho-Syndicalist Movement in Spain, 1930–1937" (Oxford University, unpublished, 1956). The record of the special CNT congress in 1931, *Memorias de Congreso Extraordinario de la C.N.T. celebrado en Madrid los Dias 11 al 16 de Junio de 1931* (Barcelona, 1931), contains a remarkable account of the vicissitudes of the confederation during the closing years of the dictatorship.

Peirats in *Los Anarquistas* . . . has an amusing account of the founding meeting of the FAI in Valencia but the most detailed narrative appears in Brademas's book as a lengthy memorandum written for the author by Miguel Jimenez, who presided at the conference. I also received colorful details of the preparation and course of this meeting from Gaston Leval and Jose Peirats, but limitations of space did not make it possible for me to include them in this volume. The best discussion I have encountered of the structure of the FAI appears in Ildefonso Gonzalez's *Il Movimiento Libertario Spagnuolo* (Naples, n.d.), selections of which were generously translated for my use from the Italian into English by Sam Dolgoff. Unfortunately, this very important survey does not as yet appear in any other language.

5. *The Road to Revolution*

Brenan's discussion of the period from 1931 to 1936 is still the finest general account of the Second Republic. Gabriel Jackson's *The Spanish Republic and the Civil War, 1931–1939* (Princeton, 1965) is very useful and provides many details that are not ordinarily available in general histories, although I share Noam Chomsky's criticisms of the book in his *The Cold War and the New Mandarins*. Hugh Thomas's *The Spanish Civil War* (New York, 1961)—a book that, for some curious reason, has acquired the reputation of being a "definitive" history of the conflict—is pretentious, superficial, and factually unreliable. For a devastating critique of Thomas's *oeuvre*, the reader should consult Vernon Richards's "July 19, 1936: Republic or Revolution?" in *Anarchy*, No. 5 (July, 1961), and Richards's introductory remarks to Gaston Leval's *Collectives in the Spanish Revolution* (London, 1975).

The best account of Spanish Anarchism from 1931 to 1936 is Brademas's already cited dissertation and its modified translation in book form into Spanish. The opening chapters (I to IX) of Peirats's *La C.N.T. en la Revolucion Espanola*, Vol. I (Buenos Aires, 1955), are indispensable for a knowledge of Anarchist activities during the period. The volume consists in large part of documents that are important in clarifying the vicissitudes of Anarchist policy. The reader will also obtain a good survey of the events leading up to the Civil War and an excellent account of the opening days of the conflict from Pierre Broue and Emile Temime's *The Revolution and the Civil War in Spain* (Cambridge, 1970), a translation from the French of one of the better general accounts of the Spanish Civil War. Certainly this volume should be read in preference to Thomas's volume. Malefakis's study of agrarian unrest in the early 1930s is immensely informative, although it is definitely unsympathetic to the Anarchists and, in its conclusion, to the Liberals. One encounters an even more marked rightist bias in Stanley Payne's *The Spanish Revolution* (New York, 1970), but the book is so well-researched and so highly informative that it makes for good reading. Salvador de Madariaga's *Spain* (New York, 1958) presents a liberal interpretation of the period and of the conflicts between the UGT and CNT.

Buenacasa's *La C.N.T., los Treinta y la F.A.I.* (Barcelona, 1933) presents the outlook of the FAI in the dispute with the CNT moderates by a leader who is by no means a spokesman for its most extreme wing. Pestana's memoir, *Lo que Aprendi* . . . should also be consulted to gain the views of one of the ablest CNT leaders. Peirats's historical works provide good accounts of the *ciclo de las insurrecciones* and Manuel Villar's *El Anarquismo y la Insurreccion de Asturias* (Buenos Aires, 1936) presents the Anarchist version of the Asturian uprising. Although most of Gaston Leval's *Collectives in the Spanish Revolution* deals with the Civil War period, Part One of the book provides a first-rate libertarian analysis of the agrarian situation prior to the revolution.

The record of the Saragossa congress of May 1936 has been republished by Ediciones "CNT" as part of its series *Prolegomenos de la Revolucion de Julio en Espana* under the title, *El Congreso Confederal de Zaragoza* (n.p., 1955). The reader should also consult Isaac Puente's *El Comunismo Libertario* (republished at Toulouse, 1947), a work which formed the basic theoretical document for the congress's discussion

of the future society. My choice of Diego Abad de Santillan's *El Or-
ganismo Economico de la Revolucion* (Barcelona, 1936), translated into
English under the title, *After the Revolution* (New York, 1937), as the
most useful of the two works was guided by the need for a more
discursive treatment. Puente's pamphlet, despite its influence, is
scarcely more than a brief outline; Santillan's book is a reflective
theoretical work as well as an informative guide to social reconstruction.

Accounts of opening days of the revolution are very numerous. I
have already singled out Broue and Temime's survey of the uprising
in the major cities of Spain. One of the most detailed accounts of the
day-by-day conflict in Madrid and Barcelona appears in Abel Paz's
Paradigma de una Revolucion (n.p., n.d.), published by Ediciones
"AIT," the concluding portion of which contains appeals in *Solidaridad Obrera* from July 19 to July 23, 1936. Portions of S. Canovas
Cervantes's *Durruti y Ascaso: La C.N.T. y la Revolucion de Julio*, published by Ediciones "Paginas Libres" (Toulouse, n.d.), deal with the
uprising in Barcelona. An assessment of the events leading to the
revolution and actual outbreak of the Civil War by one of the most
influential Anarchist "statesmen" of the period will be found in Diego
Abad de Santillan's *Por que Perdimos la Guerra* (Buenos Aires, 1940),
the opening chapters of which provide an account of the development of the Spanish Anarchist movement from the First to the Second Republic and the outbreak of the July uprising. For a sharp criticism by an English Anarchist of the FAI and CNT's performance on
the eve of the uprising as well as the Civil War, see Vernon Richard's
The Lessons of the Spanish Revolution (London, 1953).

Note on Sources

The greater part of this volume was completed in 1970 and I did
not have the benefit of any volumes cited above that were published
after 1969. Accordingly, I could not use the later volumes of Abad de
Santillan's *Contribucion a la Historia de Movimiento Obrero Espanol*, Josef
Termes's *Anarquismo y Sindicalismo en Espana*, Clara E. Lida's *Anarquismo y Revolucion en la Espana del XIX* and her accompanying volume of documents, Dolgoff and Lehning's compilations of Bakunin's
writings, Edward Malefakis's *Agrarian Reform and Peasant Revolution in
Spain*, Gerald Meaker's *The Revolutionary Left in Spain*, Abel Paz's
Durruti: Le Peuple en Armes, and the Spanish version of John
Brademas's dissertation except insofar as they contained material that
applied to the concluding chapter, "The Road to Revolution."

Wherever possible, however, these volumes were used to correct errors and, to a limited extent, expand accounts of events for which there was little available data.

Nearly all the remaining works cited in this "Bibliographical Essay" entered into the preparation of this volume. The discussion on the early history of the International in Spain relies heavily on Anselmo Lorenzo's memoirs, Nettlau's accounts of the early Spanish Anarchists, Marti, Garcia Venero, and Diaz del Moral. Buenacasa, Joan Connelly Ullman, Peirats, Bacells, and the various biographies, memoirs, and documents mentioned in the bibliographical essay should be singled out as major sources of the later events described in this book. I consulted many conventional periodicals of the day, including contemporary newspapers in Spanish, English, and French, which cast light on fairly obscure periods in the history of the Spanish Anarchist movement. I also had the benefit of individual issues of *La Revista Blanca*, *Solidaridad Obrera*, and *Tierra y Libertad* in American libraries and private collections.

Index

WITHDRAWN